CRAWL OF FAME

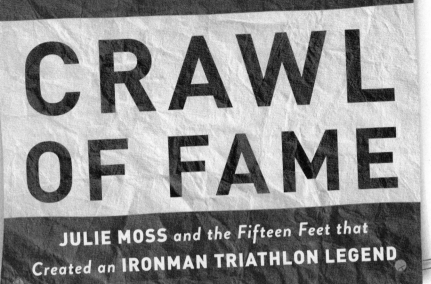

CRAWL OF FAME

JULIE MOSS *and the Fifteen Feet that*
Created an IRONMAN TRIATHLON LEGEND

JULIE MOSS

and Robert Yehling

Foreword by Armen Keteyian

PEGASUS BOOKS
NEW YORK LONDON

CRAWL OF FAME

Pegasus Books Ltd.
148 W 37th Street, 13th Floor
New York, NY 10018

First Pegasus Books edition October 2018

Interior design by Maria Fernandez

Library of Congress Cataloging-in-Publication Data is available.

ISBN: 978-1-68177-856-3

10 9 8 7 6 5 4 3 2 1

Printed in the United States of America
Distributed by W. W. Norton & Company

Happy fortieth anniversary, Ironman. . . . We've grown up together.
Your warm waters, windy lava fields, and searing marathon
challenged me to dig down and glimpse the depths of who I could be.
Your *ohana,* the athletes who have battled for their finish lines,
is the best in sport. It's been a beautiful relationship that will never end.

—Love and Mahalo, Julie

A NOTE ON THE TEXT

A long distance triathlon race that consists of a 2.4 mile swim, 112 mile bike, and 26.2 mile run. It is often referred to as the ironman distance. The IRONMAN® race that consists of this distance is the formal name of a series of long distance triathlons that is a registered trademark of the World Triathlon Corporation. For purposes of this narrative, all IRONMAN® races will be referred to as "Ironman," and references to a long distance triathlon race that is outside the purview of the World Triathlon Corporation is referred to as "ironman distance."

CONTENTS

FROM THE COAUTHOR   xi

FOREWORD BY ARMEN KETEYIAN   xv

PROLOGUE: FIFTEEN FEET . . .   xvii

1	How Do You Spell T-R-I-A-T-H-L-O-N?	1
2	Cannon Blast: Here We Go!	15
3	A Finish Like No Other	24
4	Going Viral, Circa 1982	37
5	One Article, Two Careers	50
6	Training Wheels	61
7	My Fifteen Minutes	74
8	Girl Power!	92
9	Riding the Wave: The Rise of Endurance Sports	106
10	Gripped: Finding Mark Allen	119
11	1989	142
12	Passing the Torch	155
13	Shifting Focus	168
14	Baby Grip Arrives	176
15	Out of the Spotlight	184

16   When Iron Breaks   198

17   Surfing Tsunamis: Raising Mats   214

18   A Hard Bottom   227

19   Can I Go Faster?   237

20   Mother & Son on the PCT   248

21   Kathleen   260

22   Kona 2017: What Contingency Plan?   270

23   My Iron Twin   289

24   Be Amazing at Any Age   302

EPILOGUE   319

A WEEK IN THE LIFE OF JULIE MOSS   323

ACKNOWLEDGMENTS   331

FROM THE COAUTHOR

I first met Julie Moss in 1971, when we were students at Valley Middle School in Carlsbad. She was funny, bouncy, and loved to make friends, the kind of girl with whom uber-shy boys like me could connect. She had plenty of personality but no airs, and didn't belong to cliques or try to impress others. And could she ever light up a classroom! She was the perfect girl to break a shy boy's trepidation over talking to girls, as she did mine. This was the first time she significantly touched my life.

We also attended Carlsbad High School at the same time. I was the athlete, for three years on one of San Diego County's finest cross-country teams, a strong two-miler in track, and a 1:18 half marathoner, which I ran in the 1976 San Dieguito Half Marathon at age sixteen. After Title IX passed in 1972, her freshman year, Julie took advantage of expanding girls' opportunities to try a variety of sports. She went out for softball as a freshman, basketball as a sophomore, volleyball as a junior, and tennis as a senior.

Her reflective comment in the book *30 Years of the Ironman Triathlon World Championship*, produced for the 2008 Ironman, speaks to what fueled her high school years: "The underlying theme for me is that this triathlon community is real. It's familiar, and it's familial. And always a nice source to tap into."

She has always craved community, being part of the scene, adding to it, and enlisting her considerable energy and passion to help others help themselves. She routinely offers up a light or wise moment when they can use either. Or both.

That's a good thing, because Julie Moss is responsible for transforming triathlon from a small group of endurance sports fanatics into a global sport. It happened overnight—literally—with her crawl across the finish line at the 1982 Ironman, seen by an estimated twenty million stunned viewers on ABC's *Wide World of Sports.* Some even called ABC's switchboards to see if Julie had died.

Like most Carlsbad residents, when I saw the show, I was stunned. Shocked. How did my quirky, fun-loving surfer friend become one of the greatest endurance athletes *in the world?* When did she get in such great shape? Who anywhere had such drive and determination? When I interviewed her best lifelong friends from Carlsbad, Cindy Conner, Sue Robison, and Jim Watson, we shared our astonishment, which came to us in different ways. At the time, I was the assistant sports editor at the *Blade Tribune,* a North San Diego County daily newspaper. I wrote the follow-up piece, since I knew her. Sue actually called and, while in tears, warned Julie about the emotional impact of the segment, having watched it in Wyoming an hour before. As for Cindy? "It didn't register what she did until I saw the show, and then I thought, *holy shit! What did she just do?*"

Julie's crawl was not only an iconic moment in sports history, but the bell-wether moment of her life. She took her career further than most, racing professionally for eight years, ranking as high as No. 4 in the world, and winning several major competitions. Then, in an act befitting her selfless nature, she stepped off the very big stage she'd built and switched over to support her husband, the equally legendary Mark Allen, on his record-tying run of six Ironman titles. She returned to Kona in 1997, with Mark then supporting *her* effort, and then waved farewell to a sport that gave her life purpose, direction, and success. It was time to devote her fullest energies to raising their son, Mats.

Julie came back to race in 2000 in Oceanside, and in Kona in 2003. However, it was her return to Kona for the 2012 Ironman World Championship that ignited her quest to get into the best shape possible for another shot at racing. She dove headlong into triathlon, and also launched the Iron Icons speaking seminars with Kathleen McCartney, the winner of the 1982 "crawl of fame" race. She competed in races of various lengths, her goals always growing. She stepped up her work to empower women and girls. She took a side trip and, in 2016, nearly became the oldest woman in history to re-qualify as a California State lifeguard (she had been a lifeguard in the early 1980s). She trained with a focus, determination, and discipline exceeding her best professional years.

Julie became good again. Really good. Then she set a most ambitious goal for a nearly sixty-year-old athlete: to beat her 1982 Kona time, in Kona. In April 2017, she turned the clock back thirty-five years at the Ironman North American Championship, going twenty-three minutes *faster* than her 1982 Kona result. Granted, the Woodlands course near Houston and elements are less challenging, but how many people in their late fifties can race faster than they did at twenty-three? Earlier in 2018, she matched her 1982 Kona time—11 hours, 10 minutes—in winning her age group at Ironman New Zealand by *nearly two hours.*

Crawl of Fame will tell you what happened from there—which makes Julie's story that much more inspiring and heartwarming.

During Julie's halcyon years as the world's most recognized triathlete, I occasionally ran into her. We mingled at welcoming parties for the Jeep Tri-Prix series and Nike Triterium events, urban short-course triathlons I promoted while working for Julie's manager, Murphy Reinschreiber, and his business partner, Charlie Graves, both former triathletes. (Charlie later became Mark Allen's manager.) Whenever Julie turned up at the world surfing tour events I promoted, we invited her to be a guest announcer. She had the gift of gab and ability to entertain, inspire, and bring energy to everyone on the beach with her positive attitude, as contagiously as any you will come across.

Today, Julie is an iconic Ironman and USA Triathlon Hall of Fame athlete and popular event commentator, and I'm the grateful sidekick in telling the world her story.

Meanwhile, I'm still engaged in a racing career that resumed in 1998 and included five trips to the Boston Marathon and becoming a high school coach. Much of my inspiration to return to racing, after stepping away for twenty years, came from a book I found at a Tampa bookstore in 2000: *Workouts for Working People.* The authors? Mark Allen and Julie Moss.

This string of running-related experiences also included Julie writing me two years ago to accept an offer I'd made several times: to write her long-awaited memoir. We've had wonderful times, great conversations, and nice runs, as well as a significant run-in visit with an old friend—longtime *60 Minutes* correspondent and multiple *New York Times* bestselling author Armen Keteyian. The coauthor of *The System: The Glory and Scandal of Big-Time College Football, Tiger Woods,* and other great investigative works of sports journalism, he factors significantly in Julie's story.

In 2016, I invited Julie to assist with cross-country practices at our alma mater, Carlsbad High School. It took all of five minutes for our runners to realize her gift, as Julie went to work on their mental approaches, workouts, and form. At our season-ending banquet, which Julie keynoted, runners and parents got the full picture of this ultra-fit middle-aged woman who had been helping the kids: we played the *Wide World of Sports* footage from 1982. Gasps, cheers, tears, and disbelief filled the room.

That's how much of the world, including myself, reacted in 1982—and why Julie Moss is not only an icon and legend in her sport, but one of the most important sportswomen of our lifetime. She inspires. She motivates. She competes. She excels. She makes you feel better about yourself and the world just by striking up a chat. Most of all, she puts smiles on our faces while reminding us what is truly possible if we never give up, if we never quit.

Looking back, I feel it was destiny that she experienced the most dramatic moment in triathlon's forty-year history. She was the perfect ambassador for the sport, much as my good friend and four-time Boston Marathon and New York City Marathon champ Bill Rodgers was for distance running. She connected with ordinary people like herself, a complete unknown in 1982, and gave them inspiration to rise off the couch and improve themselves. Millions have since responded. Imagine touching millions of lives . . .

Enjoy *Crawl of Fame.*

—Robert Yehling

FOREWORD
by Armen Keteyian

I just finished reading an advance copy of Chapter Five of *Crawl of Fame,* so I apologize upfront if what follows sounds a bit emotional. As expressed in that chapter, a passion for truth and fairness has fueled my journalistic, storytelling life for the better part of five decades. Actually, if one is *really* counting, six decades, dating back to eighth grade at East Hills Junior High School in Bloomfield Hills, Michigan, where I won an award for reading the most books by any boy in my class.

So it should come as no surprise that I had to stop more than once for a couple of deep breaths while taking a trip down a very personal memory lane. I mean, how many chance encounters change *both lives?* A father, mother, grandparent, coach, counselor, neighbor, wife, or boss changing one life? I get that. Happens all the time. But *two lives?* No, that's some very rare air. Yet in a kismet kind of way, that's exactly what happened back in the winter of 1982—the beginning of a beautiful friendship that remains to this day.

If you're holding this book, odds are you know the Julie Moss Story—or at least the marquee captivating-crawl-across-the-finish-line-at-Kona part of it. You know that back in February 1982, the cosmos shifted, and a bolt of black broke through and sent a 23-year-old triathlete sprawling to the ground just a hundred yards from winning the 140.6-mile torture test known as the Ironman Triathlon. As you're about to find out (as did I), it would hardly be the last time darkness dropped by for a visit, only to see the divine Ms. M rise, recover, and cross arguably more important finish lines in her life.

I love Julie. I say that as a married man of thirty-eight years. The fact in 2016 we re-connected after nearly thirty-five years—thanks to our dear, mutual friend and triathlon legend Scott Tinley—brought a level of pure joy and happiness that is hard to express. I dare say she feels the same way.

Now Julie is training to return to Kona in October. Her goal this time is to run a strong race all the way through—at age sixty. You read that right. Six zero. It's the stuff of movies, legends, maybe both, especially since she will be joined in the race by her son, Mats. Maybe, just maybe, if all goes well, she will try to best her 1982 finish time . . . a fairy tale ending. Regardless, the 2018 race is coming from Julie's heart, her personal "thank you" to all who have cheered her on.

To me, Julie's greatest gift has always been her ability to inspire. To show others that *anything* is possible, if you can somehow find the strength and courage to get on your feet and keep moving forward. Crawl, walk, swim, bike, run, it doesn't matter. An inch or a mile, it doesn't matter. Just try.

This book, in so many wonderful ways, tells that inspiring story and so much more—tracing the birth of the triathlon community by a small band of renegade athletes, the gods and goddesses of a movement, and their willingness to test the limits of human endurance.

But make no mistake: In the end, this is one woman's story—a wonder woman, if you will, whose heroic display of heart changed countless lives, including mine.

Armen Keteyian
San Clemente, CA

PROLOGUE
Fifteen Feet . . .

Fifteen feet isn't very far. When you compare it to, say, 140.6 miles, it is no more than a grain of sand on the beach. A marathon runner can cover it in three strides. You and I can walk it in a couple of seconds.

But what about crawling fifteen feet *after* swimming, cycling, and running for eleven hours beforehand? And having your body give out for the whole world to see?

Those 15 feet led to a final, agonizing thirty-second crawl that changed my life forever. I've been told they riveted a *Wide World of Sports* audience, pushed triathlon into the global spotlight, helped launch today's endurance sports boom, and in turn told women and men everywhere, "I too can push myself beyond what I thought possible. I can do anything if I give everything I have—and don't quit."

But I wasn't thinking about any of that as I lay on the ground in Kona, Hawaii, with people and their cameras hovering over me. I just thought to myself, *crawl.* I thought I could crawl, stay low, and disappear, and everyone would leave me alone so I could get to the finish line.

The second half of my crawl, something broke open: *Wait a minute. What just happened here? You just found yourself.*

I also realized my life would never be the same. I felt like I was in a cartoon where I moved really fast to the finish line, only to have it end slowly and painfully slow. *Forget about that,* said the voice inside, the voice ·I never knew existed. *What happened here? You just found a way to tap into a source you didn't know existed. If you can do this, wow, life is going to be really different.*

First, I had to crawl over the finish line . . .

Many people have written about the 1982 Ironman World Championship. Now, finally, I share my story of what legendary *Wide World of Sports* host Jim McKay famously called, "the most agonizing moment I've ever seen in sports," and everything that happened before and since. Like my inner voice said, life became really different.

—Julie Moss

CHAPTER 1
How Do You Spell T-R-I-A-T-H-L-O-N?

I sat in a marine biology class in Palomar College, wondering why I'd chosen the course. It was the hardest class I'd ever taken; there was no screwing around. I'd never worked this hard in high school, why start now? I signed up for an easier ride to a degree, much like the way I envisioned the rest of my life.

The universe had other plans—but not right away.

By the time I transferred to Cal Poly-San Luis Obispo, I had gotten caught up again in being an independent college girl . . . no curfews, no one to answer to, being my own boss—and a pretty liberal boss at that. I remember a class in statistics. After the third or fourth session, I skipped class to go surfing. After falling behind, I went to the tutor's office and asked, "Could you give me the formulas I'm probably going to have to know to pass the class?" That's how I passed the class, by going to a couple of tutoring sessions. Then I took the same muscle anatomy class as the premed students, so no punches were pulled. It was tough. After dropping it twice, I took it a third time, the semester before I graduated—and passed with a D. I found it interesting, but rote memory and I didn't get along too well.

My approach to school was simple. I did what I needed to do when pushed up the wall and it was crunch time. I was spontaneous, disorganized, and flew by the seat of my pants. My roommate and best friend Lisette and I would leave at 2:00 in the morning to go to Esalen, the mineral baths in Big Sur, when they'd open to the public for massages and you could use the cliff-top pools. We'd get back in time for that morning's final. If the surf was up, I didn't bother.

Ever hit the rewind button on your life—and see answers to how you grew into the person you are today? One advantage of reflecting is that we can hit those rewind and replay buttons, view our experiences from different angles, see a deeper purpose or direction, and grow forward with a broader perspective, a richer story.

So, for a little sporting fun that morphed into a personal growth saga, and turned me from an unknown, barely-getting-by student and surfer into "the girl who put triathlon on the map," let's hit the rewind button:

February 6, 1982: California Surfer Girl shows up in Kona well over her red head—only she doesn't know it yet.

Remember that late-1990s prime-time show *Early Edition*? Kyle Chandler (who would later star in the TV series *Friday Night Lights* and *Bloodline* on Netflix) receives a copy of the *Chicago Sun-Times* newspaper the day before its headline event occurs. With that foreknowledge, he prevents those terrible events from happening.

When my alarm clock rattled at 4:00 A.M. on February 6, my *Early Edition* headline was already printed. I just didn't know it yet. I was nervous and excited, nervous because I'd never tried something as crazy and grueling as this Ironman triathlon, and excited because . . . I'd never tried something as crazy.

I walked onto the lanai outside the small condo. In the balmy predawn darkness, the full moon reflected Hawaii's classic silver postcard light off the ocean. It did not feel like the beginning of a day that would take us into 100°F lava fields or me to the edge of my physical limits. It felt like another sweet morning in one of the world's most beautiful places.

As the moon cast her graces on me, I took a moment to reflect. I wasn't the same girl that landed on the Big Island a few weeks before. I was stronger, more confident, and starting to know a few of the triathletes I'd first seen nearly a year before on TV. I'd learned enough about triathlon since watching the coverage of the 1981 race on *Wide World of Sports*—the year they moved the Ironman from Oahu to Kailua-Kona—to understand it was an ultra-endurance sport that drew a small band of crazy adrenaline junkies who got off on swimming 2.4 miles, biking 112 miles, and running 26.2 miles. The 580 competitors were true outliers, some twenty-five years before Malcolm Gladwell famously coined the term. They must have loved what they did: there was no prize money for covering those 140.6 miles, only trophies to the top five men and women.

I got the feeling this sport was on the rise in a grassroots way, though the boost from ABC certainly helped introduce us to mainstream sports fans. But I really didn't know much; I was almost as new to this as the viewers. I'd just broken up with my boyfriend, top-ranked triathlete Reed Gregerson, so I wasn't under anyone's wing. I'd already entered the race, but when Reed and I split I was left without housing for the final week in Kona. So I called race director Valerie Silk. I asked if there was a homestay, a place where someone would let me stay for free.

As fate would have it, Valerie and I sat together on the flight from Los Angeles to Kailua-Kona. She was the best captive audience an Ironman neophyte could have. Valerie was the pioneer who secured the contract for *Wide World of Sports* to televise our fringe-sport race. During those five hours alongside her, did I pepper her with questions about the course, about hydrating, where the toughest sections were, what to expect? No. I really didn't know what to ask.

Around me, some triathletes felt like they were on the cusp of a leap forward. It wasn't a secret club or anything, more a collection of diverse individuals bonding together, like a cool high school or college team. They shared the feeling that they were doing something no one else could do. If you were in, you were in. It wasn't even about how fast you were, but that you would even show up and try this.

I would become one of them. Hopefully. No, check that: I *believed* I would get to the finish line.

I flashed back to Cal Poly-San Luis Obispo professor Dr. James Webb's smiling face and recalled his words to me months before: "I can't wait to see how this turns out." It was hard to surprise the creator of the exercise science lab at the university (now known as the James L. Webb Human Performance Lab) about anything pertaining to exercise physiology or kinesiology. He sounded more like a kid saddling up with popcorn and a Coke, dying to watch this train wreck adventure unfold. There was a reason his words skidded through my mind: *If I don't get to the finish line, if I don't finish this race, I don't graduate.* Studying and running the Ironman was my senior project. That's why I was here! It felt sort of comedic in a way; I didn't take it too seriously.

My musing over Dr. Webb unleashed a flood of feelings and images from the whole wild, zigzagging sequence of events that brought me to this lanai in the best shape of my life, getting ready to go *Star Trek*. You know, go where no man has gone before. Or, in this case, a 23-year-old surfer girl from Carlsbad, California, whose athletic background consisted of joining high school sports teams to be part of the team and wear the uniform. I just wanted the atmosphere, to be near the action but without any pressure on my shoulders.

My road to Kona started a year earlier on a cold, rainy midwinter afternoon on California's central coast, where Pacific storms sweep through with gusto. I was stuck inside, and didn't want to study, so I flipped to ABC's *Wide World of Sports*, a Saturday TV fixture that featured a variety of sports competitions, many of them quirky. It was the flagship magazine of ABC Sports, the brainchild of legendary executive Roone Arledge, who also created *Monday Night Football*. Think of *Wide World* as an early sports version of *60 Minutes*, because it inspired that format. It also inspired ESPN, which essentially replaced it. In the early years, ESPN featured many of the same wild, unheard-of sports in its round-the-clock format. It was like watching the X Games every time we viewed the show.

The show opened with host Jim McKay's distinctive voice, warm and assured, burnished from broadcasting thousands of sporting events. There was also a montage of images, with the words that still ring as gospel to baby boomer (and older) sports fans: "Spanning the globe to bring you the constant variety of sport. The thrill of victory . . . and the agony of defeat . . ." Then it showed Slovenian ski jumper Vinko Bogataj crumbling and falling over the edge of the jump.

That "agony of defeat" opening image very nearly changed after the February 1982 Ironman.

I curled up on my sofa and got comfortable. The show started with log-rolling, part of an international lumberjack competition. *Wide World of Sports* famously introduced us to dozens of sports we never knew existed. I thought it then, as I do now: it was an incredible look into the way people use their home landscapes and love of competition to create sports that involve community and competitor alike. Imagine running a dog team through frigid tundra in the Iditarod, diving off the majestic cliffs of Acapulco, paddling through nasty ocean swells between Maui and Molokai, or playing a very rugged form of polo in Mongolia. From all cultures arise sports that measure our vitality, strength, coordination, strategic mastery, speed, agility, and teamwork. Some are for fun, while others can literally decide one's social, leadership, and/or economic status for life. Among its many lasting contributions, *Wide World of Sports* gave us a rich cultural window into the rest of the world.

After the logrolling ended, there it was: *the Ironman.* Instantly, I was mesmerized. I was also astonished by how far competitors had to swim, bike, and run—140.6 miles in all. How could the human body even handle that? The location, however, was gorgeous. As a surfer and lover of nature and her forces, the raw beauty of the Big Island captivated me. I was equally captivated by the beauty of ripped, sculpted Ironmen in their Speedos, some the same age as me. While I saw plenty of eye candy on the beaches, particularly among the lifeguard crew I also wanted to join, I wasn't used to seeing so many perfectly fit bodies in one place lining up for a swim. That caught my attention right away.

Two years before, in my sophomore year at Cal Poly, I'd gone on a surf trip to Kauai. I took out a student loan for the first and only time, not to finance housing, tuition, or books, but to get a new surfboard and pay for my airfare. You know, the ingredients of an academic sabbatical. Instantly, I fell in love with the place and its atmosphere.

I glued myself to every second of the Ironman segment. During the final leg, the marathon, ABC cameras zoomed in on the competitors' faces. A national audience and an increasingly riveted coed saw their strained expressions, the look of digging as deeply into themselves as a human being can dig. Those expressions moved me in a way I still can't explain. You would think the harsh struggle and agony written across their faces would repel a non-athlete like me, and make me run 26.2 miles in the *opposite* direction. Or drive 140.6 miles.

Instead, the Ironman drew me in. While watching the athletes simultaneously compete with each other and struggle with their physical limits, I felt an intense gut reaction. My body was telling me to pay attention. To what? The bodies of the Ironmen? No problem! I have eyes too, which feasted on these beautiful men and equally striking women. However, the larger beauty of the effort mesmerized me. *What does it feel like to go there?* "There" being the limit of your physical capability. *What happens when you do?* And *why?* Why were these people willing to push themselves so hard? Okay, they're in Hawaii, a great place, but why *push it* in the land of coconuts, mai tais, leis, and lazy ocean-fed getaways?

The questions kept spinning inside.

When they got to the marathon, I saw the impact of the race with greater acuity. The highly talented (and gorgeous) Scott Molina led until he fell apart in the lava fields, where high winds whipped through a 100°F day. Here's this absolute darling lying on a stretcher, the one peers and press would soon call "The Terminator" due to his lethal way of ending your thoughts of winning. I couldn't wait to see the next fit, great-looking twentysomething grab control . . . but instead, it was thirty-four-year-old John Howard, the 1971 Pan American Games road cycling gold medalist, four-time U.S. National Road Cycling champion, and three-time Olympian. In 1985, three years after finishing second in the inaugural Race Across America, he would also set the world pedaled vehicle record of 152.2 miles per hour on the Bonneville Salt Flats in Utah. However, John didn't have the same classic, technically sound running form as many of the others. He had skinny little arms and big legs that belong to cyclists who spend hours a day in the saddle. Nothing against John, who went on to win after finishing third the year before, but my heart broke for Scott Molina as he lay on that stretcher.

So many moments captivated me. One I never saw. Maybe I blinked and missed it, but I never saw a woman swimming, biking, or running. It wasn't until after the main segment, when they rolled the closing credits, that *Wide World of Sports* viewers saw first-place woman Linda Sweeney cross the finish line. That was disappointing. *Where were the women? They were out there competing and racing hard too.*

Afterward, my brain and body buzzed. I couldn't stop thinking about Scott Molina and wondering why anyone would keep pushing until they fell into a stretcher. Was Scott even going to be okay?

Shortly after watching the race, a crazy idea hit me: I should do my senior kinesiology project on the Ironman! I was heading into my senior year at Cal Poly, and I needed something original—why not? I always listen to my intuition, for an original or unique angle, and this notion shot straight out of my gut. I could fly over, interview the triathletes, get on closer terms with those smart, gorgeous people, study the science behind pushing yourself to the edge of your mortality, then head home and write it up. Pretty cool project, right? Well, the driven, quirky, and outrageous side of me, which once pushed a little girl through many hours and crashes to lose her training wheels and ride a bicycle, then to death's edge in massive surf, thought my own idea a little dull. So I spiced it up: *Why don't you learn about the Ironman by running the Ironman?*

I took a look in the mirror. I still carried half of the dreaded Freshman Fifteen weight. Biking and running were not my sports of choice, though I loved to swim, and surfing had made me a powerful swimmer. Also, isn't 140.6 miles something you drive in a car—for several hours—without facing the heat-bearing, soul-crushing headwinds of the Big Island?

It didn't matter: I was fixated. My brain brought along my heart and competitive drive, and it wasn't about to let go.

Time to get to work. First, I had to convince Dr. Webb to approve the Ironman study for my senior project. As my final graduation requirement, it needed to reflect my entire college experience. I spent a couple weeks putting together my proposal. He looked it over, lifted his head, and asked me two questions:

"Julie, have you ever been a competitive athlete in swimming, biking, or running?"

"No."

"Have you ever gone the Ironman distance for a swim, bike, or run?"

"No."

He leaned back in his chair. After a long silence, a sly grin flashed across his face. "It's definitely an original senior project . . . and Julie, I can't wait to see how this turns out," he said.

I wasn't quite sure if he was referring to the success of the project, or the train wreck he foresaw. Nonetheless, Dr. Webb encouraged me to take the risk, and to not let my inexperience stop me. He pointed out that an essential part of a college education is to dream those big, fearless dreams. But how big did it really need to be? Ironman big? For a girl that had never run a 10K? Would I become one of those crazy adrenaline junkies who keeps chasing unattainable goals forever?

After Dr. Webb's approval, I reassessed my situation. The only part of this race I could do well was swim. I grew up surfing, which led to my becoming a San Luis Obispo County and, later, California State lifeguard.

Then there was the 138.2 miles of this race that take place on land. Could I run a full marathon? Could my bike even pedal 112 miles? *I don't think so.* Still, it came out of mothballs to chase the dream. When I got a summer lifeguarding job at Lopez Lake, I commuted the thirty miles from my home in Shell Beach by bike. Without realizing it, I was getting a base. I went with Lisette and bought Nike Waffle Trainers, and started running to burn off my Freshman Fifteen. We ran to the beginning of the Cal Poly San Luis Obispo trail, down a road to start the trail, which continued onto miles of rolling hills and ranches bordering the campus. But instead of going through the cattle gate, and onto this fine trail run, I turned around. It was maybe 2.2 miles round-trip, the most I could do. The running piece didn't thrill me much.

The summer before, I had gone home to North San Diego County and met a lifeguard. Reed. Never shy about introducing myself, I knew many of the lifeguards, but I hadn't seen *this* guy. He was from Northern California, a recent economics graduate of UC-Davis, located in the same town near Sacramento that was also home to the Man, Dave Scott, triathlon's first dominant champion. After sitting in the tower all day, Reed would change to these weird leather black-laced shoes and black wool shorts, get on his bike, and ride. He told me how he liked to fly fish and tie his own flies; he was very unique. He had a fresh perspective on life, and was full of integrity. I spent the better part of the summer trying to figure out how he would notice me. I'd even get up at 5:00 A.M. and bake banana bread to drop off at his tower! Though I was as surf-and-sand as they come, I wasn't the prototypical knockout blond California girl that would draw the average lifeguard's attention. I was (and am) a redhead with fair skin.

However, I overcompensated for my freckles with personality, that different kind of "it" factor that some call a "girl-next-door" appeal. Personality, charm, and the positive energy I enjoy and like to extend came through for me, big-time, combined with a singular laser focus on the object of my affection.

At the end of the summer, we started dating. He was planning to do a cross-country solo bike trip, so he took off the following winter, but not before talking to me about triathlons. I believe that's the first time I conversed about a sport that was started by the San Diego Track Club and some lifeguards on September 25, 1974, right in my backyard, at San Diego's Mission Bay. The initial promotional flyer read:

> *The First Annual Mission Bay Triathlon, a race consisting of segments of running, bicycle riding, and swimming, will start at the causeway to Fiesta Island at 5:45 P.M. September 25. The event will consist of 6 miles of running (longest continuous stretch, 2.8 miles), 5 miles of bicycle riding (all at once), and 500 yards of swimming (longest continuous stretch, 250 yards). Approximately 2 miles of running will be barefoot on grass and sand. Each participant must bring his own bicycle. Awards will be presented to the first five finishers.*

Many of the earliest triathletes were lifeguards who wanted a more challenging format than the run-swim-run-swim routine of state and national lifeguard competitions. Reed also had a cycling friend, Dennis Hearst, whose girlfriend was Kathleen McCartney; all were connected to this very early triathlon scene. Reed thought he might be interested in it too.

While Reed was on his cross-country bike trip, I watched the Ironman on TV. I knew he was fascinated by the race . . . and now I was too.

My research project was entitled, "Physiological and Training Considerations in Preparation of the World Ironman Triathlon." After reviewing the requirements, and knowing I did not train like Reed Gregerson or Dave Scott, I faked my way through training and the race. *Really, Julie? Faking it?* That's what a certain sixty-year-old would say to the twenty-three-year-old if they walked past each other today. Moreover, with Reed now in my life, training for Ironman became as much about pursuing a relationship as it did about trying to reach the finish line and graduate. We were ill-suited to work out together, though. I'd start out on the bike with him, but turn around halfway so he could carry on with his own training.

I had to turn in a progress report during the Fall 1981 semester. Here's the thing with a progress report: you have to show some progress. In the late summer, I completed my first triathlon, a 70.3-mile Half Ironman, now known as an Ironman 70.3, in Santa Barbara. I got a flat tire, sat on the side of the road, and ate my sandwich while the guy I'd been riding next to stopped and unselfishly offered to help me fix my tire. Some competitive drive, right? It was rough. Once we started riding again, I decided to stick with this Good Samaritan who had graciously helped me out, but I left him behind six miles into the run. It was like, "You're too slow. I've gotta go, see ya."

Only later did I recognize this as an early sign of my natural endurance, tenacity, and competitiveness. I did learn, quickly, that triathlon is an individual event and when the going gets tough, you better be willing to go it alone.

I was so happy to finish, even though I was hours behind women's winner Kathleen McCartney.

For me, it was Mission Accomplished. Reed was planning to compete in the Oakland Marathon on November 5, and I figured I'd better go too.

I jumped in with this idea that I'd run a 3:30 marathon—despite never covering more than thirteen miles in any long run. I don't know why 3:30 sounded so appealing and attainable; maybe I'd heard people talking about marathons and thought, "That sounds like a good number." It does average out to exactly eight minutes per mile; maybe that was it. As it turned out, I ran 3:39, despite blowing up at twenty miles. I suffered through the final 10K. Really suffered.

But that wasn't the worst suffering in November. A few weeks later, Reed and I split up. It was the worst thing that had ever happened to me—and I brought it on myself.

Young love, when combined with long distance, insecurity, and low self-esteem, can sabotage a relationship. These accelerants blew up my relationship with Reed. Slowly and painfully, I took responsibility for self-sabotaging actions. I cried buckets of tears through this process. I had to take responsibility for all the parts of my life that I'd sabotaged and coasted through. No more riding coattails, no more romantic notions of training into the sunset together. No more settling for doing the minimum to get by.

When my love life came to a crashing halt, it was time to get real, to pick myself up, and refocus on getting to the finish line in Kona. Heartache and regret morphed into this motivating idea that I owed it to myself and, in some awkward misguided way, also to Reed, to do better, to be better, to show up and race with integrity. The one thing to prove was to graduate from Cal Poly, and in doing so validate my self-worth. The road to graduation led directly through Kona.

I proceeded to do exactly what you're not supposed to do when training for an Ironman—too many miles too close to the race. But I didn't realize or understand any of that. In January 1982, I ran another marathon, and started riding the bike more. Three weeks after that, on February 6, I ran the Ironman. That's three marathons in three months . . . with a rather long swim and bike ride thrown in.

Days after the second marathon, I flew to Kona.

◆

I showed up in Hawaii overtrained in running and undertrained on the swim and bike. What little I'd learned about training for an Ironman over the past months led me to conclude I hadn't done enough for a race this length. I'd never swum or biked the Ironman distance in one shot. I'd only started and finished two triathlons of any kind, the Del Mar Days sprint triathlon and Santa Barbara 70.3-miler.

Since I didn't know any Ironman triathletes but Reed, I was prepared to figure things out on my own. For the first week, I trusted my intuition. I was aware of certain miles I needed for a buildup to the race, and focused on hitting the numbers. What I wasn't prepared for was the support of the triathletes, or the organic community forming before my eyes. I discovered Kailua-Kona was filled with welcoming members of a brand-new tribe. The Hawaiian word for family is *ohana*, and I'd just found mine. I didn't realize how much I craved a support system or how much I'd thrive under the positive mentorship of hundreds of endurance athletes. My newfound ohana made workouts feel less like work and more like fun. Every day was a new aloha adventure.

There was just one problem. I trained my ass off in Hawaii, building conditioning and base, when I should have been tapering. They are the opposite ends of the long-race training spectrum, with entirely different goal outcomes. Ahhh, bright-eyed ignorance! Fortunately, I had my own ohana living in Waimea, my second cousin Frank. He commuted from Waimea to Parker Ranch, where he worked as a paniolo, a cowboy. I threw my bike in the back of his pickup for the drive to the northern interior of the Big Island, just south of the Pu'u O Umi Natural Area Reserve. From the backside of the island to Parker Ranch, I'd get on the bike and go down this long downhill, hit the Queen Kaahumanu (Queen K) highway, then pedal another twenty-five miles into town—about thirty miles in all. I made this commute roundtrip every day so I could hang out with the other triathletes.

At the end of my first week in Hawaii, they held a bike time trial on the course, for which they provided aid stations along with a sag wagon, so you could ride the full 112 miles without stopping. I had to ride thirty miles just to get to the start. By the time we got to the finish, I still had to ride six miles back to town to meet Cousin Frank for my lift back to Waimea.

A 150-mile day, two weeks before the race. Shouldn't I be backing off? What's backing off? In one of his Trihistory.com blogs, legendary Big Four triathlete and good friend Scott Tinley put it like this: "Intending to use the remaining (time) to ramp up her performance on the bike, she decided to add said commute distance to her planned bike training, which overall amounted to almost 400 miles the week before the race."

Here's something I learned: you don't do that and expect to finish a race standing up. I'd "hit the wall" at the Oakland Marathon at twenty miles, when my glycogen stores dried up and the body started pulling sustenance from its own muscle cells. You can go from smooth striding to cramped walking in a matter of seconds. I'd also hit the wall at twenty-three miles in the Mission Bay Marathon, so if I kept progressing, I'd make it through all 26.2 miles of the Ironman marathon without locking up. Barely. That was the math I was hanging onto.

My other issue, which I didn't really know *was* an issue, concerned my apparel. I showed up in Hawaii with a tank top, shorts, and running shoes, the basic wardrobe for any good long run . . . right? Well, shortly before the race, after one of my training swims, a man named Frank Finizio, who I'd met on the bike time trial, approached. "What are you gonna wear?" he asked. I followed the unspoken second half of his question pretty easily . . . *in the three phases of the Ironman?*

"This cotton tank top [Olympic speed skating gold medalist and top cyclist] Eric Heiden signed after doing a criterium in San Luis Obispo, and I've got some shorts."

"No, you need a lycra speedsuit."

"Well, that's nice, but . . ."

"No, no, no, I've got a friend in Orange County who can overnight one so you can race in it." That's Ironman ohana.

I stitched everything together on a student's budget. My biggest expense was my $295 Univega bike and the $85 Ironman entry fee. Dooley McCluskey's, the Carlsbad bar where my brother Marshall worked, sponsored my airfare. I used my training Speedo for the swim, the free speedsuit from Frank, free lodging, and a free trucker's cap from the swag bag. I didn't wear sunglasses, and I put a sweatband on underneath the hat. My helmet was not a cyclist's helmet, but a skateboarding helmet that cost less and featured more air holes. I also wore front-hooking bra to save time, but the hook broke during my transition from cycling to running.

With my equipment set, if you can call it that, I was ready to race. Except for one last detail that could prove to me the costliest: I hadn't seen my ex-boyfriend in my first two weeks in Kona. The thought of running into Reed became the albatross around my neck. I knew that even a brief encounter had the potential to throw me into a tailspin, and I couldn't afford to face him on race morning. A negative reaction could put my whole race under a cloud of pain and regret. I had spent weeks working hard to move forward and focus on my training. I needed my heart to be strong when the cannon blasted to start the race.

What happened? I took matters into my own hands and knocked on his condo door at the beginning of race week. The word that I'd use to describe our brief encounter is *graceful*. It left me with a sense of relief and peace. Seeing him was bittersweet, but I knew I was going to be okay. Even if I was there to prove something to him more than myself, as I later admitted to *Triathlete* magazine.

Three nights before the race, competitors got together for an Ironman carbo-loading party. There were 580 people entered (up from 380 the year before; thank you, *Wide World of Sports*), but as the new kid on the block, I didn't know many elite triathletes. Apparently, a couple knew about me. Kathleen had, like me, watched her first Ironman the year before. While I cozied up in front of my TV, she stood on the Kona seawall to watch her boyfriend (and future husband), Dennis Hearst. Many pundits considered her a prerace favorite, and she'd also clocked the winning time in the recent Ironman bike time trial.

For some crazy reason, though, Kathleen focused on the gossip circulating about all my final training miles. My time trial wasn't too shabby, either, even with a thirty-mile warm up. But it was still hard to imagine anyone concerned about me, when this was all so new—the race, the faces, my obvious inexperience. I did love one thing about it: the positive attention directed at me. I wasn't used to that.

The whole scene at Kona, capped by the carbo-load party, was so grassroots and low-key that it was *fun*. But fun was about to turn into something else entirely.

CHAPTER 2

Cannon Blast: Here We Go!

Where's the aloha spirit? Where did my ohana go?

Three weeks of new friendships, fun times, and workouts in the spirit of shared purpose evaporated before my eyes. Down at the Kailua Pier, race day became all business for athletes, crew, and officials alike. Everyone was so serious! The specter of the upcoming race engulfed the pier like a thick fog, or vog, the air pollution that develops when an erupting volcano's gases and particles interact with moisture in sunlit air. In other words, highly unsettling to me.

Nonetheless, I was lucky to be free of the expectations that others carried into their races. Some athletes came to win, others to place as highly as possible. Some came to take their shot at this slowly growing juggernaut of endurance sports events, maybe get some good press, or pick up a sponsor from the slim pickings available. I wanted *nothing* to do with that energy. Whatever these people were going through, their personalities had changed overnight, becoming moody, even unfriendly in some cases. It reminded me of thoroughbreds at the starting gate. If this is what competition felt like, I didn't want any part of it. I wanted my happy ohana back.

My mantra was much simpler: *I just have to finish.* I paid my dues in the lava fields by hammering long bike rides in preparation, I earned my spot on the starting line, and paid then-$85 entry fee. I joined 579 other starters at the water, ready to roll, ready to head off for the fifth running of the Ironman World Championship. I didn't come to win, or even to compete. I just wanted to ensure my graduation. With only two marathons and two triathlons, that added up to less than Ironman distance under my belt, plus furious last-minute training on the Big Island, I didn't exactly have the background of a serious contender. I didn't care either.

I just have to finish. For my degree. For myself.

During my seventeen days of training and meeting people on the Big Island, I'd learned a few more things. I also started meeting the subjects of articles I'd read on triathlon for my Cal Poly research paper. One of the most prominent was Tom Warren, profiled in a major *Sports Illustrated* story in May 1979, three months after he won the second Ironman. His profile fit my initial perception of Ironman and its athletes to a T: the fledgling sport and its enthusiasts were operating on a remote, borderline sane island. In reality, though, the Ironman was born on quite populated Oahu, where fifteen hearty souls tried it in 1978, and another fifteen set out a year later. Twelve finished each time, including the first two winners, Gordon Haller and Tom Warren. The competitors in 1979 gained further street cred by surviving horrendous conditions for 140.6 miles of anything—gale force winds, huge swells, and stinging rain from a storm that dumped five *feet* of rain on the east coast of the Big Island. It was so nasty that a twenty-year navy veteran assigned to the rescue crew couldn't get his boat out of the harbor to reach competitors. Right there, most would call it a day and head for high ground and a beer. However, stuff like this drew me in, just like the 1981 Ironman television segment.

As I met more triathletes, and learned why they were so impassioned, something else struck me: nearly all were very smart and insanely driven, Tom Warren among them. Dive beneath this man of a million different workout routines, and you found a focused, hard-working physics degree recipient, owner of several homes and apartments, and proprietor of one of the best beach bars in San Diego. In 1975, he also started a great San Diego race and tradition, the Tug's Tavern Swim-Run-Swim. It consisted of a half-mile swim around Crystal Pier in Pacific Beach, followed by a five-mile run on the sand to the Mission Beach Jetty and back, with a swim around the pier and a run to the finish.

Others I met included doctors, real estate investors, business owners, exercise physiology majors and graduates, and people cooking up ideas toward the decade-long explosion in entrepreneurship that was ramping up. These athletes were brainy, thoughtful risk-taskers, driven by possibility and excellence, possessors of tremendous work ethics, and, to the young woman in me, very good-looking. Did I mention that before?

The other thing I began to understand was how significant Southern California was to triathlon. Hawaii might be the launching pad for the Ironman concept and Ironman World Championship, but San Diego County is the cradle of triathlon. It makes total sense: where else can you find perfect, moderate training weather nearly every day of the year, or landscape that varies from beaches and rolling hills to mountains—all within a ninety-minute drive? Where could you find countless running trails in open coastal foothills and scenic cycling routes, an ocean in which to swim, and so many young, health-conscious fitness freaks? And stores and restaurants that served natural, organic food? In the 1970s, we were the place.

We Southern Californians are known for setting fitness and fashion trends. Put wheels on surfboard-shaped decks, and you have skateboards. Match choreographed exercise routines to music, and you have Jazzercise. Take polyethylene foam and pour it into a mold about half the size of a surfboard, and you have the boogie board. It made perfect sense that some San Diego lifeguards who liked to run and swim would add bike riding to create a whole new athletic animal. Which leads to the next question: what do you call three sports strung together? A multisport relay? Triangle? Swim-Bike-Runathon? Don Shanahan, codirector of the inaugural Mission Bay Triathlon in 1974, crafted a clever hybrid of "tri" (for three) and the "athlon" suffix attached to multi-sport competitions (pentathlon, duathlon, decathlon, biathlon). He settled on *triathlon* because the trophy maker called him and didn't know how to spell the word. Apparently, that's when Don realized he had found a unique name for a unique sport.

Almost eight years later, I carbo-loaded in Kona among early creators and top competitors. Newcomers like me looked at people like Scott and Jeff Tinley, Scott Molina, 1980 winner Dave Scott, returning champ John Howard, Sally Edwards, Lyn Brooks, Claire McCarthy, and Ardis Bow as the stars of our tiny sport. These people were deadly serious about winning and excelling, with guys like ST (Scott Tinley) also learning everything they could about training techniques, equipment, using race conditions to your advantage, and borrowing conditioning ideas from fitness buffs of all different walks and talks. I might be running Ironman to get my college degree, which I cared deeply about, but triathlon was ST's *life*. He was the first and, I would argue, still the most knowledgeable "professor" on triathlon and its history. Which makes sense—today, Scott is an exercise physiology professor, prolific author, and a testament to continual, lifelong learning and the ability to turn your athletic talent into a deeply meaningful and serviceful life. He carries a PhD in cultural studies from Claremont Graduate University, and two master's degrees from San Diego State—a master's of Fine Art in fiction writing/literature, and a master's in social psychology of sport. He also has a BA in Recreation and Leisure Management. Really.

I took all of this in while asking myself, *would I ever commit to the sport like this? Would I commit to* anything *like this?* Sometimes we run into moments where we bear witness to people germinating something very special with their shared purpose. That's how I felt around this crew, though I couldn't imagine how a sport so far on the outer, extreme frontiers of performance could grow much. Or who was going to be the "forcing function" to elevate it to another level.

I felt something else too: a palpable camaraderie between people who probably (and obviously, in some cases) were rebels, social outcasts, or "different" in the eyes of conventional society. Well, they *were* different: they were smarter, more fit, and about to do something crazier than anyone I knew. It touched that part of me that loved being on the team, regardless of my position. I loved their vibe, and their belief that anything and everything is possible if you believe in yourself. Get that piece down, and then the world opens up for you to help you make it happen.

I came to Hawaii to see how my world might open up. So I fit right in.

◆

Time to go. With the sweet, beautiful vibe of common purpose replaced by the thick, tense racer's edge, we waded sixty meters offshore. I watched others position their bodies, shoot quick looks at each other, and tread water . . . without speaking. The huge mood shift throttled me, so I decided to get away from everyone. With all those bodies in the water, that might be hard, but I would try. After all, I wasn't in it to win it, just to finish . . .

Finally, the cannon blasted. *We're off!*

A year earlier, that same blast shook a seawall spectator to the core, causing her to seek her own Ironman goals. By the time Kathleen McCartney returned to Kona, she had trained for ten months, won three races, and done so convincingly. Now, she was the prerace favorite. The Ironman cannon blast can be a powerful thing.

However, Kathleen's last few days hadn't gone well. Far from it. Three mornings before the cannon blast, she woke up unable to stand without fainting. By later that morning, she was in the hospital, receiving tests for problems ranging from a serious virus to dehydration. She never received a certain diagnosis, though many (including her) suspected food poisoning. Not sure what she ate at the carbo-load dinner, but it must've been something. When she showed up at the starting line, she looked more like an ailing athlete who just wanted to get it over with than one who would become a part of sports history in eleven hours.

I swam away from the pack and starting-line stress, letting the balmy 76°F water settle me as I pushed forward. Once my breathing relaxed, I found a fluid inner zone, just blue water and motion. It was the same feeling I knew when surfing alone, in my aquatic environment, my soul's open-ocean playground. I started looking at the coral patterns, which I'd learned from swimming the course for days before the race. I knew where the coral took on sand, where it showed clearly. I immersed further in the quietness of being underwater as I stroked, disregarding the water churning like a hungry school of piranha beside me.

The course was simple. We swam a clockwise circuit, starting at Kailua Pier and going south for a little over a mile before turning around at Captain Beans Booze Cruise Boat—a perfectly ironic detail to a perfectly unique race. We kept the buoys on our right, the only directional thing we needed to remember. (That day's course would finish on the east side of the pier.) As we neared the swim exit, I began to hear spectators lining the seawall, which ran parallel to the rectangular course. Their excitement and positive energy erased the prerace tension. *That's more like it!*

An hour and eleven minutes after entering the water, I ran up the ramp on the far side of the pier to my first Ironman transition area, ducking into the women's change tent. I changed into my Wonder Woman Lycra skinsuit, stuffed my Snickers bar in my back pocket, and ran out of the change tent to grab my bike off the rack. I really loved the spectator energy surrounding the transition area. There's a little part of me that liked that attention, which I rarely had growing up. I liked it even better that some of the attention was directed at me.

Bring on the next Aloha Adventure. All 112 miles of it!

Bolstered by the swim, I rode smoothly toward the lava fields, loving the beautiful Hawaiian names of the roads: Palani Road to Kuakini Highway, a left to Makala Boulevard, a right toward the Queen Kaahumanu Highway . . . How can a fourteen-letter alphabet create words so sweet and gentle? I always feel the warmth and lushness of *aloha* gather on my tongue whenever I read or say the words. My favorite has to be the wedge-tail triggerfish, a tiny fish whose Hawaiian name is actually longer when spelled in standard twelve-point type: *humuhumunukunukuāpuaʻa* (pronounced ʼhumuʼhumuʼnukuʼnukuʼwaāpuʼwɐʔə). It means, "triggerfish with a snout like a pig." I later taught my son, Mats, how to spell it. I just love that word.

Now, thanks to my Ironman appearances, I have different, more specific, race-oriented associations for these road names, but as I rode my first Ironman bike leg, I was totally enthralled with the upwelling spirit of this place, the spirit of aloha, that had erased the vibe of a tense starting scene.

Twenty-five miles into my ride, the camera truck for ABC's *Wide World of Sports* drove up. I looked around—who were they following? *Why are you here?* Me? Really? *Why am I on your radar? Just getting quick shots of people doing their first Ironman?* Or maybe they noticed my battle to open a melted Snickers bar, my primary food source. I'd waited patiently to see if I could make it past Waikoloa Road, where for weeks I'd had to hang a right and head mauka—on the mountain side of the road—for a long climb to rendezvous with Cousin Frank, before I opened my sweet treat. I argued with myself over and over, "I want it, but I'm not going to have it now, not until I get past the turnoff to Parker Ranch." At that point on the Queen K, I reached into my back pocket . . .

Squish. It was totally melted. So much for delayed gratification. I tried to navigate the wrapper with one hand and my handlebar with the other while keeping up a comfortably brisk pace. As I started smearing chocolate on the white cotton handlebar tape, ABC drove up. *Right then.* I continued struggling with the melted chocolate, licking the wrapper to catch the drips. Chocolate dripped down my arm. I smeared a bit on my face. *Was America watching too?* I couldn't help but wonder.

This led to my next decision, made from the pure vanity of a girl getting her fifteen seconds on a show she loved. I needed all 350 calories of that king-sized Snickers bar, maybe not at that moment, but certainly later. Each calorie would make all the difference in the world. I didn't know or appreciate that. The only thing I appreciated was that the ABC cameras were on me and my face was a mess. *I can't be a chocolate mess on national TV!*

I did the only thing that makes sense when you're a young woman getting her first "Up Close and Personal," I chucked the uneaten Snickers bar into a fountain grass tuft in the lava field, quickly wiped off my face, sat up tall in my seat, waited for the camera crew to roll up, and flashed a big smile. "Hi! Aloha!" I exclaimed.

What a warm greeting, right? That decision turned out to be the most crucial of the day . . . and a big-time rookie mistake.

However, that was not on my mind. I had *Wide World of Sports'* attention, so we started a back-and-forth conversation, a TV-competitor relationship. We enjoyed each other's company in desolate conditions, unless you like howling winds, 100°F temperatures, moonscape surroundings, and no one else to talk to. I welcomed the company as much as the attention. Every time the van came back around, I felt like it was my private entourage. I really soaked it up and made sure to smile big-time.

The rest of the ride went smoothly, and the ABC camera truck rolled up a few more times to check in. We attempted "shaka brah" hand gestures, chatted it up, and had a good time. In Hawaii, the shaka sign—pinky finger and thumb up, middle three fingers down—symbolizes aloha spirit. It means "hang loose" or "right on," and reminds people not to worry or rush. *Everything's gonna be alright . . .*

Everything was definitely alright. My ride was pleasant, far from the misery some others suffered in the lava fields. I enjoyed much of it. As we closed in on the transition area—Queen K Highway down the hill on Palani Road, left on Kuakini Highway, right on Kuakini Boulevard, a sharp left onto Ali'i Drive, six miles to the sharp descent to Keauhou Bay to the Kona Surf Hotel and end of the ride—I felt like I was having a decent race, with plenty of energy still left in the tank.

When I reached the transition area, I received news from a race official that none of my friends would believe possible when it came to me competing in a sporting event: "You're the second-place woman."

Second? Really? Wow! *How did I get into second?*

The gears in my head reconfigured what was possible. I'd originally planned to move deliberately through the transition area, making sure everything was totally set for the marathon run ahead. *I'm in second place! Holy shit!* Not now. Change of plan. I hurried into the changing room at the Kona Surf Hotel, trailed by two volunteers eagerly waiting to help me. As I later reflected on how focused and intent they were to get me back on course, I realized *they* knew the race was on, and that I—the Cinderella girl, the girl next door, the unknown newbie—was in the thick of it. I wasn't sure what to make of it, but my brain quieted long enough for my newfound competitive instincts to kick in.

Meanwhile, in my rush to change into my run gear, I suffered a wardrobe malfunction. The hook of my bra broke cleanly off (a moment I love to mime when Kathleen and I give our Iron Icons presentation). Immediately, I sized up the two volunteers, *size* being the operative word. One woman was too big, but the other was just right.

I looked her in the eye. "Could you please give me your bra?"

Without hesitation, and to my eternal gratitude, she stripped off her Bud Light T-shirt, took off her bra, and handed it to me. Nothing else to say or discuss. She acted out of care for my well-being. The spirit of ohana, rising yet again. At this moment, while in a transition area after a nearly six-hour, 112-mile ride, filled with new ideas of what was possible, I fell in love with this woman and all other race volunteers. They are the unsung heroes of every event. We simply can't get through the race without them.

Of course, my "just right" volunteer was now more *unslung* than unsung. But she was my hero all the same.

I started the marathon filled with gratitude and adrenaline, a feeling of well-being that could best be expressed by something bestselling author Deepak Chopra said years later: "Gratitude opens the door to . . . the power, the wisdom, the creativity of the universe." It pays to live in gratitude. I also felt good. I'd survived the incident with the Snickers bar; America would see my smile without chocolate covering my face or body. I'd found a replacement bra. *The race drama is finally behind me.*

Meanwhile, after a difficult swim, and impacted by her weakened condition, Kathleen *did* load up on food and drink while riding in the lava fields. She had spent three days vomiting and getting IVs, watching her Ironman dreams swirl down the drain. Not exactly where you want to be mentally. In order to even be permitted to start, she had to get the official Ironman doctor to sign off on her hospital stay. Kathleen had also done a prerace interview with ABC; the cameras were also following her as an actual race favorite. Winning races draws attention, that's for sure.

"I started to feel better in the lava fields," Kathleen said. "I think just getting through the past few days, surviving the swim, and feeling the nutrition start to work, gave me a good feeling. I started to feel like I could race more strongly if I could get through the bike."

Thanks to smart refueling, and feeling better as she sweated out the last of her sickness, Kathleen managed to move up to sixth entering the marathon.

We had 114.4 miles down . . . and the hardest 26.2 to go.

CHAPTER 3
A Finish Like No Other

I left the transition area for the marathon with growing confidence. I'd run two marathons during my preparation for Ironman, so I felt like I knew how to do this. It was familiar, not a huge undertaking in my mind, despite the bike and swim that preceded it.

I started clicking off miles. The race seemed smoother than I thought possible after swimming and biking for seven hours. Then again, how would I know? I was deep into unknown territory. I loved the repeat visits from the ABC camera truck. Their attention, along with sitting in second place, started a new thought: maybe I *am* a serious athlete. TV trucks? Conversations with sportscasters? People peeling off bras to help me? Definitely a sign . . .

I was about to go where Julie Moss had never gone before, in any sports competition, at any time: into the lead.

Five miles into the marathon, I caught Pat Hines, a professional cyclist who had built her lead in the lava fields. However, the stress fracture in her foot caught up with her. She could barely walk. Something about this race drew people to extend themselves, take risks, and operate with a toughness beyond what they'd do in shorter or less significant races. I also learned that if you want to run Ironman and be competitive, this is the mindset to adopt.

Funny enough, I didn't realize I was actually leading until the ABC camera crew yelled from their van, "We're with you the rest of the way, Julie!"

Suddenly, I was leading the Ironman. *Leading the Ironman?* I think the only reason why I wasn't blown away was because I wasn't sure I believed what the ABC people were telling me. I ran smoothly and evenly, letting this notion of being in the lead take root. I looked around and behind for the other women, still not quite trusting the information.

Then it dawned on me that I had not seen any girls on the course since passing Pat. The ABC crew was right. I was really leading.

Talk about a massive shift! I started the day believing I could finish the Ironman. I also thought I could be one of the better competitors, since I'd finished just behind Kathleen in a training ride on the Big Island. I thought I had a chance to beat her. But to really be leading? *No.*

"People were starting to notice Julie before the race," Scott Tinley recalled. "We heard about this newcomer putting in ridiculous miles, three or four hundred miles a week during a time you're supposed to be tapering. A lot of people took notice, because who would do that so close to the race?"

Now in first place, I started thinking about the formerly unimaginable— *winning.* I'd never won anything in my life. I'd never *thought* about winning any sports event I'd entered. How do you go from that place to winning the hardest single-day multi-sport event in the world? Suddenly, just like Scott, Kathleen, and the more experienced triathletes, I began to think that to win I would have to push far beyond my comfort zone, a zone pressed only when I "bonked" late in the Oakland and Mission Bay Marathons. And when I nearly drowned surfing in Central California. The other top competitors had pushed into that territory before, but for me, it was like stepping off the earth and landing in a faraway galaxy. I did not know the pain, energy, or effort an "ultimate push" would entail. But I had to get ready for it.

While continuing to run steadily, I picked up a new friend to keep me company. Rohan Phillips, a men's competitor, opened with a somewhat pedestrian 1-hour, 31-minute swim, but rode an impressive 5-hour,

35-minute leg on the bike, which put him with me midway through the marathon. At first, I was annoyed, because I thought he'd blown up his race and wanted to run with the lead woman to grab some *Wide World of Sports* exposure. A photobomber, circa 1982. On top of that, he spoke with a really thick Australian accent, which made it hard for me to understand him. And he loved to talk. So do I, but not when focusing on the latter stages of a race or workout, when you need your mind to keep your exhausted body moving and you need to be mindful of every feeling inside and out, not to mention keeping an eye on competitors. "You can keep talking, but I'm going to be quiet and listen," I told him. I wanted to hang onto my energy, something counterintuitive to my normal outgoing personality, but necessary. He did say something pretty funny: "I'll just hang around you to get my picture in the paper."

Rohan and I decided to push each other. We formed the type of bond that happens spontaneously during long races and often leads to enduring friendships, especially if the race is significant for you. In the Ironman, it gets magnified, like everything else. As my body began to break down, my connection to this total stranger began to strengthen. I'll always fondly remember how selfless Rohan was, staying with me, even after we stopped talking. He never left my side.

I gained confidence from the continual validation of having my own television camera crew. However, unbeknownst to me, a blond storm gathered her forces several miles back. *Kathleen.* In our one common competition, the 70.3-miler, half of an Ironman, she'd beaten me by *two hours*. When Kathleen left the transition area in Kona, she was twenty minutes behind Pat and eighteen minutes behind me.

That was then. This was now, and she was gaining. Fast. Six miles into the marathon, she moved past Pat into second place, feeling rejuvenated from smart hydration and nutrition. Once again, she looked far more like the California poster girl many chose to win the race than the person hospitalized a few days before.

After receiving the first news of Kathleen's position, I made my second rookie mistake. With about eight miles to go, I heard she was eight minutes behind me. She'd made up ten minutes of her deficit, with the toughest miles to come. I started thinking, "She's here. She's got me now. You were winning the race and now you're second." That's inexperience rearing its ugly head. In reality, I was eight minutes *ahead,* about a mile at the pace we were running. With eight miles to go. Simple race management offers a simple solution to this situation: maintain my pace, stay steady and solid, don't speed up, but don't give up any pace either. *Make her catch me.* I just needed to forget about Kathleen and run the final miles consistently.

Instead, I panicked. I reacted like she was eight *seconds* behind. I pushed again, speeding it up, the worst thing you can do when dead tired, void of nutrition, and protecting a modest lead. Which wasn't even that modest. Eight minutes is usually an insurmountable late-race advantage, but right now, nothing made sense. I'm pretty sure that when race director Valerie Silk awoke on race morning (if she even slept the night before), she didn't envision an unknown redhead leading a prerace favorite just out of the hospital.

Kathleen's view of the situation is revealing. As she recalls, "By staying positive and patient, my mental strength allowed my physical strength to catch up. Running through the lava fields in the late afternoon, it was over 100°F. Up in the distance, I saw the most awesome sight . . . the turnaround marker . . . the two-story inflatable Bud Light can! As awesome as a giant can of Bud or Bud Light looks to *any* college student, I saw a sight that rivaled even that . . ."

The sight was *me.* I was firmly attached to this crazy idea of winning, of pushing faster to lock down this most absurd victory. It came with the *Wide World of Sports* crew shadowing my every move, filming me as I keep going faster, picking it up through the late miles.

When I spotted Kathleen at the eighteen-mile turnaround, she looked scary strong and fast. Definitely a threat; I'd made a smart move in picking up the pace. So I thought. What really unnerved me was how her rainbow hair ribbon coordinated perfectly with her rainbow running outfit. She was like a goddess—blond hair pulled in a ponytail, a perfectly matched outfit from her JDavid team (the first elite racing team in triathlon), the rainbow hair ribbon. That damned ribbon! She had a wholesome, blond, and beautiful Christie Brinkley look, a Madison Avenue ideal of an Ironman women's champion. She matched up well in team photos with her JDavid teammate, men's leader Scott Tinley. I wasn't the classic-looking athlete, I wasn't intimidating, and I was kind of dorky, putting out my vibe of "fake it 'til you make it."

As I put my eyes back on the road, I could only think, *she's so put together, making this look so easy. Who does that?*

Certainly not me! I was racing in a Bud Light trucker's hat from the swag bag we received, and the shoulder straps continued to slip from the bra I borrowed in the change tent. The Snickers bar, the bra . . . I took these issues in stride and dealt with them. But Kathleen's ribbon inserted doubt into my psyche. It also told me that she had all the details figured out, and she was coming for me. She could've been the scariest, most buff athlete on earth, a divine package of femininity and rippling muscles rolled into one, but the ribbon and coordinated outfit stuck. When we bring it up in our Iron Icons presentations, she talks about how she wore the ribbon underneath her swim cap, how it all comes down to the details. She was focusing on the details.

I didn't even know what the details were.

Kathleen's thoughts at the turnaround had nothing to do with rainbow ribbon fashion details or cover girl finish-line photo opportunities. Well, they did have to do with the finish line, namely, getting there ahead of me. "Up ahead I saw Julie," she recalled. "She was in first place, running toward me. But as Julie got closer, it was obvious her form was breaking down and she didn't look too good.

"I looked her in the eye. Then I looked down at my watch to get a split. Eight minutes down with eight miles to go. My legs burning, my body pushing itself to the limit, I knew I had to dig deep with every ounce of strength. But, if I could keep up this pace . . . I believed I could catch Julie. Every minute I chipped off the lead, my confidence grew."

Besides my body now beginning to feel the loss of that melted Snickers bar, I was dealing with a runner on the move. Worse, I had no idea how to manage a race from the lead. The next time my new BFFs from ABC pulled around, I asked, "Hey guys, find out how far back she is," in a voice that sounded distinctly Valley Girl. I also yelled out to spectators, "Can you see how far back she is for me?"

Kathleen was trying to take the lead from me!

From somewhere deep inside, far further than I'd felt anything before, a realization or insight moved through me like a command: *I don't want this taken away!* I'd never felt such possessiveness over a result before. I responded to this surge of inner whatever-it-was by promptly recasting Kathleen into my archrival, the archenemy for a day. Wonder Woman would prevail. *But which one?*

My brain screamed at my legs and body to push, speed up, fire ahead, ignore the pain. I was focused, trying to account for every stride, make it my best effort, but my body started protesting like a five-year-old throwing a hurricane tantrum. *I want to stop! Now! I'm going to hurt you if you don't let me stop!*

Suddenly, I couldn't fire anymore.

I hit *it*. The wall. Bonk! Every marathoner and ultramarathoner knows the feeling. When our glycogen stores deplete, our bodies literally begin to feed on themselves for protein, sugar, the fuel to keep going. The wall arrives quickly, in a matter of minutes or even seconds, and it can instantly turn your race on its head. If you've ever finished a marathon, you've witnessed the scene during the last six to ten miles, with active racers passing those who dropped out. Or you've bonked and had to labor through the rest of the race, sometimes running, sometimes walking, mostly doing the "marathon shuffle." Pushing ahead after you bonk is like trying to paddle out toward monster waves after being beaten up and held down by the five waves that preceded it. It's extremely difficult.

The race punched back, repeatedly and hard. I bonked first at about twenty miles, then hit the wall again at twenty-three. Kathleen was still a few minutes behind, but gaining. I knew it, but I also knew that *I deserved to win this race.* After struggling on the hot roads, this race took on an importance I'd never experienced.

Something was emerging from inside myself, beyond anything I could reach consciously. It was this tenacity and grit, an instinct as deep as DNA itself . . . *keep digging. Don't give up. Push like you've never pushed.* I started feeling this added tenacity when the ABC camera trucks gave me attention, then more so when I was leading. Suddenly, the switch flipped . . . *you deserve to be here. You earned this. It's okay. You just might be good at something, and that's all right. Don't hold back. Just go with us.*

Who was *us?* I didn't know. I only knew something cracked open, something silent and hidden until this moment; I was interacting and even conversing with my inner self for the first time in a competitive situation. *My inner voice.* My physical breakdown was allowing this other part to emerge, a component I never attended to or even acknowledged—my self-worth.

Before, the ego was involved—how do I look in front of the camera? Are they getting good shots of me? Where's *my* ribbon? That was being stripped away, like peeling layers of paint to get to the bare wall. As I opened up to this voice, this articulation of self-worth, this feeling I deserved to win, a strange energy moved through me that kept me going long after my physical reserves had been exhausted.

It also brought out the fighter in me. My self-worth was worth fighting for, to the outermost limits of my capacity to perform, if necessary. I'd never dreamed of leading the Ironman. Now, I was willing to suffer through these final miles to hang onto this new feeling of being good at something and being *worthy* of it.

No matter what happened as Kathleen and I headed for home, this moment of realization, which visited me in my time of greatest struggle, became the turning point of my race. And later, my life.

Kathleen, a crafty racer though admittedly ambivalent about competition itself, found an interesting new reference point to gauge the distance between us. "Running the final miles of the marathon, I'm also running out of time!" she recalled. "I feel like I'm gaining on Julie, but I can't tell how far ahead she is as I strain to see her along Queen K Highway. Then, I look up and see that Julie and I each have our own ABC helicopter. With each mile, I can see our helicopters are getting closer together!"

I began to manage my deteriorating physical condition. I walked a little more, only through aid stations at first. I shoved down oranges and coke but wasn't feeling fueled by those calories. Soon, I couldn't make it the mile that separated one aid station from the next without a couple of walk breaks. Halfway from one to the other, I'd have to walk. I put my hands on my hips to give my arms a rest, but then that inner voice commanded me: *Get going. Go again.* I found a way to push hard every time my body wanted to stop . . . until all I could manage was walking.

I reached the final 1.2 miles in the lead, but struggling big-time. I looked ahead at the long downhill into Ali'i Drive and the finish at Kailua-Kona pier. The borrowed bra distracted me. My unsettled and bloated stomach felt like a full blender running on low. As soon as I started running into town, it switched from a low rumble to liquefy. The water, coke, banana, and orange slices had whirred into a frothy fruit smoothie that wanted to explode from my body. *How am I going to run down this hill?*

Along with my growing need to use the restroom came an even more distasteful thought: *She's coming!*

I focused on the Sizzler restaurant halfway down Palani hill, about a mile from the finish. If I could run down the hill and duck into the restroom, then I could avert an emergency and get back on course.

My old nemesis from the Snickers bar episode, vanity, struck its final pose: *Is the ABC guy going to get off the van and follow me into the restaurant with his camera? Are the commentators going to say, "She's in the Sizzler! She's going into the ladies room in the Sizzler!"* Another next troubling image rumbled in my head: *I'm in the ladies room with my camera guy just outside the stall when a second ABC crew member bursts in, yelling, "Get out here! Kathleen McCartney's now in the lead!"*

Not going to happen. I'm not getting passed while sitting in the Sizzler stall. Talk about disgraceful! I had to take my chances and play it out.

I ran right past the Sizzler, then turned left onto Kuakini Highway for a half mile. Fortunately and thankfully, my gut settled down.

We turned right onto Hualalai Road, and reached a slight downhill. Suddenly, without warning, my legs buckled beneath me. When I crashed to the ground, everything in my turbulent gut spilled out. *Everything.* Worst of all, ABC recorded it all.

I was terrified. My legs wouldn't respond. My limbs felt like a splayed cat. I was humiliated that my body lost control. Suddenly, I went from being an upright race leader to a woman exposed in the most vulnerable way, which I'd later describe to *Sports Illustrated* as "a hot chocolate mess."

All the while, Kathleen closed in, her pace steady, relentless. Fear and panic squeezed my chest. My mind screamed *Go! Go! Go!* But the impulses never reached my legs. The disconnect felt as wide as Waimea Canyon. My extremities were rolling down their sleeves and calling it a day.

Kathleen remembers the increasingly surreal scene as she ran toward it. "I make the turn at 'Hot Corner,' where traditionally, the crowd is cheering wildly as you run the last quarter mile to the finish line. I've dreamed of running down Ali'i Drive for a year. But when I turn the corner and I'm actually here . . . all I get is this solemn, obligatory, anti-climactic . . . *clap, clap, clap.* Their lukewarm response is so unexpected that I feel confused . . . I'm thinking, 'What's going on?' Suddenly, I hear someone shout out from the crowd, 'You can still catch her!'"

Kathleen did not know I was on the ground.

For the first time, the idea of quitting started to surface. Never mind that I was leading the Ironman. When your body pushes itself to its extreme physical edge, it's really hard to focus. I was laid out, humiliated; it's still on YouTube for everyone to see. The ego said, "Just lay back; it'll all go away." I liked that idea. I wanted to lay on the pavement and disappear . . .

For three minutes, I sat on the ground, staring at the street, a camera truck *right there.* Then I stood up, and saw the mess on my shorts and legs. All. Over. Me. Diana Nyad, the Olympic swimmer-turned-commentator, delicately described the moment on *Wide World of Sports*: "In situations of extreme stress you sometimes lose control over bodily functions."

I had to work through my humiliation, get underneath it, meet the ego where it tries to sabotage when we're most vulnerable—and fight back.

No, Julie, you want this.

GET UP!

Again, the inner voice roared from deep within, as commanding as a hungry lioness and filled with wisdom well beyond anything I consciously knew. That silent inner roar canceled everything else out—the fear, the panic, the humiliation, the crowd, the camera . . . even the thought of Kathleen.

My mind cleared. *Julie, use your arms!*

First, I had to figure something out: how to stand. My legs weren't working anymore. The voice in my head and gut didn't exactly say, "shut the fuck up," though it was inwardly implied! It was more like a louder version of "*GET UP!* Clear the mechanism. Forget about everything else."

I placed my arms in front of me to form a tripod to support my legs. It took a couple of tries to get my balance right, but then it worked.

I stood again. *Once I can stand, I can walk. Once I can walk, I have to try and run . . .* I made it around the next corner, onto famed Ali'i Drive, the finish line so close . . .

And collapsed again, just under a huge centuries-old banyan tree on Ali'i Drive.

I always felt that I would reach the finish line. It was just a matter of getting there more quickly. Could I figure it out in time? I still held the lead. I approached the wall of spectators on both sides of the flagging used to keep them off the road. It looked to me like the Tournament of Roses Parade, so festive and noisy, with spectators spilling in the street so close to me.

I got up quickly and tried to run. Bad move. I fell for the third time. Race officials rushed to pick me up, which sent my brain into survival mode: *Will I be disqualified? I can't let them touch me or try to hold me up. I'll be disqualified!* They were trying to hold me up and I was thinking, *I'm DQed if they touch me.* I tried to push them away, but when I did, I started falling again, right into one of them. I grabbed hold of him like my life depended on staying up. Then I pushed him away and staggered on.

Twenty yards from the finish, I spotted my mom among the spectators. She held out a plumeria lei to put around my neck, but I waved her off. The motion of leaning forward to receive the lei would have sent me to the ground. I wobbled another five yards. The finish line was *right there.* I couldn't win the Ironman Championship without running across the finish, right? My mind braced for one last final run, just a few strides. What are a few more strides after just running about 27,000 of them? I would cross the line, throw my arms into the air, and soak it in. *Julie Moss: 1982 Bud Light Ironman World Champion.*

That is not how it ended.

I fell for the fourth and final time. I struggled to my hands and knees, but my arms were too weak to lift me up. My legs were frozen, done, unable to hold my 115 pounds any longer. Raucous moments before, the spectators grew eerily quiet, nearly silent, like skyfall when an eclipse covers the sun. I couldn't see their faces, but I could feel their arms trying to lift me up, worried people and their wonderful energy helping me along.

Out of the corner of my eye, I spotted rainbows again. Kathleen. *That damned rainbow uniform and hair ribbon!* Without further ado, she passed me and crossed the finish line. She didn't even know she'd won until someone told her. "I couldn't see the finish line," she said. "I knew I must be close to catching Julie. But where was she? I had no idea what she had gone through, and I didn't see her the last mile, so I figured I was coming in second.

"I wove around dozens of spectators who spilled out into the street, blinded by the bright lights. There was nowhere left for me to go; the ABC camera van blocked the road. In the midst of the chaos, I was forced to stop. I yelled out, 'Where's the finish line?'"

"You're standing on it. You've won!" someone yelled.

"Suddenly, a finish tape appeared, a medal was placed around my neck and I asked, 'Am I first?'"

Sadly for Kathleen, the crowd was emotionally drained by the time she arrived. Drained, distracted, and riveted on my struggle. "I noticed something different about the crowd," Kathleen told *Triathlete* magazine. "Rather than happy and screaming, the crowd was very emotional." Because of that, she never received the typical rousing cheers an Ironman champion hears at the finish.

It was quite a sight as Scott Tinley watched from the curb with 1979 winner Tom Warren. Scott was a bit tired: two hours before, he'd triumphantly thrown the monkey of Dave Scott off his back and captured a hard-fought Ironman overall victory, igniting one of the great careers in triathlon history.

"I'm on the curb, right by the finish line and ABC truck, tired, hungry, can't find my wife, can't find food . . . can't even find a beer," ST recalled. "All of a sudden, all hell breaks loose at the finish line, Kathleen not even knowing she'd won, and a few seconds later, here comes Julie. It was pure chaos. And then I heard shouting in the ABC production truck behind me, everyone realizing what they had was *great TV,* trying to figure out who had the best footage—you could feel their whole plans for the show changing on the spot. They knew they had something they'd probably never see again."

While Scott was taking in the race dramatics from the curb, growing thirstier by the second, excruciating pain surged through me, the worst of the day. Strangely, it wasn't physical pain. Even though I could not stand up, I did not hurt so much physically. However, I was devastated by the emotional pain and disappointment of having a dream ripped away—the dream of winning Ironman, hatched not four hours before on the marathon course.

I had nothing left to give, nothing to offer this race, nothing inside. Still, my inner voice said, less urgently now that the imminent threat was gone: *Crawl. Crawl to the finish.*

So I did. I dragged myself those final few yards, one arm in front of the other, head down, inspired by a growing awareness that I was crawling not only across the line, but into the power to uncap all limitations of what I thought possible. A face-to-face encounter with the Wonder Woman buried deep inside. I let go of the humiliation, let go of the disappointment, and let go of the win. All I held onto, like a lifeline, was getting across that line. Armen Keteyian, writing for the *San Diego Union,* stated it clearly a month later:

All you could think was, "Oh God, she's going to fall again. She's 15 feet from the finish line, 15 lousy feet from all the glory she deserves, and she's going to fall again. Dammit, she's not going to make it."

Eleven hours, ten minutes, and nine seconds after the cannon blasted at Kailua Pier, I reached my hand across the finish line. I broke 1980 Ironman champion Robin Beck's women's record by twelve minutes. I also finished six minutes ahead of Tom Warren's overall winning time from 1979! Kathleen only beat me by twenty-nine seconds. Speaking of gratitude, can you imagine how grateful she was to even start the race two days after laying in a hospital bed, her dream of winning down the toilet? And then *winning?* Gratitude is one of our greatest allies.

My finishing moment became frozen in time, thanks to *Wide World of Sports* and photojournalist Carol Hogan, a recreational triathlete whose husband Bob was an Ironman competitor and Southern California lifeguard competition legend. Carol shot the photo of me leaning on one arm, trying to struggle to my feet, now an iconic image in triathlon history. I told Armen Keteyian, "When I saw the picture at the finish line, I thought, 'That's what dead people look like.'"

With my hand firmly on the line, a smile stretched across my face. It spread throughout my body. I closed my eyes, and kept smiling. It was finally over.

I am an Ironman.

What you don't see in Carol's iconic photo is the "caption," my words to the volunteers at that very moment: "I'm so sorry; I'm such a mess. Take me and drop me into the bay!"

Instead, I dropped into a whole new life.

CHAPTER 4
Going Viral, Circa 1982

W hen I give motivational speeches, people sometimes ask, "As you crawled across the line, did you know the impact you would make around the world?"

How I'd love to revise history to say, "Sure, I knew that my race and the way I finished would elevate a sport worldwide and inspire women and men to find what is possible within themselves." I'd love to say that, except it isn't true.

What held true is that, for some time after finishing the Ironman Triathlon, I healed physically much faster than I did emotionally. The humiliation stuck with me for a long while. Yes, I'd experienced that incredible moment of authenticity, and felt awesome about finishing. I'd also ensured my graduation because of it! But how did that play against what fans in Kona experienced and *Wide World of Sports* viewers would watch: a 23-year-old coed losing it just before reaching the finish line?

I spent my first post-race hour trying to get it together in the medic tent. I knew Diana Nyad was waiting to interview me for *Wide World of Sports*. Diana had established quite a name for herself as an endurance swimmer—in 1979, she swam 102 miles from the Bahamas to Florida. Then in 2013, at age sixty-four, she swam the 110 miles from Havana to

Key West without a shark cage . . . and people think Ironman triathletes are crazy? As I think back to our interview, I still love what I said: "This is the first time I've found something that I wanted so bad, I was willing to crawl on my hands and knees to get it."

I meant it. I'd been knocked down by my broken relationship before flying to Kona, and I needed something to validate myself. Why? I had used my relationship to try and find validation through someone else. The Ironman provided a new and memorable source of validation. All but the messy ending, of course.

During my brief prerace get-together with Reed, I sought closure. In return, I learned something about anchoring in your own authenticity: it's not about anybody else. *What am I going to do?* At the crucial stage of my race, no one else could have influenced me physically, psychologically, or emotionally. Kathleen was pressing me to go harder than I wanted, but there was a point where she didn't exist in my mind. That's a pure thing about athletics; maybe that's what I saw on the faces of the athletes on *Wide World of Sports* the year before, when I kept wondering, "What is pulling me in here?" The journey of wanting an experience from your deepest heart transforms into a pure love and belief in yourself. Validation comes from within, this whole thing of, "It's okay. Keep going. Keep going deeper. Keep diving in. Your truth and trust come from within."

I wanted to convey this to Diana, but didn't. I didn't have the words yet.

The other thing about my race is that I didn't take advantage of any established swimming, cycling, and running communities, fledgling though they were. And I certainly didn't have any mentors or support group once I flew home to Carlsbad. Even though the sport had existed for eight years, I still had to spell "triathlon" to nearly everybody. Plus, men's winner Scott Tinley, a triathlon purist through and through, was initially concerned the "freak show" was taking away from the real athletes.

I was the "freak show," of course.

After the post-race interview, my mother and brother took me to dinner. All I wanted was a hamburger and a chocolate milkshake. But they didn't serve milkshakes. I took two bites of the hamburger, looked at my mom, and said, "I gotta go." We headed back to her condo, and I slept. My body was still revving hard, loaded with adrenaline, still inwardly listening to the "push, push, push" command it had obeyed faithfully until it could obey no more. Decompressing from a long race is never easy. By the following morning's sunrise, I did manage to get to sleep.

The next evening, we arrived at the awards ceremony in the Kona Surf Hotel ballroom. They called up the top five overall women, from fifth place to first. Two women tied for third place in 11 hours, 51 minutes: Lyn Brooks, who would eventually become the first woman to complete twenty *consecutive* Ironman World Championship; and Sally Edwards, the reigning Western States 100-mile champion and second-place finisher in the 1981 Ironman. She would create six companies (including Fleet Feet Sports, a national shoe chain) and write more than twenty books on endurance sports. She's a legendary endurance sports athlete, and deservedly so. That startled me. How in the world did I beat someone who won a race that scrambled up, over, sideways, down, and through the High Sierras and California Gold Country, its nasty river canyons, rocky trails, and high heat, a race that featured over twenty thousand vertical feet of ascents and descents? When a good friend told me he'd paced someone for thirty-five miles at Western States, I told him he was fanatical. The pot calling the kettle black, right? That's how I feel about ultramarathons. They're beyond what I can do. Yet on my new turf, Kona, I'd beaten a 100-mile champion. Definitely a "wow" moment.

When the emcee called my name, something incredible happened: the capacity crowd of about two thousand stood up and gave me a standing ovation. Word had already started to get out about my race. I soaked that up . . . it was like, *yeahhhh.* A little adulation never hurt anyone, right? I was amazed that so many people seemed to know what had happened. When they called Kathleen, everyone remained standing as the 1982 Ironman champion strode to the stage. She didn't quite know where to stand. She walked to the opposite side of me, so that we bookended the other three top finishers.

The energy bloom was incredible when I was called up. I can close my eyes right now, and it sweeps through me anew. What a feeling. It came along with the realization that, for the first time in my life, I was truly proud of myself. And to be so honored by my peers? I'll remember that ovation as long as I live.

Scott Tinley viewed the awards ceremony, and the thirty-six hours that preceded it, in a manner that is quite interesting when you think about it today. "In one way, Julie's iconic moment began with the mistake of not taking nutrition," he said. "If she'd sipped four ounces of coke at Mile 25 of the marathon, the world would be a different place. She wins the race as a budding rookie, a nice little upset over Kathleen, and we wait another four or five years for triathlon to organically grow into a professional sport. Because she didn't drink, we had the ultimate 'agony of defeat' moment that changed our sport instantaneously."

As soon as I returned home to Carlsbad following a week of R&R with my family on Maui, Diana called to inform me that ABC had decided to move up the original April airing of the Ironman to the following weekend. Thirteen days after the race. Apparently, everyone at ABC from executives to production assistants were stunned by the footage, which meant they envisioned something else flashing in bright neon lights: high weekend ratings. ST heard the first of those conversations go down from his curbside perch at the finish line. Commentator Jim Lampley, now a legendary sportscaster, told *Triathlete* magazine, "We got back to New York and knew we had the most extraordinary thing. People in edit rooms were blown away. . . . We knew we had to get it on the air in exactly the right way."

Part of "exactly the right way" included dealing with the visual image of me losing control of my body and its functions. For that sensitive discussion, the producers dispatched Diana, who gave me a call.

"We need to address the fact that you started your period during the race," Diana said. "Did you start your period?"

"No, that wasn't my period," I said.

"Oh . . . well, we're going to show the finish—show your finish—but we will handle it delicately."

My thought was to handle it *honestly*. I felt compelled to tell the truth. It would have been much easier to play the menstrual card, but lying would have dishonored all that I'd been through and all that I'd just discovered about myself. In this case, the authenticity of the moment trumped my ego's screaming plea to shift the story to something more acceptable.

ABC handled it very delicately, to the backing music of "Dion Blue" from masterful jazz flautist Tim Weisberg, and with minimal discussion of my humiliating moment. "Dion Blue" conveyed the melodic grace and power to remind you how beautiful our journeys through life can be. It is so uplifting, a transcendent, lovely 3½-minute work of art. You've probably heard it on a movie or TV soundtrack. "Dion Blue" marked the first time *Wide World of Sports* had ever synched a segment to a specific piece of music.

I only wonder how that scene would have been handled in today's drama-infused broadcasting world. Certainly, my loss of control would have been brought up and deconstructed on the spot, to create more sensationalism and better ratings. And then broken into small clips, maybe a meme or poo emoji for humor, and blasted on social media, put on Vimeo and YouTube . . . wait. It is on YouTube!

To prove my point: In 2010, *ESPN The Magazine* ran a feature story called "The Tao of Poo: It Happens." My experience kicked off the piece, which also featured Michael Jordan and others who have "lost it"—literally—in the heat of competition. When "it" happens, I don't have to explain what that means, or how humiliating it was. But, when you look at who they interviewed for the piece, turns out I was in pretty impressive company.

On February 19, *Wide World of Sports* aired the segment. I watched with friends at a packed Dooley McCluskey's, a popular bar in my hometown of Carlsbad. The co-owners, Bob Burke and Steve Densham, were my first-ever sponsors. They contributed my airfare to Hawaii, for which I'll be forever grateful: *Here, Julie. Take this plane ticket and go change your life.* Looks that way now, doesn't it? A nice group of friends arrived to watch the show with me, along with local newspaper publisher Tom Missett and LA area reporter Chris Mortensen, who would later enjoy a great career covering the NFL for ESPN.

Right before I left my house for Dooley McCluskey's, my childhood friend, Sue Robison, called me from Laramie, Wyoming, where she was wrapping up her bachelor's degree at the University of Wyoming. She was in tears. "Julie, you've gotta get yourself ready. I knew you were on the show, but . . . *oh my God.* I had no idea—I can't believe my best friend just put herself through something like this!" Sue was an hour ahead of West Coast time. She had just seen the segment.

"Ready? Ready for what?"

I found out a few minutes later. As the show aired, I started to cry. I wanted to help myself win that race all over again! When I saw myself about 100 yards from the finish, getting up from my second fall, I said out loud, "Just because you can stand up, and you can start to walk, doesn't mean you have to start running again." Two weeks later, I'm suddenly a racing expert, right?

"I've known Julie since we were in sixth grade," Sue recalls. "She was always a little crazy in a fun way, a little bratty, and definitely not someone I'd expect to transform into this incredible athlete. When I saw her on the show, I kept asking myself, 'Is this really Julie?' It just was so far removed from the Julie I knew, this thing she was doing, and how she took herself right to the edge. None of my friends had ever seen something like this. Neither had the rest of the world, when you look at the craziness that happened after the show."

"I remember being in a hotel room in Santa Cruz, on a sales trip for the surf clothing I was repping," Jim Watson added. "I watched the segment, and was in tears. *Julie? Are you shitting me?* You look at Julie now, all her wins and accomplishments, the great athlete she is, and it's easy to forget that she wasn't always such a great athlete. I just didn't know she had it in her. Amazing."

Two years later, Sue saw what it was like for me to lead an Ironman up close and personal. In 1985, I arranged for *Wide World of Sports* to hire Sue as a film logger. She sat for fourteen hours in the ABC van, no stops for food or restrooms, and dutifully logged film canisters and shot sequence times while talking with Diana Nyad. Throughout the bike segment, she rode right in front of me—because I was leading. I ended up blowing up and not finishing, the first of a difficult patch of DNFs (did not finish) that followed the 1982 race.

But Sue wasn't done having fun. "One night, Julie couldn't join us, but ABC took me out to a fancy restaurant, sport coats required, that kind of thing," she recalls. "I'm not a sports person, but I know how big the careers of Jimmy Roberts and Al Trautwig became. They were my dinner companions. We were having a great time, and then in walks Tom Selleck. This was when he starred in *Magnum, P.I.* I've never been around something like this, and I'm still a young girl, and . . . *Tom Selleck?* That was amazing, Julie giving me that experience."

Back to the segment. I expected to see the typical ten-minute *Wide World of Sports* segment sandwiched between commercials, with a studio lead-in from Jim McKay and on-site coverage with Jim Lampley and Diana Nyad. Plus Diana's interview with me. That's not what aired. ABC totally changed the way they put together the show. Our segment went on and on, taking up twenty minutes of the hour-long format. My final quarter mile was completely played out, warts, chocolate mess, crawl to the finish and all. To cap it off, Jim McKay closed the telecast by calling the twenty-minute segment "perhaps the most dramatic moment in the history of *Wide World*."

The next day, I got a call from ABC Studios. The caller said, "We've had such a huge response from the Ironman, we'd like to fly you and Kathleen McCartney out to New York to be in-studio with Jim McKay next Saturday."

Really? All for bonking, falling a few times, trying to get back up, and crawling to the finish? While many had already told me how amazing my performance was and how it inspired them (how? *I fell and crawled!*), I couldn't imagine how the entire country would feel. I *could*, however, picture a farmer in Nebraska, or schoolteacher in Ohio, going, "You wonder what these nutty kids are smoking out there in California. Why would someone do that to themselves?"

As it turned out, "huge response" was an understatement. The ABC Studios switchboard lit up with calls. By 1982 standards, we were going viral! That wasn't all. Following the telecast, Roone Arledge offered congratulations to his crew, praise he rarely extended. Top executives from CBS and NBC called ABC, both astonished and envious. An ABC spokesman later told Armen Keteyian, "We've had more calls on that show than any in recent memory. I can't remember anything like it. It was an amazing thing . . . it gave people the impetus to go on with their own lives."

The shockwave spread across the world as fast as a tsunami after a catastrophic earthquake. When you consider there was no Internet, social media, or texting, and people just picked up the phone . . . I was surprised. They called ABC Studios by the thousands and asked questions. What really got me were the questions themselves: "What happened to the girl?" "Was she able to walk afterward?" "Did she survive?'"

The narrator for a separate three-minute Videos4Motivation piece on my finish (available on YouTube) was Phil Liggett, now the voice of the Tour de France and the preeminent announcer in cycling. (I later worked with Phil in a London studio, doing voiceover.) With his crisp British voice offering a subtle flair for the dramatic, Phil described it like this: "Julie Moss crawled to the finish in one of the most memorable moments in the history of ABC *Wide World of Sports*. Millions of Americans watched, mesmerized by Moss's courage and determination. Everyone who saw it was moved, and history has shown us that from that day forward, the Ironman would never be the same."

Later, I learned something else. Before a network airs major shows, it screens them to producers and staff members for feedback, to work out final kinks, and make sure everyone approves of the telecast. Apparently, the vibe about this segment was a little different. Word got out, and the screening room filled quickly with network executives and staffers alike. Another show in production stopped, and its cast and crew watched. The noise in the room afterward was . . . well, there was no noise. Viewers were astonished and silent. ABC green-lighted the broadcast.

Meanwhile, before the sports world could start writing that new Ironman history to which Phil Liggett alluded, they had to make sure the damsel in distress was still around, right? Hence, the live interview with Jim McKay.

For we baby boomers, Jim (who died in 2008) is a sports broadcasting institution, right there with Dodgers broadcaster Vin Scully, the late Lakers play-by-play man Chick Hearn, and the late Curt Gowdy and Pat Summerall. Jim had much to do with Americans' views of sports and our interest in them. We might be a nation of rabid sports fans now, but back then, we were also a nation of rabid sports participants looking for new athletic outlets. *Wide World of Sports* gave us new ideas seemingly every Saturday, when they uncovered yet another sport taking place somewhere on earth. I spent many Saturday afternoons watching *Wide World of Sports* and listening to Jim's smooth, engaging way of presenting the weirdest or most obscure sports so informatively that you walked away *knowing* what that sport was about. Then, if you could, you tried it.

Since *Wide World of Sports* premiered in 1961, Jim watched and covered thousands of events as its host. The show continued until 1998, an amazing thirty-seven-year run. While fighting back tears, Jim came into our homes and informed us about the massacre of Israeli athletes at the 1972 Summer Olympics in Munich (where another Carlsbad girl, Cindy Gilbert, competed in the high jump just after turning fifteen).

After flying first-class at ABC's expense, we arrived for the interview. Kathleen was dressed in a business suit, white skirt, and matching blazer, while I was wearing a jeans and a top . . . a San Diego surfer girl. It was a borrowed outfit, at that. "Just before the show, Julie called me and said, 'Cindy, I have to fly to New York for *Wide World* and don't have anything to wear!'" recalled Cindy Conner, one of my besties. "I was working in the surf industry, so didn't know what I had, but she came over and we got a few things out that she wore on the show."

During the interview, they replayed the Ironman footage. Once again, I welled up. Keep in mind that we're live on America's favorite sports show, and I'm in the beginning stages of losing it. Jim McKay said, "Julie, I can see you're really tearing up here."

I tried not to wipe my eyes. It was really hard to watch myself go through that again. Also, people were starting to recognize me as the girl who literally gave everything she had at Ironman. It was all so raw, the power of so many people seeing it, the seismic reaction that prompted ABC to fly us to New York . . . not too easy to hold back the tears.

I've had a chance to think about that moment, and to see Jim McKay—who has seen it all—so visibly moved. I was too nervous to appreciate it then. For the world's most popular sports host to be moved like that still touches me. I also remember something else about our day: how nice and genuine he was, how comfortable he made us feel, and how our exchange felt as natural and mellow as, well, three people chatting casually about an event they're all spectating. Except that two of us *were* the event, in the eyes of ABC.

Among those who watched both segments was Frieda Zamba, a painfully shy seventeen-year-old Florida girl with mad surfing skills. "I remember watching Julie crawl across the line—I mean, it ran over and over on the news, on sportscasts, *Wide World of Sports* . . . it was everywhere for awhile," she recalled. "When I saw Julie do what she did, as a complete unknown, it gave me the courage to see what I could do against the top pros in surfing."

Four months later, the women's surfing world found out. They didn't like it. Frieda and her friend-manager-future husband, Flea Shaw, flew to San Diego for the Mazda Women's Surf Sport Championships. In Solana Beach, not five miles from where I live today, Frieda made her pro debut by blowing away world champion Margo Oberg, world tour leader Debbie Beacham, and the rest of the world's best with an aggressive, powerful surfing style they'd never seen before. She was stronger, faster, hungrier, a goofy foot like myself, an absolute machine in the waves. And, I might add, a beautiful machine: Frieda Zamba is a striking woman, right down to the six-pack abs she still sports today as she teaches private lessons from her Costa Rica home.

Frieda revolutionized women's surfing five months after I did my thing at Ironman. She went on to win four world titles, including three in a row from 1984–86, and made power surfing a standard in women's competition. She became my hero in the sport, a Wonder Woman who combined power, grace, and style in a way we hadn't seen before. Also, I loved her commitment to fitness, to cross-training long before it became part of being a strong pro surfer. She was ripped—and, as I later learned, quite the runner as a high schooler.

"That's nice of Julie to say, because she's been my hero since I saw *Wide World of Sports,*" Frieda said. "What she did gave me the belief that maybe I could do something with my surfing too. I was looking at a track scholarship then, and I'd run cross-country and got offers on that too, but I really wanted to surf and try to see the world. It's not a coincidence I got started a few months after she did. I got the courage to try to be a pro surfer, in part, because of what she did. She and I also both got some funny looks from the established people in our sports; I know that during my event, I had to sit alone on the grass at Solana Beach, keep my head focused, because of comments a couple of the girls were making about me.

"I just hope someday we can get together on the same stage, meet each other, and do a program together, because I pretty much think we feel the same way about the year 1982."

Well, Frieda, let's see if we can bring our mutual admiration society together. I've always wanted to meet and surf with her. I'm a huge fan. I can definitely see a triathlon-surfing symposium or two in our future . . .

After the studio interview was over, Jimmy Roberts walked us out to the car, along with fellow production assistant Robbie Cowen. Besides working on the original segment for fourteen hours a day for six days under rush-job circumstances, with Roone Arledge breathing down his neck, Roberts found the Tim Weisberg piece in ABC's music library. "We don't get excited about too many things, but even before we edited the tape, Bryce [producer Bryce Weisman] knew we had something very special," Jimmy told Armen for the *San Diego Union*. "All of us felt the same way. This was a story we were all very attached to."

Sports fans know Jimmy today as an eleven-time Emmy-winning sports anchor and studio host, the closest thing we have to Jim McKay in today's lineup. If he strikes you as friendly and engaging, well, he is. On the day we met him, he was just as lovely.

Robbie is equally accomplished behind the camera, with a career that spans some 2,500 live and edited sports productions that include the Olympics, Kentucky Derbies, Super Bowls, World Series, World Cups, Indy 500s, and U.S. Open Golf Championships. Through his company, Cowen Productions, he has also headed up the ESPN SportsCentury Series, World Chess Championships, and *The Sports Reporters*, which ran for twenty years.

As we reached the curb, Jimmy said, "Girls, take the limo and sightsee." He then directed the driver to go where we wanted.

They're giving the keys to the New York kingdom to two California girls? Whatever will we do?

Quite a bit! We stayed at the Plaza, brought along our mothers, and kicked around Manhattan for a day or two. We went sightseeing at the World Trade Center, Tiffany's, and the Metropolitan Museum of Art, shopped at Macy's, and had lunch at the Russian Tea Room, among other mini-adventures. Definitely different than how I thought I would spend those days—recovering at Tamarack, Terramar, State Beach, or one of the other Carlsbad surf spots.

As we left Macy's, a man who had also been in the store stopped me on the street. "Saw you on TV and wanted to tell you how wonderful you are and to welcome you to New York," he said.

Filled with that great New York moment, Kathleen and I returned to the Plaza. We ordered chocolate cheesecake and champagne from room service, and watched our show together. That was a very nice moment, sharing something between us that would link us forever in sports history. Let's not forget, Kathleen won the 1982 Ironman. She will always be the champion of that event. Because of the way I finished, with the circumstances eclipsing her come-from-behind victory in the public eye, I have always felt empathy toward the other competitors who may have felt slighted that I stole the show.

The way I see it, Kathleen and I both had something to be proud of. It was an even exchange, so we felt we could share this together. Which was good, because after *Wide World of Sports,* we led completely separate lives, intersecting only at races, and not very often at that. We remained friendly rivals, if you can call it that, until we turned our thirty-year acquaintance into a friendship in 2012 to race our thirtieth anniversary Ironman together and then launch Iron Icons.

As everyone who has worked with the media from either side of the camera knows, when one big TV splash happens, others follow. I received a lot of requests, still really surprised at how apparently inspiring and motivating viewers found my performance. My earliest responses were pretty guarded, not because of crawling across the line, but because of the indelible image of the humiliation that still lingered. I was almost waiting for someone to make that little comment, which a couple of insensitive people did with nervous laughter, followed by, "You shit your pants on national TV."

I was really sensitive about this. How sensitive? Shortly after the in-studio interview with Jim McKay, David Letterman's booking agent wanted me to come on his late-night show. "No," I replied. I was afraid that David was such a loose cannon, he might take our conversation *there*. Unfortunately, and sadly, I didn't understand that Letterman was a devoted sports fan. I also didn't realize that he saw my race not as comic relief, but through the same prism others saw it—the motivating, inspiring side. I thought if I went on his show and he started teasing me, I would laugh along, out of nervousness, at the deprecating humor. I just knew it would ruin the way people viewed my race. I learned to protect the sacredness of that experience because of the early feedback. It was really special, not for me to make fun of, nor anyone else. Today, I regret not going on Letterman. It's one of the very few regrets in my career.

Meanwhile, my close friends still have a way of working the "crapping my pants on national TV" line into our conversations every so often. I laugh it off, because I now can. I'm always going to get comments about it, since that *Wide World of Sports* finish-line footage is now a regular staple on YouTube.

But missed late-night opportunities aside, one of the other defining moments of that Ironman was a phone call I received from Armen Keteyian.

CHAPTER 5
One Article, Two Careers

E very so often, we pioneers of triathlon get together away from Kona for awards ceremonies, seminars, fundraising events, or similar gatherings. We began when triathlon was a tiny sport, hooked our stars and hopes to the thought of racing for a living, and watched it really work out for some of us. Our shared experiences forged lifelong bonds, even among the fierce competitors we all were—and still are, in some cases.

It was into such a festive spirit that I walked in early August 2016. Scott Tinley, Bob Babbitt, and I emceed Tri Legends, an evening of discussion and fun that was hosted by Skip McDowell, owner of Nytro Multisport, a popular spot for endurance sports athletes in Encinitas, California. The evening was a fundraiser for the Challenged Athletes Foundation, an advocacy group for physically challenged performers headed by executive director Virginia Tinley, Scott's wife. For two hours, 1979 Ironman champ Tom Warren, 1981 winners John Howard and Linda Sweeney, 1982 titlists Kathleen McCartney and Scott Tinley, Jeff Tinley, and others shared stories and experiences to a packed house. Four other faces fit for a triathlon Mount Rushmore—Mark Allen, Dave Scott, Scott Molina, and Paula Newby-Fraser—beamed in on video feeds with their twenty Ironman World Championships between them.

Shortly before we began, I welcomed and visited with some fans in the front of the store. I looked up, and a most wonderful man walked inside with his wife—the great sports journalist, eleven-time Emmy Award winner, and longtime *60 Minutes* contributing correspondent, Armen Keteyian. No, he was not investigating me—although months before, his hard-hitting *60 Minutes* piece exposed the latest Russian doping scheme and started a domino effect that left Russia largely out of the 2016 Summer Olympics and 2018 Winter Olympics. Truth be told, you don't want Armen knocking on your door for *that* reason. He didn't get to be a *New York Times* bestselling author, and a symbol of integrity, interviewing skill, and versatility within the journalism world because he asked softball questions or his investigative pieces fell short. He is relentless, tireless, and driven to find out the truth and crux of the story—no matter where he goes to get it. In other words, a *60 Minutes* man.

I know Armen in a much different way. I know him as the man whose incredible story on me in the *San Diego Union* following the February 1982 Ironman, and later as the *Sporting News* "Feature of the Year," set a lot of wheels into motion.

A former starting shortstop and second baseman at San Diego State, Armen understood athletics and athletes. As a human being, the empathy he brings to his life and work is the kind of stuff you wish all sports stories could capture. Besides that, we shared something quite remarkable, when you think of it: our paths first crossed when he watched me on TV, crossed again on Carlsbad State Beach, and then our respective careers shot into the stratosphere. The intersection of our destinies was not a coincidence.

Millions have watched Armen operate from the heights of sports and news broadcast journalism. Many have also read one or more of his hard-hitting, bestselling sports exposes like *The System,* a mind-boggling look at the millions of dollars that direct the flow of college football and its elite teams. Before that, Armen was a sportswriter in Escondido, near Carlsbad. He became a writer-reporter at *Sports Illustrated,* a news and sports correspondent for ABC and CBS, a sideline reporter at top NFL games and Final Four basketball games, and a multiple award-winning journalist. He then went to HBO's *Real Sports with Bryant Gumbel* and CBS News, where he was the network's chief investigative correspondent, then *60 Minutes* and *60 Minutes Sports*. If you follow sports at all, or sports scandals, you've seen something he either wrote or broadcast over the past thirty-five years.

Yet few know what triggered the ascent of Armen's career. Besides enormous effort on his part, there was a little stroke of magic. That's how the bond between us occurred.

Armen and his darling wife of thirty-eight years, Dede, and I chatted until the Tri Legends program started. Soon enough, Armen found himself participating when Scott Tinley and Bob Babbitt lobbed a couple of questions his way. How fun it was for Armen, who felt like he stumbled into a homecoming that was, in some ways, his own. He helped to promote the very first United States Triathlon Series events in early 1982, a fact that few Armen Keteyian fans know.

"Damn, I'm so happy we came down here," Armen told my cowriter over coffee at an artsy Encinitas sidewalk café after they sat together at the Tri Legends program. Robert and Armen have known each other since they dug up stories as young North San Diego County sportswriters in the late 1970s. "We just flew in from New York," Armen said. "I had to stop for a couple hours at the Denver Broncos complex and interview John Elway for *60 Minutes Sports*. Then Tinley got in touch and told me Julie would be at this. I told Dede, 'We're going,' and as soon as we unloaded our stuff in San Clemente, we jumped on the freeway. I did not want to miss this chance to see Julie again."

How do two people on entirely different career tracks and backgrounds rush into each others' lives like shooting stars, and share an afternoon on the beach that becomes a catalytic event in both their careers?

It started when my life arrived at its defining moment: with me on the ground, in Kona, face-up on the finish line.

"I was riveted," Armen remembers. "I could not believe what I was watching. I'd already spent years around all sorts of great athletes, in all sports, and seen my share of great performances, but this was beyond that. The will, courage, and one 'oh my God' moment after another. You couldn't help but get chills and tears at the incredible test of will, and the reservoir of courage—to fall, to get up, to fall, to get up, to cross the finish line . . ."

From his earliest days at the *Escondido Times-Advocate,* Armen could sniff out stories. His former colleagues and rival sportswriters remember well his knack for "scooping" them, getting the story first, and then deploying his tenacious, aggressive quest to get the best quotes, the best insights . . . and most of all, the *truth.* He did not suffer liars or athletes speaking in clichés lightly. More important, he looked for the best story he could find with the facts or circumstances that presented themselves.

When Armen saw my race on *Wide World of Sports,* his inner bloodhound came out, along with the instinctive quality all good writers and journalists possess and trust when they sense a good story in their midst. He got in touch with me a few weeks after Ironman, after Kathleen and I had done the in-studio interview with Jim McKay. We decided to meet on the beach in Carlsbad.

After the interview, Armen knew what to do. "It was such a great story, an amazing story, that I did some reporting on my own. I found out something else happened with this telecast. Roone Arledge [head of ABC Sports], who later hired me as an ABC News correspondent, seriously considered replacing the *Wide World of Sports* 'agony of defeat' show-opening montage [ski jumper Vinko Bogataj crumbling and falling off the ramp] with Julie. That's all I needed to hear in terms of significance. Then I found out [eventual eleven-time Emmy winning sportscaster] Jimmy Roberts, of all people, was the production assistant who'd found the song 'Dion Blue' by Tim Weisberg. I had the sources, and the story. It was so gripping."

In both the *Union* story and a later conversation, Armen recalls much of our afternoon on the beach, right down to how overwhelmed I felt by what had happened in Kona. "I remember Julie being waifish, sweet," he says. "When I watched her playing with the sand on the beach, she didn't seem quite as 'larger than life' as she appeared on *Wide World of Sports.* She was humble, which immediately set her apart from a lot of athletes I'd covered. No question she'd been hit by this shock wave of celebrity, but you couldn't find any arrogance in Julie, not one ounce. There was this serenity, this cuteness; not a naïveté but a true sweetness about her. That was rare. She could've been any number of other things, like cocky, conceited, already feeling entitled . . . she was none of those things. That made her story all the more appealing.

"What became clear to me was that she wasn't sure what she was going to do. I could relate to that; I wasn't sure what I was going to do, either, after turning down a job at *Sports Illustrated.* Julie was still absorbing all the things coming her way. She was protective of the moment, of Kathleen . . . I mean, how many people reveal themselves in that way? On network television? Back then, *Wide World* was appointment television on Saturday afternoons for people who loved their sports. Twenty to thirty million people saw her struggle."

The *Sports Illustrated* job. *Oh that.* If you were a young sportswriter, or fancied a magazine career, could you imagine turning down an offer from *SI*? In 1982, you simply did not do that and live to face your colleagues, all of whom would run through brick walls to get that opportunity. *SI* was Mount Everest for sportswriters, complete with fifteen million devout weekly readers and occasional book and TV opportunities. If you made it to *SI,* you were the rock star who just hopped from three weekend sets at local clubs to headlining arenas.

Yet, in January 1982, Armen turned down the job he always wanted.

He originally applied because he felt constricted in his writing. Two years of daily, early deadlines at the *Times-Advocate,* and its emphasis on stripped-down, "just the facts, ma'am" sportswriting pinched his style. He wanted to write longer stories, dive deeper into his subjects, put his truth-seeking and fact-finding tenacity to work on a larger stage. He freelanced for the *San Diego Union* and *San Diego Magazine,* finding the longer-form journalism he sought. He also took a public relations job at the Phillips Organisation, which included among its clients Ektelon, the world's largest racquetball equipment manufacturer (in 1980, racquetball was highly popular in the U.S.), and Speedo, the swimwear manufacturer. For Phillips, he wrote articles on racquetball champions and Olympic swimming gold medalist John Naber, a Speedo-sponsored athlete, which he then placed in trade magazines.

Then *Sports Illustrated* came calling. "I had sent a number of clips to *SI*," he recalls, "and was reading that masthead like it was the Rosetta Stone to see if some reporter had been promoted, or was not listed on the masthead any longer. I was in contact with Jane Bachman, who we knew as Bambi, the chief of reporters. One day, she made the offer, the culmination of a year's worth of sending clips and making an annoyance of myself with the magazine."

What happened next tested Armen's priorities to the limit. "I came home with the offer," he says. "Dede and I were living in North Park [San Diego] in a two-bedroom house with two dogs, two cars, and she's working for California Leisure Consultants, a big-time event management company. We were both twenty-nine years old and making about $60,000 between us. We had a pretty good life going. When the mag calls me, it's the dead of winter in New York. The city was then a hellhole, all the drug problems, rampant crime, the whole Son of Sam situation [the murder spree of the late 1970s serial killer]. Dee was eight months pregnant with our first daughter, Kristen. She told me in no uncertain terms, 'There's no way I'm moving to New York City in the dead of winter, eight months pregnant. You can't take this job.'

"So I had to tell a magazine I'd been spending the better part of a year pursuing that I can't take the job. Those jobs came up about once in a blue moon. People just didn't leave."

Little did Armen know that fate was merely postponing his moment. Through the Phillips Organisation, Armen found himself inside the triathlon world just as the sport was picking up steam. A pair of athletes with business sense, Carl Thomas and Jim Curl, visited the office looking for a sponsor for their new baby: the United States Triathlon Series. All of the triathletes in San Diego—pretty much every significant triathlete, minus Dave Scott, who lived in Northern California—were excited about the possibility. A Phillips vice president (and later TV producer) Frank Pace, used his various connections and brought Bud Light to the table. The sponsorship coup immediately put the USTS on the map. "I remember writing a feature on Scott Tinley for *City Sports m*agazine in San Diego," Armen recalls. "I was starting to acquaint myself with this burgeoning triathlon movement. I was involved in a peripheral fashion, setting up public relations for the USTS. At the same time, I was figuring out what I was going to do next."

"Next" was the story on me. After our day at the beach, Armen went to Mission Valley, to the *San Diego Union* offices, where he laid down one of the longest sports features in that paper's 150-year history. Like an athlete who *knows* a great race or game is brewing, a feeling he recognized from college baseball, Armen sensed something about my race and what he would do with it. His biggest concern: Would the *Union* cut down the story's 4,500-word length, an opus in a world where 1,500-word stories were often considered too long? He hoped not, because this piece *felt* different than any he'd written.

"I wrote it fairly quickly. I didn't struggle with it. For me, writing goes one of two ways—I can either struggle over something and rewrite it to death; or it comes out in a burst," he says. "This was a burst, a long burst—a lot of words. It was inside me, finding its way out. I write emotionally, and I'm pretty vested. I'm not the guy you want to hire to do the deadline piece, but feature writing has always been my forte. Having an ability to be empathetic to the subject has been a gift, in some ways. I think that empathy, and having been an athlete—though certainly not at Julie's level—gives me an understanding."

Fortunately, the *Union*'s sports editor, Barry Lorge, was an East Coast transplant who preferred a more literary sportswriting approach. Lorge often got ribbed from hardboiled sportswriters who liked their stories and paragraphs short and their words simple. But whenever Lorge saw a story that needed to be told in layers rather than confined to a strict column inch count, he opened up the room.

"It took an excruciatingly long time for him to edit my story, with me sitting there on the terminal, waiting," Armen says. "Barry was notorious for being a stickler, very meticulous. I'm thinking, 'For fuck's sake, he's tearing it apart.' Or, 'he hates it,' or 'he's rewriting it.' As a freelancer, I was in no position to ask him what was taking so long, but it took over three hours. He went through it with a fine-tooth comb. I knew my story was good, but it was so long. I had no idea what they were going to do.

"Finally, Barry came over and said, 'This is an incredible story. We're going to run it at full length. And we're gonna run it tomorrow.'

"*Holy cow!* I looked at my story after he finished. I know what I wrote, and outside of a few grammatical changes and tightening a few words, he didn't edit it much. To his ever-loving credit, he knew it was special, and he wanted to protect it, to make it really shine."

What a story, indeed! When I saw it, I felt exactly the same as the day I watched my race on *Wide World of Sports*—totally blown away, overwhelmed by what I'd just unleashed, and astonished that someone would write a piece like this on *me*. If that wasn't enough, here is how Armen introduced me to *San Diego Union* readers in his story:

> *All you could think was, "Oh God, she's going to fall again. She's 15 feet from the finish line, 15 lousy feet from all the glory she deserves, and she's going to fall again. Dammit, she's not going to make it."*
>
> *For nearly 12 hours, she had given everything the human spirit can ask of the human body. The race, this 140.6-mile torture test called the triathlon, had been hers since five miles into the marathon. She had passed the previous tests—the 2.4-mile swim in the Pacific, the 112-mile bike ride. Now, with 15 feet to go in the 26.2-mile run, her world was falling apart. The finish line was almost close enough to touch, but she looked as if she couldn't possibly get there.*

A few paragraphs later:

> *This happened February 6. Thirteen days later, in living rooms across America, millions of people watching ABC's* Wide World of Sports *saw the tapes of this utterly compelling spectacle and sat stunned, collectively thinking the only possible thought: "If anything is fair in this world, let Julie Moss get up right now. Let her walk, stagger or crawl those last 15 feet. Let her finish. Let her be the women's winner of the Ironman World Championships. Please . . ."*

In the background, a haunting, beautiful instrumental tune played on . . . there was nothing left to say now. It was only Moss and that mysterious music. All the crowd could do was hope . . .

No one can describe the sight of an athlete such as this, beyond the limits of exhaustion, crawling to a finish line. Nobody tried. Only the music played on.

Later in the piece, I tell him, "Have you ever seen pictures of dead people? When I saw the picture of the finish line, I thought, 'That's what dead people look like.' But you know what? My eyes were closed, but I was smiling. I knew, finally, it was all over."

But it wasn't over. It was just beginning—for both of us.

After Armen's story ran, he sent the clip to Bambi Bachman at *Sports Illustrated,* hoping against hope she would find a desk for him. He'd noticed name-shuffling again on the *SI* masthead, during his personal weekly tea-leaf reading. In those pre-Internet, pre-PDF, pre-links days, you sat and waited for the mail to arrive . . . then prayed, hoped, cajoled, and did whatever else to will that phone to ring. Armen wanted badly to grab the phone and follow up, but that could be construed as the act of an overly anxious, insecure writer—not the poise you want to show The Greatest Sports Magazine on Earth.

So he waited. Ten days later, the phone rang. "Armen, it's Bambi."

"Hey, how's it going?"

"Well, we have another opening, and we want to offer you the job."

"Great!"

Then she added this missive: "We're not going to ask you a third time."

"Got it."

"I went back to Dee," Armen recalls. "Kristen had been born on Feb. 18, but now it was early April. Dede felt a lot differently about going to New York, now that our daughter was born and warm weather was coming. My first day at *SI* was on June 6, 1982.

"There's no question that my story on Julie clinched my being hired by *Sports Illustrated.* That was the catalyst for them to come back after my turn-down. Would they have come back had that story not run? I don't know, but looking at the scheme of things, how they work at *SI*, probably not. Plain and simple, the story changed my life."

There was more. Not only did Bambi Bachman like the story but so did the editors at *The Sporting News,* a St. Louis-published magazine that many hardcore sports enthusiasts preferred, particularly for its baseball and football coverage. *Sports Illustrated* added atmosphere and the majesty of events to its coverage, while *The Sporting News* was all about the x's, o's, and effort. Very down-to-earth.

Imagine lightning striking you twice—rapidly—and changing everything. I had my "double taps" with the Ironman finish and media explosion that followed. Now, the lightning found Armen for its second strike.

"A few months later, I got a call, kind of a muddled voice, saying, 'Hey, it's *The Sporting News.* We've got your story on Julie Moss, it's in the book, and we're sending you $250,'" he recalls, deep memory transmitting the visceral excitement of that moment into his elevated voice. "It's like, wow, getting $250 just to put my already-written story in their *Best Sports Stories* book? I was thrilled to be included. I religiously pored through that book every year; after all, it's the best sportswriting by the best sportswriters, and I was a sportswriter.

"The book comes, and the check arrives. I'm looking in the main body for my story; I don't even bother looking at the award-winning stories. What would that have to do with me? All of a sudden, I see my name listed with John Underwood, John Schulian, and Thomas Boswell, three sportswriting legends. Three Mount Rushmores of sportswriting—and me. And I won the damn thing [as Best Feature of the Year]! I had no idea—I just thought I was getting $250 and a book with my story included."

Armen took the fullest advantage of seven years at *Sports Illustrated,* working his way into what has become a monumental journalism and writing career. I see the importance of the subjects he's tackled and stories he's written (and corrupt programs, coaches, and systems he exposed, as well as the countless wonderful pieces on athletes and newsmakers) as his greatest legacy. But through it all, after four decades of deadlines and many hard-edged stories and books, he remains the same empathetic, loving, and deeply perceptive man who committed himself to greatness and impeccable integrity, and then made it happen. But I still don't want him knocking on my door if I did anything wrong!

Armen and I are the bookends of an exclusive mutual admiration club. We are joined at hip and heart by what happened to our careers as the result of my race and his story, which he recently compared with the thousands of events he has covered.

"It ranks right up at the top. I was at the Tour de France for five of Lance Armstrong's seven victories, I've covered two Super Bowls, seven Final Fours, college football title games, been to the Masters, the Indy 500, and seen Mike Tyson bite Evander Holyfield's ear off," Armen says. "I've been to a lot of big events, but for pure drama in the essence of sport, just *finding* yourself, somehow, some way, in the most demanding of circumstances . . . there's a reason this story has stayed with me all these years, and why millions of people still can instantly recall Julie's finish in that race. I feel like I was merely a carrier of her story.

"It's almost like surviving a tsunami. You survive something that wipes out one part of your life and moves you into another part. She came out the other side with a deep appreciation for what she'd experienced, and she was protective of it even then. She wasn't giving it away. That to me was very real, very impressive.

"I remember thinking I wanted to do justice, to honor her in the way she deserved. There are not a lot of Julie Mosses in the world. Since then, God knows I've seen people suffer in sports, and in the Tour de France, you see suffering that's almost unmatched in athletics. But I don't think I've seen courage like hers in a sporting setting."

Now I had to figure out a way to bottle the momentum and notoriety I'd achieved from the race, expand my reach, and make a living at this sport that called to me—and was sending me into a future beyond anything I had imagined.

CHAPTER 6
Training Wheels

And though she be but little, she is fierce.

—William Shakespeare,
A Midsummer Night's Dream

Like nearly all kids in 1960s America, I got my first sense of speed, distance, focused intention, and the power of my own efforts on a bicycle. It started the day my dad, Don Moss, decided that my older brother, Marshall, was old enough to ride on two wheels, so he removed his trainers—but not mine. I didn't quite see the fairness in that. Since Marshall was only fourteen months older than me, I wanted my training wheels to come off too. So I asked Dad with the singularly focused passion and attitude a four-year-old girl possesses, which is to say a lot. He complied. I was determined to start riding on two wheels that day! As my family members recalled, I didn't just try to keep myself balanced and upright a few times and then pack it in. I stayed with it for hours. I wouldn't come inside until I figured out how this bike worked and how my body worked to keep it balanced so I could ride as fast as the other kids screaming down our hilly streets on their Western Auto-bought Huffys and Stingrays.

Finally, just before dark, I came in, red curls flying in all directions and my knees bloodied. I was all smiles; I'd figured it out! Part of my effort came from trying to get the approval of my dad, who I imagined would be thrilled and delighted to see his baby girl, only daughter, and youngest of two children racing down the streets on two wheels, "war wounds," Chatty Cathy dolls, and Easy-Bake Ovens be damned. In order to win his affection, I wasn't coming in until I knew how to ride the bike. My parents watched me struggle, but they never swooped in to "make it all right." They let me have those moments to figure it out. That became a fundamental building block. I will be forever thankful to them for that.

It was so wonderful to see the twinkle in Dad's blue eyes after he took off the training wheels. I say that because, sadly, it was one of the few times I can remember him directly approving something I did—or even taking note of it. He was not in the picture long enough, only for my first eight years. We once had a strong connection, but that faded long ago. In many ways, my drive to succeed and push to the outermost limit originated during those early years when he was around to reward me with his smile and pull me up onto his lap. His memory now sits deep in my shadow, behind my rearview mirror, a ghost whose approval and affection I always craved. But rarely received. Except for that day on the bike. It was one of several significant threads from my lively, active childhood that, unbeknownst to me, fed into my becoming a triathlete.

I know how Dad would view me now: he'd be my biggest fan. He'd also surely take credit for igniting my appetite for endurance and risk. He loved to take credit for me being a girl from his own heart, a tomboy at that. I wonder if he knows that, in some way, he helped start my appetite for endurance and risk. Sports, business and life coaches, and mentors understand that anything we say or any instruction we give, and the way we give it and respond to the result can become *the* words or encouragement athletes need to believe in themselves—and elevate to the next level. We might think of it as inconsequential, no big deal, but in reality, we've just unlocked a gate within that athlete, bringing them one step closer to their greatness. That's what Dad did for me, but sadly, he never stuck around long enough to see how his baby girl would utilize the gifts of hope and confidence he gave her that day.

◆

My parents were very much together on October 8, 1958. When my Mom, the former Eloise Julie Carleton, went into labor, they drove to the hospital. The greeting nurse promptly sent my dad to cool his jets in the "Fathers' Waiting Room." Remember, this was before Lamaze, birthing centers, and nervous new fathers in delivery rooms became an everyday part of having a baby. My mother waited in her room until she couldn't handle the contraction pain further. She asked for whatever relaxants and painkillers could help her through.

Shortly after that, I was born.

When the nurse gave me to my dad, he wasn't happy at first to see me. Or my flaming red hair. There was something else too. He told the nurse, "Take that girl child back and bring me my son." The poor duty nurse turned around and took me back to the nursery. My dad was set on having two boys, and already had one, Marshall, who was one year old. Dad even bet the obstetrician double or nothing on my circumcision. I can't blame him for being so confident; I was the first Moss girl in several generations.

My parents decided to call me Julie Donna. I was named for my French great-grandmother, Julie; my middle name comes from my father, Don. However, once the birth certificate was signed, my mom thought, why not switch Donna to Dawn? When she asked about getting the name changed, the nurse told her it was way too much work. She said this with such an authoritative, almost ominous tone that my mom accepted it. Institutions and their standard practices were rarely questioned in the late 1950s, almost never by women. As fiercely independent as I am, I'm not sure I could have tolerated an adult life in that *Mad Men* era.

Once I was old enough to fully understand the story behind my name, I started disliking it. I can appreciate my mom was in a vulnerable state and not feeling very feisty, having just given birth to a girl when her husband wanted a boy, but I wish she would have fought harder for the middle name. She did fight and prevail when my dad wanted to name my older brother Peter instead of Marshall, a nice triumph for her. I just can't imagine going up to my brother today and saying, "Hi, Pete Moss." I thought it was funny though. So did my Dad.

For those reasons, I associate my middle name with giving up and not fighting for what you want. On a deeper level, I associate it with my father not fighting for me either.

Carlsbad, California, was an ideal town for any kid. Imagine growing up in a combination of Main Street USA, the beach, ranch- and oceanfront-style cottages and houses, rugged foothills with trails that fanned out dozens of miles in all directions, a eucalyptus grove miles in size that is your personal playground, lagoons that offered fishing, boating, water skiing, and swimming, and vibrant neighborhoods where kids played and parents hung out constantly. Throw in abundant warmth and sunshine, and you had a cozy town of 15,000 that posed very well for any postcard shoot or Beach Boys song. In fact, it posed so well that, beginning in the late 1980s, Carlsbad morphed into a prime tourist resort destination, how it is best known today. It also grew to 120,000, but that's another story.

One of Carlsbad's greatest assets was our neighborhoods. While the city's history stretches back to the *Californios*, the rancho owners of the 19th century, Carlsbad didn't incorporate until 1952. City planners built new neighborhoods with families and droves of playing children squarely in mind. Some homes had fences, but very few had gates. Play dates? That would be all day every day, interrupted only by school. Texting your kids? Our parents gave us our instructions before school every morning. Often, we didn't talk to them again until dinner. Parents didn't care much whose yards we ran around in, or which fences we climbed, as long as we finished our homework and got home for dinner and bed. We didn't care either, as long as we could satisfy our playtime thirst with random garden hose water and maybe pick up a quick snack from someone's mother. Plus, we lived a quarter mile from Hosp Grove, a huge eucalyptus grove planted in the 19th century for railroad tie lumber—until workers realized eucalyptus wood is far too soft. "The Forest," as we knew it, was about three square miles in size, a small world to playing children. We trampled up and down the huge hills, through Box Canyon and on the many trails for hours on end, trails that still serve Carlsbad High's cross-country team in practice after being the Lancers' home course for three decades.

My childhood took place on Belle Lane, a cul-de-sac. My parents purchased our home in the mid-1960s for $24,000. No kidding. Now, you're looking at about $1 million for a comparable house and location. It's also where the first indication of my lot in life would appear, my earliest bike ride being one of them.

Another Belle Lane incident involved Jay Jardine, a neighborhood boy Marshall's age. (Later in life, Jay would write and play cartoon soundtracks for Hanna-Barbera, and mentor and influence two generations of local rock musicians.) One day, Jay and I decided to take the surrey down our steep driveway for a spin around the cul-de-sac. The problem? My grandfather's Thunderbird was parked at the bottom of the drive, blocking our way. In the house, the adults were busy celebrating some occasion or another with food and cocktails; parents seemed to celebrate a lot. There were always parties. I was supremely confident that the surrey would somehow make it past my Grandpa Marshall's car. It was an innate confidence, a *knowing* we could pull it off, without second guesses and double-takes dragging my certainty down. Maybe the confidence originated from my growing up on Disney movies and Roald Dahl books, where random acts of magic and wonderment abounded. However, this surrey was no Chitty Chitty Bang Bang, as much as I believed we could magically make it avoid or fly over the Thunderbird. Still, I must have been convincing: Jay was behind the wheel of the surrey, ready to go.

Moments later, we took off down the hill—and broadsided the passenger door of the Thunderbird. Jay and I were unscathed, but the Thunderbird had a big dent. The collision was loud. Needless to say, the cocktail party came to a screeching halt.

That wasn't the only trouble I stirred up. I arrived at Magnolia Elementary School dressed in beautiful handmade dresses sewn by my maternal Grandma T, Lucille Tubach. I wore tights and matching ribbons in my hair and started every day looking the part of the angelic little girl. Then we sat, eight or ten students to a table—and I started talking. I always got in trouble for talking. I ended up at the thinking table most days, alone, strongly encouraged by the teacher to talk silently—with my brain. Maybe I should blame my Chatty Cathy doll. When the day ended, I headed home, ribbons missing from my hair, holes in my dirty tights—something about those playground recesses and my love of action—and a dejected look on my face from having to sit at the thinking table.

My mom would ask me what I'd thought about at the table. I usually answered "nothing." When telling the story many years later, she speculated I was sitting at that table thinking of what I'd like to do to my teacher!

Maybe I wasn't the best-behaved kid, nor the one who followed instructions to the letter, but I did have people I looked up to, mainly through books, TV shows, and movies. I sought out those I admired, both fictional and real, because I couldn't easily find them in my daily life. They were characters, not yet a regular part of our society, because their heroic, powerful ways weren't readily accepted. Yet.

First on the list were Pippi Longstocking and Scout Finch. Both were strong girls, tomboys. They played in the dirt, embarked on various adventures, and beat up obnoxious or bullying boys. I absorbed these stories in the way small children instinctively wrap their hearts and souls around characters, taking Pippi and Scout deep into my heart. Then I headed off to kindergarten, full of *their* assuredness, and spoke out directly, loudly, and confidently. Off to the thinking table I went. Now that I reflect on that, it was my first expression of feminism. I was five.

Pippi Longstocking was such a huge influence on girls of my generation, and she had red hair to boot. She was such a symbol of the qualities we associate with confident, self-assured women, I was thrilled to see her literary essence return in surprising ways. She reemerged through the pen of Stieg Larsson, whose Millennium series, beginning with *The Girl with the Dragon Tattoo*, has enthralled millions with its fiercely unconventional, dark, and socially awkward anti-heroine, Lisbeth Salander. Larsson was deeply impacted by fellow Swedish author Astrid Lindgren, who created Pippi. If I wrote a Lisbeth/Pippi book, it would be, *The Girl Who Colored Outside the Lines*. The May 23, 2010, edition of the *New York Times* wrote of Lisbeth's character:

"They need only read the tales of Pippi Longstocking . . . who has been a soul mate to generations of children longing to color outside the lines. . . . Mr. Larsson especially liked the idea of a grown-up Pippi, a dysfunctional girl, probably with attention deficit disorder, who would have had a hard time finding a place in society but would nonetheless take a firm hand in directing her own destiny."

Sadly, Mr. Larsson never saw his Millennium books in print; he died before *The Girl With the Dragon Tattoo* was published. In an interview before his death, he noted, "My point of departure was what Pippi Longstocking would be like as an adult. Would she be called a sociopath because she looked upon society in a different way?"

Maybe, but she would also be called *strong and assured.* Just like my other heroine, Scout Finch, the headstrong, spunky, routinely barefoot, "unladylike" heroine in overalls at the center of *To Kill A Mockingbird.* Gregory Peck's portrayal of Atticus Finch got all the headlines, but to me, Harper Lee's greatest genius was planting Scout in the story. Scout is very much like the scrappy fireplug Idgie Threadgoode, portrayed by Mary Stuart Masterson in the award-winning 1991 movie *Fried Green Tomatoes.* Like Idgie, Scout avoided dresses, threw punches like a boy, climbed trees, and swung from tires. She was outspoken and opinionated . . . right up my alley. She was the badass feminist role model a young tomboy like me needed to tell her it was okay to *be yourself.*

Like millions of others, and like my mothers' generation, my growing fascination with strong, problem-solving girls continued with the Nancy Drew mysteries. I read as many of the 175 books as the library carried, and found my ideas of what a girl could do and how she could act continuing to expand. Not only did they expand within myself, but, as I looked at the world, Nancy, Pippi, and Scout also expanded the square box of social conventionalism that was apparently my lot for being born a girl. *I don't think so!* Nancy's draw for me was her intelligence, style, and ability to solve mysteries. I wasn't the only one moved to action by her character, either: Hillary Clinton, Oprah Winfrey, former Supreme Court Justice Sandra Day O'Connor, and current Justice Ruth Bader Ginsburg all cite Nancy Drew as early inspiration. (The book series began in 1930.) When I sat back and thought about Nancy Drew's impact on my early years, I came across a list of her role model attributes that still ring true every day of my life—she's fearless, well-rounded, a feminist (even if she did not call herself that—she was not afraid to take charge of her own life), and even today, more than fifty years after she solved her first crime, she has staying power.

I also had a couple of favorite male authors whose imaginative, fantastical works awakened parts of me I would fully experience and express later. This began with books about the ocean, particularly when they spoke of its power, mystery, and beautiful creatures. I loved Karana, the twelve-year-old girl trying to survive in Scott O'Dell's *Island of the Blue Dolphins*, but it was Frank Bonham's *The Loud, Resounding Sea* that awakened my dreams of riding waves. It's about a team of oceanographers, lab assistants, and Horace Morris, a sea-struck hermit. Assistant Skip Turner tries to "shoot" (surf through) Scripps Pier, hits the pilings, and is rescued by a dolphin, with whom he has a friendship afterward. The mix of surfing, deep-sea diving, and sea life really connected with me, which wasn't too hard, since I lived in a beach town.

The author who truly sent my imagination soaring was Roald Dahl. I read *Charlie and the Chocolate Factory* and watched the original *Willy Wonka & the Chocolate Factory* starring the great Gene Wilder, but I adored some of Dahl's other stories. When I thought Jay Jardine and I could drive our little surrey around the parked T-bird, I was recreating *Chitty Chitty Bang Bang* in my head. Roald Dahl wrote the movie's screenplay.

My favorite was the first edition of *The Magic Finger,* in which a little girl (who never reveals her name—love it!) gets back at her neighbors who are killing animals by holding up her finger and stopping them. Talk about a powerful girl! You could also hold the book up to the light, and the pictures would turn into these wonderful, almost animated images. *The Magic Finger* is a really cool book. There's even a fantastic audio narration by Academy Award–winning actress Kate Winslet on roalddahl.com. *The Magic Finger* is about achieving our dreams and finding and using our innate power, but Dahl was very realistic about the obstacles we would face along the way. In this case, the girl transformed people who made her angry by pointing her magic finger at them. When a teacher rebukes her for misspelling "cat," for instance, guess what? The teacher is transformed into a cat. It offers a moral lesson in a funny, lightly frightening way.

If you were a kid in the 1960s and 1970s, you often circled the television set with your family to watch the network news, then feast on an incredible lineup of shows. Given the gold mine of great shows, you'd never know we were limited to the three network channels. It was a golden age, and like every other kid, I had my favorites. My early reading preferences seemed to cross over, because the first TV show hero with whom I identified was a she—Honey West, played by Anne Francis. *Honey West* only aired for one season, when I was seven, but it made a huge impact. It was almost unheard of to see a female private eye in a lead role in the midsixties. I was mesmerized by the self-assuredness and determination of Honey, a private investigator who honored her father by taking charge of his agency. I also loved what she wore, such a fashionable alternative to my scruffy book heroes like Pippi and Scout. Honey stopped at nothing to solve her cases, which made her a role model to me. *Whatever it takes to get something done.* Once, my mom even took me to a department store to meet Anne Francis. She had already left, but I was able to get a Honey West doll.

Honey West was just the beginning. More and more, shows with strong female characters popped up—charming, confident, deliciously mischievous take-charge characters with whom I found myself identifying more and more, whether it was Mary Ann from *Gilligan's Island,* Catwoman, or even Sister Bertrille in *The Flying Nun.* Then there was my all-time favorite cool, fashionable California girl, Julie Barnes from *The Mod Squad.* Baby boomers can close their eyes and still see the tall, leggy, gorgeous girl with sunlit blond hair, a great personality, and badass martial arts skills if you ran afoul of the law. Later, I had to deal with a real-life Julie Barnes and all of her charms and talents when Kathleen McCartney entered my racing life. There are millions of fifty-five- to sixty-year-old men out there for whom Julie was Crush Number One. I had a different kind of crush on her: a Girl Power crush. My fascination with strong, powerful characters rolled right into the seventies, featuring people like Gloria Stivic from *All in the Family,* and of course, *Wonder Woman* (for whom fellow Carlsbad athlete Cindy Gilbert, an Olympian, stunt doubled at times).

One of the coolest things I've experienced in writing this book is how seemingly unrelated examples, experiences, details, or connections appear. Like the source of many of these characters. Behind every strong woman is a strong mother, right? The unofficial "mother" of Mary Ann, Jeannie, Gloria, and many others is Irma Kalish. Irma and her late husband, Austin (known as Rocky in the TV world), warmed up by writing episodes of the huge 1950s live hit *The Colgate Comedy Hour,* and sent us laughing ourselves to sleep with now-classic '60s fare like *F Troop, Family Affair,* and *My Three Sons.* Later in the 1970s, she cowrote countless episodes of *Maude, Too Close for Comfort, The Facts of Life, Carter Country,* and *Good Times,* among others, all racial, social, or women's lib groundbreakers in their own way.

Now ninety-four years of age at this writing, Irma brought great pedigree to network television in the late 1950s as an assured, powerful woman with an incredible sense of humor. That she wrote some of my favorite characters and filled them with these qualities makes her a heroine to me. That she knew of my own up-close-and-personal appointment with Girl Power fame at the 1982 Ironman was even more astonishing.

"I remember that moment, because some of the young girls on set were talking about it for weeks afterward," Irma said. "We were always told what our place was—especially in my time—what not to do with our own dreams, how to be strong and supportive for our husbands, but not necessarily for ourselves. What Julie did illustrates what Rocky and I tried to show with our stronger female characters—you can be charming, funny, sweet, wear dresses, *and* take charge of your life in ways that will change your life, bring out your gifts and strengths, and make a positive impression on the people around you. And," she added, "you can make them laugh too. Laughter is so important to being healthy.

"I thought often about young girls and women growing up, like Julie, and how something Jeannie or Gloria said, or something they did, might make them feel better and more certain of themselves. When I hear about girls who watched our shows becoming self-assured women, it warms my heart. If they have a little mischievous side, all the better!"

There was also a very real character I loved: Nancy Sinatra, whose live TV performances of her song "These Boots Are Made for Walkin'," and her appearances to troops serving in Vietnam, made her *the bomb* among men nationwide, as their wives looked at them and laughingly thought, "You wish . . ." As Nancy danced, pranced, and sang with her minidresses, go-go boots, and legs that seemed to keep on going, I dialed into something far different: her power, energy, and *style*. Between Honey West, Nancy, and Julie Barnes, I knew that whatever happened in my life, dressing stylishly and colorfully would be part of it. Now, we know this combination of styles as "boho" or "boho chic"—and it's still my style.

Nancy was the subject of a report I wrote in second grade about people we admired. My subject was scrutinized and deemed inappropriate by my teacher, Mrs. Noise. She brought it up at my next parent-teacher conference, only her principal complaint wasn't about the content. It was about my habit of singing the song in class:

> *These boots are made for walking*
> *And that's just what they'll do*
> *One of these days these boots*
> *Are gonna walk all over you . . .*

Nancy's song still makes me want to get up and dance. The melody and what it represented for me—style, power, grace, beauty—will stay with me forever.

Mrs. Noise told me not to sing that song anymore, because I was tone-deaf. Sadly, I never tried to sing in public again. I still feel awkward even singing "Happy Birthday," but I make myself leave singing birthday messages for my family and close friends. I hated second grade, and this was the biggest reason. It is a stark reminder of why I feel we, as parents, mentors, teachers, bosses, siblings, coaches, and friends, owe it to our kids and grandkids to give them positive messaging, and dial into how they can become the best of themselves in what they do. Who knows? I might have become a better singer. But that fire was extinguished by one mean teacher. Now, I'd rather spend eleven hours running an Ironman than sing in public.

As I grew older, I continued doing girls' things, but with the mischievous spirit and skinned-up knees of a tomboy. In fifth grade, like most girls, I played with Barbies. No Kens invited. Jenny Jones and I spent hours sewing outfits for them. Jenny was an amazing seamstress, as well as a badass surfer. Mr. Jones and Jenny's brother, David, were devoted surfers and taught Jenny to ride a longboard. With her strong build, Jenny had no problem carrying her heavy nine-foot longboard down to Tamarack Beach, known locally as The Rack. I didn't know how to surf, but I'd read *The Loud, Resounding Sea* and lived near the beach—and it appealed to me. I don't know why I didn't start with Jenny and take advantage of her dad and David as my mentors, and along with that, a guaranteed place in the waves without aggressive locals chasing me away.

While the surf bug first visited me then, it didn't sink its teeth into me for good until the summer before I started high school. The shortboard revolution of the late '60s had taken over surfing, and longboards were considered "old people's boards." If you were young and desperately trying to fit in, you weren't caught dead on them. I started on shortboards, no longer than six feet. It was very difficult to get the hang of it, because the shorter the board, the more side-to-side movement it has, and the less your stability on the deck, where you stand. By high school, Jenny and I no longer hung out together, but occasionally I would see her surfing and admire how graceful and fluid her style was on both short and longboards.

Then there was high school. The majority of great triathletes come from great high school and/or college sports careers. Some are even high school or collegiate all-Americans. I was not one of them. Not even close. Every time I tried out at Carlsbad High School, I just wanted to be part of the team. That was my goal—not necessarily to play, not to make a headline, or score the winning run, but to be a part of it. I didn't like being called into basketball games; riding the bench was fine with me! Softball was okay, because I knew where I had to be in the outfield, and I could run pretty fast. With volleyball, we practiced dolphin diving constantly; later, I used it as a San Diego County lifeguard. On our tennis team, I played No. 4 doubles—the lowest-ranked position. The idea of serving and having the ball come firing back at me? I didn't do too well. But I did earn a varsity letter!

I still get the thrill of contributing to a team. For two seasons, through a wonderful series of circumstances, I contributed directly to my alma mater as an occasional assistant to the Carlsbad High School cross-country team. We dream of things as little girls, and we move on, but I honestly did not see myself coaching a high school sport. I promise you that my high school coaches wouldn't have seen that possibility either. But that's the thrill of life, its magical twists and turns. When you put your energy and focus in the right direction, act with intention, and remain open to possibilities you may not see at the time, they seem to breathe themselves into existence.

Sometimes, those opportunities arrive in droves. Whether you're ready or not.

CHAPTER 7
My Fifteen Minutes

Imagine yourself a 23-year-old surfer girl who becomes the most recognized triathlete in the world almost overnight. You weren't on anyone's radar, but you wanted to be. (We all would, in some way.) Suddenly, after the most popular sports show in the U.S. features you, sponsors, TV and movie producers, media, corporations, and race directors seek you out, and they keep coming. "Julie the Unbreakable arrived right when America needed her most; she showed she had the sand to stick it out when most of us were wondering, privately, how many of us did," bestselling author Christopher McDougall wrote in *Natural Born Heroes.*

When America needed her most . . . It's hard for anyone to imagine being perceived in this way. Certainly this otherwise ordinary college kid.

Sudden fame carries a dual effect. A head-swelling impact can accompany the leap to international recognition. Or crawl. I'm not sure how you avoid it, especially when it hits like a tsunami to wash aside the life you knew. Articles come out, TV stations call, people start talking, and you start believing your own press. In my case, you also suffer through the terrifying feeling of pretending to be a professional athlete when you are really not. How to handle all of this?

I went with the fake-it-'til-you-make-it approach.

This scary, crazy, wild, and wonderful ride followed the 1982 Ironman, *Wide World of Sports*, and Armen Keteyian's article. It took me a while to inwardly absorb and appreciate the accolades and superlatives, but I was not shy about my outer reaction. I generally did what many young people do when we get our fifteen minutes of fame—ate it up like Michelin five-star cuisine. I walked toward the attention, rather than from it; I loved being noticed. "When Julie walks into a room, you definitely know she's there," Lisette says. "Her energy and confidence draw you in, she loves people, and she can hold conversations with anyone."

The truth of it all? I needed to believe my own press to feel like I belonged with the other women athletes. Never mind I'd just finished second in the most important triathlon. As long as I continued protecting myself from the humiliation of "losing control of bodily functions" in the final meters, as Diana Nyad put it, I was all-in. I still did not understand why so many people drew inspiration from my race, since I didn't win and I had to crawl, rather than run, across the line.

Little did I know my fifteen minutes would span four decades.

After declining David Letterman's invitation, I was contacted by ProServ, a prestigious athlete management firm. Among others, ProServ managed the careers of NBA superstar Moses Malone and two of America's sporting sweethearts, U.S. Open tennis champ Tracy Austin and 1979 world figure skating champion Tai Babilonia. I decided not to sign, for the stated reason that I wanted to train and race on my own. "Basically, that's not what I'm into," I told Armen in the *San Diego Union*. "Do I promote and go while the going's good? I asked myself what's my goal. I know it's to do well in October [in 1982, Ironman was contested twice]. I kind of had to draw the line."

There is another reason: I had no idea what it took to be a professional athlete. The frightened little girl beneath my confident public persona arose when the suggestion came up. She thought, *I'm not ready. I'm not as ready as these other girls.* I was afraid ProServ would call my bluff. So I never let them.

Meanwhile, I kept processing my race, connecting some dots, learning to articulate the deeper meaning of my effort, what it meant not to quit, to give everything . . . literally. "You know the neatest thing? An athlete rarely has a chance to take himself or herself to the limit, and then go on," I told Armen. "I know if I ever have to, I can do it. I can take it to the very end. Not many people can say that. And it's a feeling I can hang on to forever."

These realizations formed the most authentic part of my Ironman experience. I began to describe them more often. I wasn't comfortable talking about the messy bits, and I still felt inwardly unsettled by the credit I was receiving for the surge in triathlon and endurance sports worldwide. I had no idea what the sport was going to become. I told an interviewer in 2017, "It was this strange event that happened once a year and was televised. I loved being in Hawaii. I was soaking it all up. The idea of having to do a race was not exactly an afterthought, but I wasn't too worried about the race until the gun went off."

Wish I would've remembered that simple wisdom a few times since, like in Kona in 2017! It's the perfect way to do an Ironman: hold no expectations, remain completely in the moment. Out of the mouths of babes . . .

I started sharpening my message. By tapping into the larger experience of my race, I found I could better accept the impact of it. I told my story to hundreds of journalists, which further clarified the moment. This repeated telling planted an anchor that slowly moored the experience into my body, mind, and soul, where it could always empower me and positively impact the lives of others. Twenty years later, when I returned to Kona for the twenty-fifth anniversary Ironman, I told Kevin Mackinnon of Ironman.com, "Everyone has a defining moment, and mine got captured on film. Every time the tape's played and I hear Tim Weisberg's flute, it hits this deep emotional chord that says I discovered something new about myself on that day, and people get to see it." A few years later, I pointed out to Julia Morrill of *Sports Illustrated*, "What I did that day wasn't pretty to see. What shined through was the humanness of my struggle. The determination is inside everybody."

Once the post-race buzz subsided . . . well, it didn't, not for a long time. It seemed everyone wanted to hear my story. I wasn't used to that. I was the little-noticed schoolgirl who showed off with crazy antics to gain attention.

Now, the spotlight fell right onto me. Thankfully, I love people—and triathlon fans. My relationship to the fans has always been strong.

Attention rained on me like a Hawaiian downpour. Invitations flowed in from sources you might expect—and plenty you wouldn't. Right after the *Wide World of Sports* airing, I was invited to New Zealand for *Survival of the Fittest*, a popular CBS TV show. I also was featured in the "Jock" section of *People* magazine, and received an invitation to speak to an IBM convention in Hawaii. Me? On stage? Speaking to audiences? Competing on a televised event halfway around the world? Sounds great!

Think of *Survival of the Fittest* as a proto-*Survivor*, involving real sports feats rather than contestants arguing over the most innocuous things. Our diverse, renowned "cast" included two-time *Survival of the Fittest* champion Kevin Swigert, a cross-country skier from Idaho; world-class white water kayaker Dan Schnurrenberger; mountain climbing superstar Lynn Hill, the first woman to climb the "nose" of El Capitan in California's Yosemite Valley; recently crowned Ironman champ Scott Tinley; and a few others whose names escape me. Plus myself.

We were taken to the interior of the South Island and housed on the Lake Wanaka shoreline. We helicoptered to the Mount Aspiring National Park region, and jet boated to our river swim location on the Clutha River, one of the glacier-fed rivers that interlaced the park. Jet boating is thrilling, adventurous, and exciting, a robust New Zealand thing. We enjoyed it immensely. We then swam the Clutha River through Grade 2 and Grade 3 rapids, with "wave" faces sometimes hitting three to five feet, plus the challenges you'd associate with a fast-moving river, like dangerous currents, eddies, exposed rocks, and broken water.

In our cross-country competition, we ran trails to the summit of a 500-foot rock, and then clipped in and rappelled down the face, aided by a top belayer (an expert who controls the safety rope for climbers). In order to move down the sheer face, we had to lift the entire rope to create enough slack. For me, there was a problem: the rope was too heavy. Even when I leaned back with all my weight, I couldn't get the rope to slide through my harness. As I struggled, I caught the attention of the belayer and exchanged eye glances. *I can't lift the rope.* He got my drift. As I yanked on the line, he released the rope, inch by inch. We continued this dance until my body outweighed the remaining rope. Without his help, I would have dangled in my harness until they unclipped me.

Next up was the whitewater kayaking, an aerial obstacle course with commando lines and Burma bridges (think of a challenging "monkey" rope bridge), along with a jousting match twenty feet above the Clutha River. The *Washington Post* called it "a tailored-for-television sporting circus . . . First prize will be $15,000 and the title of leanest, meanest, grittiest athlete in the whole macho world."

That's a little much. You cannot compare a made-for-TV event to an Ironman—at all—but you have to appreciate the promotional gusto. I thought Dan Schnurrenberger found the only valid point in common: "It's not always the best athletes that win," he told the *Washington Post*. "Sometimes, it's who has the most willpower."

Sadly, we girls dealt with some gender bias. We were not included in the scree competition, where athletes run, bounce, and skid down the loose mountain chip rock (scree). If the scree is small and deep enough, you can "ski" it in your boots, essentially riding a miniature rockslide. What great fun! But not for the girls. Too dangerous for women, they said. That saddened me. However, it was 1982 and women and men were not considered equal by most TV producers, nor the insurance companies hounding them about the financial and legal necessity of "keeping it safer for the girls."

Much later, I learned a funny backstory about our *Survival of the Fittest* experience. It came from the resident expert on all things triathlon, Scott Tinley. In a piece on his Trihistory.com site entitled "Ripples from the 1982 Ironman Triathlon & The Crawl Felt Round The World," ST recalled his first run-in with *Survival of the Fittest* executive producer Barry Frank, president of Trans World International, the television division of IMG, the world's largest sports management firm. The studly, blond, newly-crowned Ironman champion met the short, thick New York executive puffing his cigar at a small bar on Lake Wanaka. It was a match made in . . . TV world.

Frank ordered Scott a beer. After ST suggested he looked a bit out of place, Barry Frank replied, "So are you, Hot Shot. I know that because I'm the reason you're here." *Fair enough.* "Glad you could make it. I enjoyed watching you win in Kona a few weeks ago."

After ST thanked Frank for the invite and beer, he noticed Frank looking past him, toward the door. He asked if the producer was expecting anyone else. "Julie," Frank said. "Julie Moss is the new star."

My sudden appearance on the scene bothered ST a bit at first. He thought of me as an outsider (true enough) who had turned triathlon into a freak show of sorts, or at least its perception by *Wide World of Sports* viewers. I certainly didn't mean to; it's not like I pre-scripted my race, or the final 100 meters. Or the fifteen feet that I crawled. As this perception connected with my personal insecurities, I thought, "Am I a freak? Have I turned the sport into a freak show?"

ST is a smart and perceptive man, sometimes strong with his opinions. He's also capable of pulling the lens back, taking a longer view, and changing said opinions if he sees beyond his original take. It didn't take long for him to realize a surge in Ironman and triathlon was about to get underway. Barry Frank's remark made it clear. "I knew then that the ripples of the 1982 Ironman and Moss's Big Crawl, not three weeks prior, would lap at the shores of triathlon for decades after the scrapes on her knees healed," he wrote.

Initially, ST struggled with the idea that an everyday girl had changed the sport. "It was almost too dramatic," he told the *Los Angeles Times* in 1985. "There were some people that thought the thing was play-acted. That real life wasn't like this."

Funny how we perceive things. Chris McDougall portrayed the public perception 180° differently in *Natural Born Heroes*:

"At first these contests were treated as Battles of the Freaks, until Julie Moss—twenty-three years old, still in college, and One of Us—jolted our eyes from the winners in the front of the pack toward the heroes in the back. TV was soon [actually, already—my note] *zooming in to cover these gritty Everymen."*

I think "One of Us" and "Everymen" sound much better than "freak show." I would add that *Sports Illustrated* and ABC saw the pre-1982 Ironman competitors the same way as McDougall—which is why *SI* covered the 1979 race, and *Wide World of Sports* added the event to its annual roster.

McDougall also pointed out something else: how my finish started a new way of approaching races. "Instantly an anthem was born: 'Just Finishing Is Winning.'" Hear that saying a few times at youth soccer matches, weekend 10Ks, or other participatory sports events? I'm of two minds about this "gold star" sentiment—the participant in me encourages it, while the racer and champion finishes to *win*. "Just Finishing Is Winning" is now woven into our youth, scholastic, and recreational sports culture.

Back to Scott Tinley. ST and I have come a long way since 1982, and so has his take on an Ironman race for which he should forever be feted as a great champion, since he won so impressively and established himself as the greatest rival to Dave Scott. Had a certain freckle-faced, Bud Light cap-wearing interloper not appeared, he would've carried the day. In *30 Years of the Ironman Triathlon World Championship,* Scott reflected. "It was a courageous thing. Julie was young. She didn't know. She was a college coed. She was innocent, and therein lies the heroic deed."

New Zealand also produced a welcome return to my love life. My ex-boyfriend Reed, who finished fifth in the Ironman and whom I still missed terribly, had mapped out a personal bike tour of New Zealand. When I was invited to *Survival of the Fittest,* I realized our trips overlapped. Perfect! After I informed him of this coincidence, he cautiously suggested I bring my bike along, and some panniers and camping gear.

Perfect. Time to try again. After the *Survival of the Fittest* shoot, we rode much of his bike tour, which cracked open the door for us getting back together. We returned to Southern California as a tentative couple.

I was busy from the moment the plane taxied. I was approached for a made-for-TV movie, *Challenge of a Lifetime,* starring the great Penny Marshall. Penny is entertainment royalty to us baby boomers, the star of the 1970s smash sitcom *Laverne & Shirley* and later, a brilliant movie director and producer. In *Challenge of a Lifetime,* Penny starred as a newly divorced woman trying to show her son (played by future star of the *Weekend at Bernie's* movies, Jonathan Silverman) she could pull herself together. To play a triathlete, she copied my Kona running outfit, minus the trucker hat, but including the damned bra straps. I was given screen credit as a technical consultant, which allowed me to work and hang out with a trio of great Olympians: gymnast Bart Conner, figure skater Cathy Rigby, and seven-time gold medal–winning swimmer Mark Spitz. Bart and Cathy played triathletes, while Mark was cast as the race announcer.

One day, I went to Penny's house to run through the best training routine for her. I parked my VW Squareback up the street, because God forbid it leaves oil on Penny Marshall's driveway! It was great fun to work with her, and to travel with the crew to Hawaii, film scenes, and experience life behind the camera. This free trip to give advice on being a triathlete was definitely more fun than torrential rains in Southern California.

While working on the film, I spent time with the team from Specialized Bicycles, which provided bikes to cast and crew. I hung out inside the truck that housed the bikes, chatting with the rep . . . and gaining a sponsorship after a really nice conversation. That's how I got my first Specialized Allez bike sponsorship. *Could it really be this easy?*

Meantime, interest in triathlon surged far beyond what the pioneers in San Diego and Kona could have imagined. According to *Triathlon Magazine,* the sport's first international publication, 60,000 people entered about 400 triathlons worldwide in 1982. In 1983, those numbers jumped to 250,000 runners and 1,000 triathlons; by 1985, we had 1.1 *million* participants in 2,100 triathlons, along with our own domestic tour, the Bud Light United States Triathlon Series (USTS). The growth was that fast, and I was cited as the catalyst. As Chris McDougall noted in *Natural Born Heroes,* people didn't look at me as a postcard-perfect athlete with the body of Adonis or Athena (aka Scott Tinley or Kathleen McCartney). They saw me as the energetic neighbor girl who took on and faced down a challenge. In me, they imagined themselves surviving a brutal course, high heat and wind, dehydration, subpar training, and her own limits. They saw Don Moss's little girl riding and falling, getting up, and falling again, until she got the hang of riding a bicycle. The message was pretty simple: "If she can do it, I can do it—or at least something that makes me feel better about myself." Participation soared through the roof.

In this way, my star shone differently from champion triathletes. Or athletes, really; as Jim McKay noted, few had experienced a more dramatic "agony of defeat" moment. I was regarded as the author of an earth-shattering event that vaulted Ironman and triathlon onto the world map. I found myself reminding people I did not win, that Kathleen was the 1982 Ironman champion. It didn't matter. I was in high demand.

Most athletes work their entire careers to get their signature moment, say, a Super Bowl title or long-overdue Olympic gold medal. Mine came in my *first* athletic achievement. Consequently, I became one of very few triathletes to receive appearance fees—a check for showing up to race. That led me to think, *I've earned my paycheck before I even start this race.* They didn't have much prize money then, which made the appearance fees even more special. My attitude was, *I'm here because I'm sponsored and I did this and I don't have to work like that.*

I fell into a cushy place compared to my peers, who scrambled every day to synch their work and training schedules while paying for equipment and races. They wanted triathlon to be their profession. Triathlon *was* my new profession. Fortunately, no race directors or early sponsors expected me to repeat my Kona effort. I would just welcome everything that came my way. *I'm going to keep doing this until I'm not earning money at it anymore, or it stops being fun,* I thought.

With that kind of reinforcement, race in and race out, why push to the limit? I began to feel like I didn't *need* to shift into a higher gear to assure a great career. Nor did I want to experience that end-of-the-line distress again. I put in long training days, for sure, but I wouldn't fully commit to becoming a great athlete. Why would I, or anyone, want to go through that pain again? The thought scared the hell out of me.

After my Ironman, I sought out running races and triathlons. My early results made clear a couple of things: I had the ability to attain the highest level, but I didn't know how to get to the top, nor did I fully appreciate the work required. Consequently, I blew up again in the run segment of my second Ironman, in October 1982. Once again, I raced more for the sake of pleasing Reed and competing with him but with the added pressure of pleasing my sponsors. I was in good shape after the bike, but the run course bit me hard. I finished fourteenth, not exactly what the world expected from the runner-up of eight months prior.

When 1983 rolled around, triathlon was a far different sport than the previous year. My first victory came at the 1983 Bud Light USTS event in San Diego. Finally, I felt like I belonged with the other elites.

The feeling didn't last long. I headed back to Kona for Ironman, but Reed was done with the race. Now working in Santa Rosa, he planned to return to school for his second computer science degree. When I called from Kona to confirm his arrival, he told me he wasn't coming and our relationship was over. I immediately flew to San Francisco to see if he meant it. He did. I flew back to Hawaii, crushed. Predictably, I finished a weak seventeenth. "I've come to realize that I never was a true athlete," I said a year later. "I was always doing it for some other reason." That reason being to impress the man I desperately wanted in my life.

As sadly as 1983 could have ended, my final race put a light-hearted and victorious spin onto it. In late November, I headed to Rio de Janeiro for the Golden Cup Triathlon. I was in it to win it, for sure, but this was Rio, and the place was *raging*. A magazine article shows me being held horizontally by fellow competitors Dean Harper and Robert Roller on the crowded beach, with the caption: "Gidget goes to Ipanema."

That gives you an idea of the fun we had.

Our course consisted of a 1-mile ocean swim, 32-mile bike ride, and a 10K run to the finish on Copacabana Beach. If you watched the 2016 Rio Olympic road cycling races, then you saw some of the hills on which we competed. I settled the race early, grabbing a big lead in the swim, stretching it out on the bike, and winning by fourteen minutes, one of my most decisive victories.

When I looked down at my race singlet after crossing the line, I was horrified: it was inside out! Instead of reading PAN AM, for the iconic airline that sponsored the event, it read MA NAP. Since I had a vested interest in flying home safely, I quickly fixed my shirt to appease our generous sponsor.

I converted my relationship woes into training energy for the 1984 season and committed wholeheartedly this time. As a result, I jumped to fourth place on the year-end rankings and finished second to Colleen Cannon in the Nice World Championships. Bummed by my recent Kona efforts, I'd already been contemplating retirement from Ironman races—if not triathlon itself—but in Nice I proved to myself I could still compete.

Later in the year, I won the women's division of the Off Road Triathlon, held in Santa Rosa, California. The race was rugged and unique, to my liking: a 175-yard swim in a lagoon, a 9-mile bike ride on dusty dirt roads, and a 6-mile ride on tough, technical, rocky trails. I'd driven all night from Bass Lake, near Yosemite, after racing in the USTS Nationals and staying late for the after-party, so I wasn't ideally rested. I held the lead after the swim, but fell back on the bike, as my Specialized Stumpjumper wasn't enough to keep me from feeling out of control in places. However, I clocked a thirty-seven-minute run to move into fourteenth place overall and the first woman. The men's winner? Reed Gregerson.

One of my most important rites of passage into serious triathlete status was getting into the group workouts with triathletes training out of San Diego County, which is to say, virtually every elite except for Dave Scott, who remained in Northern California. We had three big workouts: a set of fierce intervals at the UC San Diego outdoor pool; a bike ride from Del Mar to Dana Point and back; and the Tuesday run, a 90-minute fartlek workout in Rancho Santa Fe, hosted by Scott Molina. Fartlek, the Swedish word for "speed play," was popularized by the legendary coach Arthur Lydiard, who guided Herb Elliott to the 1960 Olympic gold medal and world record in the 1,500-meter run. The concept is simple: run hard for a designated number of minutes, then run at recovery pace for roughly the same time. Then knock off another interval. The lengths of intervals and rests change, but ideally, each interval is faster than the previous one. *It's all about how you finish.* Scott Molina took it further, leading the guys to a sub-5-minute final mile, but he was not the toughest in the group. That would've been Mark Allen.

My key workout was the bike ride. We began and ended at Carlos & Annie's restaurant in Del Mar. The Del Mar crew rode north fifty miles to Dana Point, through the Marine Corps base at Camp Pendleton, picking up group members along the way. Dale Basescu, Mark Allen, and Charlie Graves often joined in Cardiff or Solana Beach, while Sylviane and Patricia

Puntous, Marc Surprenant, Mark Montgomery, Kenny Souza, and I would often meet the pack in Encinitas. Our ride up was fun—joking, trading places in the pack, laughing, and getting a quick bite at our halfway mark in Dana Point. Then we turned around, dug in, and rode home like the world-class triathletes we were, with far less talking and much more intensity. "Coming back, you are on your own. No one waits for anyone," Dale told a *Triathlete* magazine writer.

By now, I started wrapping my press around myself like Olympic champions draping flags on their shoulders for the victory lap. Some of my comments make me cringe when I read them now. My sassy, smart-ass side came out big-time in the "Material Girl" cover article from the November 1985 issue of *Tri-Athlete* magazine. I was made up as a hot ginger model, with bare shoulders, curled and pouffed-out New Wave hair, bling around my neck and wrists, and plenty of sassiness. And sexiness. The author, Bill Katovsky, was the founder of *Tri-Athlete* (which later merged with *Triathlon* to become *Triathlete*). When he ran *Tri-Athlete*, Bill tended to do crazy things. He even put me on a cover one time wearing a sausage-case leather miniskirt and holding a kid's tricycle!

For this article, Bill decided to play on the badass attitude of Madonna, who also burst out of nowhere, crucifix dangling from her chest, to shock the world. She did it with her album *Like a Virgin*, her song "Material Girl," and nonstop video rotation on MTV. I adopted much of her attitude in the ten-page feature (the largest I've ever received).

When we conducted the interview, I had just won the Yanmar Japan Ironman, which led to Bill's telling first question: "You've finally won a race that counts . . . is it a dream that's finally come true?"

That speaks to my priorities then that it took three and a half years after *almost* winning in Kona to finally win an Ironman event, even though much of the world (except my close friends) regarded me as a superstar. The fact it happened months after I signed a five-year deal with Bridgestone Tires, a Japanese company, didn't hurt. In Japan, victory brings honor to athlete and sponsors alike, and I wanted my sponsor to feel very, very honored—and to continue feeling that way.

My answer revealed a lot about my headspace: "After the race, I spent ten days traveling in the Far East." I'd headed off to China to visit Robin Donaldson, one of the girls in my high school surfing crew. "I didn't even think it would be worth talking about when I got home. I was pleasantly surprised that word did get around and people took notice." I heard that Mark Allen said, "God, we're going to have to go down to San Diego, and try to pry her head out of the 747." (Probably because my ego would be incorrigible.)

Then, in another response, I revealed how unfamiliar *winning* was to me. "Before the Japan race, I had an athletic breakthrough. I felt I had finally come of age in terms of where I'm at in the sport. I had an inner feeling of contentment the entire time I was racing. It wasn't a smile that meant I was going to win; it was a relaxed, calm inner knowledge that if I didn't screw up, I was going to win that race. I kept saying to myself, 'Don't start smiling now, because you haven't gotten to the finish line. Just take one step at a time. Afterward you can smile all you want.' I went on a smiling binge for about a week."

False modesty aside, I told Bill that Japan was a huge victory for me. It also validated a comment I'd made in *Triathlon* earlier in the year, one my fellow competitors weren't accustomed to hearing from me: "I have an ideal that I still want to achieve. It is to enter a race where I know I have done everything I can in preparing and training to win it. I would love to see how I feel about the outcome under those circumstances," I said.

I arrived in Japan a couple weeks prior. Bridgestone officials kept me busy with events and appearances. "I really felt like part of a team," I said of Bridgestone at the time, "and after they arranged the seminars, set up the bike mechanics' tents at the race and everything else, it was my turn—I really wanted to win the race for Bridgestone."

I also prepared for my race differently, visiting meditation gardens and shrines in Kyoto and using mantras for the first time in competition. I'd spoken to Mark Allen about visualization, which he used for racing. My goal was to overcome another Achilles heel, trying too hard too soon in Ironman-length races and making terrible tactical mistakes as a result, such as speeding up with eight miles to go in a marathon when you have an eight-minute lead. This time, I felt calm, knowing what I had to do to win. Except I almost missed the bike check-in, because Kathleen McCartney and I were absorbed in a shopping spree. Of all reasons . . .

Race headquarters were in Hikone, a resort town of 12,000 in Shiga Prefecture, on the shores of massive Lake Biwa, the water-filled crater of an ancient volcano about 250 miles east of Tokyo. It is a beautiful, mountainous region. The Lake Biwa surface was subject to sudden changes in wave size and water temperature when the winds whipped up. We found out what happens firsthand when a bypassing typhoon brushes the area.

The start was epic. The event aired live to an estimated 60 million Japanese viewers. Samurai warriors performed a ceremony, accompanied by fireworks and boats spraying fountains of colored water. Tens of thousands watched as the major fired a black powder, hand-held cannon to start the race. The recoil knocked him on his butt.

I had a strong swim despite the wind, clocking one hour, three minutes and six seconds for the 2.4 miles. I emerged from the water in fourth place—*overall.* Only Dave Scott, Scott Molina, and women's leader Robin Beck were ahead of me. Sally Edwards, Ardis Bow, and Kathleen, my chief competitors, all trailed. This was Kathleen's first Ironman in almost two years. She had "retired" after the 1983 season, so she didn't expect much of herself. I knew better after watching her morph from hospitalized sick person to 1982 Ironman champion in a day's time.

As I left the transition area to ride, the threatening skies opened up. The course was harrowing, with narrow eight-foot-wide roads, no shoulders, and dropoffs hundreds of feet in height. Imagine riding at high speed along California's Big Sur coastline and negotiating the cliffside curves minus guardrails. That was the challenge. I relished it. This time, a melted Snickers bar did not ruin my day. I brought far healthier Japanese snacks, like *inari*, a seasoned and fried tofu bean pouch filled with vinegared sushi rice and topped with sesame seeds, roe (fish eggs), and avocado. I then attacked every hill and squeezed the juice from each mile. My plan on the bike was simple: to get so far ahead that the run *could not* take me down. I wanted at least ten minutes before starting the run. As it turned out, I hammered the bike, and reached the transition with a thirty-two-minute advantage.

The most welcoming layout was the marathon course, flat and fast. I extended my lead over Sally Edwards while reciting my mantra: "Patience. Patience." I didn't overcook the opening miles, my fatal flaw in Ironmans past. A few hours later, I stood in Konki Park alongside Dave Scott and Scott Molina, third place overall, in addition to winning the women's race by fifty-one minutes over Sally. Spectators and media were amazed that the only people who beat me out of 424 finishers were half of triathlon's Big Four. "I don't think anything like that will ever happen to me again," I told the press.

As for Kathleen? Considering it was her first race in eighteen months, she did great, finishing fourth among women, an hour and nineteen minutes behind me. Yet, I couldn't help think of our history. *No finish-line drive-bys this time, honey . . .*

In the "Material Girl" story, I had not yet embraced consistently winning and performing at the championship level, even though results like Japan showed I was doing just that. "The sport is going to do what it's going to do—it doesn't need me," I said. "I don't see myself having a big impact on the direction of triathlons, yet I perceive my attitude toward the sport as having a big impact on what I plan to do. I used to take a blasé attitude, 'Well, we'll see what comes up next year and then the next year.' Now, instead of just looking ahead to the next season, I'm looking ahead to three years down the road. I'm really thinking career now."

Did I believe this deep down? Perhaps. But it wasn't set in stone, or even a consistent thought. I loved the sex appeal and sizzle of the sport, and the bling that came from being famous because of it. "What a lot of people forget about those first few years is that Julie became famous to the general public first because of *Wide World of Sports* and how everyone reacted, and then she became famous within her sport later," Sue Robison points out. "That's backward from how it normally works."

Plus, it was the mideighties, triathlon was rising like a bullet, and the Southern California beach lifestyle was crossing over into music, fashion, surfing, and beach-oriented sports. The 1984 Olympics in Los Angeles galvanized this buzz. I was right in the middle of it and the influence of triathlon on it. I kept seizing the moment. "I suppose I'm a material girl," I told *Tri-Athlete,* playing being the athlete picked for the "Madonna" cover. "The business side of the sport is what interests me now. When I got back from Japan, I went out to dinner with several friends. After a few bottles of sake, I said that I only saw three or four triathletes who were really going to make it, and I wanted to be in that group. Once you see yourself in that position, it's important to start taking the proper steps." A Madonna-like comment, to be sure.

I constantly took steps to shine in the eyes of promoters and the media. Today, we call this branding. Triathlon became a major PR mission for me. Unlike many of my American peers, I competed in Europe, where appearance fees were plentiful and prize money was improving. Plus, fan response was through the roof. European fans are rabid about their sports, and a mighty endurance challenge plays into their deepest, most revered legends and myths. We were treated as heroes, pure and simple, and it factored into how I started to view my role. "I feel that's one of my underlying goals—to spread the sport of triathlon worldwide," I told *Tri-Athlete.*

I also picked up on something else. If you were a non–ball sports athlete in the 1980s (in any era, really), you had to make yourself louder and bigger to get attention, and dollars. Since I sat atop the mantle of a sport, in a sense, I made sure to be noticed. It's far easier to portray yourself with the bravado of a Madonna than to reveal insecurities of your true self. This led to a cringeworthy comment in the "Material Girl" interview:

"My idea of fun has changed. Fun is flying first class, or at least business class, to new countries. When I'm traveling now I see guys and girls with their backpacks who haven't had a bath in days. Well, that used to be my idea of fun. Now my idea of fun is being met at the airport by journalists and photographers, being whisked off to interviews and having interpreters run around with me wherever I go."

Or, how about this blast? "It's really hard to get out in the morning and go for a run. They're just piled up at my doorstep. Sometimes I can't find the paper . . . but I still like doing triathlons, because it's fun, and oh gee, I like doing them because I can meet guys and go to really neat places and go shopping."

Never mind that I never had a boyfriend in high school because I was, you know, the *good* friend, the *trusted* friend, the girl with personality, the girl who tried too hard to be funny. I had no clue what it took to be in a relationship. I was barely comfortable in my own skin, let alone trying to be part of a couple. Now, less than a decade later, I'm suddenly driving guys off my doorstep?

Like I said, plenty to cringe about.

After my Japan victory, I decided to go for it all—winning the 1985 Ironman. I was in great shape, and now knew how to win the long race. I had overcome my poor run history at the distance, and I felt ready. I was coming to Kona to win, period, nothing else. Much had changed since 1982. Fully seventy-five percent of the field was running in its first Ironman, and they came from thirty-four countries. Also, the 1,250 entrants were more than double the 590 starters in 1982—and selected from over 12,000 applicants.

I had changed too. At least I wanted to believe it. I swam strongly, despite the remnants of a hurricane pushing big swells into the swim basin. I forged a lead on the bike while Sue rode ahead in the *Wide World of Sports* camera van, logging film as a hired gun. By the time I reached the transition, I was three minutes ahead of Joanne Ernst, with rising star Paula Newby-Fraser seventh and Kathleen in fourteenth.

Then we had to run. I'd given too much to the bike, and by four miles started suffering bladder pain. Joanne promptly caught me and surged ahead while I flailed. By the eleven-mile mark, she held a nine-minute lead. I started walking before the twenty-mile mark and dropped out a mile later, due to the presence of blood in my urine. Not to mention the heartbroken feeling of being stifled by Kona yet again. Joanne wound up finishing second to Sylviane Puntous, with previously unknown Liz Bulman getting third.

About six weeks later, I'd recovered enough to finish a strong second to Joy Hansen in the Kauai Loves You Triathlon. Joy and her twin sister, Joan, were a top sister duo, eclipsed only by the Puntous twins, Sylviane and Patricia. I exited the swim in sixth, then rode the best bike time of all women. During the bike, Joy and I had a bit of a problem with a pack of male competitors trying to get us to join them but, in so doing, exposing us to drafting violations. Joy was diplomatic in the way she asked the guys to get out of our way. Only they wouldn't go. I got sick of wasting valuable focus and energy worrying about us getting disqualified, so I asked them more directly. They heard me loud and clear and pedaled away from us en route to Hanalei.

I also found myself on the cover of *The High Performance Triathlete,* a new book of tips and stories by Katherine Vaz and Barclay Kruse. I was thrilled to be on the cover of a book! To cap my eventful season, Kathleen and I showed up at the Triathlete of the Year awards in competing outfits, giving the media an apparel angle to vamp about. It was a fun evening.

Even though I enjoyed strong popularity and was now achieving consistently good results, a question kept burning inside, one that nags and prods because *you* know what it's really asking: "What can I really do if I train properly?"

It was time to find out.

CHAPTER 8
Girl Power!

"Courage starts with showing up and letting ourselves be seen."
—Dr. Brené Brown, author, *Daring Greatly*

Like millions of others, it thrilled me to watch Shalane Flanagan, the top U.S. women's road racer of the past ten years, and her magnificent victory in the 2017 New York City Marathon. Not only did she run her heart out, she was the first American woman to win the famed race in decades.

Fully energized from catching the race on TV, I headed to my afternoon yoga class. The young female instructor talked about how wearing a Wonder Woman costume at Halloween allowed a powerful, fierce, empowered persona to emerge that made bold choices and was fearless. What struck me, though, was her need to wear a costume to achieve that outcome. She talked about peeling off the costume and embodying the Wonder Woman persona, as if diving into her alter ego and then reemerging as a fully integrated woman. I thought about how, when training for an Ironman, I'm in that empowered, dynamic, full place. Though it isn't a costume and mask, layers of limitation and self-protection are stripped off. Anything is possible and everything attainable.

As we started our postures, I thought about "stripping off" what we hide behind, how we feel compelled to put on a costume so we can feel like someone more powerful, charismatic, or beautiful than our natural authentic selves. When we do that—and we all do, to some degree—what do we hide behind?

Funnily enough, some think I'm beyond hiding. After crawling and lying across a finish line, emptied and exhausted, what else is there to hide from, right? But I have costumes too. For one thing, I'm always self-conscious in the yoga room. I wear a tank top, even in superheated rooms above 90°F when everyone else is wearing trendy little yoga bras, unconcerned about how many rolls show on their tummies while they tuck into the happy baby pose.

We continued our postures as the young woman's remarks moved through me, eventually activating my inner voice. It had something very simple and direct to say: "STOP HIDING. Strip it off." It was time for my own personal reveal. I peeled off my tank top and finished our session in my yoga bra and tights. I've been doing yoga for ten years, and practicing in that particular studio for six. It was the first time I showed my stomach in a class.

A simple, common rule of yoga is to not compare your practice, postures, or physique to another student. Especially don't compare six-pack abs or tummy rolls! By keeping your eyes on your own mat, you help create a non-judgmental environment in which everyone feels safe and focuses on their own practice. While I know this, my perfectionist side felt better covered up so I wouldn't worry about being judged—the things you're supposed to leave outside the yoga room. I've taken pictures doing yoga poses, midriff exposed, but I have artistic control of those. It's much different than stripping down in a public setting.

It was a powerful moment. Here I was, a nearly sixty-year-old woman doing empowering things, but unwilling to be seen. The yoga class "reveal" was an "Aha!" moment of moving deeper into my authentic self. That is what being an empowered girl and woman is all about.

Sometimes, the people in our lives take different views of our transformative, life-changing moments. Maybe they don't understand what has happened with us, or more specifically, how these moments indelibly change us.

Friends or family may think they know you or me inside and out, only to be faced with the more empowered you, someone who's expanded beyond their existing perception. It doesn't change overnight; after all, they built that perception over the time they have known you. Sometimes a lifetime. Great change creates initial discomfort. When we're uncomfortable, what do we do? Often, we pull back and revert to our old worldview—and throw on a costume and mask to disguise how we really feel.

Take my breakthrough moment in Kona. *We* know that sea-change moments are deeply personal, but when they happen, they are often so subtle that no one else notices the shift. Or these moments need time to percolate, to reveal their greater meaning, purpose, or message. What feels seismic to you or me might be little noticed by others. Or not noticed at all. At first.

In Kona, the triathlon world wasn't talking about the transformative moment I experienced on the finish line. They were buzzing about the unlikelihood of an endurance sports neophyte nearly winning the Ironman. You know, the freak show to which Scott Tinley alluded. That perception concerned me. Today I would not have allowed such labels to erode my power, nor impact my vulnerability.

People will debate all day if we've changed or not. There's nothing we can do about idle chatter. Ultimately, though, girl power is how *we* act after a changing moment, when we do something that makes us an outlier to ourselves. How do we return to our everyday lives and maintain the energy and momentum? How do we describe it without being questioned or criticized? How do we move forward? Into what are we moving? When something seismic happens, it may put you on a pedestal and make world headlines—but what about bringing it into your everyday life?

As we continued our yoga postures, I thought about these questions and the Wonder Women in our lives; what prompted them to step into their power and light. I thought about Shalane, who stepped from an already great competitive career into her fullest power to win her first major global marathon. None of her 200-plus race victories mattered as much as New York. She *really* stepped forward. She even stated beforehand that New York might be her last marathon *if,* for some wonderful amazing reason, she won. She wanted to script her ending, conclude her career on her terms. (In actuality, she stepped to the line in the 2018 Boston Marathon after stating it might be her final Boston.) Though our dreams are unfulfilled now, she pointed out, our ongoing efforts will lead to gratification, even if delayed.

I cannot imagine Shalane's patience or desire to keep going through age thirty-six to win the big one. We're not talking about a college senior who showed up out of nowhere to make good on a thesis project. Shalane holds U.S. women's records at 3,000 meters, 5,000 meters, and 15 kilometers. Going into New York, she was the third fastest U.S. women's marathoner of all time, behind 2017 Boston Marathon runner-up Jordan Hasay, and U.S. record holder and 2004 Olympic bronze medalist Deena Kastor. Shalane's mother, Cheryl Bridges Treworgy, set the women's world marathon record in the 1971 Culver City (California) Marathon, running 2:49:40. Shalane ran 2:26:53 in New York. Shalane won the silver medal at 10,000 meters in the 2008 Olympics and a bronze in the 2011 World Cross Country Championships. She's suffered through several near misses in her hometown Boston Marathon, including 2018, when she finished sixth. In 2016, she finished sixth in the Rio Olympics.

Shalane's sacrifice to achieve these results was profound. She postponed getting pregnant though she's a wonderful mother to two teenage foster girls. She understood that her dream might come down the road, in the future. She was willing to wait. Obviously, she always thought it attainable. Now, hopefully, she can move into her next dream, bringing new life into the world to join her, her husband, and daughters.

Her story also speaks of a major obstacle to girl power—dealing with regrets. What do we regret? Why do we regret it? What happens to our vision, willpower, and energy when we live in that state? Would we regret *not* participating, not giving another shot or two—or three—to what we seek deeply? This piece is huge, its components unique to each person. It deals directly with our deepest dreams and goals, and whether or not we are going to chase them. Only you know what can give you the greatest gratification, just as I know what gives me greatest fulfillment. Here's what Shalane told ESPN after the 2017 Boston Marathon, in which she finished third: "I'm not good with regrets, and I would just regret not giving it one last go at two more major marathons. I definitely want to start a family. I've loved my experience with my foster girls. My cookbook has been extremely rewarding and I'm working on a second one . . . but I feel like there's still some unfinished business. How my career ends is super important to me. It doesn't mean I'm going to win a major, but at least I'm going to try to win a major marathon in the U.S., and I need at least two more events." That's a girl anchored into her purpose, her goal, her mission. Her power.

Shalane's understanding of her girl power is evident. She's a huge advocate/force for women training other women/bringing up rising female stars in her sport through various pitfalls—and after reading about everything from convicted serial sex abuser Larry Nassar to what's happening in USA swimming, lord knows what's out there. That's another element to girl power—helping others and mentoring. She embodies it so well.

On the personal side, Shalane callused her body and mind to handle prolonged discomfort at a very high stress level. That stress included the mighty task of beating world record holder Mary Keitany, the three-time defending New York champion. Then she converted the tense, amplified energy of New Yorkers shaken by yet another terrorist attack. (A terrorist killed eight pedestrians in lower Manhattan's Battery Park City five days before the race.) She "made the shift" from wanting something out of lack (the elusive first major) to feeling gratitude in the moment. When the race got tough, she thought of others. She got out of her head. She rose above her physical discomfort and connected with something bigger. In so doing, Shalane became the first American woman since Miki Gorman in 1977 to win New York.

What a Wonder Woman! Everything lined up for her to step into her power. She used her "superpower" to focus toward others while staying within herself. In the last two miles, she was trying hard *not* to smile, or cry. She had the race won and yet, she never turned around to check Keitany's position. Instead, she celebrated with the spectators. She celebrated her mightiest self.

This great performance exemplifies the power we need to practice in our lives. Sometimes, it presents itself in the most surprising, inopportune moments, like it did with me. At other times, we build and wait patiently, setting ourselves up for the moment when we step fully into our power. That's Shalane's story. You and I hold something great within ourselves, something that affirms the unlimited potential of life and creation. It emerges when we shed our "costume" of excuses, regrets, and inability (or unwillingness) to step forth. We peel back the layers, and find the Wonder Woman within us. It is such an intentional, humbling place to be.

It's about putting ourselves in a position that requires us to push outside our comfort zones. And, ladies, we push until we've pushed ourselves into a more powerful, authentic place.

My first experience with girl power was like diving into the Great Unknown. In 1982, a seismic wave of perceived empowerment fanned out from Kona to the world via the media. The stories mentioned grit, determination to finish, and the fearlessness of touching the outer limits of my physical capabilities. Some thought survival too. ABC switchboards lit up after *Wide World of Sports* with people asking, "Did she survive?" Other comments included:

- "ABC Sports has called this one of the most defining moments in sport. 'This' was Julie Moss desperately trying to get to the finish line . . . 'This' was the event that inspired millions of people, the event that started so many people in the sport, the event that has *iced* the expression that 'just finishing the Ironman is the victory.'"—*30 Years of the IRONMAN Triathlon World Championship*

- "No one can describe the sight of an athlete such as this, beyond the limits of exhaustion, crawling to a finish line. Nobody tried."—Armen Keteyian, *San Diego Union* and *The Sporting News*

- "It was real. For McCartney, a happy ending. For Moss, a bitter defeat. Well, that's the funny thing. Though she didn't win, Moss's effort the last hundred yards had hit a nerve."—*Los Angeles Times*

These excerpts illustrate a breakthrough, a dismantling of old expectations, an entering into the new. "Everyone has a defining moment; mine just got captured on film," I told Kevin Mackinnon for Ironman.com. "Every time the tape's played, it hits this deep emotional chord that says I discovered something new about myself, and other people get to see it."

What do we do *with* that defining moment? What will you do with yours? It's the question we all face, or have faced. The way we respond determines whether our moment becomes the beginning of a personal transformation, or a blown opportunity.

I became a Wonder Woman to many. I wasn't comfortable with it at first, but when athletes do something mind-blowing in our culture, we elevate them, give them catchy nicknames, admire them as examples of what we secretly (or not so secretly) wish we could do if we only had time to train more, if we were sponsored, if we didn't have to work 9 to 5 . . . *if, if, if.* We've been elevating athletes since Ancient Greeks created the ancient Olympiad and feted their superstars, comparing them to gods and goddesses.

I'd tapped my inner Wonder Woman, my girl power, though I really didn't know it. The race connected me to very powerful inner resources, like the laws of attraction, magnetism, and toughness that build empowered women. They felt like newborn babies at first; I had to nurture these released qualities.

For many women and girls in my generation, that was new ground. I was one of them. As a late-stage baby boomer, I spent a childhood listening to my mom's dream for me: to marry well, to "earn" the "coveted" MRS. Degree from the school of life. I guess.

All of a sudden, my soul echoed, "No, you are okay just as you are. You don't need a boyfriend or blond hair or anything else to define who you are." A nice soul call, but it was striking up against the inner world of the redheaded, freckle-faced girl trying to match up with beautiful blondes on the beach. Actually, it was surfing with the guys that helped me first realize, "I'm not going to *not* be out here just because I'm a girl."

Triathlon completed my personal emergence. As one of the few women competing in Ironman in the early years, I didn't know what to expect or how I would be viewed, always shaky territory for me. So I just went for it. Then, to have men look at me like, "You can do something I can't do, or even think about doing," reinforced something mighty within me—that I could navigate the world on an even playing field. That's what I've been doing since. A lot of women have told me that watching my Ironman motivated them to try a 5K, or a 10K, or even a half marathon or full marathon. Some jumped straight to triathlons, Half Ironmans and even full Ironmans. All of them felt more power within themselves.

It took a while for me to understand what "being empowered" means. I kept thinking, "I have to do everything big." I always felt the need to find big moments to assert myself. For a while, I became kind of a caricature. At least that's what I think now when I read the old articles. *Who is this person—who's not very nice? She's so self-centered. Who is that?* Insecurity drove a lot of my decisions. But, like so many watershed moments, the lessons I've gleaned have evolved over my life, like taking something new and different from our favorite self-help or business leadership book every time we open it up.

My legacy has nothing to do with making money or winning a bunch of races. It has to do with being part of a priceless, empowering moment when *I did not quit,* when *I finished.* It also has to do with learning the hard way how not to trip over my own achievements. What I would have given for a mentor, someone who saw the greater potential! I badly needed an older, wiser woman to say, "You've had a very special moment. This is not something that just comes along," and then work with me to draw it out, define it, express it through what I said, how I lived, and how I presented myself. That's why it took me so long to green-light this book. The process of fully owning the moment has taken time. I needed to manifest and share my inner Wonder Woman before I felt comfortable telling my story. Every time I talk to a young girl or woman, I remember how no one was really there for me. I'm right there for the next generations.

Our girl power shows up in different shapes and forms. Two manifestations for me were in how I learned to view pain, and how I dealt with the men in triathlon. I have a theory as to why women run nearly the same times as men in endurance sports events: we tolerate pain better. And we focus better when in pain. It also happens to be well-documented scientific fact. We've been engineered accordingly too. We have babies. We go through labor. We tend not to lash out when someone or something hurts us, but to process the pain and (hopefully) emerge stronger. We endure and tolerate a lot—at times, more than we should.

I figured this out after giving birth to my son, Mats, in 1994. He was my only child, my only birthing experience, but the kid gave me my money's worth! He just needed to get *outside*—the story of his life.

During labor, I called the nurse and asked, "The doctor just told me I'm dilated six centimeters . . . how much more do I need?"

"About four centimeters," she said.

"How long does that take?"

"About four hours or so."

"Well, I can jog a marathon in four hours and handle that."

So, I equated the pain of those final four hours with the marathon's final miles, which made it easier to handle. We all have our ways.

As an athlete, I know that the best way to work through pain is to *surrender to it*. When we can surrender, the power that pain holds over us diminishes. At first, I didn't understand how to surrender. I thought I could choke off or somehow bargain with pain. Pain laughs at that approach, and then sends you a few extra spasms for the hell of it. And it can be hell!

I first made the connection between pain and surrender during a really deep tissue massage. Know how we tend to tense up when massage therapists hit our sore spots? That's the exact opposite of what we're supposed to do. So I thought, *what if I just give in to this, surrender to the massage? Is it going to kill me? No!* As I tried to give in, I breathed deeper, my muscles relaxed, and it worked. I've since trained myself to go into that place in the latter stages of an Ironman or a Half Ironman.

In Spring 2016, when I was trying to become the oldest female certified lifeguard in California, we worked all week with a big south swell, which greatly increased surf size and created a swift south-to-north ocean current. I didn't want to telegraph that our back-to-back days were taking their toll on me and I was wiped out. Funny thing was, the younger trainees didn't think twice about voicing their complaints; I may have been the only one not whining. During the "mega vitamin," the only endurance event of our training (400-meter swim, 5-mile run, 400-meter swim), I exited the first swim with my heart rate spiking, not where you want it when starting a five-mile run. To bring my heart rate down, I focused on my breathing. *Four breaths in . . . four breaths out . . . smile.* I got so zoned out that I didn't realize I'd won the women's race.

Breath is a central key to our power. We have to inhale to feed oxygen to our bodies, to live. It's automatic. But we tend to rush our exhalations, or be shallow with them. Slow, deep exhalations solve that. They are like a basic sitting meditation technique or a moving meditation. If you can stay in that space, and breathe through the pain and discomfort, or tension or stress, you can move for what seems like forever, and do it smoothly. Some also call this sweet, gentle, and euphoric place "the zone" or "runner's high." It's a powerful place, because we feel limitless, free, and invincible. No fences, no boundaries, no walls. It is our appointment with our freest, most liberated, most powerful self.

Going through pain doesn't mean the fear of it disappears. I think of the biggest pain moments I've had, and yes, I fear going back there. What if I don't want to go there in a race—but have to in order to achieve my goal? What if I don't want to revisit the pain and discomfort required to come from behind, or to add thirty minutes to my toughest brick workout?

I've learned to work out the pain piece privately, building my calluses without people watching. The idea of others watching me through such a challenge is claustrophobic. *How will they view me?* That's why, for years, I avoided the California Ironman 70.3 Oceanside, a wonderful race next to my hometown. When I raced in Japan, France, or Australia, it was no big deal—the spectators knew me as a foreign triathlete. In Oceanside, people know me personally, some for decades, and I feel the pressure of performing for them, of finding that next gear. In 2016, I decided to run the race but to take a different approach: I entered underprepared, with no expectations. I thoroughly enjoyed the "Hey Julie!" and "Go girl!" shout-outs from spectators. What a heartwarming experience. Hometown fans always give you the sweetest love on the course . . . I just needed to realize that.

I've also learned another vital component of expressing girl power: how to navigate male-dominated arenas, surfing and racing being two of them. For better or worse, some women pin their attention and focus on their men, often subjugating their dreams and visions. I fell into that trap as a young woman, whether it was with Reed in 1982 or other situations. Since then, I've learned to straddle the fence between strident independence in my own life, and being a loving, supportive partner in a relationship.

At first, women athletes of my generation struggled for respect from men. It was like climbing up a sheer rock face with bare hands and feet. Triathlon, the first significant post–Title IX sport to emerge (snowboarding was the second), was different: it treated women and men equally from day one, from distances to (eventually) prize money. "I am fairly certain we were the first national governing body to promote equality for men and women," Sally Edwards said during the fortieth anniversary of the Mission Bay Triathlon, the sport's debut. "A sanctioned race by Tri-Fed would have no gender discrimination. That set the standard that men and women were equal in sports. It's a landmark moment for a sport's organization in the early 1980s to come out with the fact that we would be promoting gender equality."

Girl power has produced some parity all along. In 1979, the second year of the Ironman, twelve people completed the race. Among those was fifth-place Lyn Lemaire. In 1988, Paula Newby-Fraser obliterated the women's course record at Ironman with a performance that would have won the first five Ironmans outright! Let's not forget ultramarathon running legends Ann Trason and Pam Reed, who beat women and men alike in events from the Western States 100 (miles) to the Badwater 135, or Diana Nyad, the *Wide World of Sports* commentator during my big race and, in 2013, the only human to swim from Cuba to Florida without a shark cage. Know that Beatles song "When I'm Sixty-Four?" Well, that's what Diana did!

I had a much different experience with men while surfing—or, should I say, trying to talk my way into waves while dealing with their insensitive comments. I didn't know the word "misogyny," but in the lineup, I battled it firsthand. I remember thinking, "These guys are so full of shit." No subject seemed to be off limits: recent conquests, true-or-false, explicit details, and all. I thought, "Why would any girl want to subject herself to this?" *Be invisible,* I told myself.

Later, this school of hard knocks served my launches and landings into lifeguarding and triathlon really well. From my surfing experiences, I learned how to hold onto my own power, my essential truth, while navigating the comments, egos, and moments of aggression that happened in just about every surf session. My #MeToo moments came in the seemingly benign form of crude surf session chatter, very real and impactful, though not of the devastating caliber other women have faced for decades in the workplace.

"One of the things I love most about Julie is her willingness to get out there and surf, be one of us," Jim Watson says. "I remember in 1981 or 1982, my friends Steve McKellar, Paul Buckner, and I took Julie up to Trestles [a top-notch surf spot about twenty miles north of Carlsbad, near the resort town of San Clemente]. She fit right in—with the conversations, the jokes, catching waves, the way we got on each other. She gave as well as she took, which made her stand out . . . and one thing Julie will never tell you, but I will, is that she was a good surfer. Still is."

Now for a reality check, focusing on the *responsibility* and *accountability* of owning our power. Early on, if I'd truly earned my spot in the lineup by *surfing well*, I would've gotten more waves. There's a scene in the 2002 movie *Blue Crush* in which Anne Marie, played by Kate Bosworth, refuses to catch a wave. In the ocean, you have to earn respect. That's when other surfers will help you get waves. There are always respectful guys who will do that. But invariably, I would get into a perfect spot, take off, drop in—and blow it. Blow it once, and that can be it for awhile. If you ride the wave and make a statement, you'll get another wave. You'll blend into the pack. If not, then it's time to start improving.

I'm often asked, "When do I know I'm operating from my personal power? When do I feel my inner Wonder Woman?"

When something connects with my heart, I'm on my way. I crave those heart-connecting moments in competition now. I used to concentrate on blowing the public's mind again and again. In retrospect, that is eye candy, window dressing, a big tease compared to the greater depth, taking my sport and its people into my heart. Living and anchoring into my power honors that authentic place I discovered when I was twenty-three. I always want to live from that place of authenticity and vulnerability, reaching out, helping others, putting them ahead of myself . . . paying it forward. I always want to seize my moments when they present themselves.

I think of the Wonder Women in my life today. My best friend and college roomie, Lisette Whitaker, is one. The owner of Lionheart Coaching and Counseling (the name of her business says a lot), Lisette operates within her deeper authenticity and sense of purpose. She does so by helping other people—including me, more times than I can count. How do you celebrate with a girl like Lisette? Well, in April, we celebrated her sixtieth birthday by running the Paris Marathon! Another friend, Diana Kutlow, recently experienced the job interviewing process at age fifty-nine. Not easy. However, she bucked up and landed a position with Hands of Peace as director of development. Their mission is to create dialogue among Palestinians, Israelis, and Americans to pursue peace and freedom. They bring the groups together for two-week camps, one in Israel, one in the U.S. How amazing would it be to illuminate and empower the children of a feud stretching back thousands of years, to raise their voices as leaders of change?

Then there are my two closest childhood friends, Cindy Conner and Sue Robison, both sterling examples of powerful women doing great things to empower others. Cindy recently retired from thirty years as a law enforcement officer and mentor to countless other officers—not to mention running upward of fifty half marathons in her spare time. In January 2018, she was injured in a horrendous accident, requiring months of hospitalization and rehab before walking again—but she's coming back to hopefully run and ski again. She knows no other way. Sue has started girls (and boys) on their paths to inner and outer strength as a primary school teacher for thirty-plus years. Sue, Cindy, Diana, and Lisette shine in their empowered selves every day of their lives.

I am also reminded of Dr. Tricia DeLaMora, an Ironman qualifier I met at Dig Me Beach in Kona in 2017. During the bike portion in the Ironman Santa Rosa, her eleventh career Ironman competition, Tricia stopped to administer CPR to a competitor who collapsed, saving the athlete's life.

When I first heard this story, I assumed Tricia dropped out, and the Ironman World Championship wanted to honor her sacrifice with an entry. She did receive that Ambassador Athlete entry directly from Ironman race announcer Mike Reilly.

"So you had to end your race . . . ," I said.

She had a surprise for me. "No, no, I got to finish. Once I knew he was safe, I got to finish."

What a Wonder Woman!

CHAPTER 9
Riding the Wave: The Rise of Endurance Sports

W e paddled out to catch some waves. My friends Robin, Cindy, and Emily joined me, surrounded by the Carlsbad surf community, a mixture of men and boys, "soul surfers" who took a natural, almost nativist approach to the lifestyle. Some caught their waves and headed to work with soaked hair and big smiles. We kids, all eager grommet shredders (aggressive novices), learned our lessons, some on a very large stage.

By 1985, when pro surfing was as much on the rise as triathlon, two of the Association of Surfing Professionals (ASP) World Tour's Top 16 and seven of the Professional Surfing Association of America's (PSAA) Top 20 hailed from Carlsbad. So did innovative event producer and dear friend Jim Watson, director of the Stubbies Pro International Surfing Tournament. Jimmy also played a small role in the development of triathlon. Jimmy worked with my agent/manager, Murphy Reinschreiber, and producer Denis White to hold the 1986 Nike Triterium, a proto-urban circuit race in Oceanside, where the California Ironman 70.3 is now contested.

One of the two ASP stars, six-time Top 16 finisher Joey Buran, had something in common with me: he made his signature career statement in Hawaii, in his case winning the 1984 Pipeline Masters. Then he founded the PSAA, giving career opportunities to hundreds of young pros. Often the toughness and tenacity of the Carlsbad crew made the difference in close heats, and they developed an international reputation for winning.

When I look at Carlsbad during my coming-of-age years through an historic prism, I see an amazing convergence of personalities and energies. Carlsbad housed the only Top 16 world pros in the mainland U.S., Joey Buran and David Barr. Local newspaper editor Steve Hawk's kid brother, Tony, was doing things on a skateboard as an eight-year-old that people had never seen. Jim Watson; my coauthor, Robert Yehling; and others were turning surf contests into well-oiled, well-promoted events, and teaching surfers how to be professional athletes. At my alma mater, Carlsbad High, the football program was cranking out performers like future NFL stars Glen Kozlowski, who won a Super Bowl ring with the mighty 1985 Chicago Bears, and Ted Johnson, who played ten seasons with New England before becoming "ground zero" that triggered the NFL concussion issue, after *Sports Illustrated* documented his battle with football-related early-onset dementia a decade ago. In the high jump arena, Cindy Gilbert was winding down her Olympic career (she currently coaches the event at Carlsbad High), and Sue McNeal was winding hers up. And I was not the only woman in town getting people off the couch to exercise. Downtown in the old Mayfair Market, Judi Sheppard Missett was revolutionizing movement to music with Jazzercise, and she and husband, Jack, were beginning to fan out their thousands of franchises.

"I don't know if there was something in the water during that time, but it was pretty amazing," Jim Watson recalled. "I like to think it was a bunch of us who were raised to work hard and do something with ourselves, and then we saw these opportunities and we acted. We didn't feel like we had a lot of limits or rules, either, which I think is very, very important to how everything took off."

We all grow up with local heroes. None was bigger for me than Barbie Baron, the owner of Offshore Surf Shop, the community surf gathering spot.

Barbie was a top pro in the 1970s and a sharp businesswoman who, with her Offshore partner Scot Tammen, groomed three generations of Carlsbad locals while selling them boards, accessories, and clothing. She was like the den mother, giving direction and guidance to waterlogged kids like me with love for who we were, who she saw us becoming, and her contagious "surf stoke." She prodded more than a few indecisive young phenoms to enter surf competitions and change their lives. This woman has lived a long-empowered life, a true Wonder Woman.

I got to know Barbie better while working at Novak's (now Harbor Fish Café). We served up the "bomber sauce" created by Mr. Novak, who had come out of retirement to run the kitchen. Any Carlsbad local over forty-five probably still carries that taste in their memory. It drew in hungry surfers and visitors like honey to a swarm of starving bees. My friend Sue Robison, like me a big Novak's fan, has come closest to replicating the original (and still secret) sauce.

Several years ago, Barbie decided to run a few triathlons around her fiftieth birthday. After not being in touch for years, we reconnected over her training program. Now, I was the mentor and she the protégé. What a great way to pay someone back! More recently, we shared stories at her fabulous retirement party. I still idolize her.

I've also had the honor of surfing with another legend, Linda Benson, the first woman to ride the thunderous twenty- to thirty-footers of Oahu's Waimea Bay. Linda was the living embodiment and stunt double of Gidget, the classic California beach movie series, which starred Sandra Dee and, later, Sally Field. Linda was a multiple U.S. and West Coast champion in the 1960s and the inspiration for countless younger surfers. When we paddled out near my Cardiff home, I was amazed at how well this woman moved after fifty-five-plus years of surfing. She grew especially excited when the bigger set waves arrived too! She maneuvered her big board without wearing a wetsuit. My kind of girl.

Surfing is kind of like dropping into a movie thriller, except the pursuer is big, real, and either yielding or relentless, depending on how well you paddle, position yourself on the wave, dive, or bail out. Or just scream and hold your breath! I love that adrenaline surge, feeling like a world champion after long rides, then stroking like hell to get back out before the next set of waves unloads on my head. Surfing is a constant parade of figuring things out—wave heights, direction, interval between breaks, currents, winds, tides, where to paddle for best position, where and whether to take off . . . and do I keep riding, or cut out? Or wipe out? Decisions come much faster in surfing than triathlon, but the choices and options are similar in their complexity.

For me, surfing isn't about being a man or a woman; it's about being one with the ocean, staying out for hours to catch more waves, observe the reef, or absorb the rhythm of the sea. It is an endurance sport, especially when the waves are big. I love that feeling of both endurance and absorption.

As I became a more proficient surfer during my teens and early twenties, I found myself in risky situations. While I was living and training in Los Osos, near San Luis Obispo, Reed and I drove to a horseshoe-shaped spot, but it was crowded. So we continued farther down a rutted dirt road until we saw a promising break, reminiscent of Robert August and Mike Hynson's surfing safaris in the epic 1966 film *The Endless Summer.* That movie spurred me to seek my own endless summer, along with countless others. I'm still chasing summer.

We paddled out atop what I'll call "The Day of Reckoning Reef." It is considered a secret spot, and in the common respect among surfers, you don't divulge names and locations of secret spots—especially if you're not truly a local! Soon, the water shifted ominously, rearing up into huge, menacing walls . . . aimed at our heads. I thought quickly: *I'm going to end up on one set of rocks or the other. But right now, I need to push the board as far away from me as I can, and dive down.*

I was scared, very scared, but also enthralled by this mystery enveloping me, this big water holding me down, pushing me around. I thought I was going to end up on the reef. The next wave hit, and the next, and each time, I popped back up. Then I paddled in as fast as I could.

That session was probably the closest to death I've come. I'd never had a wave like that enter my life, where I honestly didn't know how my day would turn out. Or if I'd see the next day. That was pivotal: *Dive, dive into the core of your potential, find out what it is, and it might turn out okay.* In this case, I held my breath for a long time and resurfaced in one piece.

Recently, I gave a talk to the Santa Barbara Triathlon Club about complete commitment, finishing no matter what, the essence of endurance sports. I always wanted more of that commitment. I thought it would come through challenging myself and surfing mighty waves for hours at a time, but it didn't. However, one piece stuck: the ocean can become something intrinsically dangerous. Wiping out on a two-story mountain of a wave can make you think, *I survived something.* I'm willing to take my chances, not really sure if I'm going to make it out of the wave. It isn't panic; it's just this "I don't know." The ocean taught me that it isn't about winning or the accolades, but *am I going to survive? And what will I do with my changed perspective if I do survive?*

In order to fuel our dedication and commitment, we need a driving force. Passion carries us into action. Together, passion and commitment spark our outcomes and drive us to greater aspirations. No one becomes a great athlete, or great at any profession or hobby, without a strong mixture of these two qualities. It puts together the physical and emotional. Gotta have them both.

Surfing has been around for a thousand years. Polynesian royals carved koa tree trunks into 120-pound planks and paddled into waves from Samoa to Tonga, and, as the Beach Boys sang, "catch a wave and you're sitting on top of the world."

Endurance sports have been around much longer, since our distant ancestors embarked on hours- or days-long slow runs in pursuit of their prey, captured beautifully in Chris McDougall's bestselling *Born to Run.* Putting thousands of years of subsistence living aside, what is the most incredible endurance sports feat of recent times? Scientists and historians looked at the six-day foot races contested by professional British and American athletes from 1874–1888; they expended about 60,000 kcal, six times the energy an elite triathlete uses in an Ironman. What about Robert Falcon Scott's 1911–12 Antarctic expedition, in which he and his team walked up to 10 hours per day for 159 consecutive days through conditions we'd rather curl up in a blanket and read about in *National Geographic* or watch on the

Weather Channel? They expended about one million kcal, the equivalent of *one hundred* Ironman triathlons.

Ironman is certainly one of the world's toughest endurance sports tests. If you win or place highly, you're among the fittest women or men on earth. Period. However, multiday events in places like the Sahara Desert, Greece, South America, and the U.S. (think 200- and 300-mile running races, cycling's Tour de France and Race Across America, or trail runners who *run* the Pacific Crest and Appalachian Trails) would boggle anyone's mind, including this Ironman veteran's. Take the Ultraman or Ultra 515, a race held over three days on the Big Island of Hawaii. The total distance nearly equals three Ironmans. Ultraman opens with a 6.2-mile ocean swim and 90-mile cross-country bike ride that includes 6,000 feet of climbing. On day two, competitors ride another 171.4 miles—a distance longer than any stage of the Tour de France—and climb 4,000 feet. Finally, these competitors can "rest" their weary legs with a 52.4-mile double marathon. They have to finish each daily stage within twelve hours. Tempting for any endurance sports athlete, the ultimate challenge, right? I admit, that is too rich for even my blood! I am content to admire and be inspired from afar.

As I mentioned earlier, the 1980s brought along a fun, fast-paced, and adrenaline-fueled Wild West mentality: Ironman in Hawaii, hair metal bands in LA, people running 100 miles along the Western Sierra, surf contests drawing 100,000 people in Huntington Beach. We early Ironman competitors were right in the middle as participants *and* lifestyle influencers. Anything was possible, the sky the limit, and we constantly broke through that limit to higher thresholds. That's what you do in your invincible twenties, right? The possibility of outdoing our parents was there for the taking—and we seized the moment. People got off their couches and easy chairs en masse, including our parents in some cases, and began running, surfing, cycling, swimming, dancing, doing yoga or Jazzercise to MTV videos, playing rac-quetball, lifting Nautilus weights, or trying hybrid sports that popped up, like snowboarding, skateboarding . . . and triathlon.

Everything was new, exciting, and fresh. Many endurance sports athletes rushed headlong into entrepreneurship—the decade's business buzzword.

Where did *Entrepreneur* magazine locate their headquarters? In the middle of Orange County, near John Wayne Airport, the epicenter of the business of sun and fun. Much of both the surf and triathlon industries set up shop there. Enterprising sports producers, some of them former competitors, created innovative events and multiple-sport concepts. We reached for our outermost limits and pioneered new moves, techniques, strategies, or entire sports. We became the first generation of athletes to learn sports marketing for ourselves. Everything was possible *right here, right now*. We hijacked Ram Dass's "Be Here Now" approach from the sixties and gave it expression in the sports, fitness, and business worlds.

Most important, endurance sports rose up because, in the early 1980s, risk-taking was celebrated and revered. Most parents of baby boomers encouraged us to take risks, which built character and gave us new ideas of what is possible. We did not live in today's overly cautious society, where concerned parents sometimes put unfortunate lids on risk-taking, bolstered by the rise in school-related violence and a media that sometimes perpetuates a message of fear. Not to mention the messaging of "fitting in," "conforming," "thinking in the box" . . . not exactly my cup of tea. If we wanted to run a long race, start a business, or do something wild and magnificent, well, we got out there and did it. If people tried to caution or warn us off our pursuits, out of *their* fear, we shrugged it off or used it to further motivate ourselves. *You tell me it's too risky? Watch . . .*

When looking back at why endurance sports exploded, I find our risk-taking mentality and commitment to achieve to be twin magnets, attracting the elements and pulling them together. Our greatest conveniences, travel tours, competitions, and shining examples of ingenuity today started with women and men taking risks. Thomas Edison ran 10,000 experiments before nailing down the incandescent light bulb. Imagine if he'd quit after 9,000 attempts? What would have happened if Michael Jordan had quit shooting jumpers after being cut from his *junior varsity high school* basketball team? That's what the building block of greatness really looks like—deep risk, sweat and blood, and never quitting.

Another good example is Ironman. With the Ironman World Championships' current stature, it's easy to forget that it started with fifteen souls in 1978 paying $3.00 apiece (the registration fee for the 2018 Ironman is $950). The original Hawaiian Triathlon combined Oahu's three big distance events—the Waikiki Rough Water Swim, Around-Oahu Bike Ride, and Honolulu Marathon. The courses added up to 140.6 miles. The event was created, in part, to settle an argument. Who's fitter? An endurance swimmer? Lifeguard? Distance cyclist? Or marathon runner? On the rules sheet, cofounder John Collins noted, "Swim 2.4 miles! Bike 112 miles! Run 26.2 miles! Brag for the rest of your life." Then, "Whoever wins, we'll call him the Ironman."

In the November 1985 *Tri-Athlete* "Material Girl" cover story, I tried to capture the spirit. "I would like to think that if you really want something, then it's time to start working for it," I said in reference to my new contract with Bridgestone Tires. "Things aren't going to fall into your lap. I have been lucky—that moment on ABC's *Wide World of Sports* just happened. That was a nice start, but from then on it was hard work. Japan has been the culmination of strategic planning from a business and sponsorship point of view. My agent, Murphy Reinschreiber, and I pitched to Bridgestone that I was one of the top female triathletes in the world. And Bridgestone went for it. From that point on, I had to prove myself. The moment I arrived in Japan it was lectures, clinics, and press conferences. It was a major buildup—the way you'd treat any woman who was favored to win an Ironman race."

When you think about it, every time someone competes in an Ironman today or tries a multihour, multisport, or multistate competition, the resulting effort echoes back on the can-do, all-in spirit of the eighties. Every time someone comes up to me and says, "You were the reason I decided to try an Ironman (or running, or swimming, or choose your activity)," I've felt grateful and proud to be a part of such a pivotal moment and time that carries forth today.

With our rising endurance-sports stature came a new level of respect for others and myself. I began to accept that others respected me. Even stars from other professional sports put us on pedestals, and I loved it. It's like, "You did *what*?" As a guest of a *Monday Night Football* luncheon hosted by ABC, I walked among a group of NFL players in New York. These big men looked at me like, "Whoa, you know what she did?" I loved that instant recognition.

It brings to mind Pam Reed, the five-time winner of the infamous Badwater ultramarathon. How BAD is Badwater? Very. From the bottom of Death Valley, 282 feet below sea level, the hale and hearty run 135 miles to the portal of Mount Whitney, elevation 9,000 feet above—in mid-July. Temperatures of 120°F and a body-parching five percent humidity are common; so are hallucinations, delusional thinking, and other weird things that happen under extreme duress from overexertion and surface road heat that can fry eggs—let alone the soles of running shoes. Pam is beyond badass. She channels her inner Wonder Woman in an amazing way. After competing in gymnastics as a teenager, Pam started thinking about running long distances, spurred on in part by my *Wide World of Sports* moment. Today, she reigns as one of the toughest champions we've seen in American sport.

Take my situation, multiply it by hundreds of equally supercharged athletes with visions of their own, and it produced the melting pot of athletes, marketers, promoters, visionaries, and dreamers that constellated from the 1982 Ironman and helped thousands, and then a few million, find endurance sports of all kinds. With marathon racing already booming, thanks to the efforts of Frank Shorter, Bill Rodgers, Alberto Salazar, and later Joan Benoit Samuelson, the world was ready for another take on that 26.2-mile race.

About a year after *Wide World of Sports* used my 1982 finish to promote its next Ironman telecast, a *New York Times* headline read, TRIATHLON THRIVES ON WIDE WORLD. Any sociologist will tell you that when a performance or event leaps into the public consciousness and dissolves barriers about what is possible, quantum growth follows. The media and savvy promoters, marketers, and businessmen took it from there. I was still on *Wide World of Sports'* mind in 1986, when I was among the athletes seated in the studio audience for their twenty-fifth-anniversary show. I shook hands with Muhammad Ali and chatted with other legends. When Jim McKay discussed the heart as being the intangible key to performance, I could hardly believe it when a studio camera panned the crowd and homed in on me.

The crazy thing is, I never sought out these opportunities. I still don't. They tend to find me. It seems hard to believe in our "promote thyself at all costs" world, but it's the truth. To me, it's a measure of aligning mind, heart, and soul to the place where passion, personal interests, commitment, and livelihood intersect. When we align, we operate within the law of attraction—receiving what we give. I gave all of myself to Kona, and by extension, to millions on TV. I received a livelihood, a career, and a platform to continue giving of myself. From that, I received more blessings—friends, experiences, opportunities. My future husband. That's how it works. The presence of that magnetism is why I found it hard to think beyond triathlon, even though it didn't offer much of a career early on. I didn't have a next step. Thankfully, opportunities kept popping. Give, and gratefully receive. Be sure to accept gifts when offered; otherwise, we may slow the main valve of the law of attraction.

The same year as my Ironman, the Bud Light U.S. Triathlon Series took off. It was the brainchild of Jim Curl and Carl Thomas, and consisted of a seven-event schedule at Torrey Pines State Beach in June 1982. It blossomed into our multimillion-dollar, twenty-five-to-thirty-event domestic circuit, bringing in athletes from all walks and disciplines. Maybe, just maybe, they too could compete in a triathlon and become good at it. Additional events exploded like firecrackers around the world, causing a fourfold increase in participation in two years (from 250,000 to 1.1 million), one of the greatest participation spikes in sports. We had an adoring media filling our sails, helmed by two magazines of our own—*Triathlon*, the upgrade of *Swim Bike Run*, and *Triathlete*, which followed its rival out of the gate by six months.

The 1984 Los Angeles Summer Olympics excited the world about participatory sports. While neither triathlon nor surfing was included (triathlon became an Olympic sport in 2000; surfing debuts in 2020), runners, cyclists, and swimmers were on hand—and the hometown Americans put on a show for the ages. Heroes and heroines emerged every day. One of the biggest was inaugural women's marathon champ Joan Benoit Samuelson, who broke an International Olympic Committee glass ceiling. Not easy, with the all-male crew running the show. Incredibly, prior to 1984, the IOC thought the marathon too dangerous for women! Other instant household names ranged from track and field superstars Carl Lewis, Flo-Jo, Mary Decker Slaney, and Jackie Joyner-Kersee to gymnast Mary Lou Retton, cycling gold medalists Alexi Grewal and Connie Carpenter, and swimmers Tracy Caulkins and Mary T. Meagher. Distance running was solid after the decade-long boom fueled by Shorter, Rodgers, Grete Waitz, and Salazar; if you weren't lacing up before the Olympics, you were afterward. For the first time, the Olympics were fed to us 24/7 by reporters hammering out story after story about performances and lifestyles for the new round-the-clock outlets.

Lifestyle was the operative word. Everywhere you turned, athletes, announcers, sponsors, and reporters were chatting up this or that lifestyle. The surfing lifestyle. The beach lifestyle. The skateboard lifestyle. The fitness lifestyle. The combination of super-fit bodies and ever-increasing footage of beach- or scenery-oriented competitions from Hawaii and California fueled the buzz. By mid-decade, it seemed *everyone* wanted their piece of a lifestyle that afforded a growing number of men and women, many with master's and PhD degrees and thriving professional careers, the opportunity to run around in neon ST shorts, Oakley Factory Pilot Sunglasses, Nike Sock Racers, and sports bras. The sweat glistened on their tanned skin as their finely tuned, toned bodies belted out the miles in spectacular locales. Who *wouldn't* want to train to look and feel like this? To visit beautiful places? To practice this lifestyle?

Television loved what it was seeing. Triathlon had *Wide World of Sports* and, later in the decade, NBC, ESPN, and regional networks like Los Angeles–based Prime Ticket (now Fox Sports West). Surfing lived on Prime Ticket, MTV, and ESPN, the latter thanks to a ten-event-per-year contract Alan Gibby of DynoComm Productions signed in 1983. Gibby went on to produce surfing, snowboarding, skateboarding, and the other X Games sports long before the X Games were thought of. This type of lifestyle sports programming started with Roone Arledge and *Wide World of Sports*. Gibby, Prime Ticket producer Don Meek, and others turned lifestyle sports into *regular* TV programming. When Bud Light started using triathletes for commercials on all three networks, and scored a TV deal of its own for the USTS, the circle was complete.

Sports bras and bare midriff workouts were symbols of our new lifestyle. The prevalence of sports bras reminded me of my borrowed bra moment in the 1982 Ironman. Later, it reminded me of an ecstatic Brandi Chastain pulling off her game jersey to reveal her black sports bra after hitting the winning penalty kick in the 1999 World Cup soccer finals—the goal that exploded youth soccer program participation in America. The *Sports Illustrated* cover, photographed by Robert Beck (who lived in Carlsbad for years while also shooting for surfing magazines), was voted *SI*'s second most iconic cover in its sixty-plus-year history. I might add, the sports bra also celebrated its fortieth anniversary in 2017. Know how it was originally created? By sewing two jockstraps together. True story.

With colorful stories like this, the sporting lifestyle became every sports marketer's dream. They pinned their products and logos on the backs of photogenic, well-spoken, studly endurance sports stars. We'd admired the likes of tennis champions Billie Jean King, Chris Evert, Martina Navratilova, 1960 Olympic sprint champ Wilma Rudolph, and breakthrough distance runners like Kathrine Switzer (the first woman to run the Boston Marathon), Cheryl Bridges (the first American to hold a world marathon record), and distance aces Francie Larrieu and Mary Decker. Suddenly, we were welcoming in uber-chic, ultra-fit personalities like Kathleen McCartney; American surfing greats Frieda Zamba, Lisa Andersen, and the late Rell Sunn; running superstars Sally Edwards, Joan Benoit Samuelson; and Flo-Jo; Olympic heptathlon champ Jackie Joyner-Kersee; and more.

My other sport, surfing, already had this down. Former world champions Ian Cairns and Peter Townend created the Association of Surfing Professionals World Tour with all of the above in mind. They were true trailblazers. Ian and PT envisioned surfer-athletes traveling the world, earning good prize money, getting paid well by sponsors, and representing self, event, sponsor, and sport to an increasingly interested world. They brought along Australian surf companies like Billabong, Quiksilver, and Stubbies, whose clothing lines featured splashy colors with catchy graphics on trunks, shirts, shorts, and pants alike. That led to a marriage of fashion, lifestyle, and entertainment with New Wave radio stations like 91X and KROQ in Southern California. Later, in 1989, Quiksilver morphed its new-look women's surf wear into its own label. Roxy provided a distinctly feminine, athletic look, from sleek bikinis and swimsuits with athletically cut lines to women's board shorts; we didn't have to cobble together or alter the least masculine-looking surf clothes anymore.

Professional surfing became a reluctant but eventual adopter of gender equality. Much of that was due to two great Floridian world champions, Frieda Zamba in the 1980s and Lisa Andersen in the 1990s. Both are beautiful girls with distinctly graceful *and* powerful surfing styles. In fact, just four months after my Ironman moment, Frieda stunned the world by showing up at age seventeen and beating the world's greatest surfers at the prestigious Mazda Women's Surf Sport Championships in Solana Beach, a true outlier moment. After her win, the other competitors started throwing in more aggressive maneuvers. She literally changed the sport in one magical weekend.

The word in the lineup was that Frieda and Lisa were "as aggressive on the waves as guys." In the 1980s, that was a high compliment; still is, to many. Frieda and Lisa triggered an influx of girls unafraid to charge waves of all sizes and uncork ridiculous power moves on them. Roxy, and later other women's surf wear companies, drove industry growth concurrently. Fast forward twenty years: in 2014, the World Surf League (formerly the ASP World Tour) announced full parity between men's and women's average prize purses per event and size of field. Other sports, whether it is tennis or soccer have a ways to go to catch up. Conversely, and sadly, the female U.S. national soccer team *still* only receives about *five percent* of the salaries accorded their male counterparts—and they're World Cup champions! The U.S. men's national team didn't even qualify for the 2018 tournament. In golf, the LPGA Tour announced a record $68.75 million would be awarded in prize money in 2018. Great news, right? It is—until you look across the fairway and see that the men are competing for nearly $250 million. Also, the all-time women's prize money winner, the great Annika Sörenstam, earned about $23 million—or roughly twenty percent of all-time men's leader Tiger Woods. We've still got a long way to go.

I look at girls like Frieda and Lisa when I trace the roots of the advertising and media messages that built the image of the woman athlete as we know her now: ultra fit, chic, smart and assured, successful, and awesome in every way. Girl power.

CHAPTER 10
Gripped: Finding Mark Allen

L ove and relationships have always mattered to me. A lot. Within them, though, I sometimes question my self-worth and whether I'm doing enough for my man. Unfortunately, this little shadow is the residual effect of my father leaving when I was very young.

I love being in a relationship, being in love, being there for each other, finding points in common that tighten the bond, and discovering new points that further strengthen it and feed the relationship with new and fresh experiences. Renowned behavioral expert Brené Brown speaks directly to me on love when she says: "Love is not something we give or get; it is something that we nurture and grow, a connection that can only be cultivated between two people when it exists within each one of them—we can only love others as much as we love ourselves."

In 1982, my relationship served as the initial motivating factor for going to Kona. If completing my college senior project was the driver, getting my relationship back was the engine. I desperately wanted my ex-boyfriend, Reed, to take notice and see I was a changed woman, worthy of a second chance. I wanted him back.

After my *Survival of the Fittest* shoot, I joined him on his bike tour of New Zealand's North and South Islands, then accompanied him on to Australia, where we visited his friends. We remained together for another year or so, until he broke up with me right before another Ironman.

Maybe I needed to look at relationships another way . . . or maybe the man of my future was in my life the whole time.

During the month between the 1982 Ironman and *Survival of the Fittest*, I drove the sixty miles from Carlsbad to Huntington Beach at zero dark thirty to take care of some important business: my lifeguard test. It was a two-part fitness test, combining a 1,000-yard open water swim with a twenty-minute time limit, followed by the run-swim-run, a continuous circuit with a 200-yard run, 400-yard swim, and 200-yard run. The time limit was ten minutes. In my three previous attempts, I always passed the 1,000-yard swim well beneath the cutoff time, but my fast-twitch muscles always failed me in the run-swim-run. Also, wetsuits were not allowed, a crucial factor when stroking through chilly winter waters. I was pretty cold after the 1,000-yard swim. By the time the run-swim-run followed, I was hypothermic and couldn't feel my fingers or toes.

However, this was a new year, a new beach, and a new lifeguard candidate.

The 1,000-yard swim went well, as usual. Thirty minutes later, we started the run-swim-run. I even brought my ski gloves with hand warmer packets so I could feel my fingers. As we sprinted in the soft sand toward the first flag, I leaned into the turn that redirected us toward the water. A guy tried to snake my running line. I planted an aggressive elbow to shove him behind me.

As we began the swim, I dolphined through the surf to blunt the impact of the incoming waves. A thought struck me: *Where did that competitive aggression come from?* After a moment, I realized I felt differently about myself after the Ironman, more certain, more self-assured. I didn't know if I'd make the fitness test cut this time, or qualify to be a lifeguard, but I sure as hell knew how to fight for myself. When I felt that guy trying to shove past, I shoved right back. I wasn't going to let him take away my advantage. If I could fight for the finish line in Kona, I could fight for position in a ten-minute run-swim-run. I was not going to be shoved aside by any man or woman, boy or girl.

Welcome to the new me.

I settled onto my assigned tower for day one as a California State lifeguard. I looked down the beach and watched my new supervisor drive toward me in his jeep.

It was Mark Allen.

Mark and I met in 1979 and became casual friends, like "Hey, Mark, how's it going?" He knew me as one of the girls that would run four miles from Tamarack Beach in Carlsbad to the lifeguard headquarters in Ponto, and then pop into the garage for a quick flirt with guards working the off season. There was always a lot of laughing and making noise. Then my friend and I would run back to Tamarack.

We remember our first meeting in different ways. When *City Sports* magazine did a feature on us in the early 1990s, Mark said, "I was in the maintenance area doing some work under one of the jeeps. Suddenly, she walks in with a friend. It had been really quiet; now it's just talk talk talk talk. Then they leave. Dead silence. I pulled myself out and just stared."

My view from above the jeep? "He was peeping at us from under the truck," I told *City Sports*. "I saw that he had these ridiculously long sideburns and that someone needed to tell him they were O-U-T. It's funny, when I met his dad years later, he had the same bad sideburns."

Not exactly love at first sight . . . but certainly the seeds of a new friendship.

As we talked on the beach, I learned something about my new boss: even *he* saw me in a different light after Ironman. Instead of thinking, "who's this crazy girl who shows up at the shop garage?" Mark thought I was nine feet tall.

But now it was June, and I was a nervous rookie. All I was thinking about was not letting someone die on my first day. Saving lives takes priority over flirting!

Mark and I had spoken a couple times after Ironman. We ran into each other at the inaugural La Jolla Half Marathon (which I have run many times since, winning once). It was held in April, after Mark watched the *Wide World of Sports* coverage and decided he wanted to become a triathlete, but before he felt confident running a half marathon. Hard to imagine now that our sport's version of Zorro, the somewhat mysterious man who left his signature "Grip" on countless triathletes en route to six Ironman titles, could be uncomfortable about *any* 13.1-mile race. He retired as the most dominating runner in triathlon history.

Like everyone else, though, he had a starting point. "I saw you on TV and you were amazing," he said.

My first response was somewhat deadpan. "Well, I don't know about *amazing*. I crawled, I lost. But thanks."

"No, really. You inspired me."

I peered into Mark's eyes, something I'm known to do when uncomfortable with a person or the content of our conversation. *How could I inspire him?* He peered right back with his sharp, focused green eyes, not dropping contact for a second. He meant every word he said. My race had stirred something within him. Between the way he complimented me, and those green eyes and striking looks, I was a bit rattled. More to the point, I gushed.

It felt awkward to be on the receiving end of such praise, especially from someone I admired as both a standout in lifeguard competitions and as a friend. Trying to get noticed fell into my comfort zone. However, *being* noticed and praised did not. Mark's words helped launch my long journey to find peace with the conflicted belief of being good enough, without feeling I always had to try extra hard or "go big" to bring it out.

Mark was seeking something that could satisfy his quest for the ultimate challenge, and he saw it through my degree of effort in a forbidding race. Just like that, the light went on and his future flashed before his eyes. Mark Allen, the NCAA Division II all-American swimmer from UC-San Diego, was going to halt his road into the medical profession and become an Ironman triathlete.

Within this tanned, totally fit, stunning man who could leap off any *Baywatch* poster, I sensed a giant at the sport if he committed. In his green eyes was the intense concentration that great champions possess. At the least, he would become very good. He earned his first nickname, "Animallen," from his beastly performances in lifeguard competitions up and down the coast—which involve running, the final leg of the triathlon.

"If anybody should be doing triathlons, it's you," I said. "You'd kick ass. It's not that different from a lifeguard competition."

It wasn't. Triathlon has three set disciplines—swim, bike, run. Lifeguard competitions come in different forms, but essentially, you're running on soft sand and swimming in surf. In both cases, you're switching abruptly from one form of motion to the other, bringing in different muscle groups, and trying to recover while simultaneously pushing like hell. That's why so many lifeguards were phenomenal triathletes in the early years. Their candidate classes are filled with high school and college swimmers and water polo players, and all triathlons begin with the swim.

Mark's next comment surprised me. "As a matter of fact, I'm going to. I'm doing the next Ironman in October," he said.

I started gushing again. Maybe I gave it a little extra gush. "Are you serious? That's awesome! You'll probably win it."

I thought for a moment about what I said, and that my boyfriend happened to also be a lifeguard supervisor, one Mark knew. "Don't tell Reed I said that!"

Back to my job. With lifeguarding, the shoe was on the other foot, since I was embarking on a new learning curve. I find the best way to learn something is to locate an expert and open up his or her reservoir of wisdom, listening to and drawing inspiration or skill from that expertise. But I was self-conscious, a rookie guard on my first day on the job. Now Mark pulls up.

We watched the surf continue to build. Suddenly, the rip current swept a man off his feet and pulled him out. I looked at Mark. "Yeah, I'm going in."

I took the phone off the hook, followed the (tower) procedure, and started to scamper down the ladder. Mark said, "You might want to take your can."

Typically, lifeguards take their "cans"—buoys—everywhere. It is standard operating procedure. In the moment, my mind focused squarely on the man struggling in the water, *I* was *so* embarrassed. Mark might have thought me nine feet tall, but in that moment, with my gorgeous supervisor watching me space out on my can, I felt like a complete barney. In other words, a clueless novice.

◆

Meanwhile, Reed was on his way down from Santa Rosa, California, to spend the summer guarding. "Maybe you guys should train together," I suggested to Mark. It seemed like a good match: Mark was a solid swimmer and sneaky strong runner chomping at the triathlon challenge, and Reed was the fifth-place Ironman finisher with a strong cycling background. It was a matter of how those guys worked it.

I continued to guard while squeezing in my Ironman training, and Reed and Mark started to train together. They both had some latitude on the job as supervisors, from which they built creative workouts. They would ask their shotguns (passengers) to drive their jeeps along the shoreline of Black's Beach, a clothing-optional spot near the UC-San Diego campus that also features awesome waves. They ran alongside their jeeps and peeled off two- or three-mile intervals on State time. They focused primarily on surges and long sprints, so it didn't put them on the State's radar (till now!). They'd also find early morning bike rides and other ways to train, sometimes including me.

In October 1982, Reed and I made sure Mark was well hosted for his first Ironman. We gave him the pullout couch in the one-bedroom condo we rented on the Big Island, offering creature comforts to ensure a smooth Ironman debut. Though I must say, "smooth" and "Kona" better describe a cup of coffee than the Ironman. Given how Mark eventually soared to "The Greatest Endurance Athlete of All Time," as declared by *Outside* and *ESPN* magazines in 1996, it might surprise you that he DNFed his first Ironman—Did Not Finish. I'm not surprised. Kona has its way with you, no matter how prepared you think you are. I didn't do that well, either, finishing fourteenth after imploding on the run. Sadly, that particular story line would mess with more of my future Ironmans.

Our results did not deter us. Mark was hooked, I was hooked, and the world was becoming hooked on triathlon. However, Reed was done. He sensed that computer science was about to explode into something that would draw in consumers as well as companies. His prescience was spot-on. Two years later, Apple introduced the MacIntosh computer and Microsoft the Windows operating platform, revolutionizing personal computing. Reed went on to start ZaneRay, a Rockies-based web design and development company that helps create brands and sell products. In 2015, ZaneRay was named one of *Outside* magazine's 100 Best Places to Work. It aptly reflects the outdoor-first, balance of work and play, and eco-conscious values of its president. Reed always had an unwavering vision of how to go after his ideal life. I'm really happy for him.

Mark and I bolted forward in our careers. The rapidly growing Bud Light USTS circuit and other smaller-course triathlons became significant events. However, for any serious competitive triathlete willing to give the ultimate effort, it was all about Kona. We gladly boarded a fast-moving train.

It was becoming a fast-moving gravy train as well. Since I was known outside triathlon as well as within it, my sponsorship opportunities drew from mainstream corporate America, along with run, bike, and swim companies. I picked up endorsements like Yoplait yogurt and Mizuno running shoes while collecting appearance fees and, soon, prize money. On the other hand, Mark focused on becoming a top-of-the-line triathlete, made possible when he joined the JDavid Team, the sport's first elite professional unit. He didn't have time for much else, except occasional surf trips. He ate, slept, and breathed training and races, and didn't take long to start beating the reigning stars. His athletic talent was extraordinary. He showed strong ability as a runner, he already carried strong swimming credentials, and he was quickly learning the bike. Could I envision a career he has boiled down as "1-6-21-Infinity"? As in, *victory in the first Triathlon World Championship, six Ironman World Championships, 21 consecutive races between 1988-90—and Greatest Endurance Sports Athlete ever?*

Not yet, but I saw a diamond in the rough, capable of dominance.

As we trained together and became closer friends, I was drawn to something behind that handsome face: his mind. Mark Allen has one of the best minds I've ever known. He retains everything. Tell him something once, and he locks it in. I'm the opposite. Mark was singularly focused from the beginning. He also possessed a premed degree from UCSD, acing his MCAT exams along the way; his easy grasp of the science of sport gave him a strong edge. He invested time and energy into learning and mastering that extra bit of research, science, and strategy that champions seem to possess above others. He did acupuncture and extra activities like hyperbaric treatments to keep his body running at an extremely high performance level. He was always on the forefront of any new trends in nutrition, exercise physiology and aerodynamic technology, a proto–tech nerd. He served as a star client for Phil Maffetone's early work in nutrition. (Maffetone is founder of the MAF program, combining nutrition, supplements, and health and fitness tools and apps.)

The same opportunities available to Mark were also available to me, but they weren't *for* me. He was looking for every which way to refine his body, mind, and technique, and he had both the athletic drive and intellectual brilliance to tie them together. I have little patience for hyperbaric chambers, nutritionists, and all the rest. I couldn't have cared less about the nerdy science side. I loved triathlon for the flow, fun, and rawness of it all.

This wasn't to say Mark didn't love to have fun. He did—no two ways about it. However, the public didn't see his fun side often. When he locked into his zone, the Grip zone, the zone that broke great triathletes for more than a decade . . . I was around his intensity a lot. I thought, *if that's what it takes, I don't know.* I totally related to the fun, casual, loose side, but didn't have the drive to do whatever it took to become a champion. Mark did.

For Mark, it was always about excellence—the ability to show up to a race and *bring it.* Few athletes in any sport could match his ability to focus in the middle of huge events, and then focus *more* while red-lining from exertion and exhaustion. Fewer still dominated their sport *and* advanced it in the mainstream world by being the sport's very face. When I consider these qualities, I think of athletes like Michael Jordan, Serena Williams, Steffi Graf, Paula Newby-Fraser, Kelly Slater, Lindsey Vonn, and Roger Federer. These athletes operate from a rarefied space. So did Mark. The built-in discipline from swimming twice a day for years in high school and college was beyond anything I'd experienced. I spent a couple *months* training for my first Ironman, not years. When I was around Mark, it was almost like, "I don't want to do that." Remember the Gatorade ads? "Be like Mark, be like Mike." Like I said, there are not too many athletes to which you can compare Mark.

◆

We remained friends through the 1984 season and enjoyed a nice comfort level. I felt I really knew who he was. He was in a long-distance relationship with his fiancée, Bunny, who was enrolled in medical school in Texas. Mark tried to visit her often, but the distance was taking its toll and their relationship was moving onto shaky ground. I thought about what it would be like to move forward as more than friends, for sure, but for obvious reasons, it stayed on the friendship level. We trained together, hung out together, saw each other at races, and got together for meals. We both loved food and the making of good meals. We bonded over food.

Mark was hopeful his relationship would work out, and I honestly was hopeful it would not.

Our time arrived at the end of the 1984 season. So I thought. Mark was newly single and I couldn't wait to fill the vacancy in his life. We had a brief fling before he left for an extended trip to compete in the Superstars of Cyprus event. It was similar to my *Superstars* competition from 1982, but with a European flair, including shooting contests and the use of polo horses. Afterward, Mark continued his travels and sent me postcards to track his journey.

Just before the new year, he returned home. I was living in a small apartment in Encinitas, one block from popular Moonlight Beach, my first time without roommates. I bought a little Christmas tree and decorated it with handmade ornaments. I cut out tree and wreath shapes and pasted on photos from the *Triathlon* and *Triathlete* magazines lying around. The fact I was alone for Christmas, coupled with reading too much into the postcards, gave me a brilliant idea: cover the tree with pictures of Mark! My troubling habit of trying too hard to secure a man and keep myself centered in his thoughts and heart was now in holiday turbo-drive. Remember when *he* thought *I* was nine feet tall?

When Mark walked into my apartment and looked at the tree, shock spread across his face. He laughed nervously. *Wow.* Not quite the reaction I had imagined and hoped for. My inability to cope with self-doubt, mixed with a need to prove myself essential, had driven off Reed—twice. Now I was at it again.

We rang in the new year with the Hangover 100, a New Year's Day century bike ride. Mark suffered badly during the final twenty miles, most likely working off all those decadent European pastries and glasses of red wine. I, on the other hand, was floating above him and the others, somewhere on cloud nine. I couldn't have felt better. I was riding into 1985 on the wheel of the man I wanted.

For Mark's birthday on January 12, we went to dinner at an upscale restaurant in Del Mar. We also ordered a bottle of wine. Afterward, while waiting for the dessert menus, I soaked up the candle-lit ambiance and nice wine buzz. Then Mark looked into my eyes with one of his intense gazes. I knew he was feeling exactly the same way: *how lucky we are to be together.* He told me how much he appreciated the support I'd given him during his emotional roller coaster of the past months, and how he was now free to pursue his dream life . . .

. . . one that did not include a new relationship.

Not where I saw this conversation going.

We'd shared only a couple weeks together, so it hardly seemed worthy of a public scene, but I was heartbroken and suggested we skip dessert. On the drive home, I kept thinking about that damned Christmas tree, wondering why I needed to try so hard. Look what happened? My action to show Mark how much I cared for him resulted in an equal and opposite reaction: he pulled away.

It took years to sort out my base motivation for being this way. I now know the Christmas Stalker Tree was the action of a strong, yet deeply insecure little girl insisting again that her dad take off her training wheels—in this case, for new love. It never dawned on me that Mark's plan might be different.

I definitely knew his plan now. My tree might not have mattered after all. Mark was emerging as the best all-around triathlete in the world, and he was chasing the dream. After he began a winning streak at the Nice World Championships, the only major piece missing in his collection was an Ironman title. His potential dominance led Nike to swoop in and sign him in 1984 for the best endorsement contract yet given to a triathlete: $50,000 per year plus performance bonuses. He became the highest-paid triathlete in the world.

I was not far behind, thanks to my sponsorships with Yoplait, Mizuno, Speedo, and Specialized bikes, and race appearance fees. While Mark was rising like a bullet to the top, I was already in a lofty catbird seat after two solid years of capitalizing on opportunities presented by my crawl of fame.

Still, I tried to win Mark over. Sometimes, I took my efforts pretty far. Once we took a long group training ride between Lake Wohlford and Pauma Valley, in the rugged northeast San Diego County foothills. It featured a lot of climbing, some of it steep. I tried to keep up with Mark and his workout group, which including ST (Scott Tinley), Scott Molina, Mark Montgomery, and Kenny Souza, all star triathletes. Not easy. Finally, I passed ST and thought, *I'm staying on Grip's wheel.* My motivation was a little different than ST's, who was slugging out the miles with Mark in mano a mano style. As I dropped plenty of sweat and rubber on the steep, twisting roads, I thought, *This must be love. I'm so into this guy that I'm literally going to stay right on his wheel.*

I also thought of how Mark received his triathlon nickname, "Grip," a symbol of fear and respect in professional triathlon. Opponents quickly associated "Grip" with "race over" if Mark caught or led them in a race. Conventional wisdom held that Mark became Grip because once he *gripped* you, you were done. Interestingly, that's a very accurate way to describe his races. He rarely fell behind again once he took the lead, but *you* sure did. Mark was triathlon's version of the late, great American distance running star Steve Prefontaine, who *simultaneously* held all U.S. track records from 1,500 meters to 10,000 meters before he died in a car crash at age twenty-four. Like Mark, Pre was fantastic at all distances. He was also the greatest frontrunner in U.S. track and field history. Pre also helped create Nike, for which Mark was running. Countless high school cross-country kids still run around the U.S. with motivational quotes from Pre planted on the backs of their team T-shirts, more than forty years after his death.

The "Grip" origin story is poetic and catchy, but the nickname originated in a different way. One day early in his career, Mark joined ST and my future manager, triathlete and top-flight swimmer Murphy Reinschreiber, for a ride in the brutal Otay Mesa hills east of San Diego (now home to the U.S. Olympic Training Center). As a kid in 1966, Murphy won twelve of thirteen races at the California State Fair swim meet. His victim every time? Future six-time Ironman champ Dave Scott.

ST and Murphy were seasoned cyclists, but Mark dropped them repeatedly during their three-hour ride. Ever the clinical, analytical mind, ST tried to sort out why it happened. He concluded that Mark's hand position on the handlebars made the difference. With a standard hand position, you put your hands on the outer sides of the top portion of the handlebar, next to the brake levers. If you want to move fast or become more aerodynamic, you typically drop your hands to the bullhorns or lower section of the bars. When you climb, you slide them toward the center and get into a more upright position. All the while, you're balancing a strong grip with relaxation and comfort. Don't grip too hard or too soft.

Well, when the boys sped up or started downhill, Mark gripped the bullhorns like his life depended on it—and kept dropping ST and Murphy. ST caught up and watched him, and noticed how Mark held the handlebars. He told Murphy, "See that? It's the grip of death."

The next time they rode together, Mark heard his new nickname from ST. Soon enough, "Grip" became synonymous with the death-to-your-race grip belonging to a man who believed he could out-suffer all others. If you can out-suffer someone in this sport, and bring Mark's level of talent, you're going to the top.

Eventually, Mark and I regained the comfortable rhythm of our friendship. On New Year's Eve of 1985, there was a shift. We quietly spent the evening together, with no fanfare or scary Christmas Stalker Tree, not even a particularly romantic ambiance. We simply hung out and enjoyed our new connection. I sometimes joke that my persistence finally wore Mark down, but truly, it was my unwavering belief in him.

Mark and I were very compatible. We'd circled the same triathlon orbit for three years, and we knew each other well. I tried to show him that I was a good addition to his life as a friend, and maybe something more. I aligned myself with his athletic vision, but I held a bigger vision for him than he carried. Did he know how big he could be in the sport? I wasn't sure. He had no Plan B—it was triathlon or nothing. Medical school was long gone from his radar. He was so gifted, and I wanted to see him get to the very top.

"Mark owes a lot of his career to Julie," my friend Sue Robison told my coauthor. "You think about it, she already had her place in the sport, she already knew what you had to do at Ironman, and she knew how to support him. It's one thing to be a partner or spouse like me—who isn't in the sports world—and support your athlete, but when your partner is cooking nutritional meals for training, and giving training advice and course knowledge like the knowledge she has of Kona . . . Julie saw Mark's future greatness more clearly than he did, and she knew how to get him there."

We began living together in 1986 after returning from training in Boulder, Colorado, where Mark and most of the elite triathlon world gathered for high-altitude, mountain-fed workouts. We found a unique home in Vista, about forty miles northeast of San Diego and near my hometown of Carlsbad. *Sunset* magazine even ran a photo spread of the house. Set on an acre of land, it was nestled into the ground, with big plastic conducting tubes forming a wall that divided the living room and bedroom. Each tube carried a different pretty color. It looked like a rainbow. Outside, you could almost grow grass on the roof, because the house was built into the side of a hill. A total hippie house. Our first mortgage was $1,000 per month, split three ways among Mark, myself, and Alana, the girlfriend of Mark's massage therapist. She'd remain our housemate for years.

Meanwhile, our careers were flying—and so were we, all over the world. I was coming off my strong 1985 season, and Mark was becoming nearly unbeatable in major triathlons besides Kona (he did not compete there in 1985). Triathlon's fabled Big Four now asserted their reign over the sport. Mark was among them, joining ST, Scott Molina ("The Terminator"), and Dave Scott ("The Man").

Grip. ST. The Terminator. The Man. The Big Four are still our sport's Mount Rushmore, two to three decades after these guys last saddled up as champions.

We traveled to Nice, where Mark won the fourth of his ten Nice Triathlons, and did the Bud Light USTS circuit. I was already backing off the USTS, preferring to race in Europe, which earned some flak from my peers.

I started hearing the term "cherry picker," which implied that I avoided competition in the U.S. to chase easier paychecks abroad. I saw it differently. Europe meant travel, always a huge priority. It also meant appearance fees and prize money in excess of USTS purses.

Sometimes, I'd travel to Europe for one of Mark's races, and then we'd take a couple days to become tourists. In 1986, we celebrated Mark's fifth consecutive win in Nice and my fourth-place finish by renting a red convertible BMW and driving to San Remo, Italy. On the return, just as we crossed the port of Nice, the Beamer died. We had to push through a roundabout and up the sidewalk of the old city, and then walk back to the hotel at 10:00 P.M. When we stopped along the way in Monaco, I bought Mark a new cologne, Drakkar Noir. To this day, whenever I smell Drakkar Noir, I'm transported to our rented BMW speeding along the Mediterranean coastline, my hair blowing in the wind, so in love.

As we spent more time together, I explored the nuances of the man with whom I wanted to share my life. I learned that Mark's "Grip" persona—the intimidating, unsmiling, cold-cocked eyes, superhuman focus, a physical machine built to break you—only appeared during races and focused training sessions. He rarely took his inner iron warrior mentality home. Home was our sanctuary, a place to reboot and relax. Home fueled his artistic side; he's keenly interested in art and cooking. It gave him a chance to be his quiet, reserved, somewhat shy natural self. He liked to kick back, observe people, and chill, to be part of the social action without having to contribute too much. He loved to laugh, especially around the dinner table. I treasure those memories—dinner parties, friends coming together, telling stories around food. No matter the culture—Italian, Jewish, French, a bunch of starving triathletes—you gather around food and you relax and talk. We've been doing it since our most ancient forbears huddled around a cave fire.

Mark loved to surf too. Whenever he had a chance during the off-season, he paddled into the lineup. Or we did. During the season, he wasn't inclined to surf, no matter how much he loved it. However, once he had down time, he grabbed his board and caught waves.

There were exceptions to this rule. After racing the World Sprint Championships in early 1987 in Perth, Australia, we learned last-minute that Scott and Virginia Tinley were flying over to Tavarua, a Tahitian island with magnificent, booming surf. We quickly booked flights and paid Australian dollars, which made it really inexpensive. When we got to Tavarua, we rented boards from island locals, stayed five days, and surfed our hearts out. Unfortunately, Virginia had to skip the welcoming Kava ceremony pulled together for us, but for all the right reasons: she was newly pregnant with their daughter, Torrie, who is now thirty.

We took several wonderful off-season surf trips. Mark embarked on some on his own as well. One in particular tapped into his spiritual side, already emerging when we got together. Mark was constantly searching for a way to grow within himself and to better the planet in the process, an exquisitely rich and interesting period in anyone's life. Since he was a kid, his mother, Sharon, a practicing Buddhist, had discussed the tenets of Buddhism, such as dissolving the ego and the power of visualization. They also talked about how Mark's career might lead him to serve others, the earliest antecedent of his successful online coaching career and books, which have benefitted many. Sharon wanted Mark to understand that he had the potential to impact many lives. She helped him embrace that in his heart and soul, where selfless service begins. I also understand Grandma Sharon held similar conversations with my son, Mats, as he braced for his first Kona.

Mark's quest accelerated on surf trips to mainland Mexico. As California State lifeguards, he and his friends could go on the dole, collect unemployment, and become seasonal guards. They would head to Mexico or Central America to surf. What amazing trips! Mark knew a little about shamanism in general, but a visceral spiritual experience in deep mainland Mexico ramped up his quest. He was always intrigued and drawn to the shamanistic, spiritual side of Mexico, especially after reading the Don Juan books of UCLA anthropologist Carlos Castaneda, whose work introduced several million baby boomers to shamanism.

From there it was a progression, a hero's journey: *How do I overcome my hardships? What's my true calling? How do I get there? I'll do whatever it takes!* Triathlon was his first hero's journey, in the classic Joseph Campbell, Ancient

Greek sense. Mark had to overcome his physician-father questioning, "When are you going to get a real job?" He broke away from the path his family had pre-laid for him. He sought his own way. The hero's journey is different for each person and never easy to reach the other side.

Spiritually, I had a short stint with transcendental meditation at Cal Poly, a popular pursuit then. I received my mantra and kind of dropped it (though I used the mantra word "patience" while winning Ironman Japan). For Mark, it was a calling, always near and dear, whether from something he was reading or listening to. He was an open channel. He understood that the key to fulfillment didn't run through supreme mind-body fitness, but rather through spirit. He was looking to refine his interior landscape, to find what was unique for him. His path. I supported every step, because I felt it enriched him and us. My spiritual seeds would grow later when I discovered yoga.

Three years sped by. Our relationship flourished while we jetted from place to place, enjoying the spoils of being top triathletes. When the Julie & Mark Show arrived, we drew plenty of attention. I was always the perky, outgoing one who loved media interviews and the community spirit. He was more laid-back, focused, already in race mode. Triathlon was really booming, economically and popularly. It was the best time ever to be part of a sport. Just imagine being in your late twenties, one of the more recognizable figures, *and* living with Mark Allen. I loved my life.

Then it got even better. Though it didn't feel that way at first.

When we arrived in Chile on January 1, 1989, I'd been dealing with a recurring pit in my stomach. Celebrations would pass, such as my birthday, Christmas, New Year's, Valentine's Day, days I thought might culminate with a ring on my finger . . . but never did. Mark bought me flowers, champagne, or something nice he picked from Victoria's Secret, but not the tiny box with a ring in it. I was beginning to think that if we didn't get engaged soon, maybe it wasn't meant to be. I started thinking, if Mark's not the one for me, I can hardly wait to meet the next one. How cool is he going to be if he's a step up from Mark Allen? Then, the follow-up, mind-stopper question, "Who could that be?"

Mark had planned to propose in Paris, atop the Eiffel Tower en route to our November 1988 race in Réunion Island, off the Eastern Africa coast. Could anything be more romantic?

I never found out. When we reached the top of the Eiffel Tower, it was windy and freezing, biting cold. This California surfer girl said, "Okay, let's go. It's too cold."

With that, I blew my shot at the romantic proposal. I only learned about his intentions later.

I surrendered to whatever would happen next. That was good, because I had been dropping hints, apparently too many. I told Mark I wasn't going to concern myself with it any more. "I felt you let go of that [trying to get engaged]. I felt you relax, and I was allowed to decide, 'this is what I want,'" he told me long afterward.

We flew to Chile for the 70.3 Pucon, then known as Triatlon de Pucon. Mark won the men's title, gaining momentum for what would become one of the greatest multiyear winning streaks in professional sports history.

The day after the race, we decided to hike Villarrica, a 9,000-foot-tall volcano that overlooked the lake in which we swam in our triathlon. While it was 80°F at the lake, very summerlike (it *was* summer; Chile is in the southern hemisphere), the volcano could turn from sunny skies to blizzard conditions with hardly a moment's notice. Neither of us, nor our fellow competitors, was properly dressed for a sudden shift in temperature or conditions. While our Chilean guides donned proper climbing gear, we wore running tights, running shirts, and rented hiking boots—and backup wind pants and wind jackets provided by the hiking outfitter. Except me; they didn't have my petite size. I wore running tights that offered a little body grip if I slipped, and a little warmth if it got cold . . . but not much.

We started quickly, grinding out miles like triathletes do, enjoying the warm weather as we stripped down to T-shirts hiking through the snow. We hiked quickly when we could, earning a reprimand from the group leader: "Slow down, kick your boots into the slide of the slope. You don't know this mountain. It can get dangerous. People have died here."

Those words would soon prove prophetic.

As we started to climb, the conditions began to deteriorate. Thick dark clouds rolled in, including a swirl that wrapped itself around Villarrica like a halo. Visibility vanished. We threw on our limited layers as the temperature plummeted, and rain turned to snow. Our leader gave us lessons on using ice axes, how if you start to slip, you turn around, dig the ax into the other side of the hill, and hang on.

We kept climbing, up and up. And up. We got wetter and colder as we negotiated the steep terrain. By the time we stopped to rest and snack at a local shrine, the near-zero degree temperatures left us shivering in our soaked clothes. We still faced the toughest part of the climb, a ninety-minute segment that would end near the summit. With doubt and anxiety spreading among us, one woman dropped from the hike.

It took us thirty minutes to complete the next one hundred yards. We took fifteen steps, rested for thirty seconds, then plodded forward again, the conditions and altitude slowing us down. Our pleasant 80°F lakeshore day had turned into a monstrous winter beast, with fifty-mile-per-hour winds, rain and snow, and unfamiliar trails and terrain hampering our every step. Furthermore, some fought the early, shivering stages of hypothermia. A couple group members also slipped on the increasingly slick, icy ground; other hikers circled back to help.

The group leader made his way over to me, since I was the most underdressed. He asked me if I wanted to go back. "If we continue to the top," I asked, "will we be able to see anything more than we can right now?"

"No."

That made a tough decision easy. We stopped climbing and immediately started back down the mountain. I didn't hear any complaints. We were freezing, underdressed (especially me), and couldn't see—the surface clouds had reduced visibility to thirty yards. Villarrica would have to live another day without us.

After the ice axe lesson, we started sliding down the mountain, opting for lesser effort and greater fun. Our guide was not amused; he promptly tied a woman and two other hikers to him with a rope leash after the woman slid too far. He sternly warned us that we were next if we tried to slide again.

Suitably chastised, we prepared to continue. After taking a quick seat during the tie-off, I stood up and leaned on Mark's shoulder. I accidentally pushed him slightly, ever so slightly—and knocked him off balance due to ground conditions as slippery as a hockey rink. He started slipping and sliding . . . and sliding some more . . . and more . . .

He wasn't slowing or stopping . . . he was picking up speed! He swung his ice axe and tried to dig into the snow and ice, but the axe slipped out of his hands.

"Marrrrrrrrk!" I screamed at the top of my lungs.

He disappeared into the fog.

Shit! While freaking at the clear and present danger of losing my boyfriend, I tried to think. *Which switchback did we just come up?* We'd walked along a number of rocky ledges that fell into nothing. I don't like being on the edge—of cliffs and ledges, anyway—so these horrified me. If you tumbled over the side of one of these ledges, you were gone.

For all I knew, Mark was careening toward or over a ledge, ice sliding on borrowed slick pants that provided lots of speed. The person I loved most in the world was somewhere down that slope, in grave danger, because I pushed him while trying to gain my balance . . .

I took off down the hill, not giving a damn what the guide said. I slid, slowing myself with my boot heels. "Marrrk! Marrrk! Where are you?" I screamed as I kept sliding, looking for him, hoping he would answer.

About one hundred yards from our group, I heard a noise. I saw a big lava rock formation, which would have crushed anyone who smacked it head-on. By a sheer stroke of luck, and his own efforts, Mark had tumbled into it without sustaining anything more than a few bumps and bruises. We embraced tightly, then I started quaking inside. *I almost lost my man!*

After the group reached us, we wanted to get off this diablo volcano. We made quick work of our descent, taking only an hour to reach the bottom. Unfortunately, our support vehicles had not yet arrived, thinking we would summit Villarrica and return a couple hours later. We waited it out at a rustic trail hut with a fire made of scrap wood, eating our rain-soaked cheese sandwiches, and drying our clothing by the fire.

Finally, our jeeps showed up, and we returned to the hotel and enjoyed extra-long showers. "I don't think the micro-adventure can be much bigger than what we did today," Mark told me later. "I've had enough adventure for awhile . . . but what do you think about a mountain bike ride to waterfalls tomorrow?"

"Maybe we'll see what the weather looks like," I quipped.

Mark then said something else. "I could tell by the way you were screaming and calling out how much you cared about me."

In that moment on Villarrica, during our shared terror, something significant had cracked and broken loose inside him.

Those words were music to my ears, especially since I wasn't feeling my most attractive. I was a pasty-skinned redhead who flew into brown-skinned Chile from the northern hemisphere winter, carrying a few extra pounds from holiday dining, and wearing borrowed clothes because my luggage hadn't arrived. I didn't feel very feminine, but it didn't matter. Mark was safe and we were good. That's what mattered.

A few days after returning to Santiago, we visited Vina del Mar beach, where the Chilean locals spend their summer days. Surfers always like to flock to where the locals hang out, as opposed to beaches mostly frequented by visiting tourists. A hot beach with warm water in January? Count us in!

We arrived at about 10:00 A.M. It wasn't crowded, so we put our towels down, swam, napped, and enjoyed a nice, beachy day. Every time we woke up or turned around, we noticed more people packing themselves onto the sand. Before too long, they stood, sat and lay inches away. We started to feel buried inside a patchwork quilt of towels, along with the sight of the day: three young women lying in front of us, their three brown Chilean butts spilling from the tiny pieces of cloth covering them. Next to me, one Mark Allen wore a huge Cheshire Cat grin. I rolled my eyes and laughed. "Really, Mark? You enjoying this?"

For a few minutes I teased him about his astute observation of the girls' *potos*. We both enjoyed his animated post-race side, relaxed and frisky. Then he turned to me, suddenly serious. "So, do you think we're going to get married this year?" he asked.

What? You're asking me . . . now! I was stunned, incredulous. "What? No! We're not having this conversation with this going on right in front of us!" I pointed my finger toward the senoritas and counted—*uno, dos, tres.* "Wherever this is going . . . not with the *tres potos* in my face!"

Since Mark never proposed atop the Eiffel Tower, this was the first time I heard a marriage statement made with intent. After years of waiting, was I going to let him off the hook with a "not now"? Was I going to do so because of my ruffled ego over three thong-clad girls with cocoa-colored butts that we'd never see again? No . . .

This really wasn't the time. Not while sitting in a borrowed Speedo. I wasn't feeling it. Nor was I seeing the obvious beyond this silly beach scene: that Mark liked what he saw every time he looked at me. The Chilean girls were window dressing, not even a blip on his screen.

We returned to our hotel. To my great delight and relief, my luggage had arrived. I put on a nice dress, and we enjoyed a wonderful dinner on Chilean time, not seating until 8:30 or so. We returned at midnight, or maybe even later.

Once we reached the room, I could tell Mark was tired. Mark Allen is no good to anybody when he's tired, and he wanted nothing more than a deep sleep. I stared out the window of our high-rise hotel room, feasting on the lights of Santiago. It was such a beautiful setting, as romantic as can be. I lay next to him. "Remember that conversation we started on the beach?" I asked.

"What conversation?"

"You know the conversation."

He nodded, and then closed his eyes. "I'm really tired. Can we talk about it in the morning?"

I sat bolt upright. "If you want to have any hope of getting any sleep tonight, you might want to have this conversation."

We discussed what it would be like to get married, blend our lives, and make this partnership work. Being a fiery romantic at heart, I'd always thought my engagement would invoke elements that make great movies and fairy tales. I'm no different from many other girls; I carried dreams of a storybook wedding that began with the perfect proposal.

However, this conversation turned out to be pragmatic, a real heart-to-heart. Mark was thirty-one and I was thirty, not two kids racing from campus to chapel. We knew each other's strengths and weaknesses. We knew our family histories, as well as each other's former love interests. We discussed what we both did and did not want in our marriage. He knew my insecurities and accepted them, except for one: my use of cutting humor. My go-to defense mechanism is a finely honed sarcasm that, unfortunately, sometimes comes across more like the literal meaning of the Greek root *sarkasmos:* "to tear the flesh, bite the lips in rage, sneer; remarks made to hurt someone's feelings." Mark wanted no part of such "humor." He made it very clear.

I knew it was not easy for Mark to be so brutally honest in what should have been a romantic moment, but his words hit my heart stronger and with more lasting impact than "I love you." He was challenging me to be my best self, to bring that person into our marriage. It was our most profound moment, and I fully embraced his words and the life we envisioned.

During this talk, Mark also said he'd wanted to propose to me atop the Eiffel Tower. I closed my eyes and swallowed before I could speak. *Why did I have to say something about being cold up there?* He wanted to give me the most beautiful proposal, as he knew about my romantic proclivities. That drew me even closer to him.

I had what I wanted: a loving relationship with a strong, reliable man, *and* my career. My six-year run as a professional triathlete was so fulfilling that, at first, I didn't feel a huge desire to throw everything into training and racing again. I wanted to pour myself into our engagement. If I needed to cut a workout short to muster the energy to make dinner, no problem—I cut it short. It wasn't a sacrifice; I was totally down with that. I felt comfort in letting him carry the pressure of showing up at big races with the target on his back. We knew and fully appreciated our good fortune of being marquee figures in the sport. We often worked within that spirit to share our house with up-and-coming athletes, giving them a dirt-cheap, "pay-it-forward" rent. For the longest time, I felt like I was making dinners for four, or six, or eight. I didn't really know how to cook for two!

When we flew into Chile, I didn't know where our relationship would go next. Would it even continue? I had to release my expectations. A week later, after nearly losing Mark on a volcano, we departed as an engaged couple—proof of what can and often does happen when we let go of expectations and "trying too hard." When we try too hard, we grab the wheel of ego-control and steer it away from our greatest authenticity, though we think the opposite. Sometimes, we beach ourselves. Or smash ourselves into the rocks. By releasing my expectations, I gave my innermost authentic self—and, more so, his—some breathing room to find the truth of who we were to each other.

Now I knew. Now we knew.

CHAPTER 11
1989

If you sorted my ten professional seasons into word clouds, my clouds would look like a map of the stars, weighted by magnitude. About three-quarters of the way through, you'd find a huge sun, around which the rest of my competitive career seemed to pale by comparison.

That's 1989, my best professional season, my BIG YEAR, the year everything came together. I was newly engaged, my fiancé was en route to making triathlon history, and my life and body were in great working order. I was fit, focused, and energized by the alignment of my life. I never expected my peak year to happen at age thirty, but endurance sports can be stingy until you've already offered the road plenty of experience, sweat, and tears. Then you're ready. I took advantage.

My Big Year shot to another level in New Zealand, about a month after I nearly pushed Mark off the face of the earth in Chile. We flew down to train with our friends and rivals, future triathlon legends Erin Baker, Scott Molina, and Colleen Cannon. We promptly told Erin, Scott, Colleen, and her husband, Howard Kaushansky, that we were engaged, and shared our wild Chilean story. One of them, likely Scott, joked, "Oh, so you had to almost kill him to get him to propose! Really? You had to shove him off a volcano to shake something loose in him."

ABOVE: Mark, Mats, and Julie Following five-day vision quest in Alaska. *Image from the Moss family archives.* BELOW: Mile seventeen of the Boston Marathon in 1991, at the beginning of Newton Hills, when I nearly made Olympic trials. My final time was 2:47. *Image courtesy of Sue Robison.*

The picture-perfect
family—Don, Eloise,
Marshall, and Julie Moss.
*Image from the Moss family
archives.*

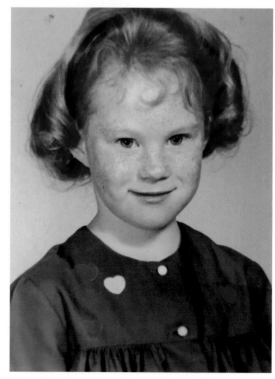

Kindergarten, Spring 1964,
and already sporting a smart-aleck
look. *Image from the Moss family
archives.*

On the bike in Kona, 1982, riding my Univega, and wearing a skateboard helmet with my new Lycra Wonder Woman skinsuit. *Image from the Moss family archives.*

Early in the run portion of Ironman 1982, well before the trouble at the end. *Image from the Moss family archives.*

LEFT: Coming out of the swim portion of Ironman 1982 in Kona and heading toward boardwalk and on to transition. *Image from the Moss family archives.* BELOW: My day job after Ironman 1982: lifeguarding in North San Diego County. *Image courtesy of Sue Robison.*

Pushing hard on the run during Ironman Japan 1986. *Image courtesy of Bridgestone.*

On the bike in Bridgestone gear, 1985. *Image courtesy of Lois Schwartz.*

Speedo promo shot of Scott Tinley and me running together, inscribed by Scott as follows: "We were so much older then, we're younger than that now." *Image courtesy of Scott Tinley.*

Bearing down on the bike. *Image courtesy of Lois Schwartz.*

Ironman Japan 1986, wearing #3, which was my overall finish the year before. *Image courtesy of Bridgestone.*

ABOVE: Gracing the cover of *Triathlon* magazine, which included my dual interview alongside Kathleen McCartney. *Copyright © of* Triathlon *magazine.*

BELOW: The spread in *Triathlon*—one of many times people have asked Kathleen and me about the 1982 race. *Copyright © Claudia Kunin/*Triathlon *Magazine.*

Moss & McCartney

Looking back on the sport's most dramatic moment.

by Kent Black

I T WAS A SCANT THREE YEARS AGO, BUT THE INCIDENT has already passed into the realm of triathlon mythology. Julie Moss was just embarrassed when she collapsed within 15 feet of the finish line at the February 1982 Bud Light Ironman Triathlon and was forced to crawl the final yards of the 140-mile long race. Kathleen McCartney was pleasantly surprised to discover that she narrowly won the race—only later did she realize what had happened to Moss. Neither imagined the impact that finish would have on the armchair athletes of the world.

It was a race finish so dramatic, so shocking, that it would be dismissed as absurd if it tried to pass as fiction. But when ABC broadcast the "Wide World of Sports" Ironman segment, there was no doubt that it was real, no doubt that here was one hell of a race.

The man who contrived the Ironman, John Collins, had tried to dissuade ABC from filming the race. "I told them it'd be like watching grass grow," he remembers. ABC told Collins that they would make the race interesting that first year they wanted to film it. Moss and McCartney saved them the trouble and ABC has been back more every year since. The triathlon had been an obscure ritual for a handful of fitness cultists; the "Moss and McCartney" episode helped make it one of the fastest growing sports on earth.

Since the February '82 Ironman, the lives and careers of Kathleen McCartney and Julie Moss have taken anything but predictable turns. Though there's been no end to the analysis of that fateful race by observers, the two competitors are still trying to figure out what it all meant. Experts can form opinions and judgments, and transform the mundane into the essential; but personal insights often wait for the passage of time.

Kent Black is a Pasadena, California-based freelance writer.

Catching a hometown wave. *Image courtesy of Mark Allen.*

ABOVE: Reed and I hosting Mark Allen in October 1982, his first Ironman. *Image from the Moss family archives.* BELOW: With Erin Baker, one of the greatest triathletes in the 1980s and early 1990s, with whom I trained in 1989, my best year. *Image from the Moss family archives.*

ABOVE: An adoring and in-love couple. *Image from the Moss family archives.*
BELOW: Mark and Julie hiking an icy slope in Villarica, 1991. *Image courtesy of Emilio de Soto.*

Champions' Kiss after winning
Sater, Sweden together in 1991.
Image from the Moss family archives.

Our Christmas Card in 1994,
taken in Kona during Ironman
week. This time, Mark is a
specator! *Image courtesy of Shana
Menaker.*

Running the Mission Bay Half Marathon on my wedding morning. I ran 1:24, complete with a bridal hat! *Image from the Moss family archives.*

ABOVE: Mark, Mats, and I in a sweet moment. *Image courtesy of Colleen Morgans Photography.* BELOW: One of my favorite portraits of my mother, Eloise Julie Tubach. *Image from the Moss family archives.*

Mark holds Mats as I wave to spectators after my return to Ironman in 1997. *Image from the Moss family archives.*

What a return! After seven years away, I ran my second-fastest
career Ironman in 1997. *Image courtesy of MFA.*

I came back again in 2003—and ran a 10:57 at age forty-five. *Image courtesy of MFA.*

Striking a USA Triathlon Hall of Fame pose at my 2014 induction. *Image courtesy of Paul Phillips/Competitive Image.*

ABOVE: Yoga has been a central part of my life for a decade, and one of my secrets to racing well later in life. *Image courtesy of Topher Riley.* BELOW: Talking to fans during #RunWithJulie, our pre-event group run through HOKA ONE ONE. *Image courtesy of Paul Phillips/HOKA ONE ONE.*

In 2016, Mats hiked the entire 2,650-mile Pacific Crest Trail—and definitely looked the part! *Image from the Moss family archives.*

Kathleen and I running together at Torrey Pines in San Diego. *Image from the Moss family archives.*

ABOVE: I'm all smiles after a strong hometown run at the 2017 Ironman 70.3 Oceanside. *Image from the Moss family archives.* BELOW: Few things light me up more than hearing inspiring stories like those I hear on the #RunWithJulie outings. *Image courtesy of HOKA ONE ONE.*

My Iron Twin, Khalil Binebine.
Courtesy of Julie Moss.

Team Binebine before the start of
Dubai 70.3. Left to Right: Bachir,
Julie , Gwilym , and Khalil.
Courtesy of Julie Moss.

I nodded and laughed. "Yeah, something like that."

That became our running joke—shoving Mark off a volcano to gain his favor. If the others had been there on that frigid, slippery slope and felt the horror and fear screaming through me while I slid ass-first through the ice fog in my running gear, yelling for the love of my life . . .

My relationship was in an ideal position for me to take a long, mighty swing at the two goals I had yet to meet: 1) a full season of top training and top performances; and 2) winning in Kona. I didn't sacrifice anything at all by mixing my engagement and work. I was even receiving *da kine* opportunities by being with Mark. He was now the endurance sports face of Nike and Oakley and, increasingly, the triathlon world. His ascent took the pressure off me; he was now the focus. Seven years of partially carrying a sport's mantle was a lot of weight to lift, and was a distraction too, from training and racing. Now I could relax and back off a little, and mean what I told many: "Mark's career is so much more important than mine." My place in the sport was cemented. However, I was also concerned how people would view me if I suddenly tanked the rankings after getting engaged.

In between our racing plans, interesting moments and decisions arose, on the course and inside my head. Several times, race officials, media, or broadcasters would ask, "Julie, why don't you do more TV work? You're a natural on camera. You really enjoy it." I'd done some TV, as a guest announcer at several triathlons and professional surfing events, and as a voiceover analyst. I loved it, especially as I developed skills, but two major problems precluded a broadcasting career. First, my soon-to-be husband and I weren't about to move to LA or New York, nor would I do so and enter a long-distance relationship. Why do that when I could travel, race, and be paid well for both? And live in Boulder, Colorado, during the summer, and a great beach town, Cardiff-by-the-Sea, during the winter? With the man I loved? I enjoyed such a nice lifestyle.

As we began planning workouts in New Zealand, I looked around the room. Mark had started a long winning streak. Scott was focusing more on long races after spending the past six years as the most successful Bud Light USTS performer in history and, in many eyes, the greatest short-course triathlete who ever lived. Colleen was a World Champion in 1984, and National Champion in 1988 and 1990; later, she founded Women's Quest, devoted to educating women about body image, nutrition, and a fun, active lifestyle. What great work! Meanwhile, Erin battled back and forth for supremacy with Paula Newby-Fraser, she of the eye-popping 1988 Ironman victory. Why was it eye-popping? Erin ran a 9:12:14 at Kona, shattering her previous mark by twenty-three minutes—and finished second to Paula. By *eleven minutes*. Furthermore, Paula finished eleventh overall in the race, just thirty minutes behind the overall winner, none other than Erin's partner, Scott Molina.

While assessing our crew, something very solid to my soul and sure to my mind ignited me: *become a great athlete, right here, right now.* New Zealand afforded me a chance to seize the moment. It was quiet, with no distractions, and I was with the best athletes in the world, along with several Kiwi multisports competitors who joined us from time to time. My companions had done the hard work for years, getting up every morning in darkness and training without shortcuts or excuses. Surrounded by these real stars, I thought, why not see what I can do? What will happen if I work at it every day?

I set out with the others, trying to replicate their training schedules, posting good, strong days from the outset, but not *their* strong days. Erin, Colleen, Mark, and Scott operated in a higher realm. For example, I would swim 300 meters to keep up with their *400-meter* workout. And I'm known as a strong swimmer. When we set out on the bike, I stayed in back and tried to keep up. It hit me very quickly that, while I might be a known triathlete who won some races, I was not in their league. I knew it, and it made me more determined to match them. Because I was training with people who knew the ins and outs of training, pacing, nutrition, and recovery, I was getting the right kind of workouts—those that produce results. I figured out how to be consistent, how to build fitness, and how to *build into* particular races, a refined skill at which my fiancé happened to be masterful.

With my shift in training intensity came a consequent inner shift to face tougher questions that no one could answer but myself: *What kind of athlete do you think you can be? What do you want to do here? You have an opportunity; take advantage of it.* Another question loomed: would my mind, accustomed to six years of *almost getting there,* be resolute enough? I'd never successfully trained from the start of a season to its finish, although 1985 was solid. I wanted to know what it felt like to show up at a race, give my fullest effort, and not worry about the paycheck.

My career reboot switched from the glamorous side of triathlon to hammering a more committed training plan. I didn't need to impress anyone, or worry about subjugating myself.

After asking myself and answering these tough questions, I had one of those interior skirmishes to rise above my phobias, challenges, shortcomings, failures, and perceived obstacles. I looked myself squarely in the soul and announced it's time to do something: *It's not about trying to balance anymore; you've got that piece. What are you going to do now? This is your time. What are you going to do with it?*

Soon it began to click. I started pushing through old barriers that formerly distracted me or ended my workouts. I decided to do my best every day, and to not beat myself up with comparisons to the Erin Bakers and Paula Newby-Frasers of the world. They lived in another galaxy, performance-wise. Instead, I affirmed and visualized a strong season for myself. I was learning to trust that my best was good enough.

An effort like this begins with solid, stable support. And a place to call home. Erin set up Mark and me with four other athletes—two triathletes and two multiday specialists—in a rambling Victorian house in Sumner, a coastal suburb of Christchurch. Located in a coastal valley, Sumner is separated from Christchurch by rugged volcanic hill ridges and cliffs that fall into the sea in a few places. Sumner faces two of my favorite bodies of water, Pegasus Bay and the Pacific Ocean.

All of our housemates were vegetarian. Everyone was required to cook one group meal per week. Mark and I teamed to cook our requisite two dinners together, then we were free to chill out the remainder of the week till the dinner bell rang. Not too shabby, even if you weren't a vegetarian. I still ate red meat occasionally, though not often. I couldn't quite break my desire for it. In-N-Out Burger fans will appreciate why. I'd spent my first four school years in the Los Angeles suburb of Claremont, within ten miles of the second In-N-Out Burger shack ever built. I loved In-N-Out, but loved Mark more, so I gave up red meat, at least when we cooked and ate together.

Erin also arranged for us to borrow a car from her good friend and coach, John Hellemans. We looked twice at our car, a Morris Minor two-door, manufactured around 1950. It hadn't been driven in years—or, at least, since a family of spiders moved in and built an intricate web condo in the back seat. The standard transmission was a challenge, since New Zealanders drive on the opposite side of the road. Neither Mark nor I were used to shifting with our left hands, from the right-side driver's seat. We somehow managed to drive the Morris Minor back to our new digs, raze the spider condo and give it a wash. We even waxed it.

Our training sessions were intense. Our mornings always started with a swim in the AquaGym, an eight-lane, twenty-five-meter facility for which New Zealand's national sports heroine, our own Erin Baker, cut the ribbon at the site dedication. The water temperature was chilly, which motivated me to swim hard from the first stoke.

We usually followed our swims with either a bike ride or run or both. On one epic occasion, Erin and Scott decided to take our crew on a little three-day adventure. We started out on the 110-mile route from Erin's house in Lyttelton to the natural hot springs resort in Hanmer Springs. It started easily enough with a ride to Rangiora, but then we started pedaling into a relentless uphill and headwind slog for the remaining 100K. Since this was an out-and-back ride, we treated it as a weekend getaway. Howard drove the sag wagon with our gear and, being the gourmet cook he was, whipped up some great meals. Our destination was a cabin just past the Hamner Springs Township, in the Conical Hill Recreational Reserve. From there, we could step onto the trails and walk or run to the summit.

It took us a while to reach Hamner Springs as the headwind reared its unforgettable head. At one point, Erin suddenly turned her bike around and flew past me in the opposite direction, assisted by the same wind that was beating up the rest of us. I don't think the challenge of a headwind turned her around. I'm not sure if Scott said something she didn't like, but Erin can be hot-tempered, so whatever it was, she was riding the other way and not smiling. While bringing up the rear in our tiny peloton, I said to myself, "Where did Erin go? What did Scott say? Because *something* just went down."

To keep us from separating too far from each other, we designated a meet-up at a milk bar about twenty miles up the road. I pedaled hard, hoping the others didn't leave me behind. They were waiting when I arrived. "So . . . Erin?" I asked.

Scott shrugged his shoulders. "I don't know . . . maybe she went home. I don't know."

Our plan was to spend the night elsewhere, get up, and do a long run in the mountains, then hang out in Hamner Springs, a very cool resort town in the Canterbury region of South Island best known for its mineral waters, thermal pools, and spa . . . music to a triathlete's legs. Further south, the Waiau Gorge was known for its whitewater rapids and abundant salmon and trout. We'd all enjoy a little recreation paradise, soak our bodies, then ride home.

Just after I started to eat and drink, Erin arrived. She'd ridden out with us, turned and gone miles back—I presume—then turned around again and rode back against the headwind. She straddled her bike and unbuckled her helmet. I was like, "Really, Erin? You're already back? You went miles out of your way, and you're already here?"

She didn't say anything. What I did learn about Erin over our weeks of training, though, is that I've never known anyone who lives their truth as intensely or as passionately. She brings that intensity and passion to everything she does. You always know how Erin is feeling and where she stands. In the time it took Erin to catch back up to us, she worked through whatever was bugging her.

I did know one thing, though: I would only improve by training with Erin, now at her competitive peak. She was a terminator, big-time: out of her 121 career triathlon starts, she won 104, most by wide margins. How incredible is that? She was the first International Triathlon Union World Champion, secured later in 1989 in Avignon, France. Mark was the men's victor. Erin and Mark earned the right to wear the rainbow world champion's jersey in Kona. When *Triathlete* named her "Triathlete of the Decade" over Paula, the magazine noted, "We've stopped trying to figure Erin out. We just accept her as the best female triathlete that ever lived." In 1993,

Erin was installed as a Member of the Order of the British Empire (MBE), the highest award given to civilians.

After we ate and Erin caught her breath, we braced ourselves against the frosty headwind and finished the ride. We started our transition run, our second discipline of the training day. We call this "brick training." The purpose is to strengthen muscle groups for the abrupt transitions from one discipline to another, and also get the body used to the jarring effects these transitions can have. Today, I'll ride and then run, or swim and run, or run, ride the bike, and run again. And supplement it with my fourth cornerstone, yoga. Transitions and recovery, the ability to quickly bounce back from one discipline when you're embarking on the next, are critical to becoming a strong triathlete. Before our time in New Zealand, I can't remember doing any brick training.

We ran on tired legs at altitude, climbing Conical Hill. Rain started to fall, and upshifted into a strong snow shower as we moved higher. Mark and I looked at each other as thoughts of our toasty cabin enveloped me.

We ran to our cabin, warmed up, and then asked each other, "Where's Erin and Scott?" We knew they continued onward, running up the slope . . . but to where? "You know, it's freezing out, it's snowing hard, and they're somewhere alone up that mountain," I said. We weren't concerned about their ability to hunker down in nasty weather; our concern was their apparel. We'd left in tank tops and shorts.

We found Erin and Scott huddled in a small bathroom on the mountain. We started laughing when someone blurted out, "Hey, if we would've left them up there a few more hours, then maybe Scott would have proposed."

The training paid off. I felt tougher, stronger, and faster. It didn't take long to get excited over the possibility of where my extra work might take me . . . like a podium spot in Kona? I now noticed day-to-day improvements. How much further until I reached peak performance? I'd never really touched that place, though one could argue I *did* hit my available potential in 1982, and came close in Japan in 1985. I already knew Mark's potential, and Erin Baker's, Scott Molina's, and Colleen Cannon's. So did the rest of the world. I knew every day how strong and how good they were.

My first significant breakthrough came on a training run. We took a ferry to a nature preserve in the middle of Lyttelton Harbor, on the backside of Christchurch. It's a wonderful place for picnicking, as well as trail running and hiking. A *Triathlete* magazine writer tagged along with us for an article on our training crew. Nice writing assignment . . .

We started running. I was normally content to stay in the back of our pack of five. On this day, though, I felt differently. It wasn't long before I passed Colleen and moved onto Erin's shoulder. Then, a bit later, I moved around her. She was probably thinking, "I'm tired, this isn't a key workout," and I seized that moment, stepped around, passed her, and did not look back. My move and tenacity in holding position surprised her. A feeling washed over me: *I want to go harder.* Erin didn't share her surprise with me, but she did tell Scott. He mentioned it to Mark, who later told me, "Yeah, Erin said you were going to surprise some people at the World Cup, and this year in general." Sometimes, with Erin, you need to rely on a small relay team of messengers to find out what she's thinking.

Finally, it was time to test the new and improved Julie. The World Cup Gold Coast Triathlon near Brisbane, Australia, was circled on my schedule. I was ready to go. What I didn't count on was beating Paula. She had just covered Kona in 8 hours, 50 minutes—a women's record that stood for twenty years. By comparison, my lifetime best at the Ironman distance is ten hours flat.

During her career, Paula won twenty-four of twenty-nine official Ironman-sanctioned races, a record that, in today's greater parity, I doubt anyone will touch. Comparatively, Mark Allen and Dave Scott won eight official Ironman races worldwide (including six apiece in Kona), and Erin won seven. Paula also won several ultramarathons. The United States Sports Academy, CNN, and *USA Today* named her one of the top five women athletes of the final quarter of the 20th century. The others? Tennis Hall of Famers Chris Evert, Martina Navratilova, Steffi Graf, and Billie Jean King.

See why I smile when I recall 1989? *No one* was beating Paula Newby-Fraser, except Erin Baker—and then me, twice.

After the swim and bike portions of the race, I felt great, moving toward the lead while heading into the marathon. Would it be my albatross again?

Or my soaring eagle? I looked over and saw Paula dismounting her bike at the same time. We transitioned into the run together, mindful of my tendency to hit big or fail spectacularly. Conversely, Paula was a relentless machine. Just like in Japan three and a half years prior, my ability to maintain patience would make or break my race.

Right away, I dropped my water bottle. I also dropped my Nike visor, so I ran back for it and grabbed something to eat, to sneak in some extra nutrition before embarking on what would have to be the run of my life. I would not stand a chance against Paula with anything less. I also vowed to run my own race. I thought of my runs with Erin, sticking close and even passing her on that big day on the island. *I've prepared for this.*

I was ready to take on Paula. I'd never felt so confident. I was truly prepared to match strides against someone that, on any other day, outmatched and intimidated me.

We took off together at a quick pace. At the 5K mark, we passed Aussie Carol Pickard. We bookended her, running up on either side, then blew past, with me a bit ahead of Paula.

At the halfway turnaround, I caught the first-place woman, 1988 women's Tour de France third-place finisher Liz Hepple. After pushing into the lead, I took a quick look back. Where was Paula? I couldn't see her. Just like that, with 15K (9.3 miles) to go, my destiny unfurled like a long red carpet: running strong, in the lead, the fittest female athlete on earth behind me. Do I smile? Pinch myself? Celebrate finally putting it all together?

Not close. *Been there, done that, not interested.* For the next few daunting minutes, though, part of the old Julie did circle back, the one that broke down late in runs, that played not to lose, that didn't give everything. I started thinking, *Why are you running scared? Because it might fall apart on you?* Normally, this messed with my attitude, allowing competitors to pass me and end my hopes. This time, a wiser, more positive inner voice popped up: *You're fine. Just keep running.*

I recently found the 1989 World Cup Gold Coast Triathlon on YouTube, and watched it. I was really *running.* My stride was strong, my chest out, and I really look like an accomplished athlete powering through my miles with confidence and authority rather than grinding. I arrived at the starting line with the training background of a champion, and it was evident.

Finally, the finish line was only a kilometer away. I hadn't heard footsteps, seen shadows, or picked up any hint of a late-race comeback, but I knew Paula Newby-Fraser wasn't one of the two greatest women's triathletes ever because she settled for second. I kept my guard up, but took the chance of grabbing a quick peek behind me. Only empty road. This was not Kona. This was not 1982. There would be no embarrassing, late-race crash-and-burn. This was really happening!

Before entering the stadium for the finish, we ran through a short shaded section behind the bleachers and scaffolding. I was so locked into the runner's zone that I didn't hear a sound nor notice anyone alongside the road, even though several thousand people made plenty of noise. The only thing I heard was an amazing inner dialogue as I pushed for the line:

So THIS is what it's like to win a really big race on merit. WOW!

I'd trained really hard, but I didn't expect this . . .

This is from all the training. Good job, Julie. You did everything to get to this point. Here it is. You WERE the best on the day.

It's so small, really, that small inner acknowledgment. I thought it would be so big, and yet it was as sweet and simple as saying to myself, *good job. You started out this year thinking, What if I show up for a race prepared? No excuses—just show up ready to go? This is what it's like to know, for one day, your best is THE BEST.*

I ran flush into the bright lights and wall of stadium noise. Spectators and top male finishers, including Mark, cheered like hell for me. Mark won his race as well, the fourth time we'd shared the podium at a major international event (we also finished first at the 1985 Japan Ironman, 1986 Avignon Triathlon, and 1988 Sag Sater Sweden Triathlon, which was ¾ of the official Ironman distance). I dashed into the finishing chute, waving, hugging Mark, getting pictures, and giving interviews.

I had fulfilled my goal of being the best among the world's top triathletes on this particular day.

World Cup Gold Coast Triathlon was completely different from any race I'd experienced. It wasn't about winning; it was about capping off a maximum training effort with a race in which I performed at my highest level in all three disciplines.

I'm interviewed at every race in which I compete, and I love the parties, competitor pasta feeds, hanging out with friends in the sport, and side journeys within event stops. If there's a surf spot nearby and the waves are breaking, I might borrow a board and check that out too.

Not in 1989. Not on the Gold Coast. I was so focused on race performance that I didn't even bring the right outfit for the party afterward. Nor did I bring much except my workout gear, bike kit, and racing outfits. I kept asking the same question: *What do I have to do to stay ready?* Well, I needed to stay in the condo, put my feet up, and ignore the waves at Surfer's Paradise. I'd come out on race day.

Beating the No. 1 triathlete in the world is no different than taking down the greatest in any sport. You're on top of the world, if only for a race or game, and everyone hears about it. I felt as proud as anyone that's ever taken down the No. 1. There's no such thing as a perfect race—God, do I know that!—but after almost thirty years, the World Cup Gold Coast Triathlon still comes closest.

Later, I learned that Paula had visa problems that nearly prevented her from entering the race, which might have dinged her mental edge enough to make a difference. Though she never made an excuse, she was really upset. In 1989, Australia refused to admit South African or Zimbabwean athletes due to apartheid, on its dark last legs after the freeing of African National Congress leader Nelson Mandela from thirty-five years of confinement. The prevailing attitude? If you were from South Africa or Zimbabwe, you were guilty by association, no matter your views. Paula is from Zimbabwe, though she lived primarily in the U.S. for over thirty years. Erin disliked Paula intensely because of this issue, causing a peculiar tension between the superstars. Paula is a wonderful, warm, and kind woman, and I don't know I've ever heard her speak of this. As far as I was concerned, she was scrutinized only because she spent her early years in an offending country. Perception is not always fair—or accurate.

Putting Paula's visa issues aside, I reflected on my performance. It traced back to my original commitment for the season. If you commit in a certain way, you open the door to untapped potential—but you have to immerse so deeply that it's sometimes hard to see outside your bubble. It's not something you can think about or visualize. It's more like a concrete mental picture. How do you anchor your vision, or commitment, into your body and mind and lock it in so that it takes shape, grows wings, becomes real? I knew this concept intellectually. Now I *believed* it too.

After Australia, we traveled to the Japan Ironman. I won again, but only because Paula got DQed for a drafting violation on the bike. In the aftermath of my victory, the old Julie reared her head and put an asterisk on the win—*won because of Paula's misfortune.* Then my new Julie attitude snapped me out of it: *Hey! You put yourself in a position to win.* When you put yourself in a position to succeed, something very good often happens. How did I position myself? By crossing the line in second place, not third. Runners-up become race winners when a DQ occurs.

After the race, instead of diminishing my effort by saying things like, "Well, if she wouldn't have been DQed . . ." I was like, "Let's move on to Kona and see what happens." Rather than bluster on the outside (did I mention the 1985 *Tri-Athlete* magazine article?), a current of confidence built within me. My shift was complete.

Sadly, it took Paula and me years to heal our relationship afterward, the healing made necessary because I trained with her dreaded archrival. Today, we have a really nice friendship. If I had to pick one of the two superstars to train with, and one to race against, it couldn't have been more perfect than the way 1989 turned out: train with Erin, race against Paula.

I came into the 1989 Ironman World Championship with the same feeling I would later experience in 2017. I did everything I could, checked off every box, and hit my daily and weekly training goals with more precision than ever. I had two wins to show for it. I repeated the process for Kona.

When we arrived on the Big Island, I had enjoyed my best season, and Mark hadn't lost all year. He was confident he could finally turn aside his running ghosts at Kona and take down Dave Scott after six years of trying. Our joy ran far beyond big races too. We headed to Hawaii less than two months from our wedding.

Would it be a perfect ending to the season? On paper, it looked possible, especially for Mark. However, we were no longer in Japan, the Gold Coast, Europe, or a USTS event. We were dancing again with Kona, the most fickle and complicated competition partner ever. Madame Pele, the volcano goddess, would churn up much different outcomes for us.

CHAPTER 12
Passing the Torch

*S*hould I stay or should I go now?

I surveyed the situation, feeling trapped inside a Clash lyric. The question was pretty simple: Do I shout encouragement to Mark as he runs past me, and then finish my race? Or do I abandon my effort to support his? Do I stay in the race? Or do I "go"—drop out—and watch my fiancé try to supplant the King of Ironman as they slug it out side by side and stride for stride?

A tough choice, because I thought the 1989 Ironman World Championship might provide a winning conclusion to my best racing year of my life.

Many stories and a book have chronicled the showdown between Mark and reigning six-time champion Dave Scott. The race was epic, the greatest marathon duel in Ironman World Championship history. The two warriors ran side by side for 24 of the 26.2 miles, neither giving an inch or a word, neither willing to lose. In an ironic twist, Dave's six titles equaled the number of times Mark had tried and failed in Kona.

On the course, I didn't know the marathon was so hotly contested. I had enough trouble dealing with my own race. While passing my ten-mile mark, I saw them at their Mile 21. Dave kept trying to push the pace, but Mark stuck with him. Dave had once told Mark that the Ironman marathon really began at the sixteen-mile turnaround. Mark trained with that in mind. Could he hang on? Could he get over the same hump—breaking down—that typically waylays me at mid-race, and overcome another late-race disappointment?

I'd entered my rough patch. Besides struggling physically, I was thinking about a race besides my own. You can't do that in any Ironman and maintain the edge to perform well, let alone Kona; she will bend and break you. Besides rooting for Mark, my incentive was eroded by the feeling that I would break down at—you guessed it—the midway point. I came to Kona to win this race, yet five women were ahead with more strong running ladies heading my way, their leg turnover much faster than mine. I had nothing left. I could see myself slipping out of the Top 10, out of the money, a whole lot of hurt about to head my way while the most important moment of Mark's life was unfolding.

Stay? Or go?

Decision time.

We showed up in Kona on a robust momentum wave. This race was about more than facts, figures, and comparisons. It was personal. We were in love, engaged, and two months away from getting married. And Mark had spent 1989 taking dead aim on the only major triathlon he had yet to dominate. As we got swept up in the prerace hype, something occurred to me: how much fun would our wedding in December *really* be if Mark left Kona without a win?

I realized I wanted Mark to win Ironman more than myself, so we would start our marriage in a deeply positive place. I wanted Mark to have this. He worked so hard. He'd been so close. Did I have the confidence he'd do it? I figured that if he shadowed Dave, as he planned, he'd have a damned good chance.

The triathlon world had anticipated a mano a mano showdown since midseason, as Mark and Dave operated at a higher level than the rest of the field. We both enjoyed great seasons, me winning two major races and several podium appearances, and Mark riding a 9–0 undefeated streak—including his impressive, hard-fought win over Dave at the Gold Coast Triathlon.

Mark also beat Dave in St. Croix, along with winning Nice for the sixth time and taking the World Triathlon Championships in Avignon, France; did Grip finally have The Man's number? For Dave's part, he won several short-course races, and the Japan Ironman in the mind-boggling time of eight hours and one minute. Both men won on short courses too. You could almost hear the saloon doors swinging and the streets quieting in anticipation of their showdown.

Though joined in history as two of triathlon's fabled Big Four, Mark and Dave didn't socialize much. They respected each other, and were cordial in public, but they weren't what you call friends. They were very different, right down to their one shared fascination—reading the elements. Mark loved to read the surf, while Dave sharpened his forecasting game when training over the fields and hills around Davis, his home near Sacramento. While most other triathletes found heat and cold, winds, and remote settings to be a turnoff, Dave lived for these conditions. "My other calling was to be a weatherman," he once told *Outside* magazine.

Then there was Kona . . . bewitching, unyielding, ready to take but not so quick to give. Mark and I knew that better than anyone in the field, given our previous disappointments. As the buzz over and Dave mushroomed to atmospheric proportions, like you'd feel in a "match race" environment, Mark understood and appreciated the harsh reality of Kona. "When you come to the Ironman," he told *Triathlete* magazine, "you have to put everything you've done before it in the garbage can."

Our histories at Kona were checkered. I seemed to alternate between a Top 10 finish and DNF, not coming close to victory since 1982. Mark's resume read like a syllabus from the School of Close But No Cigar: DNF. Third. Fifth. DNC (Did Not Compete). Second. Second (and a trip to the hospital). Fifth (suffered two bike tire flats). These are superb results for mere mortals, but Mark wanted the only result that mattered to him. Furthermore, Dave had won five of his six Ironmans at Mark's expense. Despite Mark's season, Dave was the favorite, simply because he had delivered in crunch time at Kona and Mark had not.

I'd like to say I too came into the race with the mental mechanism clear and ready to face down my disappointments. However, Kona wasn't going to make or break my year. Also, I made the mistake of saying and deeply affirming, "If I could win just one big professional race, I'll feel complete." Then I won the Gold Coast and Japan triathlons. Maybe I shouldn't have said just one! And definitely not "complete"; that word tends to bury into the psyche, though I meant it. But in reality, once I got that win, I wanted more.

I first saw Mark on the bike course. I was in the top six after a strong swim and solid ride thus far, and he and Dave were already pushing each other. Thankfully, Mark wasn't trying to "Grip" him into submission so soon, the strategy that cost him here before. He was already doing something different. *Good.*

I saw him next on the marathon course. He and Dave remained side by side, inches apart despite having the whole road to themselves. Neither talked. Both looked straight ahead, oblivious to the entourage that, I noticed, was equally riveted. I was thrilled. *He's doing it! The new racing strategy! Something different!* I was really stoked.

I was also hurting. While not having a horrible race, I was suffering and knew it wasn't my day. My focus and concentration were compromised and distracted as well. When you can't figure out a reason to continue running while sitting in the Top 10, something's missing. *Kona, you got me again.* I wasn't surrendering to the pain, but fighting it, all the while thinking of Mark's race.

I wrestled with my choices for another half mile. If I didn't decide fast, I'd never be able to catch up with Mark and Dave, who were clocking brisk six-minute miles. Then my heart took over. I turned around, reversed course, and started running back in order to get to Mark. I jumped on a course official's scooter for a ride to the press truck, a big flatbed with a railing set up for the media. They stopped long enough for me to climb aboard as Mark and Dave finished Mile 22.

To this day, I feel I made a perfect choice.

Once on the truck, my muscles relaxed, so relieved to be finished running. I spotted Kenny Moore of *Sports Illustrated*. I divulged the *big plan*: "When they get to the bottom of the hill, Mark's going to go," I said. It was a decision Mark made during summer training in Boulder, while sitting at the dinner table. We were discussing the perfect place to make the crucial big move. If you're strong, it's at the base of the hill at the 24-mile mark, where you can use surges to further weaken an opponent's legs that already feel like they've endured fifteen rounds of body punches. Dave, no stranger to winning strategy at Kona, had his own plan too: to surge at the *top* of the hill, and use the final downhill into town to break Mark.

I was unsurprised by what I saw, but inwardly ecstatic: Mark was executing his plan. At this point, I knew it could be his day. He hadn't faded after sixteen miles, his normal "danger zone" at Kona. He looked just as strong at Mile 22.

One person who, I assumed, wasn't happy to see me on the press truck was Dave Scott. One of Dave's Ironman routines is to spot his wife, Anna, during the early stages of the marathon. He felt a nice mental lift and tended to dig deeper whenever he saw Anna and, now, his infant son, Drew. Family time was so precious to Dave that the Scotts typically spent a few days alone on the Big Island, quietly prepping, away from the hubbub of press and fans.

In Kona, Dave and Anna spotted each other a few miles into the marathon. Anna held up Drew, which lit a sizable spark under his Ironman dad. "That's not fair," Mark said as he ran alongside.

Those were the only words Mark spoke the entire race.

I'm sure Dave would consider my close proximity as an unfair advantage, a motivational cue for Mark, maybe even think I was coaching him from the truck. (How comical, the thought of *me* coaching *Mark!*) If Dave only knew how it really worked: *if* Mark noticed I was on the truck, he never let me know. I didn't get an acknowledgment. A gesture of any kind. Nothing.

Mark's way is to get deep inside "the zone" and not come out, which I fully understand as an athlete. Personal feelings have no place on race day, even when engaged couples are running. When Mark got locked in, nothing distracted him. He needed very little from the outside world besides nutrition and drinks. What worked for Dave did not work for Mark. The only thing that mattered was the next stride, and the next.

I looked around, mesmerized by the fact that the normally boisterous, chatty entourage of dozens of cyclists escorting Mark and Dave were so quiet. It was equally quiet on the press truck. Everywhere it was almost silent. No one talked. You could hear a pin drop. It felt eerie in a sense. You could only hear the runners' footsteps. They'd begun running close enough to bump shoulders if they'd wanted. They actually did bump in an aid station. They ratcheted up their battle to a test of guts, determination, and steel-minded willpower few had seen in a race of any kind, let alone an Ironman. For me, it was like jumping onto a party truck, only to find it better resembled the moonlike silence of Haleakala, the dormant volcano on neighboring Maui.

We all need something to push us when the usual motivators don't work. Maybe we call to mind our love for a spouse or concern for a sick friend, how good the food will taste when we're done—or creating something truly magical that draws in the inherent energy of a place. Nothing rolling through Mark's mind pre-Kona touched the phenomenal experience that followed.

As Mark approached the sixteen-mile mark, an image appeared to him in the lava fields. It hovered between his eyes, like a passing daydream, the face of an old shaman healer portrayed in a *Yoga Journal* ad that promoted an upcoming shamanistic training. The shaman in Mark's vision was over 100 years old. Mark had spent much time seeking the connection between his desire to win Ironman and the pain of pounding out marathon miles at a six-minute pace with Dave. It all came together at Mile 16. Mark told me it was a supernatural moment in which the shaman offered his strength—and Mark received it.

On this day, he would not falter down the stretch.

Mark focused on executing the strategy for which we'd trained all summer, and becoming the first to make a move, rather than reacting and hanging on. He emerged like a blade of forged steel. How does someone overcome a previously insurmountable challenge when mind and body aren't always enough? Mark found the answer: draw from deep inside.

Mark later told me he was trying to connect to the spiritual element of the Big Island. He made the connection that he hadn't properly tapped into the elemental energy unique to Hawaii. What happened if he did? He felt drawn to the ancient Hawaiian religion of Huna, or at least its shamanistic aspects, along with the visionaries, healers, and *heiaus,* sacred places or sites. Now, for the first time deep in a Kona race, he thought, *Why fight the pain and distress, this course? Why not just surrender to it?*

That realization is the key to Ironman—surrendering to what the elements and course give you. It's also a critical step on the hero's journey, the Wonder Woman journey. We must let go, surrender, and trust the process. It becomes hard when the world dumps its expectations on us, and, like Mark, we have to figure out how to draw power from surrender while overcoming our rivals in any type of life or work conditions that present themselves.

Mark surrendered to the place and race. He even offered up a little prayer: "Allow me to be here. Whatever you bring, allow me to be here." He did exactly what I *did not do* in 2017, or in many previous Ironmans. He took what the course and conditions gave him. He didn't force anything on the race. Out came a wisdom burnished into his muscles and mind from six losses at Kona. His past struggles with bonking, hitting the wall, further forged a superior willpower. The Grip. This time, Dave was chagrined to find out Mark *did* know how to close at Kona!

Only one question remained: how deeply would Mark reach down to win this race? Will he carry through? Blow out? Find himself back in the hospital? Great athletes push themselves to the furthest extremes to win. Mark's Kona hospitalization in 1987 from overexertion, and the resulting severe abdominal distress, reminded me of an even worse incident. In the late 1970s, the future Boston and New York Marathon champ Alberto Salazar collapsed after valiantly trying to knock four-time Boston winner Bill Rodgers off his perch in the prestigious Falmouth Road Race. Salazar gave so much that his body temperature hit 107°F—a normally fatal number. He even received last rites *at the site.* Mark's situation wasn't that bad, but it was serious enough to make anyone think twice about tackling Kona again. As for Salazar? He survived to become one of the greatest distance coaches in the world.

Mark and Dave arrived at Mile 23. Mark noticed Dave struggling slightly, so he started throwing jabs, little surges, forcing Dave to battle back. Surges work great on uphills, because you control the pace to make your opponent suffer. After they catch up, you burst again, and again, until your little surges have softened the opponent for your upcoming *big move*. The key is to make sure *your* legs can handle the opponent's responses, and to save plenty for the closing push.

Mark threw down this surge strategy after already swimming, biking, and running 137 miles, and flying through the marathon at a six-minute pace, an all-time Ironman marathon record if he could hold it. As I stood in the press truck, I knew that only a Superman could fight off surges like these. Dave certainly proved he was a Super Ironman, time after six previous times. Who would wear the cape today?

We found out very soon. When they reached the Mile 24 aid station, Mark saw his tiny opening, his "cubic centimeter of chance," as Carlos Castaneda put it in *The Teachings of Don Juan*. He took off. He didn't stop or grab a drink, but he sure as hell accelerated. "When it was time to go," he told me afterward, "it was like being shot out of a cannon." Mark was going to conquer his twin Ironman demons, Dave Scott and the final stretch!

All I could think about was how hard Mark had worked for this moment, and the triumphant, celebratory, loving vibe that would permeate our wedding.

Quickly, I jumped off the press truck and tried to shortcut to the finish line before they arrived. It wasn't easy, since I'd just swam, biked, and run all but fifteen miles of the Ironman World Championship myself.

A few minutes later, Mark crossed the line to wild cheers in a record time of 8 hours, 9 minutes, and 14 seconds. Someone gave him an American flag, which he carried across the line to accompany his wall-to-wall smile. He wrapped up his Ironman with a stunning marathon time of 2 hours, 40 minutes—a record that stood until Patrick Lange, one of an incredible crew of Germans racing today, broke it in 2016 with a 2:39:45 on his way to a third-place finish. In 2017, Lange won it all with a new course record time of 8:01:40, beating Craig Alexander's mark of 8:03:56, set in 2011.

To give you an idea of Mark's marathon, imagine yourself running an 18:55 5K. That's a very good time for any recreational runner, just over six minutes per mile. Imagine holding that pace for a marathon, *after* swimming

2.4 miles and biking 112 miles in lava fields and 100°F heat. Now hit that time with your archnemesis working to wear you down.

After almost thirty years, the same word still surfaces when I review this race: *WOW.* It felt so good to support my fiancé on the day he took over the sport.

At the finish line, I chose to let Mark's parents and family congratulate him first. We weren't married yet, and I wanted them to share the moment fully. Mark's dad, Space, was so proud. Space had criticized Mark's initial decision to make a career of triathlon racing, thinking it a fool's waste of time. Now, it must have felt like Mark won Olympic gold. Kona was the grand prize, our virtual Olympics. And Mark was Zeus, standing high atop triathlon's Mount Olympus. Seeing his son ascending as both the world's highest-paid *and* finest triathlete made him beam like any proud father. It was really heartwarming.

Meanwhile, Mark's mother, Sharon, was sobbing. I thought it was because she was so proud of her son, which is very true. But only in 2017, when I watched my son, Mats, suffer for mile after mile in his first Ironman in South Korea, did I understand Sharon's deeper feelings, how this race can reduce mothers to tears. How does a mother resist the urge to run on the course and make it somehow less exerting for her child? It's such an anti-maternal thing to watch your kid run an Ironman.

In Korea for Mats' first Ironman in 2017, I encouraged his girlfriend, Megan, to greet him first at the finish line. I'm sensitive to those who've stood on the sidelines, supporting their loved ones through training and racing. They went through it together; they should celebrate first together.

After the race, I refocused on wedding plans while Mark enjoyed the post-victory buzz. Nike flew him to Oregon for a series of promotions, and his manager, Charlie Graves, lined up other events. Special flyers were sent out, along with press releases, for the *Wide World of Sports* broadcast, what people were starting to call an "Iron War." I loved seeing Mark reap his rewards. He deserved it. He conquered his twin demons, Dave Scott and Kona, to complete a perfect 10–0 season. How anyone goes undefeated for an entire year of triathlons, I don't know. So many things can go wrong.

Our wedding took place at Neimans in Carlsbad, a restaurant my brother, Marshall, managed. Originally known as the Twin Inns and built in 1896 on the corner of Carlsbad Village Drive (formerly Elm Avenue) and Carlsbad Boulevard, the majestic, three-story white Victorian is listed on the National Register of Historic Places. For the stars of Hollywood's Golden Age, the Twin Inns became a favorite restaurant stop between Hollywood and the Del Mar Racetrack. The Duke Room was named for frequent guest John Wayne. Cindy Conner's mother used to take FBI Director J. Edgar Hoover to lunch at the Twin Inns and then off to bet the ponies at Del Mar. We Carlsbad kids took great pride in the Twin Inns' grandeur, its distinctive chicken marquee, and its history; it was built by two of Carlsbad's original land barons, Gerhard Schutte and D. D. Wadsworth. They developed the property while the Southern California Railroad connected Carlsbad to the world. In 1976, my high school senior class picture was taken there.

I spent the night before our wedding in a Carlsbad hotel with my college roomie, Lisette, and her husband, Ben. However, on our wedding day, I did something a bit differently: I got up at 4:45 A.M. and drove to Mission Bay to run with my teammates, the Magic Bullets. David Lesley, who coached me for years, paced me to a sub 1:24 half marathon, a strong workout time. I took the leftover tulle from my wedding dress and stapled it to my visor. Throughout the run, folks congratulated me as I passed them.

The downside? I was the first who wanted to leave my own wedding. I was so tired.

Our big day arrived. We would marry in the majestic central ballroom of the Twin Inns, a round room wrapped by windows. We had every reason to celebrate. We were in my hometown, with our friends, and with Mark riding the crest of his greatest life achievement. Twenty million people had just watched the Iron War on TV. We were pretty popular in our crowd of family and friends.

The guest list kept growing until we recited vows, it seemed. While trying to accommodate this ever-increasing horde, which included the who's who of triathlon, I realized how far we'd come since my first Ironman. We weren't a disconnected smattering of triathletes anymore. We were a full-blown community. In seven short years, we'd gone from being a freak show to among the most admired groups of athletes in the world. We'd also become a tight crew, for the most part.

At my wedding, I met Wendy Ingraham ("Wingnut"), who came as Mark Montgomery's date. Wendy had just returned from an ultra event in Brazil with a super tan, legs up to her neck, and a little black dress borrowed from Paula Newby-Fraser, two sizes too small. Wendy's legs were there for all to see. My first words to her were, "You know, you're not supposed to upstage the bride at her own wedding!" I was joking, and we've been good friends ever since, but Wendy, I admit, those legs were showstoppers!

"I'd never met Julie before that day," Wendy recalled. "I'd only really gotten to know who she was during the past few years, after I'd become a triathlete. I'm not sure what she was so worried about on her wedding day, because she looked fantastic, like the happiest girl on earth. And after her wedding day, we became good friends and got together whenever we could for workouts and visits."

A few years later, in 1997, "Wing," as many of us still call her, joined me in the "crawl across the line" club when she and Sian Welch finished off a historic duel in Kona by *both* crawling across.

Our wedding featured many little touches that reflected our love for each other. Our officiant, Carol Janis, wore a vestment we bought in Guatemala in 1987. Mark didn't know it was a vestment at first, thinking it a beautiful work of embroidery, but it came in handy for the ceremony. My attendants were Sue Robison, Lisette, and our housemate, Alana. Her daughter, born three years before in the hot tub of our sunroom in Vista, was our flower girl. Mark's attendants included his younger brother, Gary; his half brother, Bobby; my brother, Marshall; former triathlete George Hoover; Mark's massage therapist, Mike; and his high school friend Eric.

My mom handled the flower arrangements. A very frugal woman, she decided we could replicate a florist's touch for pennies on the dollar. Her plan was to force-bloom paperwhites, or narcissus. It's a pretty foolproof flower bulb to force. Earlier, we planted enough to make three pots of paperwhites for each of our forty tables. The scent of 120 pots of blooming paperwhites could cover up the smell of a toxic dump, but they were inexpensive and really pretty and went with our "Christmas on the Cheap" theme.

My grandfather, Henri Tubach, walked me down the aisle. Grandpa T was the world's proudest ninety-five-year-old man as we proceeded toward the wedding party, looking fabulous in his tux and tails. He and Mark decided they alone would wear tails; the other groomsmen were in standard tuxes. Grandpa T gave us a wonderful toast as well: "To Mark and Julie, may you be champion lovers for life." Today, Mats carries Henri as his middle name.

Also on hand for our big day was my father, who I decided to invite though I had not seen him since my high school graduation, thirteen years before. He came in a sign of reconciliation, which began a process of integrating him into my adult life. Sadly, he passed three years later.

For our honeymoon, we originally thought about embarking on a romantic getaway with plenty of surfing. Bali, Tahiti, Fiji, and Tavarua floated through our minds. However, we set off instead for Santa Fe and Taos, a good 800 miles from any ocean. It wasn't for lack of trying. We kept seeking places in the South Pacific, but airfares and room rates were astronomically high. Of course they were: It was December, high season for the South Pacific. We didn't know any better. For the past six years, we'd been in the enviable position of having tickets booked for races, special events, TV shoots, and our other duties. Our surf-related plan fell out the window.

During the year, we'd talked about remodeling our Cardiff home in the classic Spanish style. Now it was more than talk. We were going to use our off-season to move on it. For that reason, we chose to head to Santa Fe, eat some good food, walk around and gather ideas, and then ski in Taos for a couple of days. It was a very practical, pragmatic decision. (Remember our engagement night talk?)

I really enjoyed Santa Fe. Its centuries-old artist colony still attracts painters and sculptors who work in studios along Canyon Road, the classic main street. We walked around this architectural and archaeological wonderland, studying numerous buildings in the Spanish pueblo style we both loved. We stayed at La Fonda on the Plaza and upgraded to the King Room;

after all, I was married to the King of Ironman, right? Our room was luxurious, with indigenous, handcrafted Southwestern décor, an inviting Kiva fireplace, and a private balcony and rooftop terrace that gave us a great view. Our best meal happened at El Farol, a tapas restaurant, where we enjoyed live music, a flamenco dance show, and Wild West–style bullet holes in the front of the bar!

From Santa Fe, we drove north to Abiquiu to see the great artist Georgia O'Keeffe's home and works. I looked forward to studying her portraits of enlarged flowers, New York skyscrapers, and New Mexico landscapes from her home studio. Our visit recalled my lifelong admiration of powerful women and role models that began when I watched Anne Francis in *Honey West*. In her life and work, Georgia was very badass, "The Mother of American Modernism." She was also a great wife and creative partner to famed photographer and art promoter Alfred Stieglitz.

I could easily see parallels between Georgia and Alfred in Mark and me. Both were successful in their respective fields before joining their lives together, to grow something exclusively their own. It seemed like the life we'd begun. I also learned that my quest to be at Mark's side was not the most famous case of determination in the relationship world. From 1915 until 1946, Georgia and Alfred exchanged about 25,000 pages of letters. Sometimes, they'd write three letters of up to forty pages per day! Their letters reveal a relationship that evolved from admirers to lovers to spouses to exasperated long-marrieds. The first volume of these letters came out in 2017. Within one sits my favorite quote: "You—believing in me—that making me belief in myself—has made it possible to be myself."

With that strong, beautiful affirmation of love and commitment, we headed into the 1990s atop not only the triathlon world, but our own world as well.

CHAPTER 13
Shifting Focus

I felt done. Burned out and completely done, having achieved the goal outcomes for which I'd been striving since 1982: a strong relationship, success in triathlon, and finding purpose in my life. Ironman, triathlon, and I grew up together. I felt great purpose in racing and promoting the sport. Plus, I was in love and married to the fittest man in the world. My 1989 season was so fantastic, with the two major victories and Mark's first Ironman World Championship, I wondered: *Is this it? Does it get any better than this?* After all, I was thirty-one—how does it get better *after* thirty?

What else could there be?

Every professional athlete faces this question and feeling at some point, and it's an issue. Scott Tinley writes beautifully in his book, *Racing the Sunset,* about how tough it is for an athlete to walk away from the cheering, adulation, and adrenaline of competition and being on center stage. Not to mention walking away from something at which you've been a major success. I'd been racing for nine seasons, a long haul in professional triathlon. I didn't know if I would ever train six to eight hours per day again, or if I even wanted to step on the line. I saw what it took for Mark to keep up his championship training. Sometimes I felt like working hard. Sometimes I didn't. The very thought of Mark's regimen drained me. Perhaps, if some competitive opportunities knocked that didn't involve racing for ten or eleven hours at a time, I would jump back in. Why throw more wear and tear on my body for a mediocre result when there were other spectacular things I could be a part of?

I spent much of 1990 distracted from racing. We were elated newlyweds remodeling our Cardiff home after the honeymoon/scouting trip to Santa Fe. The remodel was well underway by the time we left for Boulder during the summer, so we left the project with our friends and neighbors, Steve and Becky Bedford. When we came back in the fall, it was done.

Meanwhile, Mark's weekly workouts boggled my mind: 350 miles of cycling, 60 to 65 miles of running, and 10 miles of swimming, much of it at very fast speeds. Just before heading back to Kona, he knocked off five 300-meter swim intervals in under three minutes apiece. That's borderline speedboat, an "Animallen" moment. His coach, Jeff Milton, told *City Sports*, "It's the fastest I've ever seen someone do that workout."

In supporting his success, I had the distinct advantage of knowing what it took to compete for Ironman titles. I'd been telling Mark since 1982 that he could become the world's most dominant triathlete. Now that he was, he openly welcomed my decision to focus on his training and racing instead of my own. "It's helped a lot. The last couple of years when we were racing together, we'd both be stressed out at the same time. So, say someone needed to go to the store, neither of us would want to," he told our good friend at *Competitor*, publisher-editor Bob Babbitt.

Seven years later, Mark would return the favor.

We flew to Chile for the Pucon Triathlon in 1990. A year earlier, we had arrived with our relationship status an open question. At least in my mind. Now, my husband successfully defended his title, while I recorded a Top 5 finish. Later, we won the men's and women's titles at the Säter Sweden Triathlon, the fourth (and final) time we shared the podium—but our first as husband and wife. I also returned to Kona, where I lasted for six miles of the run before shutting it down to focus on Mark's successful defense of his title.

I felt ready to have a good Ironman, but my race sucked from the beginning. Without a clear vision, I had no backup plan. I couldn't muster the willpower to push past the pain and lean into the abyss into which I so willingly dove in 1982. In many ways, I'd turned into the opposite of that young woman. My perception of success left me unprepared to face the dark reality of those final miles. I resigned myself to thinking it wasn't a big deal, and if I dropped at six miles, I would at least be at the finish to meet Mark.

My decision cost me. I gave up on the most essential part of myself: the girl who would do anything to get across the finish line.

That became the motivating factor behind my races in 1991.

I burned with desire to become a better distance runner. I needed to settle a score with naysayers who didn't feel I was a strong runner. It bugged me. I'd hear things like, "She's all right in the run, but late in the race . . ." or, "she's such a good swimmer and cyclist, but that run . . ." Despite my success, I was still known as the girl who didn't run very well. What if I took all this cross-training and applied it to running? It was winter, we were in San Diego, and I knew the Olympic Trials were coming in a year. I thought, *Well, let's see what you can do.*

I started training with David Lesley and his Magic Bullet team, the group with which I ran a swift thirteen miles the morning of my wedding. This motley collection of educators, scientists, and researchers loved to run, and then head off to work and positively influence young minds, or work on their vital projects. We shared a series of soul-forging and champion-building workouts, and I found myself feeling fresh and excited about attacking workouts again. It didn't feel like competing either. I was just getting after it.

David Lesley is the only running coach I've ever had. He believed in my running and guided me as a pure runner, not as a triathlete who runs. Believe me, people make a distinction. "One of the things that impressed me right away about Julie is that she did not want to be known as a triathlete running a marathon. She wanted to be known as a marathoner trying to get into the Olympics," David recalled. "She didn't train with us all that much, but when she did, everyone was happy to have her. And I became really impressed with her work and her results; honestly, I did not see a 2:40-something marathoner in her at first. She made sure to hit the time and distance on every workout, and understood how precise I was about it. We ended up having three or four women doing 2:40-somethings."

David and I built a bond that continues to this day. He is the perfect example of a coach whose belief in you precedes your belief in yourself, one of the greatest gifts a coach can offer. David's strength was breaking down the numbers, not surprising, since he was the chair of the math department at San Diego State.

The Magic Bullets were very supportive of each other. We had some friendly, competitive rivalries, especially Sam Howland, Oonagh Bruni, and me. We met for Tuesday and Thursday workouts, and a long weekend run. On Tuesdays, we met at the Salk Institute for sprint intervals. One workout called for a series of two minutes of hard running with two-minute breaks. On another, we ran three minutes at roughly race pace, then one minute of sprinting, followed by three minutes at race speed, one minute of sprinting . . . tough stuff. On Thursdays, we'd go to the track and knock off mile repeats, which I learned to hate. The two-mile repeats on the roads served me better.

I trained with one goal: getting to the Boston Marathon, and running the Olympic standard of 2 hours, 45 minutes so I could compete in the 1992 Olympic Trials. In 1991, Mark and I headed to Boulder for our annual summer trip, where I ran extensively while he focused on Ironman. After we came home, I trained with the Magic Bullets. I wanted to run a 400-mile month over the winter, which I did, followed by these incredible sprint and interval workouts. A good example is the last big workout we did before Boston, a set of six two-mile repeats. We ran to a strict clock, starting a two-mile repeat every sixteen minutes. The faster we finished, the more rest we got. I finished in under twelve minutes each time, gaining roughly four minutes of rest. After that workout, I thought, "I'm ready."

I made it into Boston with a well-placed phone call. Dave McGillivray was the technical director, so I talked him into bringing me out. There's a lot to be said for street cred, since at that time, you normally got into Boston by one route—qualifying by time. A few years later, in 1996, David did such a good job with the 100th anniversary Boston Marathon that they promoted him to race director, where he's since presided over a huge uptick in participation. In 1995, Boston had about 9,100 runners. In 2014, the "Boston Strong" year after the horrible bombing, there were 35,000 competitors (including the 8,000 who didn't finish the tragic race)—and well over a million spectators. Every runner in 2014 can thank Dave and his team for standing resolute in the face of terrorism. They generated an atmosphere of such love, strength, courage, and support that competitors in that race still get chills when they think about it. One random fan told a finisher, "Thank you for making Boston smile again." Dave still faithfully carries out his annual tradition of running the entire course after most of the runners have finished.

To qualify for the Olympic Trials, I needed to average 6:18 per mile. The course lent itself to a strong time if I didn't push the first half too hard, which in Boston is a challenge: the first three miles are downhill, and it remains generally flat or with downhill tendencies all the way to Newton Lower Falls at seventeen miles. That's when the four Newton hills appear, culminating in the infamous Heartbreak Hill at Mile 21. None of the hills are particularly tough on their own, especially for one who trained in Southern California and Colorado, but when you put them together over a four-mile stretch, after having already run seventeen miles . . . that's why most Boston races are won or lost in the hills.

After Heartbreak, if you still have your legs, the experience is one of the most sensational in marathon—two miles of flying downhill, thousands of people screaming at you as if you're the only person on the course, and then a flat stretch that takes you past the Citgo gasoline sign and Fenway Park. *One mile to go.* A couple of turns later—*right on Hereford, left on Boylston*—and you're onto the final 600-meter finishing stretch along Boylston Street.

I had such a blast in Boston that I took Lisette back to run with me in 2004—her last marathon until the 2018 Paris Marathon, which we ran together. I even got cheeky with a guy at the top of Heartbreak, who looked like he was hurting. "Hey, where's Heartbreak Hill?" I asked.

"We just came up it," he said, huffing and puffing.

I smiled. "Okay. Thank you. Bye!"

That was my smart-ass way of letting off steam and lightening the mood. The atmosphere had become too somber. I could have said nothing, but it felt both lighthearted and even a little bit funny—to myself, anyway—to say that. I got my ten-mile PR on the first part of the course, breaking an hour, not surprising considering the layout. I slowed down in the hills, but I still averaged 6:24 per mile and ran a 2:47:19, just over two minutes off the qualifying standard. I was also the twentieth woman to cross the line. It was thrilling to almost become an Olympic Trials marathon qualifier. Maybe I *was* more than a triathlete who faded during the run . . .

I really wanted another shot at an Olympic qualifying slot, to race against stars like four-time Boston runner-up Kim Jones, Lynn Nelson, Nancy Ditz, Cathy O'Brien, forty-year-old Francie Larrieu, Lesley Ann Lehane, and others. Francie, six years older than me, made every Olympic team from 1976–92 at distances from 1,500 to 10,000 meters. She also set the world indoor mile record. (She would reach her fifth consecutive Olympics, placing third in the trials in 2:30:39.) That boggled my mind; how can *anyone* be so good at forty? Her reward was carrying the U.S. flag into the stadium in Barcelona for the opening ceremony.

I traveled to the Twin Cities Marathon in Minneapolis and tried again, but dropped out after twenty miles because I could not imagine hurting that much for another six miles. I didn't have somebody that I could latch onto. I needed someone like David Lesley running by my side, encouraging me. I felt alone.

I couldn't hold onto my pace. I'm not sure how much of it was physical, because I didn't run the full twenty-six miles. I didn't have the mental capacity to hang on. All it would have taken is one runner moving past and saying, "You're doing fine! Let's go. We're on pace to run 2:45!" I had all my paces and splits written on my arm, but there were no more fast miles within me.

From this, I began to understand how powerful it is to give voice to somebody, to approach struggling runners and say, "Hey, you can do this. Just stay with me." It picks up passing runners too. Simple acts of kind motivation in tough times work; that's why we love motivational stories. I eventually did something bigger with this when Kathleen McCartney and I started the Iron Icons speaking series in 2013.

The level of pain also astonished me. On the surface, it makes no sense: why would an Ironman triathlete who sticks it out for ten or eleven hours in furnace-like conditions struggle with pain in a twenty-six-mile race that takes less than three hours?

It's about pace. Marathon racing is much, much faster. At Boston and Twin Cities, I was running sub-6:25 miles, versus 8- to 9-minute miles in the Ironman. With a marathon, I run at my very best, mile after mile, and then I have to summon even *better* miles to finish. A former top age-group runner and finisher of more than 100 marathons, sports journalist James Raia likes to say, "A marathon is a twenty-mile run followed by a 10K race." I wasn't ready for a 10K in Minnesota.

I didn't completely abandon triathlons—at least not physically. Apparently, I was so checked out mentally that it took an afternoon of going through old race results recently to realize I'd made the podium in the Easter Island Off Road Triathlon and Margarita Island Triathlon in Venezuela in 1991. It was quite a Latin and South American year for Mark and me, since we also enjoyed a delayed honeymoon in Costa Rica that featured what we'd originally wanted in our post-wedding getaway—surf, sun, and relaxation.

If I felt burned out from racing after 1989 and 1990, it was small potatoes compared to how I felt after 1991.

By 1992, I was supporting the Virtuoso, which Mark had become. He was at the height of his powers. Between 1989 and early 1991, he put together a twenty-two-race winning streak, lost once, then won everything else in 1991—including his third straight Kona. He returned to Nice, where he'd won five times before taking two years away, and started another five-race winning streak.

After Nice, CBS needed someone to fly to London and do voiceover analysis with Phil Liggett, the future voice of the Tour de France on Eurosport (and NBC Sports Network). Would I be interested? I'd planned a trip to Italy's Lake Maggiore with my brother, Marshall. We headed to Italy and had a great time, and then I caught a train to Paris and flew to London.

I sat all day in a production booth doing voiceover with Phil. After we finished, I hurried to a kiosk in the West End and bought a ticket to the musical *Blood Brothers*. There was a bit of time to kill, so I popped into a pub for a pint. When I walked over to the Phoenix Theatre, the street was cordoned off. Within two minutes, Princess Diana pulled up in a vintage Jaguar. Not bad for twenty-four hours in London!

The broadcasting experience was fun, something worthy of exploring in the future. However, Mark and I had other plans: starting our family. We aimed for a post-Kona delivery, so Mark could have maximum time with the baby and help me during his off-season. Unfortunately, I didn't get pregnant right away. We rolled it over to 1993, and then it happened.

CHAPTER 14
Baby Grip Arrives

The pop woke me up. My water had broken, and our baby would arrive a couple of weeks early.

I was starting labor with a guest in our guestroom. A business associate of Mark's came to town on Monday, November 15; my due date was December 1. He joined us for dinner at En Fuego in Del Mar, after which we strolled up to the Del Mar Plaza. On the way back to the car, a Braxton Hicks contraction fired across my abdomen, forcing me to grab the stairwell. As I crawled into bed a bit later, I felt Thanksgiving-turkey-with-all-the-trimmings full.

Finally, at age thirty-five, after postponing parenthood for my triathlon career, I was about to become a mother.

At 2:00 A.M. I called the Best Start Birth Center. An attendant told me to pass through labor at home and to check my temperature every hour. Since my water had broken, they wanted to rule out any chance of infection. Next, I called my mother, who had remarried and lived in Sedona, Arizona, with my stepfather, John. "Pack up and come over," I said.

Our overnight guest departed about ten hours later. Mark and I walked down to nearby Cardiff Reef for a surf check. While scrabbling over the big rocks that protect the berm at Pipes Beach, our local break, my contractions began to intensify, closing in like wave intervals from a building storm.

When I talked to Best Start, they'd said to come in when contractions hit two to three minutes apart. By 5:00 P.M., fifteen hours had passed, and I was *really* ready to have this child. I put on my first and only maternity outfit, which the ever-trendy Lisette passed down. It consisted of stylish red pants and a top with colorful, embroidered ethnic designs. We'd just visited her, her husband, Ben, older son, Cyrus, and new baby, Mark in Bakersfield the week before, after spending the weekend at a retreat for Dance of the Deer, a spiritual group focused on Huichol shamanism that Mark had been following more deeply since his first Ironman victory. Before we headed back to Cardiff, she gave me the outfit.

Setty and I shared a healing ceremony at Dance of the Deer to bless and fortify our future pregnancies. After suffering through an ectopic pregnancy, which led to emergency surgery and fertility complications, she was unable to conceive for years and adopted her son Cyrus in 1990. Now she was pregnant—and protecting that pregnancy with everything in her calm, strong nature. "The reason why I did the ceremony was because Mark had a vision, which I really trusted, and he said by going through the ceremony, I would receive the healing that would help me get pregnant," Lisette said. "I thought, *why not?* Julie and I both participated . . . and we both got pregnant."

Our sons were born one month apart, Mark on October 19, and Mats on November 18. Setty's busy life and high-risk pregnancy kept her close to home, while I remained in Colorado from late May until September. We raised our sons together, erasing any regret from not sharing our pregnancies more.

We arrived at the birthing center. The Best Start midwives examined me and gave me the thumbs-down. They said I was less than three centimeters dilated—still early labor—and sent me home. I couldn't believe it. After contracting for seventeen hours, it's like I hadn't even reached T1, the first triathlon transition! Leave it to me, and the baby inside, to turn childbirth into a grueling endurance event.

By 2:00 A.M., a full twenty-four hours after labor set in, I was back on the phone, pleading with the attendants to readmit me.

They gave us the green light. I took the then-recommended two table-spoons of castor oil to promote labor, and we drove back to the birthing center. We brought along my ice chest, which I'd packed with the kind of solid nutrition you use when marathon or triathlon training. I made ice cubes out of Cytomax, and brought along GUs, lightly caffeinated electro-lyte and protein packets that provide nice energy bursts midrace. Unlike most hospitals, the birthing center encouraged expectant mothers to eat to maintain their strength. No Snickers bars on this trip!

There was a problem though. Two tablespoons of castor oil can create havoc; it certainly did with me. During our ride to the hospital, I suffered from severe nausea and vomited all over my cute maternity outfit. So sorry, Setty.

I believed my participation in endurance events would help with labor. I was used to pain. I could tolerate and work through vast amounts of it. How much harder could having a baby be? I told myself that contractions were only ninety-second pain bursts with breaks in between, whereas races were nonstop pain. The effort of a ninety-second contraction would be no different than, say, a ninety-second sprint interval after already training for several hours . . . right? It would hurt, but the pain would subside. This mental approach calmed me throughout my pregnancy. How would it work now, twenty-four hours in, with the baby seemingly content to keep hanging out in my womb?

The baby clung to its final moments in the womb. The nurses put on a belly band and instructed me to start climbing stairs, which I did, repeatedly. I worked with the pain of each contraction as I walked, focusing on my breath with each push through. I could have done this all night, were I not so exhausted from lack of sleep. Finally, the midwives and I mutually decided I needed to lie down. If I got a couple of hours of good sleep, they said, I would wake up fresh and ready to rock the baby out.

Mark and I chose Best Start because it was the longest-established freestanding birth center in Southern California; these facilities were uncommon in the early 1990s. While physicians were on call, they did not actually practice in the center. We liked that. Deliveries were handled by midwives. Best Start also featured the Bradley Method of father-coached natural childbirth, and a water birth option. Our former housemate, Alana, gave birth in our hot tub, a phenomenal experience. However, Mark and I decided that approach was a little too rustic for us.

We planned the pregnancy thoroughly. When we arrived at our second window of opportunity in February 1993, after not getting pregnant the year before, we conceived knowingly, the most intimate moment of our relationship. The baby was conceived on one of two nights. One was very moving and loving, the other completely silly and full of laughter. Much like Mats is today; he formed from the incredible energy and exchanged love of those two nights, and it helped define his essential self in a perceptible way.

I began my pregnancy like any good athlete: by squeezing in as much travel, competition, and training as I could, while I could.

Shortly after confirming my pregnancy, I lined up at the start of the Carlsbad 5000, the elite international road race held since 1986 on three major downtown streets of my childhood: Grand Avenue, Carlsbad Boulevard, and Elm Avenue (now Carlsbad Village Drive). The Carlsbad 5000 was started by the charming Steve Scott, the former American mile record holder, later the fine track and cross-country coach at Cal State University in nearby San Marcos. Steve also won the first Carlsbad 5000. Today, the race is billed as "The Fastest 5K road race in the world." With Olympic and U.S. champions hitting times of thirteen minutes for men, and low fifteen minutes for women, you can't argue. It was wild to see elites run this fast down the same streets on which we rode bikes and skateboards as kids.

I asked my doctor about running the Carlsbad 5K, since I planned to race hard after training all winter. He knew I was an Ironman and unconcerned with the distance, but what about my heart rate? I'd recently run a quick 17:39 5K and knew how hard it felt on my cardiovascular system, as well as my body. My heart pounded an average of 185 beats per minute, up from my resting pulse of 48 to 52.

The doctor asked, "Can you carry on a conversation without feeling out of breath at 185?"

"Obviously not."

His message was clear: *If I can't talk, then I can't run.* I started, but jogged and chatted with friends while they competed. I watched as Zimbabwe's

Philemon Hanneck won the men's elite race in a blazing 13:22 and Shelly Steely blitzed the women's field in 15:36.

Eleven days later, I sat in Winter Park, Colorado, for my friend Eney Jones's "Mountain Mermaid" wedding to Jeff Writer. I flew solo; Mark had left on a Dance of the Deer retreat. Eney, a two-time cover girl for *Triathlete* magazine, was a tremendous swimmer. She often led the swimming portion of races with Wing, my friend and great triathlete Wendy Ingraham. Wing and I had remained close friends since her splashy "hot legs" introduction at my wedding.

Eney planned a fun weekend of downhill skiing and cross-country skiing. Much as I wanted to fly down the mountain with everyone else, I opted for cross-country, the safer bet for a newly pregnant woman. I might be a thrill seeker and risk-taker, but I knew how to shift into mommy mode while carrying my precious child.

It didn't take long for trouble to find me though. Within two long strides on the narrow Nordic rental skis, I fell back and landed hard on my tailbone, knocking my breath out. My tailbone felt fine, so I continued skiing.

The wedding was a hit. Eney bought matching cowboy boots for her bridesmaids, which included Wing, Shannon Delaney, a college friend, and me. We did something unconventional—hiking through the late season snow to a rustic lodge, where the ceremony was held. Given our love of Colorado, and the great relationship between the Rocky Mountain State and triathletes, it seemed more fitting than pulling up in a stretch limo.

When Easter Sunday dawned the next morning, I found myself lying in a good-sized pool of blood. *WTF?* Immediately, I thought of my fall on the cross-country skis, and beat myself up over the stupidity of deciding to ski. Why did I always think I could do anything and everything? Why did I have to be the Queen of FOMO (Fear Of Missing Out)? *Was my baby all right?* Guilt, regret, and despair filled my heart. "I don't want to have my irresponsible actions put a cloud over the wedding," I told Shannon.

Still bleeding, I flew home and called my obstetrician first thing the next morning. "It sounds like a miscarriage," he said, "but come in and we'll check it out."

After physically examining me, the doctor gave me a fetal ultrasound to confirm his suspicions—that I might have suffered a miscarriage. I was crushed. What had I done? Frozen by sadness and fear, I waited as he moved the transducer across my belly, bracing for the dreadful news . . .

"The heartbeat is strong; the baby is fine," the doctor said.

Our weasel was alive and well. I'd been given a second chance. In that moment, my greatest loss became my greatest gift. The universe was giving me a do-over. I wanted to take care of this tiny baby more than anything else in my life. I finished my pregnancy risk- and incident-free.

Due to the scare, we opted for an early amniocentesis procedure at twelve weeks. There was another reason for the procedure as well. Mark's brother, David, was born with Down syndrome, a condition passed along genetically. Mark wanted to be prepared for that possibility. In addition, insurance guidelines strongly recommended an amnio for advanced maternal age, geriatric pregnancy, and high-risk pregnancies. That was me. I was only thirty-five—why the senior citizen references? We did, however, choose to learn our child's gender after the birth.

I continued to work out, but far more carefully. I lasted until October 30, two days after the 1993 Ironman. I noticed the buoys still on the swim course, and decided to go for a dip, three weeks from giving birth. As I reached the buoy in front of the Royal Kona Resort, a quarter mile out, I felt a couple of strong Braxton Hicks contractions. Since the near-miscarriage, I held my breath whenever I felt *anything* from my stomach, womb, or lower abdomen. I took some deep breaths, rolled onto my back and floated. While the contractions subsided, I thought about swimming to the mile marker buoy. However, I decided to turn around. As I swam back, I thought to myself, *how will I be able to tell if my water just broke out there?* Certainly, it could make the cut for a future *Bad Moms* movie!

It was time to become even more careful.

Later that week, Mark and I flew home for my baby shower, which took place November 7. I had such fun with the girls, which included Sue Robison and plenty of triathlon friends, including Ironman superstar Paula Newby-Fraser, Leslie Engel, Shannon Delaney, Janet Hoover, Sian Welch, Janet Wendle, and Patty Mackle, a State lifeguard friend and wife of professional triathlete Rob Mackle. My mom, Aunt Bev Castleberry, and Cousin Wendy Castleberry joined the fun.

The shower motivated me to finish the baby's room. I was given a crib previously used by several babies, their names written on the bottom with a sharpie to show the pass-along history. I repainted it into a tropical theme with blue and green sponge painting, and glued wooden tropical fish to the head and foot. Later, I added Mats's name and passed the crib to another family in short order; he only stayed in it for two days. We even had a "fashion show" moment, when I modeled a nursing bra over my elegant outfit. I wore a purple floral tunic and purple silk pants, something I made in Thailand when we ran the Phuket Triathlon the previous year.

After three hours of sleep hooked up to a fetal monitor, the midwives woke me at 6:00 A.M. I didn't feel any closer to having the baby than twenty-four hours before. They gently explained that I was having trouble surrendering to the birth process. "Labor and birth is really out of your hands," one of my attendants said, "but definitely controlled by nature. By 'going' with it, it usually makes the experience less stressful. Less stress will give you a better outcome."

She may as well have described an Ironman push. However, labor bewildered me. I was used to being in control of my body and pushing through pain, but labor is more about surrendering. The midwife also explained that pregnant athletes can have longer second-stage labor because their pelvic floor muscles do not yield as easily. The good news? I have a strong pelvic floor. The bad news? I'm a control freak.

Great.

The midwives grew increasingly concerned. They talked about lightly inducing labor by administering Pitocin, the synthetic version of oxytocin, a natural substance in our bodies that causes the uterus to contract. If your body doesn't produce enough oxytocin, Pitocin can provide the needed boost to get the job done. However, Best Start could not legally administer Pitocin, or any labor-inducing substance. We had to go to the hospital.

Mark and I walked 150 yards to Scripps Mercy Hospital. When I arrived, I'd only dilated to four centimeters. I was hooked up to an IV to receive the Pitocin. They started me on very small doses, slowly increasing until a strong, regular pattern of contractions developed. By 2:00 P.M., "Vitamin P" had kicked in, and mid- to late-stage labor finally began. We were thirty-six hours into labor . . . I could only think of it as the time equivalent of back-to-back-to-back Ironmans.

"Vitamin P" proved to be a go-no-go situation. Eight more hours passed with plenty of contractions, but no results. I begged the duty nurse to check my progress. She told me that, because of the fear of infection, she would only check me if I was considering an epidural.

"I most certainly am!" I exclaimed. I was getting a bit tired of waiting for this baby to emerge.

"You're about six centimeters now."

"What is the best I could progress naturally?"

Her reply came quickly. "About four hours."

I thought about it. Four hours . . . a marathon at a roughly nine-minute-per-mile pace. *Doable.* I thought of the effort, the pain I'd endured in Kona, always in the latter stages . . . body depleted, trying to finish . . . not going to make it on one can of Exceed nutritional drink and ice chips . . .

"Bring in the anesthesiologist," I said. Moments later, Dr. DeReamer arrived. True to his surname, he turned my late-stage labor into a dream.

Our good friend Shana Menaker offered to be our impromptu doula, or trained labor coach. Shana taught modern and improvisational dance and yoga for dancers at four different colleges in adjacent Orange County. I especially appreciated her assistance, which made it possible for Mark to completely support me. Shana was a nice buffer when things grew intense before the epidural kicked in. Mark and I made a better team with her there, holding space and coaching us.

At some point, I fell asleep again. At 5:00 A.M., two days and three hours after my first contraction, I awoke and gazed lovingly at Mark and Shana. They were sound asleep in their respective reclining chairs. I woke them up with a tired glow warming my face. "It's showtime," I said.

Two hours later, at 7:03 A.M., and with the aid of forceps, Mats was born. He "only" took fifty-three hours to make his appearance. If you're only going to have one baby, well, I got my money's worth.

CHAPTER 15
Out of the Spotlight

I n 1997, *Triathlete* magazine came calling for a story far different than my "Material Girl" cover girl appearance twelve years before. With Mark sitting at the table and Mats playing nearby, our lives could not have changed more. Nor could the conversation: *Triathlete* visited to ask Mark about his retirement, and me about my decision to return to Ironman after a seven-year absence. Meanwhile, in other news, *Outside* magazine now dubbed us "The First Family of Fitness." Heady stuff.

The visit began with a tour of our Cardiff house, described by *Triathlete* as "a beautiful Spanish Mediterranean home surrounded by bougainvillea, cactus, and willow trees." We showed them our special wall and its sculptures and masks from around the world, featuring a shamanistic aboriginal painting, *Dream Time*. Mark had collected the masks, paintings, and the ultimate aboriginal instrument, a five-foot-long didgeridoo (which he played at dinner parties), before getting serious with Huichol Shamanism. The Huichols created their own form of art, applying beeswax to a board and inlaying yarn to describe their dreams and visions. Eventually, he sold the African and aboriginal works to focus on the Huichol art.

The buzz in the triathlon world concerned Mark's retirement: would it last? He'd returned to Ironman in 1995 and won his sixth title, tying Dave Scott for the all-time men's record. A year later, he ran his final competitive triathlon, and then turned his attention to our family, shamanism, and his fledgling corporate speaking and online coaching career. One thing about Mark Allen: when he makes a final decision, he's not likely to reverse course. However, he worried like anyone else taking a chance from a sure bet to an unknown. "My immediate reaction was like everybody else, to freak out," he told *Triathlete*. "What am I going to do? Can I make enough to support my family?"

We were fine. Nike, Oakley, GT Bicycles, PR Nutrition, and Iron Men Properties still sponsored Mark. He'd received a large appearance fee at the International Triathlon Grand Prix in 1996. He'd also signed with ESPN as a commentator for three Ironman series races, and with NBC to provide expert analysis from Kona. His coaching was starting to produce income. Now the president of the Professional Triathlete Guild, Mark remained in the public eye, though he preferred the quietude of our private life. He'd also been the subject of an eighteen-page *Outside* magazine article, "The World's Fittest Man." The article shared the evolution of his coaching career, launched with his reputation, results, and scientific fitness approach. He already had one young Ironman competitor under his wing, Australian Chris Legh. The article discussed his recent appearances at Paula Newby-Fraser's and John Duke's Multisport School of Champions, and his nine-week Ironman preparatory clinic.

Doesn't sound retired, does it? But that's the thing: when professional athletes retire, we are still young, so we have to create new opportunities from our achievements and the relationships we've formed. It starts by trying to decelerate from the fast, glorious, and seductive world of center stage. "The lure of the heroic athlete has a powerful force field around it," Scott Tinley writes in his book, *Racing the Sunset*. "Sport gives them the opportunity to be a hero . . . for every athlete who passes that gate, though, the aura of hero becomes their identity, it validates their existence. Take it away and meet Mr. and Mrs. Vacuum."

Fortunately, Mark and I knew how to leave center stage and stay within the sport, not being impacted too much by the vacuum caused by the absence of training and competition. We both felt it though. Years later, in my case, I nearly became nearly consumed by it.

"It can be really difficult when you retire," ST said. "Most young athletes, especially in a sport like triathlon that doesn't normally lend itself to a long stay at the top, don't plan well for a life after the sport. They're too focused on winning and staying in the game. I'm not talking about financial planning, which is another issue, but finding something meaningful that they're passionate about. I see it across every sport; we retire when we're still young. What the hell do we do next?"

We were building our new future with our three-year-old son in tow. I couldn't have asked for more, because everything I'd most deeply wanted sat in front of me: my husband, who'd been in my life for twelve years; my beautiful son; and a wonderful, warm, loving home.

As well as lingering business to settle. It was time to return to Kona. This time I'd be lining up as a thirty-eight-year-old mother and member of the Ironman Triathlon Hall of Fame. While I was thrilled to be inducted a few years before, I still couldn't bear the thought of carrying those DNFs on my record. I had plenty to prove, and I didn't mind taking center stage again to prove it.

Before Mats was born, Mark took the off-season to rest and pursue his other interests, surfing and shamanism. I sort of felt like, "Well, I want some of that attention and support." The feeling didn't last long, but I held all this untapped energy. I'd trained and raced for nine seasons, pouring myself into a single focal point. When I stopped racing, I lost that. Now what? What did I bring to the table? ST may as well have written *Racing the Sunset* and addressed it to me. I was challenged to offer something uniquely my own, not as a supporting player, but as a real contributor. My mom, Eloise, supported my brother and me as a kindergarten teacher, then earned her Master's and became a school administrator. What was I going to do? I didn't need to work for financial reasons, but I wanted to be part of something bigger here. I didn't miss the attention I received from Ironman. I missed the feeling of *making a difference*. Athletes on center stage can exert influence and become agents of change in any number of ways.

Mats's birth shifted me out of that headspace—for a while. Initially, I handled baby-rearing duties so Mark could keep his string of Ironman

World Championships alive. He'd won his fifth straight the month before Mats was born, an unprecedented feat. Dave Scott's longest consecutive streak was three, and Paula Newby-Fraser once won four in a row among her eight total crowns. No one has matched Mark's consecutive string since, and probably never will, in today's ultra-competitive, ultra-structured environment.

Mark's selflessness ended the streak, when he decided to step away from Ironman in 1994 for Mats. Father and son were together regularly for the first year, though Mark honored his commitments to most other races. When Mark went to race in Pucon, Chile, Shannon Delaney commented that he slept the entire week. Later, he competed in the Berlin Marathon for Nike and, before dropping at Mile 22, ran several miles with German superstar Uta Pippig, she of the three-runs-per-day workouts in Boulder. Uta didn't have her best race, either, but she can be excused: earlier in 1994, she won her first of three straight Boston Marathons with a blazing 2:21:45. She would come back to win her third Berlin crown in 1995.

Mark refused to sacrifice his time as a dad in Mats's first year. It was a wonderful gesture. It also fulfilled my dream of creating a do-everything-together family. Plus, we shared a family dynamic on which I'd missed out, due to my father leaving when I was eight.

The spirit and love behind Mark's decision, and his love for Mats and me, manifested in the Christmas cards I received:

> *Merry Christmas MY Love,*
> *We have been given the beauty of Christmas in our little bundle. I don't have much in the way of presents for you this year. But I give you instead my love, help, support, all that I can to be with you in this new way. It's a completely new adventure for us. I pray it will be the best.*
> *Love, Mark*
>
> *The Weasel—Merry Christmas Mom,*
> *I can't tell you in words the love I have for you or how happy I feel to come into this family. I can only look you in the eyes with my*

love and lay across your chest touching you with my body's warmth.
We can talk later.
   Love, Mats

During the holidays, forty days after he was born, we took Mats on his first outing.

We chose to confine Mats at home for forty days. Giving birth is a profound, intense, and life-altering experience. It redefines your being mentally, emotionally, and spiritually, and it takes time to assimilate the changes for Mom, Dad, and Baby. Confinement allows the mother's body to recover from the intensity of childbirth when hormone levels change dramatically, the uterus returns to pre-pregnant size, milk production is established, and the perineum incision heals. (Did I mention I had a lot of stitches?) Many cultures around the world practice confinement. Because it takes that long to set a change of habit or lifestyle, it was vital to us that this time be honored and respected. Taking it further, my "Iron Twin," Khalil Binebine, celebrates Ramadan in a forty-day cycle, not the traditional thirty days. And didn't Jesus spend forty days alone in the wilderness?

We headed to Swami's beach, once the hermitage of Paramahansa Yogananda, who brought deeper, more spiritual yoga teachings to the United States in 1920. After starting in Boston and New York, where he drew packed houses at Carnegie Hall for lectures, he headed west and built centers from Hollywood to San Diego, still highly popular today, some sixty-five years after his passing. A sixth Yogananda-inspired community, Ananda Village, is tucked away in the Sierra Nevada foothills. Interestingly, I subscribed to Yogananda's meditation lessons years later. I marveled about living so close to where, in 1946, he wrote the bestselling *Autobiography of a Yogi*. Growing up, though, I knew Swami's as an excellent surf spot in Encinitas.

We also practiced Attachment Parenting, which breaks down into four components: co-sleeping, feeding on demand, holding and touching, and quick responsiveness to crying. Mats slept with us in the same room, in the same bed, and we adhered to his sleep schedule rather than ours whenever we could. I breastfed him for eighteen months on his schedule, rather than referring to a pediatric time chart. I loved the feeling of our family being tucked in together. I also love touch. We kept Mats physically near always, either by cradling and cuddling, or by wearing front packs. Whenever he cried, we intervened right away, not to silence his voice or make the house quieter, but to act on the source of his distress before it flew out of control.

Mark would take Mats to eat breakfast at our local spot, Miracles Cafe (well, Mark ate), and walk along the railroad tracks near our home for hours on end. They checked out sticks, rocks, and wildflowers, which often go unnoticed when running rail trails at six-minute-per-mile pace or cycling at twenty-five miles per hour. "He is totally at home in the natural world . . . you wake up in the morning and goof around with him a little bit because he is always in a goofy mood in the morning," Mark told *Triathlete*.

As soon as he could talk, Mats started asking questions. Good questions too, not just "why?" or "why not?" He asked whenever something intrigued him, and a lot of things caught his attention. As he grew into early childhood, we saw how we blended in his features, down to Mark's facial characteristics and my blue eyes. He was very playful, sometimes goofy, and quite sociable; he loved to chat and make new friends, both characteristics of my personality. He was very physical, moving around outside, curious about the natural world. He's been entirely comfortable in nature since he was born.

As a toddler, Mats was the first to awaken. We would encourage him to see "Auntie Lala," our tenant Leslie Engel. She rented the Blue Room, the mother-in-law unit adorned in three shades of Martha Stewart's blue paint. Mats would open the front door, walk onto the shared front patio, and tap on Leslie's door. She would open her door without getting out of bed, and Mats would hop up for some Auntie Lala time.

Mats and Mark drove for daily surf checks in Mark's silver Toyota truck. When they returned, it was either time for Dad to surf, or our time to head off to the park. Mats was what Jerry Seinfeld coined a "sidler" (pronounced side-ler). He would observe the other kids playing, and slowly make his way closer. He never tried too hard to make friends, but inched over until he assimilated into their group. Mats did have a BFF living on our street, Rebecca Kutlow. Becca called the shots. When they rode around in a big plastic car, Becca always drove. She had an older brother, Zach, so when it was her turn to rule the roost, she did just that. Mats and Becca spent part of every day together unless Becca had a conflicting playdate. Becca would announce, "Go home, Matsy." Thus dismissed, poor Mats would watch as her new friend arrived.

Mats and Becca are still the best of friends, more like cousins. A human rights law student at UCLA, she might be the kindest person I know. However, she was a ballbuster in her early days. A kind ballbuster is a good combination for a future lawyer. We still tease her about being an early dominatrix.

From the start, Mats became my partner in various adventures. We held season passes to the San Diego Zoo, San Diego Wild Animal Park, and Sea World. We always sought out a new animal, bug, or flower. I have many "Bad Mom" stories, including one from the Wild Animal Park. The tram driver started commenting on the animals we passed. Soon, she directed our attention to a rocky outcropping and, by name, pointed out the African Wild *Ass*. I laughed and turned to Mats, faux innocence fighting with real mischief for control of my senses. "Honey," I said, "I didn't hear what the man said. What was that animal?"

"A Wild Ass."

I couldn't help myself. "What was it?" I repeated.

"Wild Ass!" he yelled, his voice booming.

The other passengers laughed.

Mats also liked fun runs so much that we held one for his fifth birthday, starting at our house on Glasgow Ave. The kids ran down to Cardiff Elementary School, where a piñata waited to be bashed. Mark's triathlon coaching protégé, Chris Legh, and his wife, Sarah, were staying with us, so Chris and Mark kept pace with the speedy runners while Sarah and I were the sweepers, making sure everyone was finished.

Mats attended preschool at Sandy Hill, a parent-teacher cooperative school that emphasized natural settings and a play-based philosophy to support child learning, exploration, and self-esteem. It was a perfect fit, considering how we'd raised him thus far. During this time, I thought more about my how rewarding it was for my mom and best friend Sue to teach early-grade elementary school. (In a nice personal twist, Sue student-taught in my mom's kindergarten class.) Leslie would follow suit and teach second grade. I'd seriously considered a career in elementary education until Ironman sent me down a different path. Later, I saw myself teaching high school rather than elementary.

While in the classroom with Mats, it struck me that I loved this young age. Were I to teach, I would want to follow in the footsteps of the Wonder Women in my life responsible for making such a big impact on young people. Why not pursue elementary rather than secondary education? The thought lingered. Maybe I could pursue my credentials when things got more settled, and Mark was secure with his speaking and coaching . . .

Meanwhile, Mark dove deeper into shamanism through Dance of the Deer. According to the foundation's website, "The Dance of the Deer Foundation Center for Shamanic Studies exists to preserve the Huichol culture and its shamanic practices and traditions (the deer is the Huichol symbol for heart). The foundation was established in 1979 by Brant Secunda to carry on the vision of his grandfather and teacher, Don José Matsuwa, the renowned Huichol shaman. Don José's vision was to leave Brant in his place to carry on the sacred traditions and to teach Huichol shamanism."

Mark had gravitated toward shamanism for years. He was fascinated with native Mexican spiritual practices, the Huichol Indians in particular. He experienced the lava field vision in Kona, and then attended a retreat on the Big Island the following year. Mark's commitment involved pilgrimages, vision quests, holistic medical conferences, and practicing sacred traditions that, according to the website, "reunite people to the source of all life in order to help heal the earth, our communities, and ourselves."

When *Triathlete* asked Mark about how he gauged his practice, his answer warmed my heart: "Well, the microcosm you can see every day in your child. Are you selfish, or giving? Are you self-absorbed, or present for somebody else? Are you clear in your communication? You see all of that in your child. They reflect it back to you."

Mark wanted Mats and me to join him in his quest. Very much so. I'd been to a couple events, and supported his spiritual quest, but I realized it wasn't my path. Yoga was still a decade into my future. However, Dance of the Deer served as Mats's introduction to a spiritual life. We headed to retreats to Sedona and Alaska, the latter to baptize Mats while Mark went on a five-day vision quest in the deep Alaskan wilderness with no food or water. I knew Mark could handle extreme physical situations, as you might expect of a five-time Ironman champion. Still, I worried, and was relieved when he returned. His translucent eyes were shining, the eyes of one tapped into his inner light. He remained in that space for days afterward.

Mats's introduction to Dance of the Deer came at the ripe age of five days. We bought a new palm tree to plant along with my placenta, a ritual familiar to many indigenous cultures . . . but we still hadn't decided on a name. "What kind of a father am I when I can't even give my son a name?" Mark despaired.

We laid out a beautiful altar in our front yard. I was wavering between naming him Mats (after Mats Wilander, the tennis star) and Watson, after my Carlsbad surfing friends Jimmy Watson and Watson Gooch. I'd call him Wats for short. It was between those two. Mark broke the tie and we went with Mats.

We flew over to Kona for the 1994 Ironman World Championships with our eleven-month-old in tow. Neither of us raced, but Mats took his "one small step for man." He walked for the first time in Kona. How perfect was that? Meanwhile, I became the second person to be inducted into the Ironman Hall of Fame. Dave Scott was the first. I was thrilled and overwhelmed, especially considering I was a new mother, out of shape, and not exactly holding the best Kona credentials, having DNF'ed in my last two Ironmans. What humbles me the most is that it is such an exclusive club. In 2017, Chrissie Wellington became just the twenty-ninth Ironman Hall of Famer. If only I might one day erase those DNFs and again finish what I started . . .

In 1995, Mark set a goal that the triathlon world considered ridiculous: Coming back from a one-year absence to win a sixth Ironman at age thirty-seven. We heard that younger competitors were writing him off as old and out of touch. Do you know how much that motivates a great champion?

Mark was a different athlete than the one who left the Kona stage after 1993. In his absence, Greg Welch held off forty-year-old Dave Scott to win the 1994 Ironman. Mark took a close look at Dave's age and performance, and knew he could succeed again. His first Kona win had freed him up to enjoy racing, and to appreciate the other things in his life, like his son, which he couldn't do while constantly striving to win. It made our life so much better, and happiness in life is success in life.

Now, he wanted his crown back.

When we arrived for the 1995 Ironman, l looked at the young upstarts and thought, *You guys have no idea what you're dealing with. He might be chronologically ancient, but he's more powerful than ever.* Mark had spent a full year steeped in fatherhood and spiritual practices. When he returned from his vision quest, the look on his face was so calm, so powerful. These younger athletes might have watched him win the Iron War while in college, and now considered him Too Old To Beat Them.

Good luck loosening The Grip with that misperception.

With Mats and I watching and cheering, Mark stepped up for his race, the toughest since his duel with Dave. Mark addressed the challenge of defending champion Greg Welch, but his larger fight came against two young Germans, twenty-four-year-old Thomas Hellriegel and twenty-eight-year-old Rainer Müller-Hörner. Mark came into T1—the swim transition—in fourteenth place, and only moved up to ninth after the bike. I was concerned. He was thirteen minutes behind Hellriegel; he'd need to outrun the German by thirty seconds per mile over the marathon—unheard of at this level. He also had to pass eight world-class athletes along the way, while being at the center of all of their radars. With all due respect, I don't think a defending champion ever faced less pressure than Greg. Everyone wanted to see if Grip still had it. Much as I wanted, I did not coach or urge Mark on; he did not want that. Yet, he still fed off my energy. "There was always this invisible connection between us that was critical for me," he told *Triathlete.* "I told her that no matter how far behind I got, to always think positive thoughts. There was no room for negative thoughts if I was to have that one percent chance to win. She gave me her strength."

Between our constant positive thoughts, his training and unwavering belief in himself, Mark dug into an inner place only Mark Allen knows. He erased Hellriegel's thirteen-minute advantage in a comeback for the ages, unleashing an incredible 2:42 marathon, his second fastest ever in Kona. He beat Hellriegel by two minutes, Mueller by five, and Greg by nine.

After the race, Mark handed the Kona family race baton to me. I wanted my final date too, to erase those damned DNFs from my memory banks. I told him, "You know, I was thinking, when Mats is older, he will ask, 'So Daddy, you won Ironman six times. Mommy, what did you do? Oh, you dropped out the last two times?'" I did not want that to be the story Mats knew.

While I competed in other triathlons, and made strong attempts for the U.S. Olympic Marathon Trials, I'd also had Mats at age thirty-five and spent his first year doing what new mothers do—feeding, changing diapers, and tending to family, and not so much working out.

I needed a longer runway than a same-year decision. In 1996, I began to view marathons as the way back. During the fall, I trained for November's New York Marathon, with a goal of breaking three hours. It gave me something to do while Mark wrapped up his competition commitments. I ran a lot during our summer in Boulder, which made me confident I could hit my goal.

"I want to go back to Kona," I told Mark.

"Why don't you see how New York goes first?" he replied.

A wise suggestion. Lisette and I flew out and dove into the crazy Manhattan scene while Mark stayed home with Mats. My goal? To break three hours. The crowds encouraged and motivated me, and I fed off their energy—much as Shalane Flanagan did twenty years later, albeit much faster. Plus, the difference between running 2:47 and 3:00 in a marathon is major—30 seconds per mile. Though it had been six years since I ran the 2:47, I could tell the difference in pace and effort.

In the end, the PowerBar centipede got me through. The runners in that costumed chorus line allowed me inside their "cape" while grinding through the late-race Central Park hills. They dropped me with two miles to go, but helped me pick it up enough to finish at 2:59. Earlier in the year, I ran 3:18 in the LA Marathon. In seven months, I'd improved by almost a minute per mile.

I launched into training for my return to Kona.

◆

A few weeks after returning from New York, I surprised Mark on our seventh anniversary. Leslie Engel took Mats to see *101 Dalmatians*. He even wore a jacket covered with dalmatians! Back home, Mark and I dressed to the nines for an anniversary dinner, like we'd done every year since getting married. "We need to make a quick stop at Lois's house," I said, referring to Lois Schwartz, the cofounder of *Competitor* magazine with Bob Babbitt.

We walked inside—into his surprise retirement party. Lisette and Sue joined the predominately triathlon crowd as well. We used Mark's Waterford Crystal trophies for flower arrangements, and we balanced the honoring speeches and words with a nice, kindhearted roast. I'm happy to report that Mark responded to the trophy flower arrangements better than my Christmas stalker ornaments!

Mark stopped racing completely. Since his body hurt from fifteen years of intense training, he worked out or jogged very little for the first few months. Except for surfing; he surfed all the time. When he tried to resume a workout schedule, his new daily work schedule—plus family obligations—made it difficult. He famously told *Outside*, "When I was racing, I couldn't figure out why people couldn't stay fit. I thought, 'They have no excuse.' Now I know."

Now in the same boat as the rest of the working world, he carved out time to hit the weight room, ride the bike, stretch, and run. His aches stopped, his muscles strengthened, and he felt in shape again. He would never win another Ironman, but now, he embraced the bigger reason to work out: to maintain lifelong fitness for the sake of his well-being. This is the essential reason to run, ride, sweat, lift weights, or play sports, beyond races or achievements.

As Mark found his groove on the sidelines, I couldn't wait to get back in the game. It showed; the 1997 season could not have gone better. My fast start was due entirely to former pro triathlete Jenny Wood, my amazing and sassy training partner who dragged my ass around for months. Together, we logged hundreds of hours riding and running. The season officially started when Mark, Mats, and I traveled to Australia so I could qualify for Kona. I turned in my second fastest Ironman ever, finishing seventh in 10 hours and 13 seconds—70 *minutes* faster than my Kona race fifteen years before. My splits were rock solid: a 55:36 swim, 5:33:33 bike, and 3:31:04 marathon. My desire to erase the bad memories of Kona now seemed possible.

I realize not many who saw me on *Wide World of Sports* remember or even know of the Kona DNFs. Well, *I* remember them. And they had to be erased. "It's good for her to do that. She had that thing inside her that felt incomplete. She felt she let herself down the last few times she did the race. Who wants to live with that if you can correct it?" Mark told *Triathlete*.

My Ironman résumé did not square with my place in the Ironman Hall of Fame. I was known for finding whatever resolve it took to crawl across the line, not dropping out of races. I have a moral code, which I'd covered up by justifying the DNFs. I used the extreme discomfort of 1982 as my excuse. *I know how far I can go, and I'm not willing to do it.* It led to three DNFs. The first, in 1984, was legitimate; I had medical issues. Then came 1989, when Mark and Dave waged their Iron War. I couldn't focus on my race anymore. Not a good excuse. In 1990, while Mark defended his title, I dropped again to be at his finish. Another bad excuse. This is not why you line up. In all three cases, I dropped while in the Top 10.

My moral conundrum was simple. After the race was over, the cheers died down, the press filed their stories, and my justifications faded, I was left with a knotted truth inside my belly: I quit. *I fucking quit.* Something needed to be protected—the "never quit" moral fiber from 1982—and who better than me to protect it? No one else knew it was a big deal, or any deal at all. But it was to me.

During my Ironman training cycle, I faced the same problem as athletic mothers everywhere: how to find time away from my kid? I used a local daycare facility to buy some training time. Mats took one look and did not dig it one bit. He saw some poor kid getting his diaper changed from a table that dropped out of the wall, the toddler's package on full display. Mats decided he would never poop at that preschool! When I saw the look on his face as I dropped him off twice a week, I realized I had to raise the bar on my training. If my kid was putting up with a daycare he didn't like, then I owed it to him to become more efficient in my training.

That's when I *finally* got the idea of brick training—putting together two or all three triathlon disciplines by stacking one workout atop another. I literally charged through my training as if my kid's happiness depended on it, fueled by guilt. I also thought of the poor kid desperately having to poop and holding out until I got him home!

When we arrived in Kona, Mark was in full Sherpa mode, proud to support me in the first Ironman either of us ran that Mats can still remember. On the flight, I finished up Mats's Halloween costume; I considered sewing and making costumes to be part of my rite of passage into motherhood. Two weeks after Kona, he wore his favored menehune costume in the Halloween parade in Lahaina, Maui, during the Xterra (Off Road) Triathlon World Championship. Mark and I went as the Turn Down Service, wearing bed sheets with chocolate mints pinned to our chests. Mark threw in the hotel lampshade for good measure.

I raced with authority in Kona. No DNFs this time! Not only did I finally feel worthy of my Hall of Fame induction, but I finished second in my age group and nineteenth overall in the women's division, running 10:39—a half hour faster than 1982. "She is older and wiser, and she trained smarter," Mark told the press afterward. "She was not so obsessive. There was no pressure. She could have been sucked up into an unhealthy competitiveness, but she kept her perspective the whole way through."

I attributed much of my success to Mark's support, Jenny Wood, and motherhood, particularly the brick training necessitated by Mats's daycare discomfort. "You make sure to get as much as you can from each workout," I said then, "because your time is much more valuable."

I bowed out of the sport with my head held high. What a perfect way to return to retirement, to my husband and son . . .

While basking in the afterglow of Kona, storm clouds began to pop up on the horizon. Storm clouds at home. I began to worry about the degree to which Mark immersed himself when working with Dance of the Deer. His activities increased greatly during the year, often without including Mats and me. I began to wonder, *How far is this going?*

CHAPTER 16
When Iron Breaks

W here would we turn next?

Mark rolled deeper into his post-race career, which now included owning a new gym in La Jolla, California, and a new book we were writing with Bob Babbitt. Mats continued to grow; his spirit, energy, and deep intelligence lighting us up daily. Our marriage carried on, minus all but the usual stresses. I immersed myself in tending to Mark and Mats, my commitment to being a great wife and mother absolute. Deep down, though, a question nagged: *What about Julie?* I'd enjoyed the world stage for a decade before willingly ceding it to focus on motherhood and family. As the buzz wore off my latest Kona achievement, I felt an itch. It's something most great athletes who later become mothers experience, but I grew more and more isolated from those circles.

I wanted to find something. Maybe announcing? I'd enjoyed the bit of TV work I'd done. It would be nice to continue—as long as I didn't have to move to Los Angeles or New York. What about public speaking? I'd given quite a few talks, and liked sharing my experience and energy to inform or motivate the audience. The thought of teaching also stayed with me.

Meanwhile, I more keenly observed the differences in our parenting styles. Mark had been a parent-pleasing child, wanting his dad's approval, never acting out. He was the classic good kid, just like my brother, Marshall. His life rolled on discipline and structure. He created moments of greatness by trusting that his workouts would pay off, and then grinding them out. He passed the state lifeguard test at seventeen after graduating high school, and entered UC-San Diego and did mega yardage every morning and night for the swim team despite a heavy premed course load. He didn't have a lot of wiggle room for free time.

My upbringing was much different. Marshall was my mom's primary focus. She was determined to create a better man than she married. Because her spotlight was trained on him, I slid under the radar. Meanwhile, I was a parent-pleasing kid as well, until the parent I wanted to please most left us. I got by with minimal daily effort, though I was certainly smart enough to achieve good grades. Marshall and I were even tested into the mentally gifted minors program (IQ 132+) in junior high, an embarrassing proposition to share with my peers. I used my smarts as my excuse: "If I really wanted to do well, I could. I'm smart enough." I was too busy surfing and socializing, making sure I was not left behind, all the fun things about high school. "I remember having a pre-prom party at my house," Cindy Conner recalled, "and we were all there with our dates. But no one had asked Julie to the prom. Julie showed up anyway and helped with throwing the party. She found a great way to be right in the middle of it."

From his earliest years, Mats's comfort zone was different than ours. He would take his little Radio Flyer four-wheeler and race it down our driveway. The driveway wasn't steep, but he built some speed and stopped just shy of the bumper of Mark's truck. He knew when he needed to slow down—when his face was two inches from the bumper. A perfectly fine comfort zone for him, but as I watched, I bit my tongue to keep from yelling out. Never mind that when I was the same age, Jay Jardine and I plowed a surrey wagon into a car in Carlsbad. I wanted to honor Mats's comfort zone, and not impose my discomfort on him. I wanted to honor that. So I avoided yelling, "Stop!"

Mark was uncomfortable with Mats's more blatant adventures. His structured approach held that, if you take the right step, then step after step after step, you can find success. Conversely, I maintained that sometimes you stumble and fall into things. Like moments of clarity. Or Kona; I changed the sport without really knowing what I was doing. Whereas Mark, following his methodical path, took seven years to win in Kona. He never lost there again, posting six victories. Our results intersected in a great way. When they announced the ten greatest moments in Ironman history for the thirtieth anniversary celebration in 2008, my 1982 race was voted second only to the creation of the event. Right behind that was Mark's Iron War conquest of Dave Scott. To me, this shows how you can take vastly different approaches to a sport—or parenting. I see in Mats a great blend between us. With him, we got it right.

Mark had been involved with Dance of the Deer for nearly a decade. He'd attended their major functions and retreats, and served on their staff. When we traveled to the retreats as a family, it was a positive experience and I was pleased to take part and witness Mark's transformation and healing. He had found what he was seeking, a community- and family-oriented group that fed him spiritually.

As 1999 rolled around, Mark felt drawn to increase his commitment. Since Dance of the Deer was headquartered in Santa Cruz, he reasoned that living there would allow easy access to the local activities, while he continued to participate in the ongoing national and international retreats.

Mark started talking about moving us to Santa Cruz. From our beautiful Spanish Mediterranean home in sunny, warm Cardiff? *What? Why?* Why uproot to a colder, wetter climate that chills any surfer to the bone? Sure, the waves could be really good, but who wants to paddle into hypothermia? What could Santa Cruz offer Mats educationally, or me personally, that we didn't already have? What about the friends and family who fulfilled our family life, all of whom I wanted Mats to know as he got older?

I held out hope. I thought Mark was throwing out feelers for something years down the line. Mats would start kindergarten at Cardiff Elementary in the fall of 1999. Surely, we would wait until he changed schools after third grade—at least. That gave me plenty of time to change Mark's mind while Mats and I continued to live our happy lives in Cardiff.

Unfortunately, Mark moved his chess piece before I moved mine.

When Mark got the calling to do something, and committed to it, you either followed suit—or left the train.

He tightened his resolve—and our marriage entered troubled waters. I tried to save it through the way I handled difficulties then, by ignoring them. Maybe I was holding out for a miraculous shift. Maybe I believed we would be okay. Deep down, though, I knew we were in trouble. A dark cloud billowed, a disturbing perception that the shit would hit the fan if we moved to Santa Cruz. It was the inner version of the sudden weather change on Villarrica we'd experienced in Chile, only far worse.

I knew this was beyond my ability to sort out. I sought out a therapist, who lived in our neighborhood. I walked over for our first meeting and explained that my husband wished to move our family to support his spiritual path, a path different than my own. I hadn't even found a path yet. The therapist said something I'd never considered: "Navigating opposing spiritual paths is one of the most difficult obstacles a married couple can overcome."

Oh boy . . .

She added that when one partner embarks on a spiritual discovery, there is no telling what will happen to the relationship, marriage, or future. It is a deeply uncomfortable and despairing place for the other partner. She likened the experience to sailing along smoothly, and then hitting an iceberg. "It can be scary for the partner left behind, for the partner witnessing rather than seeking," she said.

There they were, words to trigger the scared little girl living inside me since my dad left thirty years before . . . *left behind.*

After we finished, I walked home to share the session with Mark. He was not sympathetic. He simply said, "Get a new therapist."

I didn't know how to shift my fear and ensuing anger into neutral. My primary role, my job, was being a wife and mother. I also loved being half of a triathlon power couple. I didn't know how to shake my feelings to remain the wife whose loving presence supported our marriage no matter what. I desperately wanted to find this in myself, but anger and fear paralyzed me.

Mark continued to move forward. As he veered further away from me, I felt left behind emotionally, helpless to stop him. I well knew the feeling of being dropped on a long climb by the Grip. My anger and growing depression plunged me into emotional quicksand, and I slowly sank. As a girl who not only thrived, but also subsisted on love, vibrant energy, and positive attitude, I found myself in a desperate place. How could I feel any worse? How could it get any worse?

Well, it did.

I focused on keeping us where we were. In Cardiff, I could trust my love for Mark, and see that his growth was good for all of us. To offset the fact that emotionally, Mark was becoming increasingly distant, I surrounded myself with those who shared in our success, relationships built over many years. They became a lifeline for me.

I focused on getting Mats ready for kindergarten, just a few months away. Cardiff Elementary served about 350 kids in grades K through 3, with a great view of the Pacific Ocean across Highway 101 as well as San Elijo Lagoon, a beautiful coastal waterway. California dreaming, all the way. I visualized Mark, Mats, and me holding hands for our ten-minute walk to campus for Mats's first day. Later, I would run along the beach and wait for him at the gate. We would walk home and he would tell me about his day. This image was so strong, so sure. I never doubted it. I never pictured another image, or another school. Or another life . . .

We packed several bags and moved to Santa Cruz on a weekend, so Mats could start kindergarten the following Monday. While Mark happily bid Cardiff farewell to plunge headlong into a new life, I slumped in the backseat with Mats for the entire seven-hour drive, fuming, hurt beyond belief. I barely spoke to Mark. When I did, it was to complain.

Finally, we arrived at our fully furnished rental home, which sat above Sunny Cove—the exact opposite of how I felt. Relocating your family to best serve all parties is something we can rally behind, even if we miss our friends or our kids complain about their new schools. Still, the spouses/parents are working together to make a better life.

This was a different story. Mark was singularly committing to a lifestyle to which I had only a peripheral connection. Fine for him, but not the life

I'd committed to. This was a whole new ball game, not the same as making mistakes in your relationship or marriage, which can be apologized for, rectified, and "worked on." We were no longer on the same team.

It was the end of the life we had known for fourteen years.

After we enrolled Mats in his new school, I tried to make the most of our new life. I liked the Gateway School from the beginning. Their mission appealed to me, especially the emphasis on gender balance, whole-person education, and using playing and laughter as vital learning tools along with nature. An adventurous, sociable, smart, and free-spirited kid like Mats would fit right in. Simple notes like the one Mats received at year's end from his kindergarten teachers, Diana and Pat, warmed the aspiring educator's heart inside me: "Dear Mats, you've been a good classmate this year, because you're a good sport and share your skills with others."

Before Christmas, I took Mats to the Tall Ships' annual procession in Santa Cruz Harbor. We spent three hours sailing both the *Lady Washington,* and a vessel whose name resonated with us, the *Hawaiian Chieftain*. I have a picture of Mats hanging from one of the masts. We learned about the ships and their trade routes, along with life on board for 19th century sailors. We also reenacted a battle between the two ships, and Mats learned how to load a cannon on command: "Fire In the Hole!" As the group leader explained, "fire in the hole" was a warning of an imminent detonation. The term originated with miners, but spread to the high seas in the 18th century. When someone yelled "fire in the hole," you ducked for cover.

The Bad Mom in me thought "Fire in the Hole" would make a perfect name for a spicy salsa. Sadly, though, it more accurately reflected my home life. On December 10, we celebrated our tenth wedding anniversary, a far less joyous event than anniversaries past. Mark had just returned from a speaking engagement in New York, and brought me a white gold band I had admired, along with an Ebel watch with a beautiful blue face.

However, no gift could mask the tension between us. We got into a fight, and I hurled that red Cartier box across the bedroom. Fighting with Mark was something I'd rarely done. It felt so foreign and wrong.

For our first Christmas in Santa Cruz, we also decorated a birdseed ornament tree on our back patio, having left our ornaments behind in Cardiff. We cut out Mats's initials in the ornaments—"MA." The old Stalker Tree skills came in handy, but the memory at that point seemed distant. We also cut out shapes of stars, diamonds, and candy canes, strung popcorn, peanuts, cranberries, dried pineapple, and dried apples, coated them with peanut butter, and put birdseed on top. It was really fun to see the birds enjoying this Christmas tree.

I had no idea what to do with my consuming love for Mark. I loved him, but hated his choices. I couldn't handle being torn apart by these opposing feelings, so I shoved my love deep down and let my new persona of being a total bitch mask the fear.

The year 2000 began with more confirmation that we were staying in Santa Cruz for the long haul. While skiing in Mammoth with Lisette and her family, we closed on our new house. Mats finished school and we returned to Cardiff to put our beautiful home on the market, the center of our family's greatest years. After returning to Santa Cruz, Mats started first grade at Gateway.

Meanwhile, Mark worked on his public speaking with famed financial planning and life strategy expert Bill Bachrach, whom he also coached in the 1998 Ironman. (I would have my own moment with Bill years later.) After figuring out his path forward, Mark had rolled everything fully into gear by 1999. We'd also finished working on a book with Bob Babbitt, *Workouts for Working People.* The premise was simple: Mark and I shared our stories, training secrets, and a simple series of workouts with readers who had trouble finding an hour a day to exercise. The cover even shows the two happy spouses, Julie and Mark, running on the beach together. Only one thing: we were the furthest thing from being happy.

I continued to hold Mark at a distance, my fear and anger now dominating my heart. Slowly, he became completely remote from me. Eventually, he let me go.

I needed to keep myself afloat and among people. I'm a sociable person who likes her quiet time—not the other way around. It was not working for me to be so isolated in Santa Cruz, hundreds of miles from my friends. I had to do something.

I turned to an old friend: racing. In April 2000, I returned to North San Diego County for the California Ironman, held in Oceanside, my old stomping grounds. It was so good to race again, to feel part of a scene I'd helped to build but toward which I now felt increasingly removed. While training, I reconnected with some old friends: Alicia Hougharty, a former pro triathlete living near in Santa Cruz, to run in the redwoods, and Marc Martinez, a California State lifeguard who worked with Mark and me, to swim at Simpkins Pool, a mile from the house. I made new friends in Nick Lewellyn at Masters swimming, and with Diana Roberts, a physical therapist and strong age group triathlete, who showed me all the local rides.

I also connected with the local surf community. Several Santa Cruz moms and I would paddle out between 9:00 and 11:00 A.M., when our kids were in school. These were the Mom Sessions. I really enjoyed riding waves again, but never got used to the ocean temperatures; Santa Cruz was not Cardiff. But what stoked my heart was the sheer number of women in the water. What a difference from Emily, Robin, Cindy, and me fighting for scraps in Carlsbad as kids; women's surfing had grown so much.

Leave it to my original favorite sport to enliven me. I loved to go to the beach in front of wetsuit inventor Jack O'Neill's house. The O'Neills have been the First Family of Surfing in Santa Cruz since Jack and his hearty friends, Fred Van Dyke and Richard Novak, bare-trunked it or wore flannel shirts while surfing in 50°F water, then warmed up with giant beach bonfires. The stories they told at those bonfire sessions are some of the richest in surfing lore, and I love good surf stories. In 1952, Jack handed Fred's wife, Betty, a neoprene suit to wear in the water. She ditched her cashmere sweater, paddled out, and stayed warm in the suit for much longer than her typical twenty-minute white-knuckle sessions. Jack called his invention a "wetsuit"; water enters the suit, then warms from one's body heat. Nearly every surfer in the world now has one. I was deeply saddened when Jack passed in July 2017, after taking ninety-four splendid trips around the sun—during which he surfed, ballooned, sailed, and headed up the wildly successful O'Neill Wetsuits operation and its great branding slogan: "It's always summer on the inside."

Next to O'Neill's is a dirt field, "The Dirt Farm." Jack was kind enough to let the community use the property to run local surf contests like the Log Jam. It was old school, all the way: you couldn't compete with a board built after 1970. You couldn't use a board leash either. If a wave separated you and your board, you swam to shore. The contest brought out Santa Cruz's big-wave titans, including Peter Mel, Jay Moriarity, Chris Gallagher, Robert "Wingnut" Weaver (later to star in *The Endless Summer II*), Marcel Soros, Darryl "Flea" Virostko, Richard Schmidt, and tough, cold-water goddesses like Candy Woodward, Anne Useldinger, Brenda Scott Rogers, and Shannon Aikman. Brenda, whose father invented Doc's Pro Plugs to protect surfers' ears from cold water, and Shannon were once part of the California Golden Girls, an elite surf team. Think of these wave-riding goddesses as Bad Girls on Boards.

Out of the water, our ships continued drifting further apart. Mark and I decided to attend couples counseling, but after six sessions, felt no closer to finding common ground. I took that to mean one thing: *When can we move back to Cardiff?* I gave that thought plenty of flight. I really wanted to go home.

My days revolved more and more around Mats's schedule. After school, we'd find an after-school adventure, or dine together, particularly at Star Bene, where he liked the gnocchi. He'd order the gorgonzola gnocchi and ask for no gorgonzola. I've always been a frugal woman; to save $12, I could learn to make gnocchi at home. I made them for us at least once a week, and later taught Mats how to make them too.

After Mats finished kindergarten in the Summer of 2000, we traveled to Cardiff as a family for our summer break. Something else excited me: triathlon was making its Olympic debut in Sydney! The race turned out to be a nail-biter, with Switzerland's Brigitte McMahon, American Michelle Jones, and Switzerland's Magali Messmer finishing their 1,500-meter swim, 40K bike, and 10K run splits in almost exactly the same time. McMahon won by two seconds over Michelle Jones, with Messmer just twenty-eight seconds behind.

As I looked at the results, I saw the complete changing of the guard in women's triathlon. Paula Newby-Fraser, Erin Baker, Wendy Ingraham, the Puntous twins, Colleen Cannon, and I were nowhere to be found. An entirely new crowd ruled the sport now, and if this Olympic Games was any indication, we were in for a fantastic new decade.

A few months later, Mark and I observed our eleventh anniversary without a dinner reservation, gifts, or "Happy Anniversary" greetings. Our anniversary tradition of dressing up like bride and groom was also long gone. Nor were any boxes filled with rings or watches. The only boxes sat in our garage, stuffed with our belongings. We still hadn't fully unpacked. This proved to be sadly convenient, as Mark would be moving out soon. Through all of this, Wendy Ingraham popped back into my life as a huge support. Wendy lived in nearby Walnut Creek, and really came through. The vibe and mood was quite different than when she'd shown up at my wedding in the hottest dress, but one thing was clear—she was a real friend, big-time.

Years later, we did a NPR radio lab program together on triathlons. I flew out to Wendy's new Colorado home to see her and her husband, Vern Smith, and her daughter, Skylar. On the drive from the airport, she mentioned she had to make a quick detour to do a radio interview for National Public Radio.

"Is it for something called Radio Lab?" I asked with a pit in my stomach.

"Yeah, how'd you know?" she replied, curious. "It won't take long."

I suddenly remembered the Radio Lab interview request from weeks earlier. When I put it all together on our drive, that I'd not responded and they'd turned to Wendy, I was horrified. *WTF.* NPR is huge. "Wing, I think I was supposed to do this interview, and I completely blew them off." I was still so distracted by what was going on at home. "Can you let them know I'm here with you in case they still want me to join in?"

Years later, while in Junior Lifeguards in Santa Cruz, Mats listened as the instructor put on an inspirational podcast . . . the Radio Lab show. After several minutes, Mats said, "That's my mom." His instructor couldn't believe it. When I picked up Mats, his instructor looked a little more awestruck by me than when I'd dropped him off.

As Mats settled into second grade, and we all dealt with the 9/11 terrorist attack, I settled into more loneliness and despair. The only person I wanted to call after the attacks was Mark, but I couldn't risk hearing the flat, detached tone in his voice. I continued to seek solace in the community of triathletes, but I didn't need tea leaves or couples counseling to see our next step.

Time to make our separation official. Months after Mark moved out, we began mediation. Once we turned off the emotions and focused on the task at hand, we were very efficient and clear about our intentions. Mediation began and ended with no fuss, no muss, nothing too emotional. We simply split everything down the middle, including custody of Mats.

"She was far more emotional and distraught after she and Reed broke up than when she and Mark divorced," Lisette recalled. "I was surprised. I kind of kept waiting for the big emotional fallout. During this time, in late 2002, her mom also died. Same reaction as when she and Mark split up: Julie didn't want to go there emotionally. I didn't see her cry for the longest time. We can only do that for so long."

All the tears had been shed and the lines drawn. The lack of emotion I showed was a combination of shock and denial that the love of my life was no longer my husband, and I would be making a life on my own in Santa Cruz to co-parent Mats.

My first consideration was returning to Cardiff, but I could never take Mats away from Mark. I couldn't imagine recreating the childhood and adolescence Marshall and I had, raised entirely by our mother, her bitterness a constant, our father nowhere to be found. Mark is one of the greatest fathers I have ever known. I couldn't imagine being readily employable and self-supporting, either, while also tending to Mats during this disruptive time. Cardiff was out.

Mark remained nearby. He purchased a house almost directly behind my house and two blocks over. If Mark walked the block and half from his house to check the surf, and I walked from my house to check it out, we never saw each other, because of the way Pleasure Point is situated. He went to the shortboard spots known as Sewers and Little Windansea to check the waves, while I scanned the peeling longboard surf at the Point.

Our avoidance of contact became the rule, rather than the exception. However, Mats navigated freely between our homes.

◆

With Mark gone, I had choices, none of them awesome. I couldn't continue to lash out, sabotage, or vent against him, because he was Mats's dad and I did not want Mats to see or feel my anger. I couldn't beg, plead, and demean myself, or compromise my dignity while trying to impose my will. I desperately wanted him to see my side of things, but that ship had sailed. Our mutual anger eroded any compassion we felt for each other.

I fell into a place where so many women tumble after a long relationship or marriage breaks down. I imagined Mark moving toward his ideal vision for his life, free of the constraints of a disapproving wife. I pictured him fully empowered, his world filled with new options, his adrenaline pumping, mastering life in the same way he mastered the Ironman.

I felt the exact opposite. And my perceptions of Mark's life, right or wrong as they were, caused me even more pain.

After a summer visit to Cardiff, Mats moved into a tiny charter school for third grade—away from his Gateway friends. However, his teacher, Mrs. Sanders, softened the landing. She remained his single favorite educator throughout his school years. Tall and robust, she greeted the kids with welcoming smile and hugs. She played tetherball with Mats on a regular basis and generally made him feel special during a tough time in his life. Mats needed a friend and Mrs. Sanders stepped up to the plate.

Meanwhile, I decided that life as a sidelined maiden was no life for me. I started dating an up-and-coming triathlete that Mark was coaching. My new friend needed to make a choice: Me? Or his coach? He found a new coach. We both had unfinished business, as he was married but separated, and I was waiting for my divorce to become final. I found myself the experienced older woman who knew how to spot and hone an athletic diamond in the rough. I could do that in my sleep. It felt good to be seen as special, and even though I sensed the limitations of this relationship, I enjoyed the sweet simplicity and sense of renewal it gave me.

During our time together, though, my friend introduced me to the last thing I would ever imagine doing. He had modeled overseas, and picked up smoking. I never smoked, because I couldn't stand the smell of tobacco, but I always liked the scent of clove cigarettes. One evening, we saw clove cigarettes in the store and bought a pack on a whim. I smoked one—and liked it. Then I smoked another. And another . . .

We stopped dating after a year, but I kept a new secret habit.

Two days before Thanksgiving, my mother died. No one was around to help me deal with this crushing moment. Mark and Mats were at a Dance of the Deer retreat in Waipio Valley, Hawaii, and Sue was also traveling with her daughters in Hawaii. Lisette was in Houston, leaving only Leslie Engel, Mats's Auntie Lala, to sit with me in Cardiff while I waited for the coroner to arrive.

One of the only silver linings of moving to Santa Cruz was that I could be away from my mom and her ever-increasing drinking. I wasn't ready to admit she had become a full-blown alcoholic, but I didn't even trust her driving Mats to the nearby Cardiff library a couple times a week. She and John, her late husband, were partners in smoking and drinking, and she started earlier and earlier in the day. Often, I could hear the ice cubes clinking in her glass when I called in the late morning.

We started visiting with Mom for shorter and shorter periods. It became hard for me to be around her and see her deteriorate.

Before Thanksgiving, I decided to visit. Marshall had taken an assignment in La Quinta to work at one of the restaurants owned by his employer, TS Restaurants. He had become my mom's caretaker and seen her through her decline. He told me, "Julie, you need to come home."

"What do you mean?"

"It's getting bad."

"How bad?"

"I'm leaving, and I need you to come down and get a sense of the situation."

I headed home on a Saturday, but stopped for a night in Santa Barbara. I really resisted going home, worried about what I'd see. I knew I had to show up by the Tuesday before Thanksgiving, when Marshall would be gone. So I pushed Saturday into Sunday, into Monday . . . into Tuesday. On the way down, I stopped at Oakley Eyewear to pick up some new gear.

I finally showed up at 4:00 P.M. on Tuesday; Marshall had left a couple hours before. The house felt dark. I went upstairs, and my mom was napping. I gave her a hug and kiss. "Mom, I'm here."

She stirred slightly. "I'm just going to sleep for awhile longer," she said.

"Great." I got on the computer to do some work for Aqua Sphere, where I served as a sales and demonstration rep for triathlon clubs and workout groups in the Bay Area.

Later, I turned on the lights downstairs. My mom came down and made herself a vodka on the rocks. She was going to smoke a cigarette. "Mom, would you please go outside to smoke?" I asked, unaware that she probably wasn't physically capable of getting herself out there.

She opted not to smoke.

We talked briefly. I don't know if it was her feeling uncomfortable, or not being able to smoke, but she headed back upstairs. She was unsteady on her feet; she'd really deteriorated physically. I now saw what my brother had been telling me. She looked ten years older. I didn't want to call attention to her unsteadiness, but after Thanksgiving, I was coming in hard to check her into a detox facility. *Give her these next couple days, be kind, don't nag or make comments . . . you're gonna save her.*

I researched facilities online for a little over an hour. As I went upstairs, I peeked in on her. I didn't see her in the bed. Was she so messed up she went to the wrong bedroom? I checked every room. Nothing.

A moment later, I found her, halfway between the bathroom and bed. The way she was laying was awkward. I knelt down to see if she was breathing. She was so cold. I think I knew she had died, but wasn't one hundred percent sure.

I got a message to Marshall; he called me right back. "I think I need to call the fire department, get the ball rolling," I said.

"Yeah, do that. I'll be back in a couple of hours."

I called the fire department, and they came with lights blazing. I recognized a couple firefighters from our years in Cardiff. They raced inside, ready to save a life. They turned Mom over and set up the defibrillator, then shocked her once. They asked for her details. I made sure to tell them, "She's a chronic smoker and a chronic alcoholic." Plus, Marshall had told me she hadn't eaten in more than a week; I relayed that information.

A look passed from one firefighter to the other. They eased back, slowing things down, taking their feet off the gas pedal. I watched the monitor. I could see it jump to life; were they bringing her back? I said a silent prayer to basically implore my mother to let go if that's what she really wanted. The spike in the monitor turned out to be a shock from the defibrillator.

I went downstairs, where Lala waited. When I saw her, something occurred to me: "I didn't give my mom a kiss goodnight."

"You still can," she said softly.

We walked upstairs and I knelt down. Mom looked so vulnerable on the ground, so I tucked a wool throw around her. I kissed her cheek and whispered, "I'm here." I lay down next to her, closed my eyes and imagined cheering for her as she crossed her own finish line.

Looking back on the latter years of my mother's life, she drank when she was happy, and drank when she wasn't. The drinking masked her depression. She'd escalated since retiring at fifty-five after a productive career in education, even though she'd remarried and moved to Sedona. She came back to Cardiff after John died. Her father, my grandfather Henry Tubach, had a long battle with depression, but lived to be ninety-eight and walked me down the aisle. Unfortunately, alcoholism runs in both sides of my family. It had just taken away my mother, and my brother battled it too.

I grew to see my mom and her life through two different prisms. Through my divorce, I came to appreciate how she single-handedly raised her two kids and earned her master's degree. She made so many sacrifices of which I wasn't aware, and did it on her own. Now she was gone—just when I needed her most.

While mourning my divorce and my mom's death, I reached again to my beloved triathlon community. Was I running forward into healing, training, and competition? Or running away from my life? Probably both. I headed to the 2003 New Zealand Ironman, where I learned I still had gas in the tank. Still, I was so emotionally wrecked, I finished in 11 hours, 11 minutes, not quite the 10:00:19 of a few years before, but enough to place third in the 40–44 age group. It felt validating to stand on a podium again!

Something else happened in New Zealand—an Australian lawyer walked into my life. He owned a coffee farm in Byron Bay and lived in Sydney. He had me at the mention of Byron Bay, one of the world's best surf spots. We flirted with a long romance until February 14, 2004, an awkward day to end any relationship.

My ongoing anger toward Mark shifted to a constant, underlying sad hum inside. Anger energized me into action, but this new, ever-present sadness idled and froze me. A perfect example was teaching. I held a lingering desire to get my teaching credential, but now felt emotionally paralyzed. It was too late to change, I reasoned, and I felt too far removed from academic learning to return to school. In telling myself this lie, I reinforced my depressing paralysis. I believed I was a victim and helpless to change my situation. This non-decision still haunts me.

I still had Mats on which to focus my love, but it was time to again become the girl who could change sport by showing the world her will and determination.

It would take a lot longer than I imagined.

CHAPTER 17
Surfing Tsunamis: Raising Mats

Sometimes, a parent sends her or his kid into a new experience and watches how things go with varying degrees of excitement, joy . . . and maybe concern. On an early March morning, as I arrived at Pleasure Point during a wake-up walk, I thought Mats needed to try something that doesn't happen often:

Riding a tsunami. Freshly brewed by a mighty Pacific earthquake.

I'd listened to the weather and news reports, looked more closely at maps and forecasts on the computer, and didn't see anything too dangerous materializing. As I stood on the cliff, two local guys talked about a tsunami that once hit while they were in the water, and how wild it was to feel the hard pull of the ocean. Pure stoke lit up their eyes. That look revealed a thrill to beat all thrills. *I want Mats to feel that.*

I ran home and woke him up. "Mats! Put your wetsuit on. I think you should paddle out!"

"What?" he replied, full of thick teenage grogginess.

"I'm not going to go out, because I need to keep my eye on you."

"Okay, Mom."

My son had already camped alone in an Italian forest at age six, run his first triathlon at eleven, traveled to more than twenty countries, earned his

Junior Lifeguard stripes, and become an all-league cross-country and water polo performer. He was also an excellent surfer. If we had a family business besides triathlon, it was surfing. He understood the thrills and safety factors, and knew how to assess his surroundings. I wasn't throwing a non-swimmer into the deep end.

We arrived a few minutes later. Quite a few onlookers stood on the cliffs, pulled together by the same coastal alerts I'd heard: the tsunami that crossed the Pacific following the March 2011 earthquake that leveled Japan's Fukushima nuclear power plant with a forty-eight-foot wave was about to hit Santa Cruz. A few surfers watched with Mats, hoping the tsunami would amount to more than the gutless one- to two-foot ripples dissolving on the rocks below.

After surveying the situation, Mats grabbed his board and looked at me excitedly. Some parents might think (and did think) I was sending him into harm's way, but Mats viewed it differently. "When I talk about this, I can kind of imagine someone thinking, 'How did your mom not get a call from social services?'" Mats recalled with a hearty chuckle. "Well, it was my decision to paddle out, so . . .

"When I first heard a tsunami was coming, I thought, 'It's barely going to be noticeable.' We'd had tsunamis, but they were like a foot. Still, I was super excited: 'Cool, I'm going to paddle out and surf a tsunami. Wild . . . not something people do every day.'

"When Mom and I arrived, the tide was normal, coming up on the cliffs. I talked to a couple people, and then walked down the cliff. When I got to the shoreline, it's like, *hello!* The tide was receding as fast I could walk on the rocks . . . a hundred feet out . . . two hundred feet . . . The rocks never show unless it's a super low tide, and no one had seen the rocks this exposed.

"There was a little surf, but nothing really. Then a set of three waves came through with about ten-foot faces. I missed the first one, caught the second one, rode it for awhile, kicked out . . . and then the same wave completely filled in the exposed rock reef and crashed against the cliffs. I decided it was time to go in, so I paddled over to the three other guys and told them I was done. We're all smiling at each other: *how cool—we just surfed the tsunami!*

"There are two channels at Pleasure Point where you can safely paddle in and out when the surf is big. They turned into raging rivers. Then these incredible longshore rip currents started running up the coast. We tried to paddle against them, but it was hopeless. I turned to the other guys and said, 'We're just going to have to ride this one out.' We got pushed a half mile down the coast. Then it switched, and we got pushed right back. It was a trip. Totally bizarre.

"I got to school late, and told my friends, 'Yeah, I just rode the tsunami!'

"'You're full of shit,' someone said.

"When they saw me smiling and heard me talk about it all day, they knew otherwise."

Well, *my* friends reacted differently.

"When Julie told me about it on the phone, I said to her, 'What the hell are you doing? You can't let him out in the water *during a tsunami!* Are you trying to be the cool mom?'" Lisette recalled. "But she knew her kid and how capable he was. She'd never urge him to go out there if he didn't have very strong surfing and swimming skills. It seems irresponsible, but when you hear him describe his experience, it's clear he had full awareness and control. In hindsight, would it have been any more irresponsible if he'd paddled out during a monster swell? When you have kids who surf, they're in the water, that's part of the deal.

"On the flip side, one time I was visiting when our boys were about nine. There was really big surf in Oceanside. Mats was in this rebellious headspace of, 'Well, if you don't want me to do it, or it seems dangerous, then I want to do it.' He was in the water bodysurfing, caught in a rip, and Julie was a wreck. She was running up and down the beach. She was really scared, and was ready to go out and get him."

It *was* Mats's final decision, though my role could be construed as a Bad Mom moment. Mats loved it! Were I seventeen years old that day, I would've paddled out. You know how powerful you feel inside after an experience like that? Too many people don't allow themselves the opportunity to try something outrageous. *Hey, here's a tsunami. Go feel it.*

Later, we drove over the narrow Santa Cruz Harbor bridge en route to school. A huge crowd lined the harbor; what was going on? We then saw the no-nonsense business end of the tsunami. The same five-foot surge that sent Mats and his surf buddies a half mile down the coast ripped through the harbor, destroying or sinking thirty boats and decimating a dock. Further north, in Mendocino and Humboldt counties, six people were swept out to sea, never to be seen again.

Meanwhile, my son grinned without stopping. The smile reappears every time he's asked about that day. Why not? Like my Kona moment, it's something incredibly unique, and unlikely to be repeated.

Meanwhile, I struggled to figure out my next steps. The subject of Mats's spiritual development through Dance of the Deer further polarized Mark and me. I tried to balance the nontraditional emphasis on traveling for retreats and missing school with more traditional options. I wanted Mats to carry forth with fullest authenticity, independence, and confidence in his choices and decisions, but also to be a fully functioning member of society.

Between co-parenting, shuttling Mats, and fielding heartbreaking questions—as in, how and why did the storybook marriage of two Ironman stars fall apart?—I contended with complications that drained me of energy and resources. Mark had to deal with these same complications, but he unilaterally chose this path to Santa Cruz that impacted both of us. He had the opportunity to make a conscious decision. I had no choice in the matter.

I knew I should buck up and move on, but I was trapped in a downward spiral. I couldn't convey to friends what I was feeling, because I struggled to make sense of it myself. I tried to slow things down while all my moorings and foundations were breaking loose or disappearing—Mark, my mom, my life. Where was my inner Wonder Woman now? I felt like a tsunami had submerged Julie-town and left it in shambles. Divorces have that impact.

After experiencing its painful effects firsthand, I will never view divorce as a positive, transformative experience. Nor will I view it as "the best thing to do for the kids." It's just too fucking hard, *especially* for kids. But life must go on, and at some point it's critical to stop letting divorce define us. My challenge felt like a never-ending headwind on a twenty-mile hill climb. I struggled with how to emerge. How would I take the reins of my life back and stand on my own?

I looked to my side. There was Mats. I felt alone in partnership, but he was right there. Already, he was my constant reinforcing rock. That would never change.

Mats started displaying bravado, awareness of his surroundings, and an active, incisive brain early on. He was a worthy mesh of Mark's structured, one-step-at-a-time approach and my more spontaneous "go for it" attitude. If Mark was a straight line, I was a zig-zag. Mats embodied both of us.

When Mats was about four, he climbed up a tree. Mark was worried he could fall and get hurt. I thought about that possibility too. But I also thought, *how amazing that he feels confident enough to be up there.* "Mats, if you got yourself up there, you have to be responsible for getting yourself back down. Can you get back down safely?" I yelled.

"Yes."

"Show Mommy how you can take a couple steps down."

"Okay." He shimmied partway down the tree.

"So now, you're responsible for keeping yourself safe in the tree."

"Okay, Mommy."

I celebrated these moments. When Mats was six, he added another: his all-night vision quest in the Italian Alps during a Dance of the Deer retreat. Can you imagine being six and alone in the woods? I can't. Mark felt fully confident. I was like, *Isn't sitting next to a fire enough?* He kept an eye on Mats, who embarked with his little backpack and sleeping bag, minus food or water, and made his little camp. "That little camping trip shaped my connection to nature. I feel at home in the mountains, in the woods," he says now.

When Mats applied for college at University of California-Santa Cruz, he revisited the vision quest in his college entrance essay. I'm guessing the UC system doesn't get many admission essays about vision quests taken at age six; I would have loved being there when they reviewed it! He wrote about watching the ants crawl, the clouds scud across the sky, and not leaving his circle until sunrise the next day. He also wrote how it helped define him. As a parent, you never know what lesson, guidance, or conversation ultimately sticks with your kid, because they're not going to tell you while they're growing up. After he wrote this, I felt good all over again about his upbringing, and the fact his father and I got his upbringing right.

"When I wrote about it, it did bring the experience into a different light. I thought, 'Maybe this is something worth talking about. This is something that was a special opportunity, a unique thing to do.' It didn't seem like a big deal when I actually did it. I looked back at my upbringing, and concluded, 'Yes, this has shaped me.'"

We did raise Mats in an unorthodox manner. "I had a different upbringing than my peers," Mats said. "The places I got to see, my parents . . . I think it's led me to see things on their own merit that might seem unorthodox to some, or out of their belief systems. Including nontraditional careers. I grew up around professional athletes, going to all these different events . . . so some of these extreme feats, or whatever, don't seem so strange. Like if someone calls and wants to do a fifty-mile hike, it's like, 'Okay, let's do it.' Nothing strange about it.

"My upbringing has given me a wide scope of what is possible. I traveled a lot and really appreciate the travel, especially with my dad at all the Dance of the Deer stuff when I was a kid. It's only when you grow up that you realize, 'that wasn't so normal.' I got to see a lot of different places in the world, places of great natural beauty, so I developed a strong love and appreciation for nature."

The long periods away from school needed to change as Mats grew older. He needed a more structured and socially interactive high school routine, not the in-school-today, in-Europe-tomorrow rhythm of his elementary and middle school years.

"I think a lot of times growing up, I felt isolated from my peers. I never had a super strong group of friends," Mats recalled. "I had friends, of course, but never felt I had that same bond as other kids do. There'd be weekends in high school where I didn't have anything else to do, so I'd drive down to Big Sur and go camping by myself. Instead of going to a party on Saturday night, I'd go hiking, or drive up the coast to go surfing. It felt worthwhile, something I could do that fed me, that felt normal to me. I found a lot of comfort in that.

"I was a solitary kid, and part of that was growing up as the only child of two parents who had big names, traveled a lot, and created their own places in life with their two feet and their minds. I spent a lot of time entertaining myself. That plays into a sport like Ironman, which is a very solitary endeavor. You spend a lot of time in your own head during racing and training. I think sometimes, triathletes are the most self-centered people on the planet, out of necessity, right? All the solitary training is appealing to me, takes me to a place where I feel comfortable."

About the time Mats graduated from sixth grade, he ran his first triathlon. "I thought that was pretty impressive, watching little Mats do a triathlon," Scott Tinley said. ST rode his mountain bike next to Mats during the run, a kind gesture from an old friend. Mats also showed the family penchant for running up front . . . but, like his mom in 1982, he got nipped at the finish line. "It's not the performance of our kids that matters as much as they know that sport is a kind of thread that stitches our collective families together," ST, now an exercise science professor at San Diego State University, said afterward. "They understand this. Any success as a parent or a teacher that I've had far eclipses anything that I ever did in sport. I think Julie would agree for herself as well; she and Mark did a great job with Mats. And I don't say this lightly."

I continued to make sure Mark remained central in Mats's life, even if it meant staying in Santa Cruz in the home we'd bought and I remodeled after the divorce. "I really appreciate that time we spent together, especially now looking back on it," Mats said. "Whether you're super excited about what you're doing or not, just the fact you have this time to spend with your dad is special.

"With Dad, I was a student at Dance of the Deer for years. For me, the biggest thing was learning to quiet the mind, always try to operate with a settled mind, finding peace in every situation, and drawing on the natural world for spiritual and mental strength and renewal."

How can I not beam when my son says things like that?

Meantime, I did something for myself. I joined Marshall at Source Seminars in Idyllwild, in the San Jacinto Mountains about two hours from Cardiff.

Among other things, Marshall had become happier and more centered since going to Source after I suggested he enter a ten-day intensive at the Yoga Room in Encinitas to help his training for the Rock 'n' Roll Marathon in San Diego. He was also trying to lose weight and stop drinking (which he did for good in 2010).

Among other things, Source reconnected me with meditation, which I'd tried in college. This time, meditation became a central spiritual practice. It also helped me undo some of the trauma and insecure feelings of my childhood.

Marshall carries a vivid memory of our time at Source. "I'd just finished my second ten-day yoga seminar at the Yoga Room in September 2002. I was seriously thinking about becoming a yoga instructor, and then my mom died. I talked to the instructor, Michelle. She told me about an inspirational, life-changing weeklong program in Idyllwild.

"When I got there, the leaders of Source, Dennis and Kanta, were a sight to behold. Dennis looked like Gandalf, with the hair and goatee, and Kanta had just done one of her annual 'cut my hair as short as I can' haircuts. *Okay.* But the energy was awesome. I thought, 'Well, this might be a way to get past my crap and start my life again.'

"After twenty minutes on a Monday afternoon, I'm crying like a four-year-old. This stuff keeps coming out, dealing with childhood trauma. The one event that emerged was that one day, while my folks were embroiled in their ugly divorce, I came home from school and went to make a snack. There was no bread, no peanut butter, maybe a few canned goods in the cupboard. But in my mind, the fridge was empty; nothing that a kid would eat. My mom came home, upset about something, and I asked, 'Hey Mom, there's no food. Can we go to the store?'

"She lost it: 'Don't you get it? Your father is leaving us, we're poor, we have no money.' I really feel like at that moment, at nine years old, that's when my life as I knew it had fallen apart.

"That's the constructed story of my childhood I had to get rid of. Source Seminars helped me shed the preconceived notions of who I was. The childhood crap is just a story, a well-crafted script we create in our minds to adapt to life. I also realized for myself that the real truth was to be found with that first kernel of real meditation, and while you might be *this small,* you're also as big as the universe.

"Julie noticed something different after I started going to Source. She went up for the first time in the summer of 2003. By December 2004, we were going for Level 3 training together. I'd already staffed the seminar a couple times, and really became involved with what they were doing. Over the course of the next several years, I traveled with them extensively. Julie and I went to India; and I went to Israel, Bulgaria, Ireland, also Self-Realization Fellowship–inspired meditation pilgrimages.

"Julie realized that her marriage was done. She received the same initial benefits I did—let go of crap stories of her childhood, stories we thought our parents told us—whether they did or not. Source has a way of pulling those threads apart to reveal who we are. She went back to Santa Cruz with this knowledge and inspiration under her belt."

The contractor remodeling my house, Tom Eagleton, ended up becoming a Source graduate and traveling to India as well. He and I formed a wonderful friendship, often taking our sons, Mats and Willie, on ski trips. All these years later, Mats is working construction for Tom—the job subsidizing his current triathlon dreams.

I loved Source, how it enabled me to make sense of my childhood, then get rid of parts of that story that weren't really true and no longer served me. I understood my mother's life better, what she went through to try to raise us alone. I kept going, and joined Marshall as a staff member—really purposeful work.

"One thing about Julie: When she puts her mind to something, she becomes phenomenal at it," Marshall said. "Julie turned out to be the greatest senior staff member Dennis and Kanta ever had. I heard it directly from Kanta: 'Marshall, you're second only to her.' She's the greatest because she knows how to read people and get them exactly what they want. The Moss siblings were the wunderkinder up there. And we liked it because we could get out of ourselves. Julie didn't have to be a mom or a divorced woman up there; I didn't have to be a drinker up there."

In 2008, when Mats reached high school age, we decided he would attend public school. Along with that, your free-spirited, adventurous, send-your-kid-into-a-tsunami-and-up-a-tree narrator of this story became a sign of the times: a helicopter parent.

I had trouble with the "helicopter parent" then, and I do now, after seeing how far some have gone in their oversight of their *nearly adult children,* and their willingness to step on any toes to fulfill the vision they see for their kid(s). In 1990, child development researchers Foster Cline and Jim Fay coined the term to refer to a parent who hovers over a child in a way that runs counter to the social responsibility of raising that child to independence. Hmmm . . . hard to imagine myself going there, but I did.

Years later, when the helicopter was grounded and Mats emerged an independent, well-balanced adult, I read something from Dr. Brené Brown that struck home:

> *Raising children who are hopeful and who have the courage to be vulnerable means stepping back and letting them experience disappointment, deal with conflict, learn how to assert themselves, and have the opportunity to fail. If we're always following our children into the arena, hushing the critics, and assuring their victory, they'll never learn that they have the ability to dare greatly on their own.*

I'd spent my whole life living the second half of this statement. Now, though, I was so focused on Mats excelling academically that I became overly hovering. I certainly wasn't helping him. While I continued to encourage his adventurous side on weekends, vacations, and holidays, I reverted to Helicopter Mom the second we focused on school. I fully expected Mats to live up to his intellectual potential, which I never did while in school. I pushed him, hard; I couldn't allow him to fail.

Mats and I had many fights over grades and time-management choices. He often let me know how I made him feel—never good enough, no matter how hard he worked. If he got an A-minus in AP calculus, a strong grade in anyone's book, I'd quickly point put that if only he'd put in a little more study and less video game time, that A-minus could be an A. In today's overheated high school scene, with everyone clocking grade point averages that didn't exist when I went to high school, that half-grade could mean the difference between admission to an A-list college and not. I would've done anything to finish high school with a 3.5 GPA, an honor roll position. Today, a 3.5 typically gets you two years at a community college. Mats was better than that, and I let him know over and over again.

When I revisit my attitude during those years, it wounds me to recall that my kid thought the way to love and approval was through achieving a slightly higher grade. It shames me. It is one of the few regrets in my life.

Helicopter parenting was my attempt to ensure success, therefore giving Mats more self-esteem and greater opportunities. I was so worried about the future that I didn't appreciate the present. Here was a kid getting excellent grades, smart as could be, and a cross-country and water polo star. I didn't take the time to celebrate his accomplishments. Later, I realized it was my fear of Mats not being "enough" that drove me. *Enough for what exactly, Julie?* I projected onto him my deep-seated childhood fear of not being good enough. OUCH.

Some decisions worked well. I introduced Mats to Junior Lifeguards, so he could experience something Mark and I enjoyed as teens. "You have to do junior guards," I told him. "You have to do it once so you have good water safety." I always wanted him to play sports and surf, but I rarely told him *what* I wanted him to do. Lifeguarding is part of the legacy that Mats comes from. Not surprisingly, he completed the program with flying colors.

In high school, I told Mats he needed to try out for sports teams, to experience and appreciate the social and competitive aspects. He chose water polo and cross-country—and became an all-Santa Cruz Coastal Athletic League performer in both. "My mom encouraged me to play water polo; that was my one and only team sport," Mats said. "I started in middle school. It was one of those things I wasn't excited about doing, but my mom said, 'Well, you're going to try it.' I ended up loving it. It's fun. You're basically hanging out with a bunch of other kids, being active, scoring goals. I loved middle school water polo, but in high school . . . I liked the social aspect of hanging out, but I played year-round, so some of the kids on my club team, when they went back to their high schools, would kick my ass when our schools met. Every game seemed to be like that; my high school team wasn't very good."

He also became a reluctant team captain. Once selected, he led the team nicely. "The Bay Area has a lot of great club water polo teams. I was kind of bottom-of-the-barrel at club level, good enough to be on the teams, but not the best guy, not even close. High school was totally different," Mats explained. "All of a sudden, I was kind of forced into the team captain role, the leading role. It was an interesting experience. I was used to being this solitary kid, so transitioning into that role was difficult. However, I picked up a lot of tools that served me well when I became an adult and got into my own life."

Mats had no such trouble with cross-country. This is a fantastic high school sport, both a team and individual pursuit. You run against yourself, an opponent, and the clock, but you score team points—so there's plenty of strategy and tactical maneuvering in those 5K races. Mats was good at it, to be expected; his dad was a superb runner, and I'd clocked a 2:47 marathon. I loved watching him, unaware that less than a decade later, I'd help coach the cross-country team at my alma mater, Carlsbad High School. When I offered pointers to my hometown Lancers, I felt a bit nostalgic.

"I'm more drawn toward individual endeavors, so I really enjoyed cross-country," Mats said. "That was probably the first time I really pushed myself athletically, because I really wanted to run as fast as I could. It was a personal challenge. Who wouldn't like trail running for three or four months a year instead of practicing on the same field or in the same pool every day?"

By the time Mats graduated, he had become his own man, with the best of Mark and I blended within him. He was forging his path as a fascinating human being. He no longer needed to be taken care of—and certainly didn't need me trying to "upgrade" him.

We healed from my high school hovering. We persevered, he excelled, and then he emerged into adulthood with a personality, quirkiness, and strength of his own. One time, I commented that one of my most significant accomplishments was being his mom. "What will you do when I grow up?" he replied.

Good question: What would I do next?

Mats intuited that I needed to nurture my own dreams. From his youthful perspective on the universe, the more time I worked on my own life, the less time I'd have to hover over his! Again, he was spot on.

I continued to repair the damage I caused our relationship. In reading Elizabeth Fishel's and Jeffrey Jensen Arnett's book, *When Will My Grown-Up Kid Grow Up?* (who I was reading it for—Mats or myself?), I found three valuable tips:

- Observe respectful boundaries: Keeping a privacy buffer was key to our relationship. All through high school, I had access to Mats through the online parent portal, and he didn't have a car until his senior year. Only after I moved back to Cardiff and Mats remained in Santa Cruz could he be free to define his identity.

- Listen more than you talk: This elusive virtue was especially challenging for me. I'd literally have to bite my tongue to keep from giving too much unsolicited advice or asking too many nosy questions.

- Do what you love together, and intimacy will follow: Surfing, skiing, hiking, and triathlon have offered many precious hours that Mats chooses to spend with me.

Mats was now a young man. A solid man at that. His upbringing now complete, what would I do? How would I find new meaning in my life? Where would I turn to find it?

I decided to return to the most solid life partner I had left, always waiting to receive me, the one I chose to leave rather than the opposite—triathlon.

But first, I had to dig myself out of another dark place. Maybe the darkest.

CHAPTER 18
A Hard Bottom

"Rock bottom became the solid foundation on which I rebuilt my life."

—J. K. Rowling

The phone rang. "Julie, we'd like you to announce for the Tri-Cal season," Darren Wood said.

The call from Darren, the husband of my 1997 training partner Jenny Wood, presented a nice opportunity to share my knowledge of triathlon and spread the love to event spectators. It also felt like a lifeline. With my despair mounting, I needed something.

Once again, my triathlon family came calling, this time with a vocation that combines three of my favorite things: striking up conversations, competition, and sharing inner victories and celebrations, the "Wonder Woman" and "Superman" moments. I felt all but empty of this inner power, and badly needed to reconnect with it.

I loved announcing. I first fell into it when I did voiceover with Phil Liggett in London. In 1990, I was hired by Turner Sports to commentate on the Goodwill Games, an international sports competition CNN founder Ted Turner created after the Soviet Union and its allies boycotted the 1984

LA Summer Olympics. Like the Olympics, they were held every four years until ending in 2001. I worked on the 1990 Goodwill Games in New York, where I had a nice connection with beach volleyball superstar Gabby Reece and her husband, big-wave surf legend Laird Hamilton, famed for riding the fifty-foot waves (and larger) at Peahi (Jaws) in Maui. Gabby covered beach volleyball, I handled triathlon, and Laird tried to find surf somewhere on the south shore of Long Island. He needed some amusement, which for him meant anything to do with the ocean. I could relate to Laird's need to keep busy and burn off excess energy.

When Tri-California called, I needed them as much as they needed me. In September 2003, I announced my first event in Pacific Grove, near Santa Cruz. Then I started announcing their entire season. First up was the Wild-flower Festival, held every May for thirty-five years near San Luis Obispo. The event includes the iconic 70.3-mile triathlon, half the Ironman distance, and Sprint Mountain Bike on Saturday, then the Olympic and Collegiate Olympic championship on Sunday. We bring in Dean Harper, the winner of the inaugural Wildflower and University of California triathlon coach, as our race expert. He's also a good friend. Our volunteer base comes from my alma mater, Cal Poly San Luis Obispo. It's great to see how much triathlon is part of the Cal Poly experience. I can remember when that experience consisted of a crazy girl trying to convince a kinesiology department chair that running an Ironman was a worthy senior thesis project.

Announcing plugged me back in. Again, I was around people I knew, an energy I loved, and a vibrant, nurturing atmosphere in which I thrived. It felt like coming home again.

I also learned more about the recreational athlete's experience. I'd never thought of triathlon in this way until becoming an announcer; I only knew the pro experience, life at the front of the pack. When my race was over, I packed up my bikes and got out of there. The awards ceremony? Sometimes I passed on that too.

As an announcer, I draw from the personal experiences of all competitors, and spend little time with the pros. It took a while to get the hang of it. In my first Tri-California event, I interviewed the pro race champion. After we finished, a more seasoned announcer, Don Ryder, approached me. "Julie, there's a little too much *you* in that interview," he said. "Let's make it more about the athlete." All along, I was thinking, *I'm going to ask the greatest questions* or *I'm going to use my experience to* . . . In other words, finding ways to insert myself. As I've learned since, it's about giving the athlete the opportunity to talk about their experience, no matter whether they finish first or 3,000th.

From the announcing tower, I look around for things, like someone holding up a sign: CHELSEA AND SAM WISH DADDY A GOOD RACE. I'll call them out on the mic: "Hey, Chelsea and Sam! How cool is *your* dad doing an Ironman?" That exchange elevates their experience and trains the spotlight on them. Announcing is all about putting the spotlight on someone else—and being a disassociated voice sometimes. I think some announcers, especially former pro athletes, focus too much on their personal experiences: "I did this and this and this . . ." Perhaps I overcompensated for doing the same too much at first, but I love making competitors happy, giving back to them. "She reads people very, very well, and senses what motivates and inspires them—and then gets them to talk openly about it," Marshall says. "She adds so much to every triathlon she announces."

Thanks, big brother . . .

The announcing gig came while I was extricating myself from the shattered mess I'd become. The darkness was unmatched in my life; there were many days and weeks when I didn't want to get up. I kept myself going for Mats, staying busy with him and his school activities. The call from Tri-California snapped me out of a place where I lacked value and purpose, compounded by that awful *Racing the Sunset* feeling: being a former professional athlete without a post-career plan.

The call also triggered a desire to compete in another Ironman, this time the twenty-fifth anniversary event in Kona. I'd last competed in 1997, and been through six years of mostly hell since. Maybe I could lose myself in the training. My prerace comments to a visiting reporter read like a metaphorical window into my inner world: "I can suffer, and suffer deeply, and for a long time, and that's a pretty scary thing. Sometimes I have some pretty deep valleys to climb out of. I do it methodically: What am I feeling right now?

Then you go into cruise mode for a while. Then your attitude shifts and you say, 'Okay, what's wrong? What do I need?' You would give just anything to stop—that seduction to stop—and you have to not give in to that.

"The heat scares the shit out of me. The heat strips me to the core . . . I've got to be smart all day. Sometimes you even need to slow down and walk, since quitting is not an option. You walk for a hundred yards. If you vomit, that's okay. That's surviving. I have my A Plan, and I have my B Plan, and I don't think beyond that. On a heart level, you must surrender to the day and bring to it what it needs."

I decided to run for two reasons: at age forty-five, I wanted to beat my 11:09 time from 1982, when I was twenty-three (that goal would circle back again); and I wanted to beat Kathleen. We even jokingly called it the "Battle of the Moms," since she now had three kids.

My first race was on reporters' minds when I arrived. "I have to keep reminding myself that that was a really amazing time in my life," I told a *Sports Illustrated* writer. "Going back to compete in the twenty-fifth anniversary is a way to honor that memory. I don't need to get anything more out of Hawaii . . . I have already received so much. All I really need to do is cross the line, which brings me back to that first race. That's all it was about, just finishing something. Whatever else happens is icing on the cake. A lot of good things have happened to me because I just got across the line that day."

I set off with 1,600 other contestants and felt strong during the swim. The online news site *SFGate*, which serves the San Francisco Bay Area, described me as "fresh as if she had just stepped out of the bath." Next we rode to Hawi, at the other end of the Big Island, our turnaround point. "It was a little nuts at the beginning of the bike, frenetic," I told Michael Maloney, the *SFGate* reporter. "Everybody started out sprinting, and they passed me, young and old, you name it, but I decided I didn't want to work hard till twenty-five miles out, past the Waikoloa Hilton. I can't remember a day when the lava fields were that calm, without wind, but that meant heat, and at Mile 70 I started getting nauseous. My stomach went bad, and I told myself, I'm going to just let my system chill, and I stopped eating and started riding aerobically."

The stage was set for another difficult run, a possible DNF, another visitation by my old demons. This time, I didn't have a husband's race to watch, or a husband, or any other excuse. I wasn't looking for one either. I endured a large cramp at the ten-mile mark, dealt with it, and remained focused. I didn't worry about others in my age group passing me, or a podium appearance; I just focused on a strong result. I crossed the line in 10 hours, 57 minutes—13 minutes better than in 1982. I was double the age, and faster. It was incredibly rewarding and vindicating. Bad Mom was officially *Badass Mom* now!

Kathleen finished an hour and a half behind me, but what really impressed me is that she somehow trained herself into race shape despite having three kids (today, she has four). We celebrated our inner victories together.

Something I later said in the thirtieth anniversary book crystallized my thoughts and feelings about my relationship with Kona: "We've grown old together. But it took me a long time to own my image. I represent something to people. Twenty years later, I'm not about being an amazing athlete. It's about having the personal qualities to not give up when things get really hard. The underlying theme for me is that this triathlon community is real. It's familiar, and it's familial. And always a nice source to tap into."

Again, a strong metaphorical statement for what I needed to reclaim, retain, and strengthen in my own life.

I bottomed out as I hit fifty—and this bottom felt worse than hard. It felt bottomless. Many of the things women fear at that age converged, even as I tried to maintain a positive public persona and remain strong for Mats. I stopped working out, gained twenty pounds, drank too much wine, and became addicted to clove cigarettes. Once a woman who changed a sport, I found myself alone in a place I didn't want to be, my soul raining tears as hard as any Pacific storm. I was a prisoner in my own backyard, where I secretly smoked, then took shower after shower to mask the smell. I felt deeply ashamed, unappealing, and unattractive to everyone, so I latched on—to Mats. I needed that emotional bond, because I had little else. When parents operate from *their* needs, teenagers tend to pull away. Mats did exactly that for some time.

I bottomed out on my purpose for living. I was depressed and addicted. It took my friends Lisette, Sue, Cindy, and Wing, along with my brother, to snap me out of it.

"Julie had a hard time letting go of Mats," Lisette recalled. "Mats was the main guy in her life. He kind of took the place of a husband. That was a real struggle. It wasn't easy for Mark, either; Mats stepped away from Dance of the Deer, central to Mark's life. What Mats did more overtly when he became eighteen was to rebel. He was very overt.

"This bottom was worse than the one Julie had after her divorce. Far worse. She avoided it for as long as she possibly could. I knew it would happen, and when it did . . . she put it off by throwing herself into being a mom, and by all the other stuff she was doing. Finally, she couldn't avoid it anymore. She had to face it, once and for all."

"She was really a mess," Sue recalled. "I remember that I called her up, did not like the tone of her voice, and I knew she was in trouble. Mats was away with Mark so I told her to get out of Santa Cruz and come stay with me and my family. When she arrived, she was really sick and I put her to bed. The next day I asked her if she wanted to go for a walk, to see if moving would help her feel better. We started, but after maybe 200 yards, we had to stop. Julie was doubled over. She couldn't continue. How was my best friend, the Ironman legend, unable to walk 200 yards?"

Besides clove cigarettes, I developed an obsession for seashells, which my brother noticed. "I call that period the 'Great Shelling,'" Marshall said. "She was gluing shells on anything that would stand still . . . picture frames, mirrors, boxes, crucifixes, anything she could find. She made these fantastic shell designs; she'd collect the shells on the beach and had bags of them. I don't know how many glue sticks she went through. It was so obsessive. She was delving into depressive behavior, shelling and smoking. If it were me, I would've been eating and drinking. She wasn't exercising at all, and was smoking clove cigarettes like crazy, numbing out."

The following March, Marshall took his own final step—he drank for the last time after battling the same insidious alcoholism that contributed to my mother's death and ran amok on both sides of my family. "I think my getting sober was an awakening to her," he said. "If I could check myself into a detox facility, then maybe she could look at what she was doing. She was just getting back into race announcing, and spending a lot of time with Lisette and Sue. When she moved here, she could feel the veil of depression slowly lift off. Then it was, 'What am I going to do?'"

What I've always done—find some fitness and see where it takes me.

Meanwhile, Cindy knew a lot about people losing contact with their greater purposes and lives. As a career officer and leader within the Los Angeles County Sheriff's Department, she saw the best and worst among fellow officers and citizens alike. "I started running when I was twenty-eight or twenty-nine, after I joined the department," she recalled. "There were a lot of crummy days on my job, and I needed that release. In law enforcement, you see one of two things: well-balanced people who make sure to take care of themselves; and people who end up in bars after *and* before work, a lot of divorces, things like that."

After I returned to Carlsbad, she grew alarmed. "I looked at her and asked, 'What's with the clove cigarettes? Why are you doing this to yourself?'" Cindy recalled. "I'd never seen her in such a mess. We were all worried about her, and I was hoping we could steer her back to the things she loved—surfing, her friends in North County, and being the positive, helpful, fun person we knew, the person who inspired millions around the world."

Cindy then took action to get me out of the dark place, and toward what I did well—making people feel good about themselves. "I took her up to LA, and she did some really nice motivational programs for the officers, just sharing her Ironman experiences and how they changed her life," Cindy said. "The officers loved her, and she loved their response. I even think there might have been a date request in there . . ."

Lisette, a life coach for many years, saw beyond my suffering. She'd also observed my breakdown building over the years. She put her professional tools to work to help her best friend find some perspective.

"Her bottoming out had the added accumulation of slowly destructive behavior eroding away her foundation," Lisette said. "In my opinion, Julie is very good on focusing her attention on others. 'My career is all about Mark now.' She was his copilot, and that was great. Same thing with

Mats; it was all about Mats, at her expense. By the time Mats went off, she no longer knew who she was. She'd lost complete contact with her inner self—including the realizations she had and steps she took forward back in 1982.

"She was in a really tough space. Then she finally owned it. When we own it, find our purpose and strength again, and move forward, great things tend to happen. That's what this whole decade has been about for her. Between her athleticism and intelligence, Julie is not your average person. Her potential is enormous and on a world scale. She's finally coming into it in her full life, not just her racing."

I smoked my last clove cigarette on July 28, 2009.

I put myself back together, reclaiming the "no quit" attitude for which I was known. It began with surfing. After riding shortboards almost my entire life, I began surfing again on a longboard. I'd played around with one when Mats and I came down for Junior Lifeguards. As I learned the differences in balance and footing, and started styling it on a longboard, I realized I should have been a longboarder all along. I surf better now than I did when I was younger.

Surfing was so incredibly healing. I couldn't believe I'd unplugged from it. That Beach Boys lyric describes how surfing makes me feel: "Catch a wave and you're sitting on top of the world." Paddling back out reminded me of the innate connection between surfing and triathlon. In surfing, there is a very big ohana, a family of surfers everywhere. We're a huge tribe. There's also an ohana among triathletes. When the two intersect, it is really fun, and it intersected often with my generation. The most noteworthy examples were Mark Allen and Scott Tinley, surfers and lifeguards well before they became triathlon legends.

I really loved my new longboard, a gift from Wingnut. I also noticed more balance, probably due to the yoga classes I was taking to return to emotional and physical relevance. The one-legged yoga postures certainly didn't hurt. When I get a good wave, it touches my heart as deeply, or more so, than a good workout. Nothing beats having someone yell, "Great wave!" When you get a great ride, part of you hopes someone saw it, and when they do . . .

When I'm surfing, I feel like I'm fourteen and with my girls Emily, Robin, and Cindy, or watching my personal idol, Barbie Baron, showing us how it's done. With triathlon, when I'm training and in really good shape, I feel twenty-three—my age at my first Ironman. I feel youthful, vibrant, powerful, and fierce. My body doesn't betray me; it lets me *think* I'm that young.

As I settled into my routine of surfing, training, and yoga, I felt better. Fitter. Younger. Yoga is all about breath, and as my lungs healed, I could breathe again. I also started to dream, to visualize a purposeful life, one that took me away from the devastation of a lost marriage and the dark years in Santa Cruz. I started to reconnect to my inner self. *How can I get beyond this and help nurture others, help them find their larger potential, become empowered in themselves?*

First, I had to reclaim my inner Wonder Woman. I'd covered her with a cloud of smoke and negative thoughts and experiences, as well as the thick armor plate around my heart slowly building for over a decade. It would take some coaxing this time.

As I worked within, I also worked out, and plunged into training and competing. You know how some advise, "Throw yourself into your work?" when you're going through something scary, difficult, or life-altering? Triathlon training was my work. It had paid the bills for many years.

I started getting my life back together. I put my Santa Cruz house on the market in April 2011. It sold within days. I had until June to move out—the month Mats graduated. A month later, I returned permanently to North San Diego County. I moved in with Sue and her husband for a month, while Marshall finished the remodel of the condo my mother left us in Cardiff. Then I moved into the place that remains home today.

Sometime late in 2011, wouldn't you know it? Kathleen McCartney called.

She wanted to know if I was planning to run the 2012 race, the thirtieth anniversary of her victory and my crawl of fame. I was feeling better, noticing some fitness, and healing well. It took me five months to say yes to Kathleen's suggestion, but the second I did, something else fabulous happened. After thirty years of circling each other's orbits, only intersecting at races, we now lived in the same general vicinity at the same time. We started training together, and finally became the friends both of us secretly wanted, but neither of us could really put together.

I flew to Kona, stepped to the starting line for my thirtieth anniversary race, and proudly made it all the way through. My time was quite slow, 12 hours and 35 minutes, but when I consider the decade that preceded that race, it was a very big inner victory.

Then Kathleen and I moved on an idea that first sprang up during a training ride, one that involved our 1982 race and a way to make it inspirational to others now.

CHAPTER 19
Can I Go Faster?

K athleen and I didn't want to end a wonderful year of reuniting, training together, and building our friendship at the Kona finish line.

We further discussed the possibility of reenacting our 1982 race, and drawing out the themes and lasting messages from it. Since we have such a great story, and stories drive themes and conversations, we decided to create a wider story that would serve audiences of women and men looking for that "spark," or place to find fitness or whatever impassions them—and then to act on it.

Kathleen and I hatched something entirely new on a training ride in the Cuyamaca Mountains, east of San Diego. "We would sometimes spend weekends riding with the 'Give 'Em Hell' bike group, this amazing group of mostly men," Kathleen said. "They were very, very good cyclists. I got Julie to go out, and one of the men was Bill Bachrach. 'Oh my God, I know Bill,' Julie said. 'He's one of the best motivational speakers in the world, and he helped coach Mark when Mark got his motivational speaking going. And Mark got him into Ironman one year and coached him in turn.'"

Kathleen and I discussed her idea further, then I rode up to Bill. "Hey, Bill," I asked, "do you think Kathleen and I have a good story to speak?"

"Absolutely."

Kathleen takes it from there. "We went back and had some Mexican food. Afterward, we said, 'We'll see you next week.'

"'Well, I'm headed to a National Speakers Association convention in less than a week. You guys should go.'"

We went to the NSA National Convention in Indianapolis and started to build our story. It was very rare for two people to publicly speak together. We got the motivation and inspiration from Bill, who said, "You could go back and forth. You could take people through the [1982] race through your different perspectives, and weave your messages through that, and have a great story. Plus, you have incredible footage to share. You just have to craft it, work hard, cold call, and get your story together. Don't wait. Get out there and do it."

With that, Iron Icons was born.

Buoyed by Bill's advice and support, we also spoke to thousands of Jazzercise franchise owners at their national convention in Las Vegas. That was redeeming for me, since Jazzercise, which started in Carlsbad, turned down my request for sponsorship in 1982. Ironically, newspaper publisher Tom Missett, the brother-in-law of founder Judi Sheppard Missett, was among those watching the *Wide World of Sports* broadcast at Dooley McCluskey's. Judi created Jazzercise in the old Mayfair Market in Carlsbad, a grocery store staple in my childhood. While I was making news in the triathlon world, she was redefining dance in a sense by putting it to remixed music and presenting it in a very hip way to a nation and world looking to move more. Like Jimmy Watson said, there must have been something in the water in Carlsbad.

Kathleen and I explored the impact we could make on people trying to gain self-esteem, lose weight, find new purpose and meaning, and empower themselves. We talked about the fitness community as a proponent of not only personal health, but family and social health. We all want to be healthy winners, right? *Aren't we all, in different ways?*

Before the 2012 Ironman, I'd told a reporter, "I hope I can incorporate all this swimming, biking, and running into my life in a way that feels more like a hobby, a lifestyle, instead of something that I cram in every ten years toward racing Ironman." I was going to talk about bringing out the inner Wonder Woman and Superman in everyone, even as she was still in the process of reemerging in me.

Lisette felt I had something else to offer through speaking: how to pick ourselves back up when we fall, hard. "When we bottom out, we have to reassess everything. Starting with, 'Why am I here?' In retrospect, that was the biggest gift she could have in her life," she said. "Didn't feel like it, and we were all very worried about her, but look at where she stands now. I believe most of this decade, how it's turned out for Julie, doesn't happen if she doesn't bottom out and doesn't have to reassess her life while hurting and not sure what her next step is—or if she even wants to take it."

For the next two years, we took those messages on the road with the Iron Icons Speaking Series. While we wrote a back-and-forth script, we made a solemn decision to speak extemporaneously after fumbling around with index cards at our first presentation.

I also made a commitment to see how fit, focused, and inspired I could become as a woman in her fifties. I vowed never again to take my health or fitness for granted. While many might have thought, "There she goes, diving back into another Ironman," my inspiration drew from a far deeper source: the place that I determined to honor in myself and bring out in others, the place of deepest inner power and authentic truth, from where our larger voice and purpose rises.

In 2013, I stepped into age-group racing. When I was a professional, I never imagined myself sticking with the sport long enough. Young rock stars know this feeling as well; who imagines still being out there at fifty or sixty when you're conquering the world at twenty-three? But I wanted to race again, and when you are aging through a sport, you move into age groups. "As my friends like to remind me," I told a reporter, "I was famous for saying, 'I'll never race as an age-grouper!' Well, you know those age-groupers are badass athletes."

I qualified for the World Ironman 70.3 Championship in Las Vegas. While dismounting the bike, I knew I had no shot of placing, but enjoyed the greatest experience with Cherie Gruenfeld, an eighteen-time Ironman age group winner, thirteen-time World Champion, two-time Ironman 70.3

World Champ, and the record holder in the women's 70–74 division. Talk about excelling into the golden years! She emailed me:

> *Julie, you came by me, and didn't offer one excuse. You just supported me, said 'Great Job.' Obviously, something bad had gone on in your race, but do you know how many athletes would have tried to explain every little thing that went wrong? And why they're so far back? You didn't do that. You supported me.*

To which I responded:

> *Cherie,*
>
> *I never imagined having so many bike issues in one race but also never considered the possibility of not finishing. The flats took me out of racing, the overwhelmed tech crews did their best but I figured that after the 3rd flat I could walk the 6k in as fast as they could get back to me. The result was the surprising gift of being able to run with a sense of gratitude and joy. I ran to honor the time I'd invested to qualify and to see my season through all the way to the finish line.*
>
> *I will be in Kona, not to race but to enjoy and support. I will look forward to seeing you there.*

Three years later, I asked Cherie if she would send a few words to say to the ladies who participated in my Hoka One One #RunWithJulie fun run before the 2017 Ironman in Kona. The words of this beautiful, powerful woman ring true for anyone:

> *I wish I were with you here today and I'm sorry I won't be there to see Julie write the bookend chapter in her unique story that started with her courageous finish in 1982. Enjoy your time with her today.*
>
> *Each of you is in for an experience of a lifetime on Saturday— whether this is your first or you've been here many times—whether*

you're racing or you're a supporter. We're all privileged to be a part of this wonderful Ironman family, in whatever capacity.

If you're racing on Saturday, I would remind you that during the long day, there will ups and there will be downs. Throughout it all, remain Calm, Courageous, and Confident. And always remember, no matter how you're feeling, that this is what you have been dreaming of and you're on your way to realizing that dream.

For those of you here supporting, your smile and encouragement from the sidelines, whether for your loved one or a stranger, will give them strength and make them race stronger.

One final word to racers: At the end of the day, regardless of whether you met your goals or fell a bit short, what you have accomplished is something very rare and very special. Whether you finish in the glaring sun or under the Kona moon, you've done something to be very proud of.

Have a wonderful race day. Go make memories that will last a lifetime.

As I started racing more consistently. I took note of the dramatic changes in triathlon since my first Kona. Advances in technology, science, nutrition, and training programs allowed our sport to evolve into a highly technical, strategic athlete-to-course operation where every calorie is measured, every mile digitally logged. Now, you qualify for Kona by winning or placing highly in your age division in official Ironman qualifying races. In 1982, I signed up, stepped to the line in my oversized T-shirt, shorts, and a Bud Light trucker's hat, and rode a ten-speed bicycle. The entry fee was $85. Today, it's $950. "In 1982, we ate bananas and oranges from the aid stations and rode with PB&J sandwiches stuffed into our back pockets," I told a reporter. "The sport has changed light years with improvements in nutrition and aerodynamics. I wouldn't consider racing Kona now without my fuel belt loaded up with electrolytes and gels."

We were wild entrepreneurs. We could get appearance fees; we could negotiate all kinds of things. It was really fun, and, thank goodness, Hawaii was seen as an exotic location, because race producers chose great locations in order to get airtime. The travel was awesome.

In 2013, one of those wild entrepreneurs—yours truly—received a wonderful honor. I joined Missy LeStrange and the late Jim MacLaren, the father of paratriathlon, as USA Triathlon Hall of Fame inductees at San Diego's posh Bahia Resort. We were the fifth selection class. Missy won fourteen age-group titles in Kona after being introduced to the sport by her Masters swim coach, the great Dave Scott. Meanwhile, MacLaren finished the 1989 Ironman in 10:42—four years after his leg was amputated. Then he suffered another accident that left him quadriplegic. That led to the creation of the Challenged Athletes Foundation (CAF).

Jim Lampley, the anchor for the *Wide World of Sports* broadcast, introduced me. "We got back to New York [with the footage of the race] and knew we had the most extraordinary thing," Jim told the audience. "People in edit rooms were blown away . . . We knew we had to get it on the air exactly the right way."

When I spoke, I tacked on a postscript: "The girl who always just showed up and got by was being transformed . . . I was being transformed into someone who felt like I deserved to be thinking of myself as someone who was good at something."

The ceremony was gracious. I felt so honored to join a great champion in Missy, and a man who changed countless lives, Jim. I wish he could have been there. We also had fun moments, such as when Alistair Brownlee came up to me and quipped of Kona in 1982, "That was the first piece of triathlon footage I saw. I don't know why I did one actually." Well, I do: Alistair is currently the two-time reigning Olympic triathlon gold medalist, and the 2018 Ironman 70.3 Dubai winner.

Celebration was in the air again a year later, when triathlon pioneers gathered at San Diego's Mission Bay to commemorate the fortieth anniversary of the sport's creation. (A rock at the entrance to Fiesta Island marks the place where triathlon began—our own Plymouth Rock!) A lot of familiar faces were there, along with people I hadn't seen in ages, including Don Shanahan, who came up with the name "triathlon." We also saw 1975–76 Mission Bay Triathlon champ Russ Jones, fellow USA Triathlon Hall of

Fame inductees Jon Noll, Scott Tinley, Jim Curl, and Bob Babbitt, Kathleen McCartney, Ironman founders John and Judy Collins, and legendary triathlon journalist Mike Plant, ST's partner with the site trihistory.com. (Mike also shot the *Crawl of Fame* front cover.)

During the event, who flies by on a mile repeat workout? Meb Keflezighi! Months earlier, Meb had won the Boston Marathon before one million screaming spectators, the year after the terrible bombing. He was the first American man in thirty years to capture Boston. He couldn't have picked a better time to help heal a city and country with his feet.

Kathleen and I moved forward with Iron Icons. As we traveled from city to city, and met with women, men, and children from all walks of life, I started focusing on our *inner* attitudes, how we approach our lives and what we see and think of ourselves. How do we size up a new project? Or life change? What lifts us off the couch to run a 5K? Or a triathlon? How do our attitudes aid (or hamper) the way we pursue our goals or bucket-list items? What can we do to empower ourselves?

In late 2015, I began focusing on the power of intention. When you have intention, one thing leads to another. You develop an interesting momentum of following through and reaching your potential time and again, and better things start to happen.

I was at a low spot after suffering a knee injury. I'd done two ninety-mile weeks, because I wanted to take off Christmas and New Year's to ski. I didn't want to feel guilty that I wasn't looking for a gym or a treadmill. On day two of our trip, a family friend playfully tackled me . . . and that was it. I watched all those miles go down the drain, and with it, my positivity. I started thinking, "What's the next chapter?" I had no idea. I thought I might be looking at surgery, taking years to get back.

For a couple of weeks, I focused on what I couldn't do. Then I thought, *I can go to the pool and use my Eney Buoy* (a gift from my friend Eney Jones), because even kicking was hurting my knees. I picked up the first thread—getting in the pool. Sure enough, it led to a lot of things—trying out for lifeguards, and getting started on this book.

With intentionality, you might pick something that doesn't seem to make sense at the time—either to you or your family—but then the pieces fall into place and it turns out to be the key to something bigger, a new chapter in your life. Cultivate the confidence. Cultivate intentionality.

In April 2016, I put my intentionality, training, injury recovery, and fitness to the test in front the crowd that makes me most nervous—hometown fans. In the race, my first local effort in a while, I had an opportunity to run a good half marathon at the end of the swim and bike. My thinking reflected my new attitude: *the swim and the bike are done, just get out there and have a good run.* The second loop was like, *okay, one more loop. That's all you have to do.* That's how you build the brick and mortar. I wanted to be that athlete who knows how to navigate any situation and adjust to races that don't go my way at first, or at all. In my earlier years, I often missed that piece.

I learned to be efficient—key to both effective training and developing a strong inner discipline and attitude. After Mats was born, I had so much less time to myself. That made me truly efficient for the first time. I started doing back-to-back workouts.

Through this, I was developing the skills of navigating training and racing *psychologically.* Ironman is, above all, a mental game. So are most races—and most challenging pursuits. No matter the situation, I began thinking, "turn it around. Make it positive. Turn it around. Use it to your advantage."

This comes back to intentionality, which operates on full awareness, taking cues when they fly onto your radar, demanding expression, or knock very quietly on your soul or heart: *pay attention to this.* At the Ironman Oceanside 70.3 race, the entry landed in my lap: "You want to do this race?" "Well, sure!" I had this focus, everything seemed to be healing . . . and I was thrilled. The results were better than I thought.

During the race, I had to walk up a set of short, sharp, steep hills. A gal said to me, "You go girl!" But I was walking! I reached the top of the hill and started running, and thought, "I'm going to come running by you in a couple minutes." When I passed the runner, I'm sure she was reconsidering her decision to run up that hill. I did the best I could in the moment, and it enabled me to run through once I'd climbed the hill.

The moment reminded me of a Paula Newby-Fraser quote: "To me when people ask if I can give them my one piece of advice, I tell them it is all in how you handle the chaos of your mind. If you can direct that into the current moment of what you're doing, it can definitely calm a lot of the chaos that goes on around competing in triathlon."

Triathlon racing, and life, come down to managing the low parts. How do we handle things when we're down? How do we handle crises? Bad breaks that hit unexpectedly—or suddenly? How do we rise above them? The actions and attitudes we adopt to rise from our darkest and most challenging moments form the positive, strengthening attitudes that carry us toward our greatest achievements. To paraphrase former Boston Marathon contender Don Kardong, they forge our souls. They also create mental toughness. If you have a strong body, strong mind, and strong belief in yourself, you can conquer your world or completely change the landscape of the one that hasn't been working for you.

By handling that one hill in Oceanside, I turned my attitude around. I've since come to look forward to these opportunities. Now, when it's going really well, I have these mind gaps, like, "Where did those four miles go?" It is almost a time-travel thing.

The day after the race, I sat my sore body down in the Village Pie Shoppe in Carlsbad to begin work on *Crawl of Fame*. I opened by recounting the 1982 race, discussing transformative life moments, and how we can develop inner attitudes so strong and resolute that nothing can take away our authenticity, power, passion, or the way we shape our lives. I burned with the desire to impact and mentor women, men, girls, and boys, to help them see what is readily available within themselves—things *we* often see in our friends, loved ones, family members, and colleagues that they don't always see in themselves. Like what I saw within Mark Allen in 1982, a global superstar ready to rise forth if he put in the work. Which he did.

I also was fired up about something else—regaining my California State Lifeguard license. What's so odd about a (then) 58-year-old trying to become a lifeguard? I give you Mats's incisive comment: "Mom leads an unorthodox life in many ways, so to her, what might be normal seems different to others." I'm sure not many 58-year-olds are channeling their inner *Baywatch* by intending to step into a tower, racing into the water, and rescuing swimmers caught in riptides . . . but I wanted to see if it was possible.

The idea of being a water person calls to me in the deep, soulful Hawaiian tradition, echoing from my heart to my DNA. I've always wanted to surf big waves, paddle across the Molokai Channel, ride stand-up paddleboards, row outrigger canoes, swim great distances, and rescue swimmers in distress. It is part of ohana, family, looking out for each other, sharing community. The camaraderie among lifeguards is close to that.

To kick off my unlikely bid to recertify, I went online, saw the requirements, and thought, *these are so doable.* Completing a 1,000-yard ocean swim in 20 minutes? *Check.* Ten minutes to complete a 200-yard soft sand run/400-yard swim/200-yard run? *Check.* Instead of showing up to join my friends in the recertification swim, I decided to officially start with the hundred young guns seeking their spots on a lifeguard tower near you. Leave it to me to choose the hardest path. I've done the same for my last two trips to Kona, qualifying the old-fashioned way despite receiving an at-large invite. I've ridden the 1982 coattails many times, in many ways, but I want to *earn* my spot in Kona, or on a lifeguard tower.

For our test, I pulled up to Ponto Beach in South Carlsbad and noticed the big surf. *The playing field's gonna level now*, I thought. I should've been nervous at being the oldest candidate by . . . a lot . . . but I had nothing to lose, and the ocean was my element. I focused on the time cutoff. I needed to feel capable of moving on, of being in sufficient shape to save someone's life. I finished twenty-second in the first open swim, and was second woman in the 200/400/200.

"We didn't think you would come," the training supervisor said afterward.

"Well, I want this."

I really did. The training proved harder than I thought, especially since I was also prepping for an Ironman 70.3 Gurye in Korea, to be held in mid-September.

When we were done, I ran into lifeguard supervisor Julie Garcia, a two-time Molokai-to-Oahu paddler. "Julie, you did so well; I'm so stoked for you," Julie said. It was so good to hear that. I think I out-bodysurfed her on a couple waves. I don't remember being such a good bodysurfer, but if you have a choice of swimming to shore or catching a wave and already catching your breath when the others come in, which do you take? More than a couple of ocean triathlon swims have ended with lifeguards-turned-triathletes leading because they caught waves on the inbound swim. One that comes to mind is the 1986 Nike Triterium in Oceanside, co-managed by my manager, Murphy Reinschrieber, which now looks like a visionary prototype of closed-circuit, short-course urban races. Mark Allen's buddy George Hoover came out of the water first, because the surf was a booming six- to eight-feet, he was an old lifeguard, and he simply caught an outside wave and bodysurfed it to shore. You're not going to swim that fast. Interestingly, one who almost never got off the beach was one Lance Armstrong, a sixteen-year-old professional triathlete from Texas who could run and bike like the wind, but had never tackled ocean surf before.

Four months later, it was time for the eight-day, eighty-hour state lifeguard training and testing program. Would I become the oldest woman to regain a tower spot? Would I return to a tower for the first time in almost thirty-five years? Would I be able to "take command of emergencies . . . initiate first aid and resuscitation procedures, and work closely with other emergency responders . . . prepare reports, remove hazards, assist the public, and advise visitors of park rules and regulations . . . operate and maintain rescue vehicles and equipment," as the job description states?

I didn't quite make it. After spending the week fulfilling the physical goals and holding my own in the competitions, my exhausted brain blanked on something that should've been second nature: CPR certification. While more involved and advanced than the trainings available to teachers and coaches, it still should've been simple. My brain just wouldn't fire. I could rescue my "victims" from the surf without a problem, but would I kill them on the beach?

As I licked my wounds, I looked forward to the Ironman 70.3 Gurye Korea. But first, I embarked on an adventure with Mats: the 2,650-mile Pacific Crest Trail, which he was soloing.

CHAPTER 20
Mother & Son on the PCT

Like many fans of Cheryl Strayed and her wonderful book, *Wild: From Lost to Found on the Pacific Crest Trail,* I entertained thoughts on hiking the PCT. Then my notion grew legs and became serious, a challenge I envisioned myself tackling and completing.

As my triathlon training and race results continued to improve in 2016, I thought seriously of hiking the PCT, the spine of a continuous mountain range that starts in the northernmost Cascades at the Canadian border and runs south to the Laguna Mountains and the Mexican border. Along the way, you walk through the Cascade, Siskiyou, Sierra Nevada, Tehachapi, San Gabriel, Big Bear, and Cuyamaca Mountains. I thought first of hiking it right away, and then possibly as a sixtieth birthday present in 2018.

My first natural love, the ocean, got in the way of any immediate PCT plans. Or to be more specific, lifeguard training. I had a choice: ocean or mountains? I chose the sea. Then Mats called and informed me he would be hiking the PCT, alone. He asked if I would join him on a few stops along the trail.

I didn't need to be asked twice. The significance of his ask hit home: my *adult* son was asking me to join him on an excursion that was in his hands, not mine. Instead of being a helicopter parent, I would be a supportive companion on the trail. We hadn't done anything particularly long-lasting or defining since I'd moved back to Cardiff, but now that he was in his early twenties, he and I could relate as adults. And nothing brings you closer (or not) than being in close quarters on a grueling hike.

From August to November 2016, I darted to a few put-in points to the PCT while continuing to prepare for (and run) Ironman Korea 70.3. I came to spend some time hiking with Mats, and enjoying the exquisite nature and wilderness on the PCT. I ended up learning a lot about him—and he offered up a very big surprise when he finished.

Mats's decision to hike the PCT was entirely his own. He started thinking about it nine months before his first step. It came at an auspicious time for him, as he was trying to figure out his next step, his place in the world—and kindling a brand-new romance with his beautiful girlfriend, Megan Speciale, at the same time. "I took a leave of absence from college. In hindsight, I wish I would've finished it up, but I knew computer programming was hard work, I was going to college for computer science, and I realized that it might be leading me to a job in Silicon Valley, in a cubicle, and that's what I'd be doing my whole life," he explained. "Not quite what I want, when I'm young and have all these other aspects of my life that I really enjoy. Part of me wanted to be a climbing bum, just buy a van, drive around, and climb everything I could. I decided to take a break from school to figure out what I wanted to do.

"I ended up in not the most glamorous of endeavors, working carpentry. I was going from being behind a computer to working outdoors all day, being active with my hands, learning new skills, building things. I liked it, a lot, but not finding what I ultimately wanted.

"Then I came up with my next plan of action: 'Maybe I'll do the PCT.' I went up to Seattle with some friends, and one of their friends told me, 'I've decided to take a sabbatical from work and hike the PCT.' I'd hiked parts of it, little parts, so I knew what the Pacific Crest Trail was, but I'd never considered doing the whole thing. As he kept talking, I thought, 'You know, that's what I want to be doing right now.' I kind of forgot about it, but a couple months later, the thought hit me again, stronger this time. I talked to my boss, and he was willing to give me the time off; he'd been a kid in his twenties who'd traveled in the world to learn more about himself, so he was very understanding. He told me, 'If you need to take a couple months off, go for it.' He was super cool."

When Mats called and told me he was doing the PCT, I reacted like mothers might in that situation: I launched into planning mode. "She bought the guidebook, searched online, trying to map it out—which is not my forte," Mats recalled. "When I go on a vacation, I buy a plane ticket and figure out the rest when I get there. I've heard she was like that when she was young—I mean, what is her 1982 Kona story really about, when you look at it from a personal perspective? It's about a girl flying to Hawaii and figuring it out when she got there—and she's inspired people ever since. But she was all business on PCT."

There you have it . . .

As we planned out Mats's PCT hike, he decided to depart in July, taking the more seasonally preferable route of south-to-north, from the Mexican border just south of Campo, California, to the Canadian border. However, he was three months late. By going in that direction, he would be crossing the Cascades in October and November. Not good unless you want a PCT experience complete with gully washer rainstorms, hurricane force wind blasts, and early-season blizzards. Mats is well suited to handle himself outdoors, but digging snow caves for survival purposes wasn't in his plans. Nor on his bucket list.

He chose to reverse course, and start at the northern terminus. A great call.

His next challenge was deeply personal. He and Megan had only recently begun dating, yet both felt their attraction to be potentially lasting. And then Mats decides it's time to hit the trail for a few months . . . Gee, I wonder where he might have seen that kind of spontaneity and desire to take mighty solo challenges . . .

"We had just met," Megan recalled.

"Which didn't make it any easier," Mats said. "We were still new and fresh, and I figured she wasn't going to stick it out for four months while I disappeared, so I thought we were going to break up when I left. I told her about it, and to my surprise, she said, 'We can make it work.'"

She laughed. "The things you men put us through!"

◆

I met up with Mats near Ashland, Oregon, six weeks into his trip. Along the way, I picked up Megan in Santa Cruz, so she could reintroduce herself to her boyfriend. I wanted to meet him in Ashland because of the incredible scenes I'd watched in the *Wild* movie, which starred Reese Witherspoon. I could also fully relate to Cheryl's story, since I too went through some years picking up the pieces and using a powerful outlet to recover—in my case, returning to triathlon. Cheryl's reconnection with her larger, more authentic self, her inner Wonder Woman, resonated with me. I felt like I was honoring her in a way by choosing Ashland to begin my latest adventure with my son.

Megan and I found Mats downtown with four or five other PCT hikers. We could smell them before we saw them. I passed around some brownies to the group, which had taken to giving themselves trail nicknames, a quirky but common thing for both PCT and Appalachian Trail through-hikers. They gave Mats the hybrid name "Jorts," as in "jean shorts." Their needs were pretty simple: hot food, cold drinks, a bath, and a laundromat.

We walked around town and found an amazing microbrewery. For the first time, I tried a nitro beer. There is something poetic, almost romantic, about a freshly-poured IPA from a nitro tap. The cascading effect is mesmerizing. The waterfall of tiny bubbles slowly yields to a caramel brew, with a fluffy, white head thick enough to float a bottle cap. While nitro is normally associated with a certain Irish brewery, more and more craft breweries are embracing the nitrogenized method. Several of the hikers filled up their growlers, small jugs that typically carry sixty-four ounces of beer. We headed to our campsite at Hyatt Lake, ate, and slept.

The next morning, Mats and I hiked around the lake, hoping to find a coffee joint at the nearby resort. No luck. We made a hearty breakfast, but Mats grew antsy with our slow pace. He was used to brewing up a cup of instant oatmeal and coffee and getting back on the trail, not the fresh fruit granola and yogurt buffet I was laying out. Oh well, Mom likes gatherings and conversations around good, nutritious food, and Mom was on the scene . . . I did hear him mention that he could already be five miles down the trail while I finished packing my car.

Finally, we were ready. Our plan was to hike thirteen miles on the PCT to Green Springs and spend the night. Thirteen miles can't be hard, right? It's a half marathon; I can run it in an hour and forty minutes. I found out otherwise when I began hiking on the rugged, steep trail. Running is a much more level energy expenditure, and much more predictable. The steepness made me work my muscles at lengths where they have a lot less strength, compared to muscle lengths used while running. Lifting my body weight up a steep incline, even with a very light pack, proved to be plain hard work.

"She was this incredible triathlete with her amazing training, so when she first thought of PCT, I thought she had the sense of, 'It's pretty easy, right? It can't be that hard,'" Megan recalled. "After she did the first overnight backpacking trip and was sore, I remember her looking at me like, 'I don't know if I can do this.'"

We spent a great night under the stars . . . until a late-arriving PCT through-hiker pitched his tent too close to mine and snored like a hibernating bear. I threw sticks at his tent, which accomplished nothing: he kept on snoring like a broken metronome, impacting my nerves. I thought of a well-placed set of fingernails crawling down a chalkboard.

The next day, I decided to run thirteen miles back to the car while Megan and Mats hiked to Callahan's Lodge, the next stop, where I would drive. My run was a bit different than a normal trail outing; I carried my sleeping bag stuffed into a daypack. Fortunately, Mats decided to haul my tent for me. Once parked at Callahan's, I walked three miles onto the trail to meet the kids. In our first two days, I'd logged thirty-one miles of hiking and running. Not bad. Mats went inside to check out the lodge, where we would be staying in a few days, and grab his free beer as a PCT hiker.

We spent the next few days in Ashland, where I'd rented an Airbnb. We kicked around all kinds of ideas for short hikes, but Mats was happy to hang out and focus on the Big Four must-haves for any PCT hiker breaking from the trail: Hot food. Cold drinks. Baths. Laundry. Fine with me. My legs were hammered from just two days. Plus, Jorts's jorts were in dire need of mending, so I stopped into an amazing artisan quilt store, Sew Creative, to buy a couple squares of flowered fabric to patch them up.

Finally, we headed off to Callahan's Lodge, but not before loading up on supplies at the Ashland Food Co-op, stopping at a post office to ship boxes, and getting a fresh beer refill at Growler Guys. When we arrived, I treated Mats and Megan to a swanky room in the lodge, with its own fireplace and hot tub, while pitching my tent on the lawn and sleeping under the stars with other PCT hikers. We played bocce, and ate one more great meal: rib eye steak with an extra dollop of garlic compound butter, herb roasted potatoes, heirloom carrots, and for dessert, berry cobbler à la mode.

The next morning, Mats was off before he could enjoy the all-you-can-eat pancake breakfast at the lodge. His next big target was the California state line, 113 miles down the PCT. As Megan and I loaded up the car to return home, I was relieved that Mats set off so eagerly. Earlier, in Ashland, he'd confessed he was *over it*. I feared he might decide to quit, but then he clarified himself. "I'm over it but I'll finish it," he said.

The trek had become hard. Very hard. But he was really happy to see us out there.

"That was really cool. I'd talked to a couple of my friends, and my parents, about meeting me out there," Mats said. "I'm so happy she made that happen. I'd done a lot of outdoor things, camping things, with my dad when I was little, but not really with my mom alone. It was special getting to share that with her."

Several weeks later, Mats and I met up again at the Kennedy Meadows General Store, a significant spot that represents the end of the Sierras and beginning of the desert. Mats was amazed to see how the environment had changed from the lush, green vegetation he'd enjoyed the entire way. Plants that have regular access to water are so much friendlier to hiker's legs. It was evident it had become a prickly cactus world.

We left Kennedy Meadows late at noon and hiked twenty-two miles to a spring, passing the 700-mile marker along the way: 1,950 miles down and 700 to go. We hiked for over an hour in the dark and found the spring. Mats spent the next forty-five minutes filtering water, and then we heated already prepared Indian food with naan bread. We shared the two-person tent that really fit 1.5 people, but it was cozy and I was exhausted.

At first light, Mats headed to Walker Pass, thirty-two miles away, while I doubled back to the car. My legs felt better than in Oregon and I moved easily, with only a bottle of spring water and nutritional bars for snacking. Since we were late in the hiking season, and southbound PCT trekkers don't often see others, I didn't pass a soul on my twenty miles back to the car.

I drove to Walker Pass, with a quick stop in the tiny Inyokern market for supplies. I gladly paid their inflated prices to buy multiple gallons of water. I didn't want to filter in the dark again. That might be a Mats thing, but it's not a Julie thing. I found the designated PCT campsite, and enjoyed being the only camper while I set up dinner and made the breakfast and lunch sandwiches he'd take the next day. Then I hung a lamp, a beacon for Mats, who put in a twelve-hour day that included hiking in the dark the final two miles. Within an hour of arrival, he was out.

After a quick cup of coffee, Mats hit the trail by 6:00 A.M. for another thirty-five-mile day. He was taking advantage of the more modest portion of the trail to bite off large chunks of distance. I offered to transport what he wouldn't need until the following evening, when I next saw him, but Mats wouldn't let me transport a thing by car. He was honoring trail integrity, hiking from start to finish without taking any shortcuts. I admired my son all over again.

After Mats left, I organized the car and then decided I wanted to see what he was seeing on the first few miles of his hike. I followed him down the trail—or should I say, *up* the trail. I climbed from switchback turn to switchback turn, until I topped the ridge line and beheld a breathtaking view. I could only imagine the spectacular view Mats had already stored. These vistas could change the way you saw the world. A little over a century ago, they seemed to work on the great naturalist John Muir, who first encouraged the creation of a series of national parks to President Teddy Roosevelt. Muir's own named trail occupies 210 miles of breathtaking Sierra views, 160 miles of which Mats had already walked, since it merged with the PCT for that stretch. Muir saw those vistas for the first time in 1868 and found his home.

Two hours later, I headed back. As the mom/trail angel, I was constantly retracing my steps. How nice it must be, I thought, for Mats to move in one direction, always gaining miles, rather than not gaining and subtracting. I got back to my car with a long day looming, and detoured to the quaint town of Kernville.

Mats had gone feral, with no change of clothes. His jorts died in Independence, California, so he hitched into town and came back with a pair of women's running shorts. I had almost purchased the same style. "What size are they?" I asked.

"Women's size small."

"Mats, I wear that size."

He looked at me. "Mom, you're an extra small."

Mats put them on, and they fit. It was weird seeing my tough, fit son squeezing into a woman's small short. He's about six-foot-one, and weighed 180 pounds when he began the PCT. Now he was at 150, on his way to an eventual 145.

The other part of going feral, or ultralight, means not carrying water, and using your filter system. Mats stripped down to the most basic elements needed to survive the final 700 miles. He didn't carry fuel to heat food, nor did he carry soap, toothpaste, or TP. In fact, he carried nothing but the one set of clothes on his back, a tent, sleeping bag, inflatable sleeping pad, tiny journal and stub of pencil, headlamp, and down jacket. His daypack only weighed ten or eleven pounds, depending on his Pop-Tart, Top Ramen, and instant oatmeal supply. He prepared everything with cold water.

Sorry, son, but give me Kona any day with its fully catered buffet . . .

At one point, Mats openly wondered if he should send his tent back. I had a concerned Mom moment, and urged him to keep it to insulate himself from not only the elements, but to feel nurtured in his very own cocoon so he could recharge his spirit. That worked, but Mats was discovering his inner grit, the willingness to sacrifice comfort to finish something. I knew the feeling. Difference was, I held onto it for hours at a time in races and brick training days, not for weeks or months on a sustained 2,650-mile hike.

Leaving Kernville, I drove along Highway 58 to Willow Springs, then headed nine miles on a dirt road to a ridge, where I spotted a PCT marker. Thank goodness I arrived during sunlight; I never would have seen the marker. I hiked a few miles along the trail, again wanting to see the view. Sometime after sunset turned to darkness, I found my car, climbed in and nodded off.

A rap on the window. A horror movie moment, for sure . . . a woman, alone, in a remote place, a rap on the window . . . and Mats's face outside. I exhaled a very deep sigh of relief.

While waiting, I realized that, despite my many thoughts about hiking PCT, I never would do this trek solo. It's too disheartening, and I like being around community and support too much. Maybe if I headed northbound with the other 2,000 hikers in the height of the season I could handle it, but to travel SoBo (southbound) with maybe 200 other hikers and be alone mile after mile would break me. I have learned that I feed and gain strength off those around me—friends, family, other racers, the crowd.

The solitude had the opposite effect on Mats. It strengthened him.

Once again, we had one hour to eat, share stories, and crawl into our sleeping bags before Mats's desire to start early and sheer exhaustion ended his day. I got up before dawn and made sandwiches and coffee by headlamp. We said our goodbyes at 6:00 A.M., and I drove to Lisette's house in Bakersfield while he headed toward Tehachapi for another thirteen-hour hiking day.

He had 600 miles to go.

Two and a half months after I first saw Mats in Ashland, I met him near the San Jacinto Mountain hamlet of Idyllwild on November 1. Set among tall pines, sweet smelling cedars, and legendary rocks, Idyllwild was a wonderful mountain village just two and a half hours from my Cardiff home. When we met up at the Paradise Café, he had 151.9 miles to go. We spent the night in the guesthouse of Sandi Castleberry, the unrelated (to me) niece of my Aunt Bev. Again, we had less than an hour to organize, eat, and prep for the morning before the lights went out.

At 5:30 A.M., Mats hit the trail, focused on covering the final 151.9 miles in the next four days. I marveled at his determination to close like this, which reminded me of how his father operated at Kona. I drove the ninety-eight miles home, knowing I would later meet Mats for dinner in Warner Springs, making a 130-mile round-trip from Cardiff after wrapping meatloaf and baked potatoes in foil to stay hot. All of this for the twenty-minute visit we would get at a tiny roadside intersection where the PCT crosses Highway 79. He ate quickly and then hiked another eight miles to a water supply at Barrel Springs, completing a fifty-mile day. WOW.

Three nights later, on November 4, I arrived in Campo and parked on the side of the dirt trail, about a mile from the terminus. Several border patrolmen, quite busy men in this section of the border, had checked in with me on their rounds, accustomed to seeing late-arriving PCT hikers. They made me feel safe in the pitch dark.

Finally, I saw a headlamp coming toward me. *Mats!* From the way the light bounced and danced on the trail, he appeared to be running. "Mats, I'm here, honey!" I called out. "I see you're running the final miles."

"No mom, I'm not running. This is my walking pace."

Thoroughly amazed, I now saw how he covered fifty miles a day for the past four days. "Do you mind hanging back for a few minutes until I finish?" he asked.

I understood completely. This final mile would become a touchstone in his life, like my 1982 Ironman. The final mile is where I discovered so much about myself, and I wanted Mats to embrace the enormity of what he had accomplished and absorb it quietly and undisturbed.

After what felt like an eternity, I drove the final mile to join him in celebration. He arrived at the southern terminus of the PCT on the Mexican border, near Campo, at 9:38 P.M. on November 4.

Mats wrote this entry into the PCT Log Journal at Campo:

(July 10–Nov 4)

Well, here's to 2650. To the months of total solitude, unforgettable friendships made, the unimaginable kindness of utter strangers, breaking up and reuniting with my girlfriend, the unimaginable love and support of friends and family. To endless suffering which is only exceeded and overshadowed by the boundless bliss and serenity

of the PCT. This has been a journey whose hardships and rewards
can only be comprehended by those who have lived it. In the words
of an unnamed NOBO, "Sometimes I just want to shake them and
scream . . . You don't know what we've been through!"

I started this thing on my own and so have I finished it. Now time
for a well earned champagne celebration on the brink of Mexico.
Here's to my predecessors and those still to come. Welcome to the
fucking coolest club on the planet!
  —Jorts

Later, Mats reflected on our time together on the PCT. "It's one of those experiences where, when people ask you about it, you have to say, 'Well, unless you want to sit here for a day and a half while I tell you about it, I can just tell you it was really cool . . . or you can experience it,'" he said. "But having my mom out there, she'd helped me plan it; she wanted to do it anyway. It was really cool to share part of the hike with her, because there are some experiences you can't put into words. It's like any other peak solitary experience: it's so important to you that you want to share it with others."

Mats's peak solitary experience, and his reflection afterward, sprang into something that caught both his father and me quite off guard. "Triathlon, and especially the Ironman in Kona, has felt like a bucket list item to me since I was a kid," he explained. "After finishing the Pacific Crest Trail, I had this place in my life where I really didn't know what I was doing next. The more I thought about Ironman, the more appealing it was, especially since [finishing] the PCT left a big hole. On the PCT, you're out there pushing yourself every day, that's the main focus, and it's especially rewarding when you're doing it in all these beautiful places.

"Then there's the mental side of PCT. Some days, you have to really will yourself into walking, or push into things you didn't really feel were possible. You might wake up at 4:00 or 5:00 A.M. and say, 'Today, I'm going to push as many miles as I can,' and that's the mental challenge. One day, I did sixty miles. You don't go that fast, but you stay up late and use a headlamp and just keep going. You're isolated and only pushing against yourself. You're by yourself. There's no one else. You're not racing, there's no competition. It's a pure form of challenging yourself.

"That's what attracted me to Ironman. I was searching for something to fill that hole of 'the next great personal challenge.' Especially where I'm at right now. I'm sure that the more you do a sport, the more competitive you get, but for the time being, I'm just going out there to see what I can do for myself. It's an opportunity for me to challenge myself physically and have a goal I'm working toward day in, day out."

Nothing says *legacy* faster than jumping into the family treasure chest and grabbing the baton.

Oh, boy. It didn't matter how many Ironmans I'd run. Despite my initial excitement, I would become another worried parent watching their kid take on the Ironman. There's the thrill of victory, the agony of defeat, and the torment of being the mother of a young Ironman athlete. I would be experiencing the third piece of that reality . . . and one of the other two as well.

CHAPTER 21
Kathleen

M y story is incomplete without bringing in the woman who, on February 6, 1982, deserved all the accolades due an Ironman champion.

America first became acquainted with Kathleen McCartney as the perfectly put together California girl who beat me at the finish line in Kona. She is the 1982 Ironman champion, not me. Yes, a few sips of coke at Mile 25 could've resulted in a different outcome, as Scott Tinley speculates, but it didn't happen that way.

From that day on, Kathleen and I were regarded by media and fans alike as rivals. Part of that perception drew from our dramatic race—if you only beat someone by 29 seconds after 11 hours and 140 miles of racing, it must be a rivalry in the making, right? This prevailing thought continued despite the fact we crossed paths like two ships navigating different courses, occasionally intersecting, but never really docking in port together. When we finally got that chance in 2012, we clicked in several ways. Now, we enjoy a nice friendship.

Kathleen's life changed as much as mine in 1982. She was one quarter away from graduating from UC-Irvine, but didn't go back right away. "The phone was ringing off the hook, I'm loving this triathlon life, this was a rare opportunity, so I focused on triathlon with the idea I'd return to college the next year to finish my degree," she recalled. "That turned into two years."

The instant name recognition that comes with winning the most-watched Ironman race in history launched her career too. In hearing her story, I'm reminded of how remarkable Kathleen is, still determined to run Kona despite debilitating injuries over the years. In ten appearances on her own, she has finished ten times. Now she has found a larger purpose, teaming with triathlon pioneer Mike Levine, who is battling pancreatic cancer. Their story, which played out in 2017, leaves few dry eyes in the house; we'll get to it.

"The Ironman experience has been so influential in my life," Kathleen said. "To have the experience to win as a twenty-two-year-old, when I was just developing my foundation for life . . . everything I learned through Ironman has carried through. It's about doing things that seem impossible, never giving up, and continuing to dream the big dreams.

"This has manifested in every way possible. The event gave me a completely different mindset. I was not a competitive athlete. I was a recreational athlete, had never been on a team, and had no reason to believe I could win an Ironman. Are you kidding? I got totally inspired when I watched people dive into the ocean on February 14, 1981, including my then-boyfriend, Dennis Hearst. As soon as the cannon blasted, I knew I would never be a spectator. I wanted to be a doer. That decision changed my life.

"I'd already done some extraordinary things, just not athletically. I took a trip around the world between high school and college. That's another thing where I felt like, 'Wow. I just did something totally outside the box.' I'd worked hard, saved the money, planned the trip . . . When you do things unique and empowering, it gives you the feeling of 'Hey, I can conquer the world.' Life is the series of choices we make. When we make big ones, they can elevate our lives to a point we didn't think possible the year before . . . or maybe the day before."

While I showed up in Kona as a neophyte in 1982, Kathleen had kept busy since watching Dennis—and quite successfully at that. Few triathlon experts remember this, but Kathleen's Ironman victory was her third of five consecutive race wins—six, if you count the 100-mile century cycling race she also won. "When I first started training for Ironman, my goal was to finish in something like fifteen hours (her winning time: 11:09). I trained with my boyfriend, now my ex-husband, and we discovered that I had a lot of endurance, natural body awareness that helped me to cycle and run."

She came to Kona red hot, off victories in the Santa Barbara Half Triathlon and Navy SEALS Triathlon. After Ironman, she captured the first two Bud Light USTS events, in San Diego and Long Beach. I finally got her in Malibu, winning a hefty $2,500, but let's be fair: 1982 was Kathleen's year. She capped it by defending her title admirably to place fourth among women in the October 1982 Ironman, the second of the year in Kona. She lost this one because she hit the wall and had to walk the final two miles of the marathon. Ironic, considering what happened eight months before.

When recalling our February race, it's easy to assume we became heated rivals, or spent all our time recapping our race dramatics—which would land us in ABC Sports Studios three weeks later. Neither was the case.

"It bothered me a little that we were portrayed as rivals," Kathleen said. "There was no particular basis for it. She hadn't done anything to me, and I hadn't done anything to her. I can't really blame the media, but I've always had trouble with that. We tried to click, but never really did, only because we spent a very limited amount of time together. The main obstacle was where we lived: When I was in San Diego, she was in Santa Cruz. When she was in San Luis Obispo, I was in Santa Barbara and then Irvine. There weren't many races in those days. Even when we were in Hawaii in 1982, we didn't see each other much.

"The finish still feels surreal to me. I didn't know I'd passed Julie; I was just happy to finish. I didn't get to congratulate her; they whisked her away. So we never had a chance to go over our race. The next time I saw her was in an awkward moment at the awards ceremony. Then she was off here, off there, and I was back home, except for our weekend in New York [at ABC]. So our experience in 1982 was so poignant, but so limiting. When we did see each other, it didn't feel warm and fuzzy, because we hadn't really had time to figure it out."

Kathleen ran well in 1983, but by the spring of 1984, she was off the circuit. Triathlon was growing, but did not yet provide a comfortable living.

She sized up her options and realized that, for her, one thing needed to happen: finish her degree.

"I thought, 'my gosh, I can't put this off any longer.' That's the reason why I pulled back," she said. "So many people were doubting I'd finish school. My course load was tough. I was making some money in triathlon, but I felt I had to have a career to support my life. I didn't know where the sport was going, so I decided to get the degree, then get a job."

That didn't last long. Running Ironman is quite seductive . . . especially for a champion. We saw each other again at the 1985 Japan Ironman. "I went as a guest of Penny McCoy and her family. She had watched my Ironman win, and we became close friends after that," Kathleen said. (Penny's father, Dave, created Mammoth Mountain Ski Resort in the central Sierra, installing the first rope tow in 1942 and the first chair lift on the massive volcanic mountain in 1955. He celebrated his one hundredth birthday in 2015.) "I was working, and Penny called and said, 'Hey, you want to go to the Japan Ironman and run with me? I'll line us up some sponsors.' I ran in the rain and finished fourth. It wasn't a bad race, especially since I hadn't done an Ironman in two years. Julie won with a fabulous race. I got the Ironman bug again."

However, one thing hobbled Kathleen—her nerves. The party line was that when Kathleen was hospitalized two days before beating me in Kona, she suffered from food poisoning. That's been written in most articles since. It took Kathleen one more hospitalization to realize food poisoning did not cause her severe discomfort. She also realized a huge difference between us: while I thrived on competition, she was not a natural competitor. Interesting to say that about a champion, but it's true.

"I've been hospitalized twice for nerves in Kona, once in 1982, and then again in October 1983. The same thing happened both times. It was horrible. I would even go down to the swim start beach, and get an overwhelming feeling of nerves and fear. I could barely get down to the beach. I think it was due to the pressure, wanting to win or at least compete at my best."

She might have been nervous, but she was still damned good. From 1982 to 1988, she fought off her nerves to finish in the Top 6 at Kona three times. We both had great races in 1988, when I ran a Kona PR 10:09 to her lifetime PR 10:19.

After the race, she left the sport to start her family with Dennis, while I stayed for two more years and then bowed out to support Mark's Ironman journey and start a family of our own. She didn't return until 2003. When she did, the triathlon world beheld a more relaxed Kathleen. "I wanted my kids to know me as the Ironman/Ironwoman, and it was finally a good time for that," she said. "I wanted them to see me set goals. They'd never seen that side of me—ever. I didn't even race triathlons; I did some marathons and half marathons, but that was all.

"I thought that I would have terrible nerves. I was approached by NBC to do a piece, and I said, 'No. I'm doing this for my kids. I'm not doing this to get attention.' I knew if I jumped back into all the activities, I would have terrible nerves and it would be a bad experience. I quietly did my training, went to Kona, and had no nerves. It was amazing. I got to run the last one hundred yards with my kids, from the banyan tree to the finish. When I was training, I kept envisioning running the end of the race with them.

"That was the turning point. I realized, 'I don't have any pressure. Nobody cares; I don't care; I'm not going to be on the podium. I'm just here because I truly love the sport and the training, how it makes me feel.' It gave me calmness . . . to this day. I sleep the night before races now, and I don't have any nerves. It's almost like a meditative feeling on the course. The key was to step away from the competitive side. If I have competitive goals or ambitions, I get nervous."

We enjoyed a nice interaction in 2003, but never reached the point of friendship. Kathleen returned to San Diego and I flew back to Santa Cruz. "We never had the opportunity to get over whatever was created; never had the time to build the substantial, meaningful friendship," Kathleen said. "There was never time to nurture it."

This was not a simmering rivalry, but two busy women raising kids . . . as single women. Mark and I were already divorced, and Kathleen and Dennis followed a few years later.

In 2011, after I moved back to Cardiff, my phone rang. It was Kathleen.

"I had reasons to go back to the 2012 Ironman, and I'd heard Julie was back," she said. "Here was the time we could finally develop a friendship and be training partners. I didn't know if she was interested, but it was a split-second decision by me. This was the first good possibility of merging our triathlon lives, since we finally lived in the same area."

This time, we concentrated on building a friendship. "I think foundationally, we're both pretty much the same people we were in the '80s. I definitely felt like she had a more relaxed approach to me, and I to her," Kathleen said. "I told her what I'd been going through with my divorce, she'd been through a divorce, and I told her about my goal. She wasn't thinking about going back to Ironman—at all. But she was really kind, and said, 'You know what? I'll be there for you as a friend. I'll support you and train with you while you go on to do Ironman.' It felt really good, two people coming together and forming a friendship. When you're going out on bike rides and spending five or six hours, you're going to get to know someone. This was the first time we'd ever trained together."

A lot of people might find that amazing, given how we were joined at the hip on the day triathlon exploded globally. How could we be in the sport for thirty years, the first several as top-shelf elites, and not have trained together? Two ships passing . . .

"We found a lot of common bonds. We know we're different people, but we respect and admire each other. It was so amazing. We had a fresh start. I was so excited that Julie came onboard for the 2012 Ironman; it was phenomenal."

Kathleen and I made Iron Icons appearances for the next few years until we decided to move into other areas as well. We rarely pass up an opportunity to speak together. We also make it a point to get together every February 6—the anniversary of our race. We ride the Ironman in Minutes, all 140.6 minutes of it. Only a few select people join us, part of Kathleen's mission to keep the anniversary gathering as organic as triathlon was in 1982.

In 2017, Kathleen and I each worked with another triathlete. While I trained with my Iron Twin, Khalil Binebine, and assisted his two-year quest to race in Kona, Kathleen took on something far different. She decided to help old-school Ironman Mike Levine return to Kona, a miracle, in that Mike is battling pancreatic cancer. Mike ran his first Ironman in October 1982 for the same reason as Mark Allen and many others: the *Wide World of Sports* telecast.

Not surprisingly, Kathleen found her wisdom and strength as an Ironman champ stretched to places she never imagined. "Mike told me that I breathed the life back into him," she said. "I never thought anyone would tell me I'd brought them back to life. I can't even put into words what that means. I dedicated basically my life to that journey with him. I was between jobs, and decided to focus exclusively on working with Mike. It was more meaningful than anything I've done."

Everything about their effort was challenging. I would have liked to train with Kathleen more, but her focus was on Mike, and rightly so. "We rode at a much different pace," she said. "We had a major training challenge. Mike's on chemo for life. He goes on for two weeks, comes off for two weeks, goes back on. To train through chemo when you're down, you can't sleep and take medication to do so, you're groggy in the morning . . . literally every day was a game-day decision. I had to keep him in a protective bubble, away from other people."

Nevertheless, Kathleen decided they were ready to go. They petitioned Ironman World Championship Executive Director Diana Bertsch for a special entry. "We'd talked about Kona since Mike had expressed interest. He sent a letter to share his story. We wondered for three months if it was going to happen. After he got in, every time I saw him, I'd say, 'Hey Mike, you're going to Kona!' We were so excited and thrilled, couldn't believe it happened," she said.

Whenever you work with someone in a life-affirming situation like this, magic happens. You may have no idea when or how, but sometime during the big day, a magical moment pops up, one on which you look back and say, "Wow." In Kona, Kathleen and Mike experienced several such moments.

"We had to split for the men's and women's swim start, which turned into a very poignant moment," Kathleen recalled. "I didn't know how his swim was going. He thought he'd come out ahead of me. We thought we'd meet at the first transition, or I'd catch him on the bike. I got to the turnaround boat and looked at my watch—thirty-four minutes. I breathed to my right every stroke, as usual, but after I went around the boat, I took a breath to my left—and there was Mike. I saw his purple cap, I had a purple cap, Julie had a purple cap; that's the cap some people wear so the NBC cameras know who to follow. He stopped to look at the swim finish; he was taking a little break. There were 2,500 people in the water—and there he was, the one time I breathed to the left. One of the most serendipitous moments of my life. It was like finding a needle in a haystack without looking.

"He was struggling. I told him to stay right behind me, draft off me, but we swam together. It was so spectacular; we'd never thought about finishing the swim together. I'll never forget our first steps out of the water. I put my arm around him, and we were both smiling, then holding hands. It was really special."

They shared other poignant moments, though not in the manner either of them had imagined—or hoped. "When we were training, Mike didn't spend a lot of time drafting me [on the bike]. He spent a lot of time fighting the wind, because we knew it would be windy on race day. I have this thing where I look over my shoulder; it's a natural thing. The plan was for me to stay ahead of Mike, keep checking on him, make sure he's riding near me. But he had to stop at every aid station, which was really bad. He'd crashed three times in training, so he became insecure about reaching down to get a water bottle. At Ironman, you need to eat and drink constantly. So we'd stop at every aid station, and I'd run around, getting him drinks, getting him food.

"When we got back on the bike, Mike didn't really let me know how badly he was feeling. I could tell that we were really slowing down; our average speed went down to twelve mph, compared to twenty to twenty-five when I was racing to win. I tried pushing the pace, but he couldn't go any faster."

Then came a crushing moment: at the forty-five-mile mark of the bike ride, Mike said, "Kath, I don't think I can make it."

"I didn't expect to hear that; I didn't have any contingency for that," Kathleen said. "I thought we were going to finish the bike, then walk or run the full marathon.

"I said, 'Mike, we're in Kona. Let's figure this out, pull over, and let medical check your pulse.' He felt dizzy, like he was going to black out. We had him checked and got him back on the road. He pulled over one more time, and I said, 'Mike, we're at fifty miles. Let's at least make it to the turnaround.' We were six miles away. We knew of a pancreatic cancer patient, Dave, recovering from his chemo in Hawi—the turnaround—and he'd read Mike's story. On race week, he contacted Mike and said, 'I just want to meet you. I'm recovering from Stage 4 chemo, you're inspiring to me, you're giving me hope.' He was waiting for us in Hawi.

"I thought the one way to see if Mike had anything left was to remind him that Dave was waiting for us in Hawi. If we could just get there, and then drop . . . I knew Mike would do something for someone else as much as he'd do something for himself."

"Kath, if we do, I will crash. I will black out. I can't," Mike said.

"Okay, we're done. Let's call it a day, but there will be no tears, no regrets. We are winning by you being at the starting line, and the journey we've had to get here. We're going to be so proud of what we've done."

Their race over, they sat for ninety minutes to wait for the sweeper vehicle, which picked up athletes who dropped early. Kathleen suggested to Mike that they borrow a cell phone and call his wife, Jan. She was monitoring him via the Ironman Tracker app, one of many nice developments since 1982.

"I'm sure she was thinking, 'Oh my God, why have they not moved for an hour and a half?' We called, and (my daughter) didn't answer," Kathleen said. "Finally, my son, Patrick, answered, then handed the phone to my daughter, Madelene. 'Be sure to ask Mike if he wants you to finish for him, in his honor,' she told me.

"I never had any intention of leaving his side—no way—but I asked. 'Kath, why don't you go on, go get your T-shirt and medal,' he told me.

"'Mike, let me make this very clear: that's *not* why I came here. I'm not leaving your side.'"

Kathleen isn't leaving the cause either. From her 1982 Ironman medal, she created a perpetual trophy to award each February 6 to someone living with pancreatic cancer. Mike Levine was the first recipient, and she made the award perpetual, so he would live long enough to pass it on.

Kathleen would love to ramp up her game to the level I've been fortunate to experience recently, but she can't. Injuries have taken a toll, specifically spinal problems and their resulting surgeries. However, through that difficult experience, she holds a wonderful perspective. "What amazes me is how fit our generation is; have you ever seen so many fifty-five, sixty, sixty-five-year-old people in this shape? It's never happened," she said. "I feel really proud that Julie, and I, and the other early triathletes and endurance sports athletes, had something to do with that.

"I'm not Kathleen from 1982. I can't do the type of training to be competitive. I can swim freely, and cycle pretty freely, but I have to avoid steep hills now. Running holds me back. I just had another serious injury in June 2017. But I had to go do Ironman. If it were my own race, I would've said, 'No, I don't think so,' but because it was for Mike, my surgeons worked with me to give me three injections so I could be there.

"This is what I like to share with people in my age range: focus on what you *can* do. It's such an important message. Don't have excuses. You never know what can happen. Part of going back was to return as someone who'd given up on running for life. A light came on: 'I can swim, I can bike . . . and I can walk a marathon.' I developed my core, worked out with weights, and my surgeon put me on an amazing protocol to get strong enough to walk the marathon. As it turns out, I ran every step of the way."

Just like she did in 1982.

CHAPTER 22
Kona 2017: What Contingency Plan?

"We must all suffer one of two things: the pain of discipline or the pain of regret and disappointment."

—Jim Rohn

I stood on stage at Nytro Multi Sport, talking with the packed crowd and my fellow Tri Legends, soaking up a great August evening as I shared emcee duties with Scott Tinley and Bob Babbitt. As I spoke, something kept tugging at me: *Are you going to say it? Are you going to really say it?*

Well, I'm known for being direct. If I wanted to own my next goal, and inject life and legitimacy into it, what better way than to make it public—with the winners of a combined thirty-five Ironman World Championships sitting on stage or beaming in via video feeds?

"I like big goals," I said, a smile stretching across my face. "So I have a new goal: I'd like to go as fast in 2017 at Kona as I did in 1982."

More than a few members of the very athletic crowd looked at each other, their faces wearing the same expression: *What?* Even ST gave me a wily sideways glance, like, *there goes Julie again . . .* "I want to see if the body can produce a time that would've won the Ironman in 1982, and to produce that time thirty-five years later."

As the crowd digested my latest leap into the unknown, I settled into the goal. I wanted to chase something so big that it held me accountable each and every day to get up with focus, drive, and connection. That makes me feel ageless, my métier now: wake up, chase your dream, and you *will not* feel your age. And enjoy many ageless adventures. You may feel a few physical limitations, and your recovery time will be longer. However, by feeling worthy of chasing that big dream in your core self, of contributing to the world with something audacious and expanding, you create an energy that causes others to take notice. In some cases, you inspire them to pursue their dreams too.

As audacious as my goal sounds, I do admit that greater bike and running shoe technology and nutrition make hitting a tough endurance time goal at an older age more feasible. I'm also a much better swimmer than in 1982, which I attribute to the flexibility and upper body strength gained from yoga. However, it's still the same engine putting one foot in front of the other in the run, and turning those pedals over. "There are many technological, technical, and nutritional advantages over the way we had it," Scott Tinley said, "and now we have refined training programs for every part of training, every part of a race. You have to account for that. However, while the rest of us are just trying to stay fit and not ache every day, Julie's turning back the clock. Her goal is far beyond me to try—but if anyone can somehow make it happen, it would be Julie."

After the Tri Legends gathering, and my excellent result a month later at the Ironman 70.3 Gurye in Korea, I looked again at my goal. It felt possible, but times are arbitrary. Was it *really* possible? Or a wild idea I allowed to fly far too deeply into my mind and imagination?

I was going to find out.

By fall 2016, I'd laid down the goal: Finish the 2017 Ironman World Championship under 11 hours, 10 minutes, my 1982 time. Impossible? Perhaps. But it reminds me of Twentieth Century Fox brass telling George Lucas that *Star Wars* would be a colossal waste of the $11 million budget they gave him, a big-time money loser. *Okay . . .* Did he listen? No. He worked day and night to prove them wrong—and did he ever! I can be just as short and dismissive when dealing with doubters and naysayers. They take our energy, question our dreams, and waste our time.

Once I put my goal into active motion, the stars began to align. I developed an excellent training program, I was injury free again, and my life was in good order. After spending the past couple of years training into this position, I would now summon my inner Wonder Woman, and subscribe to the very messages I'd been sharing—find your authentic self, live from there, never quit, be ageless and fearless with every step.

Then it almost ended, due to the biggest unforeseen circumstance: a freak injury.

During the holiday season, Mats and I took a ski trip with Lisette and her son, Mark. We stood atop the Winter Park slope in Colorado, preparing to ski down. As Mark and I were messing around, he snuck up to hug me, and I kind of twisted around. My brand-new leopard skin snowboard pants weren't stretchy, so at some point, my legs sprawled—and stopped. One thing kept moving: my knee. It popped and buckled. That forced me to cancel a planned January trail marathon, which I wanted to run to get into hill running shape. I also wanted to attack a 50K trail run in February, but I switched to a 25K to protect my tender knee. I did well, finishing sixth in the women's 50–59 age group in just over 2½ hours. I felt really strong, so I knew my knee was healed.

I'd started training in December for the initial measuring test, the Ironman North American Championships at Woodland Lake, outside Houston. I held an invitation for Kona, which took the pressure off while dealing with the knee injury. However, as I noted to Ironman World Championship director Diana Bertsch, "I will do everything in my power to earn the invite by getting out there and racing for a qualifying spot."

Time to hold up my end of the bargain.

The Ironman 70.3 California in Oceanside was next. I planned a fast training day, but wanted to drop a strong time. I ran 5:24, shaving 18 minutes off my 2016 time in the same race, and finished second in my age group. I ended with a 1:49 half marathon, after finishing with a 1:53 the year before. Four minutes doesn't sound like a lot, but it felt much different. A friend gave me two photos from the same spot, one shot in 2016, the other in 2017. In 2016, I'm digging, grinding it out, shoulders hunched, head slightly down. In the other shot, I'm smiling, head and shoulders upright, my gait strong and flowing. It was a fabulous way to enter another bit of training before Houston.

Three weeks later, I toed the line at Woodland Lake—and had a dream race. The swim went fast and smooth. So did the bike, until the last bit. After fighting a headwind for thirty miles, my frustration hit a brief trigger point at mile 110 when I yelled out, "I can't believe anybody wants to do this sporrrrrt!" *Time to get off the bike!* I also sat in the penalty box for a five-minute time drafting infraction. When they penalize you, it's not worth it to argue.

I started the first of three running loops, each about eight and a half miles. I set up my last brick training specifically to run eight miles off the bike, to have that feeling under my belt. The first loop went great. I stopped at every aid station to take care of nutrition, hit the port-a-potty, and fiddle with my socks. On the second loop, I noticed one woman in my age group sticking with me, and several others still together. After that, I headed into the unknown, having not run longer than eighteen miles in training. The landmarks along Woodland Lake seemed to pop up and pass by faster, a nice psychological visual. By Mile 23, I noticed the chase pack was gone. I felt even better. *Time to push.* When I tried, I felt twinges, cramps trying to grab hold of my calves and hamstrings. *Not yet.*

When I'd passed Mile 4—also the Mile 23 mark on the looped course—I said to myself, "When you get back here and it's the real Mile 23, you get to do a happy dance." That positive image went into the fiber of my legs and made a difference in my marathon. I was too tired to actually do the happy dance, but in my mind, I was doing it. I was also smiling a lot at runners, spectators, and volunteers, thanking them every time I passed by. There's a science around smiling, how it elevates everyone around us—and ourselves as well.

At Mile 25, we ran out, turned around, and finished. A woman came toward me, running really well; I thought she was sizing me up. I reached Mile 26, and started imploring myself to push, much like a jockey yelling into his horse's ear before the final turn: "Okay Julie, you've spent 140 miles getting to this point. Now you have to start racing. If that woman is coming, you are not getting passed in the last half mile of an Ironman marathon, not after 10 hours and 40-something minutes."

I picked it up, and started rallying people as I raced for home: "Come join me! Come on, let's go!" It was really fun to feel that good at the finish, to feel I'd used just the right amount of effort, concentration, and focus.

I crossed the line in 10 hours, 46 minutes, 51 seconds, beating my 1982 Kona time by 23 minutes and 28 seconds. "One of the most inspiring, and one of the best, examples of turning back the clock we've seen," Scott Tinley said. Carlsbad High School athletic director Amanda Waters, a former all-American basketball player in college and someone I got to know while helping the Lancers' cross-country program, added, "I can't even imagine doing something like that. Nor can almost everyone else. She makes us think we can get up and do something special again athletically too."

"When I saw what she did in Houston, I was blown away," Lisette said. "She'd been talking about breaking her Kona time for a while, and of course I believed her—this is Julie, and once she sets her mind . . . Her mental attitude and strength is so much greater than in 1982, it's like two different people are out there. But to see her actually break the time, by that much . . . she's making all of us rethink what is possible when we get to fifty or sixty. I ran my first marathon in fourteen years in Paris with Julie. I never thought I'd do that again either."

Reaction was strong and positive. *Triathlete* magazine spread the word in a nice online and print article, with the fetching subhead, "Ironman's ageless It Girl returns to Kona to literally write her final chapter." The It Girl? I loved that connotation, since the original It Girls, actress Clara Bow and socialite Zelda Fitzgerald, were *the* ultra-stylish, scene-setting flappers of the Roaring Twenties. Their energy, enthusiasm, reputation for behaving brashly in word and deed just as women were attaining the right to vote, and willingness to speak loudly in a male-dominated world made them iconic. They stood tall—and uplifted those around them, even as they faced down their own inner demons—Zelda in particular with her alcohol issues and tortured relationship with her husband, *The Great Gatsby* author F. Scott Fitzgerald. The It Girl of Triathlon? I loved it. The article started off:

In February 1982, the year of her famous collapse and the 10-yard finish-line crawl seen around the triathlon world, 23-year-old Julie Moss finished the Hawaii Ironman in a time of 11:10:19.

In April 2017, 35 years later, 58-year-old Julie Moss won her age group at the Memorial Hermann Ironman North American Championship Texas in a time of 10:46:51.

Whoa. "Right now, I'm the best athlete I've been in my life!" excitedly says Moss. "I'm back to where I was at 38 years old, when I was a pro and went sub-11 at Kona."

That a former pro athlete could even think she is her best at nearly 60 years of age seems remarkable, but to hear the ageless, irrepressible Moss tell it, it simply took her this long to get her act together, get properly motivated, and for the first time, truly fall in love with the sport that has defined her life.

I'd come a long way from 1982 . . . and from 2009. I was invited to blog about the race, and developed a David Letterman–like list of ten things that made a difference. Here are several items from the list, with side notes. The first contains within it the faux pas that almost ended my journey before I left San Diego:

- Dropping my Cervélo P3 off at Nytro Multisport after my final long ride, so TriBike Transport could deliver it to Texas. With all the hours of training, the last thing I wanted was to worry about packing and traveling with my P3. (Note to self: when your last long ride requires a driver's license to enter Camp Pendleton, do not leave said license in your stealth pocket, or it will arrive in Texas before you do and definitely complicate boarding your flight when you discover your mistake at 5:00 A.M. while standing at the ticket counter.)

- Walking through the Ironman Expo, where they handed out samples of Texas BBQ. (Y'all, I'm talkin' the full smoky combo of beef brisket, chicken, and sausage wrapped in a foil packet with your choice of mild or spicy BBQ sauce on the side for dipping. Seriously, don't mess with Texas.)

- Staying with a host family that turned out to be Ironman royalty. I reached out to the Houston Racing Triathlon Club to see if any members would be interested in hosting me. I love the added experience of staying with a local family whenever possible, and the club provided a once-in-a-lifetime experience. My host, Bonnie Wilson, was the daughter of Henry Forrest Jr., one of the original twelve Ironman finishers in 1978. Sadly, Henry passed away in 2009 from pancreatic cancer. His spirit and Ironman legacy remained a powerful presence in the family home. She shared with me that when Henry was in remission, the only thing he wanted was to gather together his family and friends for a celebration triathlon. Henry took his infant granddaughter and dragged her toes through the pool so she could swim, and then went on to push his sister in her wheelchair for her run. Bonnie reminded me of the gift of being an Ironman.

- Women Who Fly is a Hoka One One slogan. My Hoka Claytons made me feel like I was truly flying in both Oceanside and Houston. Finding a shoe that gives you maximum support and wings to soar to the finish line.

- Attending the awards while wearing the North American Champion's jacket. It wasn't pink, but it was still a look that worked. Oh, and watching the roll down in my age group and seeing another Julie—Julie Kaczor, third in my age group— go bananas when she heard her name called and punched her ticket to Kona. I gave my Champions' jacket to Bonnie's youngest daughter to help inspire her to create her own legacy.

- Earning the number one spot in my age group, then toasting the win with a cold IPA.

Triathlete asked me an interesting question: Now that I'd beaten my Kona time elsewhere, would I literally resort to crawling to beat it in Kona? The article stated, "For the sake of perfect symmetry, a Hollywood script writer might suggest that Moss could push hard enough to collapse and crawl to the finish one final time."

My response may not have been what they were looking for: "That will definitely not happen again," I said. "Once you go that far, you guard against having to do it again—so you either back off or train your ass off. And I'm having tons of fun right now training my ass off."

Texas was challenging, but I never pushed too far outside myself. I stayed inside the grace of my comfort zone, and never encountered lasting pain. I felt so positive the whole day—and it was nice to hit the time goal just three weeks after my race in Oceanside. Certainly an April for the personal record books!

When you achieve a landmark goal, the expectations ramp up. I'd served notice with my age-group win in the Ironman 70.3 Korea, finished second in Oceanside, and captured the Ironman North American Championship. *Bring it on, Kona!* Well, wait a second. Once the word got out (wind-aided by me on Facebook, admittedly), my family, friends, and well-wishers began commenting with statements like "How is that even possible?" to "I know you can do it; you've got it; look what you just did in Houston!"

Yes, it was fantastic, but Houston is not Kona. The setting, intensity, weather, course, and competition level are far more intense on the Big Island. While it's human nature to assign a comparative time from one course to another, everyone who's ever tackled Kona knows better than to fall into that trap. More than anything, I realized two things: If my training and racing continued to go strongly, I had a chance; and my training would need to become even more refined, focused, and engineered to the specific demands of Kona. I needed total consistency, no distractions, and nothing emotional to knock me off a goal that had become a consuming focal point.

I wasn't the only member of my family to eyeball Kona. Just a few months after completing the PCT, Mats decided he too wanted to race in Kona.

Mats's decision thrilled me. Sort of. He'd talked several times about fulfilling his personal legacy of racing Kona, a legacy laid down by Mark and me. I knew he could handle the challenge and training. But as a *mother*, I worried about how my son would fare, how much he would hurt and suffer . . . motherly concerns. While Mats might have expected Mark and me to jump up and down at his bold decision, we both know the euphoric ups *and* most devastating downs of Kona. We reacted accordingly.

"My parents approached my decision in different ways, which I think reflects their respective approaches as parents," Mats said. "My mom was more excited and supportive." She offered all this advice and perspective, which I of course appreciate, not just because she's my mom, but because she knows this race. They have two different roles, and it forms a nice balance. Right now, they see that I'm taking it more seriously, which is making them get more excited about helping out. My dad's been a good resource, because he's so close, he's been coaching forever, he's a great coach, and I'm not afraid to ask. My mom's taken more of a role of seeking out different opportunities."

To Mats's point, neither Mark nor I attended his first test, the Ironman 70.3 Santa Rosa. I wanted to go, but fulfilled a promise to attend the graduation of Lisette's son, Mark, from the University of Colorado. I did track him on my Ironman app. Mats served notice, placing fifth in his age group. After seeing his results, I had some confidence he would reach Kona by 2018 or maybe 2019 if I could get him into a qualifier. Which I did, in Korea.

Mats's qualifier happened two months later, a few weeks before I returned to Kona. His recap speaks to his big day, and his self-awareness. "My goal for the race, beyond the end-all goal of finishing, was to qualify for Kona," he said. "That was the whole point of Korea, to get into and do the *Kona* Ironman. Given who my parents are, I'm sure I could've gotten an at-large entry into Kona at some point, but I didn't want or need that. I needed to earn my own way into Kona. What I didn't expect was to win my age group and qualify by quite a wide margin. An Ironman is never over until it's totally over—ask my parents—but when it became apparent I was going to qualify, I eased up. I have some work to do on that issue."

Plenty of expectation, pomp, and circumstance awaited when I arrived in Kona. The primary story lines focused on men's phenoms Jan Frodeno and Lionel Sanders (who finished first and second in my hometown Ironman 70.3 Oceanside in 2018), and Daniela Ryf's bid for a three-peat over Heather Jackson, Sarah Crowley, and Lucy Charles. However, I got some love too. I also had sponsor engagements for Hoka One One, competitor dinners, a couple of VIP events, and a houseful of friends and family—in other words, another crazy week at Kona.

"One of the biggest differences between Mark and Julie was in how they approached their races, specifically Kona," Lisette said. "Mark would go into his Zen space and that would be it—he checked out of everything except his own thoughts. You know, The Grip. On the other hand, Julie seems to feed off the energy and excitement, so that when she's racing, it's like she's racing with your energy and mine, and your hopes and mine, almost as much as her own. That's one reason she's such a huge inspiration—we can *feel* her on the course, just as she *feels* our energy when she races."

I needed all the energy I could get for this race—and I was getting it from the people in my life, well-wishers, and triathlon friends. Days before the race, I received this from age-group superstar Cherie Gruenfeld:

> *I have always been so impressed with how you've lived your life since 1982. That moment showed such courage and strong will, but I know it wasn't the way you wanted the race to end and it wasn't easy for you. You could have taken that moment and handled it in any manner of ways. But what you did was to embrace it and to realize the good you could make of it. And that's what I've seen you do over the years. There are several generations of racers, women and men, who are in the sport because of you. That's a legacy to be very proud of.*
>
> *I know how hard you've worked this last year to prepare for this Kona race. Without fanfare, you've simply gone about preparing and on race day, you'll cross the finish line "in style," completing the story you've so ably written. I'm very happy to know you and I am wishing you your greatest moment ever as you run down Ali'i*

> *Drive. The only moment to top this should be (2018) when Mats*
> *runs down Ali'i Drive to the finish line.*
> *—Cherie*

On top of that, Kathleen was coming back to celebrate our thirty-fifth anniversary of the Crawl of Fame race. She was there to help Mike Levine take another spin on a course he first ran in 1982, but this time while battling pancreatic cancer. Talk about a Superman! "This was a day to come together as a triathlon family to support Mike Levine," Kathleen said. "We were greeted with leis at the finish line and we raised our '82 throwback Bud Light cans in celebration." Michael became the first recipient of a perpetual trophy Kathleen created to perpetuate living the dream through Ironman's motto, "Anything is Possible."

I would have loved to join them, but I spent a year preparing to run a different race. If my goal was an airtight bull's-eye, I was the dart zeroed in on hitting the red.

Unfortunately, Kona had different ideas. Doesn't she always? Because of the feedback from my training and racing, I had no doubt I would hit my specific goal. Hence my calm confidence. It allowed me to fine-tune my focus.

What I didn't count on was my body failing me.

I got off to a great swim, and felt fantastic early on the bike. I was in perfect early-race position to challenge 11:10. Ten miles into my ride, though, my lower back tightened. This was unexpected, something I had only experienced while climbing steep mountain grades in training. I could deal with the lower back pain, but I did not anticipate the shredding quadriceps cramps that started around Mile 70—nor how they wore at my mental attitude like storm surf shredding a coastline. I never envisioned these hours of physical suffering.

I finished the bike with my heart broken and my desire on empty. I watched the women in the change tent gearing up for the marathon battle, and I envied their determination and focus. My fight was gone. My goal of running a strong marathon was not going to happen. I could have walked/

jogged the marathon, but out of respect to the race and my fellow athletes, I had to be one hundred percent clear about my choice.

I never laced up my running shoes. I dropped from the race.

The next day, I sent a long post on Facebook. It read, in part:

> *Today is my 59th birthday and I thought I'd be waking up in Kona looking forward to a very celebratory day.*
>
> *I'm definitely going to celebrate, but this morning I'm taking the time for some introspection and reflection on the past year over my cup of coffee. My final Kona ended with the bike.*
>
> *Desire and passion will get you through almost anything. It's how I got to the finish in 1982. This morning, I'm still clear and heart solidly steadfast in my choice.*
>
> *My goal was to put together an Ironman race in Kona that would be the bookend to 1982. It would be a testament to the strength of women as they age, to longevity in endurance sports, and to the pursuit of personal excellence and audacious dreams.*
>
> *Instead, my 35th anniversary Ironman in Kona will stand as a reminder that we don't always get the fairy tale ending we script, the journey should be equal to the end result, and pursuing really big dreams takes risk but no matter how it turns out it will change you in amazing ways.*
>
> *Throughout the week, I have loved meeting you and hearing your stories. You will be one of the best parts of my Ironman week. We are all Ironman Ohana now and forever, with or without a tattoo! As for my personal ohana, the family and friends who traveled here to Kona and those who have support me back home, I love you and will be forever grateful for your generosity and kindness. I look forward to being your sherpa as you chase your dreams.*
>
> *A friend, who happens to share my birthday, texted me that today is not the end of Ironman but the start of a beautiful life.*

In retrospect, there were reasons for my trouble. Even though I gave myself plenty of time to rest, maybe I dug a little too deep. You know how, when you've felt thirsty for a long time, when you finally take a drink, it might be too late? That's how I felt afterward. My brother, Marshall, speculated my weight might be down. "I felt she went into Kona too light," he said. "She was four or five pounds under her normal race weight. Those four or five pounds mean a lot; they can be the extra power and endurance you need. I won't say that was the cause—it wasn't—but I feel it was one of many factors."

While I struggled, another story unfolded in the lava fields: my son's apprenticeship. Mats headed onto the run course with his father and Lisette to gather sage advice from Ironman's greatest male champion. "When I went to watch, right after qualifying in Korea, I had a more personal connection," Mats said. "It wasn't just something my parents did and became famous for anymore. Now I was vested. It's like the Super Bowl. It's one thing to watch it as a fan, but another when you've played in it or know you're going to play in it. Instead of just watching Kona through my mom's or dad's eyes, I was being totally nerdy during the pro race, checking splits with my dad. Seeing those athletes out there . . . those pro men went way faster than I did in Korea. I can look at that and think, 'I'm a pretty athletic kid, I train hard, I went fast,' but they're *still* the next level higher."

Lisette was with Mark and Mats when race co-favorite Lionel Sanders, one of the breakout male triathletes of the past several years, fell apart. They'd heard bits and pieces of how and why Lionel had stopped . . . then started . . . then stopped . . . then started again. The Ironman shuffle; we've all been through it. Then Mats said something about the possibility of Lionel dropping out.

"Mark stopped him right there," Lisette recalled, "and said, 'the one thing you can never do in your first Ironman is quit. If you quit, you will set the bar so high on yourself that it will be very difficult to ever finish an Ironman.' Mark told Mats about how Julie's race in 1982 was the heart and soul of Ironman. It didn't start out as people trying to beat each other, but to push themselves, and to never quit."

After the race, Mats did his best to console me. This was more than a son comforting his mom; it was also a racer trying to plug my experience into his memory bank for future reference. "We talked about her quads not loosening up," Mats said, "but I didn't really say anything; I asked questions.

I'm certainly not in any position to tell her she should've done something differently. It's her race, and she ran it her way."

I was done. I'd given most of the past thirty-five years to triathlon, to hitting a time goal that would have astonished many . . . but then what?

My fellow inductee in the USA Triathlon Hall of Fame, Missy LeStrange, started my process of finding a different perspective. I ran into Missy in the change tent after the bike. Year after year, she's risen to the Kona occasion. She's sixty-five, she keeps winning age-group, and she's amazing. Her energy was so overwhelming that I was disappointed I couldn't ride her coattails onto the run course.

That moment triggered a notion: what if my 2017 Kona was a stepping stone leading in the right direction? What if my all-in goal of breaking 11:10 wasn't a misstep—but a chance to peel back the layers of Kona itself. *What is Kona?* It's not just about hitting a time. I thought I'd earned the right to do it my way, and I missed the mark. Sue Robison painted the picture: my goal was a tiny bull's-eye, when my relationship with triathlon had always been about inclusiveness, running with others in mind, and the like. I'd become a dart on a dartboard.

I didn't want to end this way. Kona should be about giving something back by using my example to encourage others. I was missing that key piece. It's not about performance alone. It's about performance that inspires others.

Another exchange came from Ironman age-group maestro, Ellen Hart, the former U.S. record holder in the 30K run. My life inspired a fictional movie, *Tri* which was released in 2016. However, they made a movie specifically *about* Ellen's life, *Dying to be Perfect: The Ellen Hart Pena Story.* Our lives run an interesting parallel track. We're both Ironman triathletes and age-group champions. We both overcame harmful situations, an eating disorder for Ellen, and clove cigarette addiction for me. We both found our way back, with Ironman a central part of the picture, and took it further. However, she'd never hopped on a racing bike until age forty-seven, when she also started swimming. She proceeded to win five consecutive age-group world titles at Kona from 2009–13 and is a top 60–64 age-group runner today. So am I.

After finishing seventh in age group, Ellen posted a race recap far different from the flowing, fairy tale narrative she'd kept in her head and heart for months:

> *This was my first over 12 hour IM, my slowest marathon by far, the first time trudging along in the dark, first time in any race I've ever had to walk, and, my favorite—my first glow stick! My daughter had seen me race once about 9 years ago, but countless times has heard the tales of triumph. I wanted this to be the best ever—to show her, at the biggest race in the world, what I do. I envisioned coming down Ali'i Drive in first place, and seeing how proud she was of me. I talk about dancing on the stage, or painting a picture with our talents and performances in this athletic realm. This picture says it all—it felt like an uphill climb all day. The women who beat me raced really well. I didn't. And what then do you do when your best isn't good enough?*

Ellen found perspective in her effort, and in the meaning of her one disappointing race in the grander scheme. She allowed me to share this:

> *Suffering is universal—the refugee crisis in Myanmar, earthquakes in Mexico, hurricanes in Puerto Rico, violence in Las Vegas, sexual abuse everywhere. I am not presumptuous enough to compare my experience with anyone else's. But I do know we all suffer. Last Saturday for me it was physical, and then even more, emotional. I struggled again with trying to believe I am more than a list of my achievements, that I am worthy and loved just for being me. For some reason that's easy for me to give to others, and hard to give myself. It's so seductive to measure oneself by external criteria. And it's so false. I do this sport because it brings out the best in me . . . I do it for the community, friends, and people, and the challenge, healthfulness, and fun. Not very many people with serious eating disorders ever really come back to athletic competition, and hardly anyone gets to go out and do an Ironman at age 59. Hardly anyone, really.*

In my response, I noted that Kona and I weren't finished dancing yet.

> *Ellen,*
>
> *Just read your race recap and I was deeply touched.*
>
> *I saw you briefly at T2 . . . I think I was actually in your way as you tried to get into the tent. In a funny twist of irony seeing you was my brief moment of affirmation. As bad as I felt, I was still ahead of Ellen Hart!*
>
> *Reading your race recap was deeply moving and your struggle every bit as inspirational as the success you envisioned for your day. The lessons you learned will keep revealing themselves and guide you in all you pursue.*
>
> *Your heartfelt account has touched me deeply and your words will stay with me. It was like you were writing my story along with your own. Let's go out and show the world what 60-year-old ladies can do.*

A few days later, I received this:

> *Julie*
>
> *What a lovely message. Thank you. It's funny, that moment in T2 I was thinking that as bad as I felt, I had caught up to Julie Moss! As sure as I was that this Kona was my last, I would like to end on a good note. Not necessarily a win, because I think I put too much value and pressure into that, but at least a happy satisfied feeling about my experiences there.*
>
> *You are one of my favorites in the sport, not because of 1982, but because of now, who you are, and the goodness you send into the world. Stay in touch. Much love.*

After thinking about the exchange with Ellen, and then watching how Shalane Flanagan won New York a few weeks later, I returned to "beginner's mind," the mindset I occupied in 1982. *If I went back to Kona, what do I have to do? FINISH.* If I'd give up the time dream and start fresh, it would say more about my support for all athletes, and what triathlon has done for me, than hitting a personal time and calling it a career.

I went back on Facebook. My message read, in part:

> *On October 14th, I was very clear in my choice to not start the marathon in Kona. I knew going in I was being very finite with my goal of a finish time that rivaled my time in 1982.*
>
> *In retrospect, the goal of finishing Kona with a certain time missed the mark from the very beginning. I was too caught up in having the dream year with the Cinderella finish. And I became more enamored with the dream every time I hit another bull's-eye, whether in a workout or in a race.*
>
> *The dream felt real.*
>
> *In Kona at my NBC interview, I said that my year leading up Kona and racing the World Championship was a love letter to Kona, a thank you for the past 35 years. I envisioned professing my love with a fairytale performance. When it went south on the bike I didn't have the heart that Kona demands.*
>
> *Turns out this year it was a conditional love after all.*
>
> *I want another chance to rewrite my love letter. I need to rewrite my Kona ending. If I return to Kona for the 40th Anniversary, it will be with only one goal: to focus on the heart and soul of racing Kona.*
>
> *I see now that, as much as I trusted my heart to go for my dreams, I clearly missed the target in Kona. I had the wrong target. Kona is about having the heart to pick yourself up when you fall.*
>
> *So, here's to dusting myself off and starting over by looking to the past for inspiration.*

I set my new intention: to say goodbye in a way befitting this race and what it means to the athletes. It's all about finishing.

I began by assessing Shalane Flanagan's brilliant victory over Mary Keitany in New York. Shalane took Mary down out of *respect* for Mary's greatness.

When you approach an opponent with such respect, and rise above them, that's empowering. Shalane took her "costume" off, connected to the Wonder Woman within, and won. It is such an intentional, humbling place to be.

That's a great contingency plan for a marathon or Ironman. I didn't have one. Even as I rehearsed what I needed to do—getting my nutrition, backing off the bike if needed—I did not anticipate muscle failure. Instead of beating my 1982 time, I should've said, "That has served me so well, I just have to finish."

If I went back, a goal time would be the last thing anyone heard from me.

I signed up to requalify for Kona at the 2018 Ironman New Zealand, but then a thought hit: could I write Diana Bertsch, the Ironman World Championship director, and get into the fortieth anniversary race? I prefer to qualify the old-fashioned way, but I have earned some stripes in this sport, and it is okay to cash them in for special occasions.

After initial pleasantries, I got to the point:

> *Thank you again for the incredible (2017) Ironman experience and memories that I made with my family and closest friends. I can honestly say it was one of the best times I've ever had in Kona despite not finishing the race.*
>
> *I told the Legacy Athletes that each and every one of them already possessed the most powerful and compelling tool needed to get to the finish line . . . their passion for Ironman. I said their passion would help them find a way to push past their limits and discover their inner excellence.*
>
> *Sadly on race day when my body failed I lost my passion and it left me heartbroken. And as you well know Diana, you can't get to the finish in Kona without heart.*
>
> *I would like another chance to do what I didn't do this year . . . return to Kona fueled by passion, gratitude, and appreciation with the humble goal to get to the finish line, no matter what!*

It would be an honor to return to race Ironman's 40th Anniversary and share the finish line with Mats Allen and all my Ironman Ohana.

Mele Kalikimaka

Julie

Diana's reply couldn't have been a sweeter, nicer Christmas gift:

One of the most amazing marvels about this event is once you have crossed the finish line on Ali'i Drive, it is really never over. It wasn't your time to be 'done,' and not finishing was how the island will bring you back. The joy you had while here, and the learning lessons I am sure you gained, will continue to inspire not only you but others.

I was back in the race.

CHAPTER 23
My Iron Twin

What's with all the shopping bags?

The two sets of aero bike handlebars grabbed my attention first. They were loaded with shopping bags. However, neither the owners nor their bikes were ordinary at all: top-of-the-line Cervélo bikes can run up to $15,000. As I stood at the Hoka One One booth during the 2017 Ironman 70.3 Oceanside expo, and watched these two stroll my way with their overloaded bikes, I had to say something.

"Gentlemen, I hope you're not going to try and ride your bikes home with all those bags hanging off them, because that's a recipe for disaster," I said.

The men were starkly different in appearance, one from England, the other from Morocco. The Moroccan looked at me, then at the Hoka One One poster with my picture and name in large bold letters. "Hello, my name is Khalil Binebine," he said.

"Hello, I'm Julie Moss."

He broke into an electric smile that, I later learned, was typical. And contagious. "Dahhhling, we're meant to have dinner this week."

"Oh, you're *Khalil!*" OMG . . . the man about whom Jimmy Watson texted me!

Jimmy had just dined with Khalil Binebine and his spouse, Gwilym Hall, in their home near San Diego. Gwilym was the other merchandise-laden athlete in Oceanside. As they talked, Khalil brought up triathlon, his newest consuming passion, something he never tires of discussing in a life that includes overseeing a far-flung, global collection of very cutting-edge companies that can and will change the world in rejuvenating, life-sustaining ways.

"I have someone you need to meet," Jimmy told him. "Julie Moss. She's a friend of mine."

"My goodness! I've always wanted to meet her. She's the lady who literally made Ironman IRONMAN!"

"I'd been inspired by this lady for a very long time, decades before I did an Ironman," Khalil recalled. "I mean, the whole planet has seen that [*Wide World of Sports*] video. In my heart, Julie won it with her remarkable effort."

"I'd love to meet her," he told Jimmy.

Jimmy texted me from the dinner table. After I responded, he looked at Khalil and said, "Okay, let's have dinner here. Next Wednesday."

"Okay!"

"She's competing in the race in Oceanside this weekend," Jimmy added.

Just like that, I had a dinner invitation from a man I'd never met—but one who would become a major part of my life, quickly.

Serendipity speeds up what is meant to be. Thanks to my poster and Jimmy Watson, Khalil, Gwilym, and I found each other. After chatting for a few minutes, they scooped up their favorite Hoka running shoes (and mine), the Bondi 5, in every available color. So much for my admonition to not be burdened by shopping bags!

Four nights later, I arrived at their majestic home for dinner. When I walked through the door, I was delighted to see Khalil in his traditional djellaba, a loose-fitting robe customary to North Africa, paired with his not-so-traditional Gucci velvet loafers. I took a look at a beautiful array of sculptures, paintings, Persian rugs, and an indoor dining table for twenty. Khalil's house is filled with fabulous art. When I entered the foyer, the first thing I noticed was a huge, twenty-four-foot-tall kiswa tapestry, embroidered with silver and gold wire thread. Every year, a kiswa about fifty feet high is commissioned to cover the Kaaba, a small shrine made of granite in Mecca and located next to the Sacred Mosque, which Muslims consider the most holy spot on Earth. It costs about $4.5 million to make. The previous kiswa is cut into pieces and presented as gifts to visiting Muslim dignitaries. Khalil received quite a big piece from the Saudi friend who gifted it to him.

I also beheld large paintings and sculptures by Mahi Binebine, Khalil's brother, who earned his PhD in mathematics at the Sorbonne prior to pursuing his true love of painting, sculpting, and writing. His work is on permanent display at the Guggenheim Museum. His book, *Horses of God*, was made into a feature film and, in 2013, selected as the official Moroccan entry for best foreign language film at the Academy Awards. Khalil's and Mahi's beloved mother, Lala Mina, cared deeply for them while their father was secretary to the king of Morocco for thirty-seven years.

Along with Mahi's large art installations, there were a couple of smaller originals on the far dining room by Marc Chagall and Pablo Picasso.

Despite all the amazing art on display, Khalil's favorite thing to show visitors is his home gym on the lower floor. As you walk past the garage toward the gym, the vintage 1969 Rolls-Royce and new Bentley are hard to miss, but it's clearly the dueling Wahoo KICKRs, stationary trainers that can mimic Ironman courses worldwide, that catch Khalil's fancy. Next door to the gym is a yoga studio where he ends most days under the guidance of Melody, his private instructor. Melody's husband, Ryan, ran his first marathon, the New Orleans Mardi Gras Marathon, and is training for his first Ironman. Khalil casts a wide net of motivation by his example.

I learned my lesson about being a smart-ass when we popped into the home theater just off the gym. I jumped into one of the plush recliners and mentioned how unfortunate it was that there wasn't a pashmina to throw around my shoulders while watching a movie. We ended the tour and returned upstairs. Just before dinner, Khalil walked into the living room with three pashminas stacked atop each other. "Dahhhling, don't ever assume we don't have pashminas, now you have three, to match all the colors of your outfit." Lesson learned!

Clearly, these men lacked for nothing. I grew even more ecstatic when I saw platter after platter of delicious Moroccan dishes carried out of the kitchen and assembled on the patio dining table overlooking the Pacific Ocean. Remember how much I love food and gatherings around food? This was nirvana, a Moroccan feast.

An intimate dinner for twenty or more is a nightly occurrence in Khalil and Gwilym's home. They are Ironmen in their ability to host friends, business partners, family, and guests from around the world. Typical dinner conversation involves an eclectic group from as many as ten countries, the discussions always compelling. For those who can speak eight languages, like Khalil, the evening becomes a feast for the ears as well as the stomach. (Besides his parental tongues of Arabic and French, he also speaks German, Spanish, Portuguese, Hebrew, and English—plus Mandarin Chinese, which he learned when he found himself in a business arrangement with Chinese speakers. Try that sometime!)

Khalil honed in on how I could help him reach his goal of becoming a top-ranked Ironman age grouper—and earning a berth in Kona. We also realized the beginning of something more important. We'd not only become new friends, but found our other Iron Twin: we share an October birthday. Everything happens for a reason, and everything happens when it's time.

It was time. I had no idea just how remarkable our friendship would become . . . or that "when it's time" meant "you're linked from now on."

Dr. Elkhalil Binebine is one of the most remarkable human beings I know. His accomplishments are vast; he was born a fully faceted diamond, ready to shine and gleam in many ways. Khalil started bridge lessons at age three, played with his mother at five, and partnered with her to become a world champion—at nine. Predictably, he didn't stay in secondary school long; he was a college freshman at France's University of Bordeaux by age fifteen. After graduating, he earned a medical degree from the Sorbonne University, took his orthopedist credentials to the United States, and became the personal physician and friend of the billionaire *Forbes* magazine publisher Malcolm Forbes. Thirty years later, in 2016, Khalil was honored with an *entire tribute issue* of *Forbes*'s English language Eastern European edition, featuring interviews and writeups from more than thirty people who know and love him. Including me.

In 1989, Khalil threw a seventieth birthday party for Forbes in Tangiers, Morocco, that drew international media attention: Forbes sat side by side on a throne with the other "royalty" in the house, actress Elizabeth Taylor. Two hundred horsemen from the royal guard of Morocco performed, and Khalil arranged for the seven hundred party guests to be flown from and to New York on three charter jets.

Khalil's friendship with Forbes set the stage for his life that followed. Forbes advised him on ways to invest wisely, and also helped him develop a business contact list that any CEO on earth would covet. Soon Khalil was an influential investment adviser, his charm and insatiable curiosity always a big asset. So was his ability to make you feel like the most important person in his world at that moment, no matter what your station in life or how busy his schedule. That's an amazing gift, which speaks to the vast empathy and spirit that gushes from his heart and soul.

Khalil also loves sports. He has played tennis constantly since age fifteen, becoming a regional pro, and later a pro beach volleyball player. He swam, rode bikes, and ran occasionally, without ever putting the three together. Sports served as an outlet, which he needed: it makes me dizzy to think of his daily workload. The night before our Ironman Dubai 70.3 in 2018, he slept for ninety minutes, after taking a meeting he'd been pursuing for *six years*. His vision is vast too.

By 2000, Khalil left medicine to focus on a formidable venture capital fund he had built. Soon, lightning struck again, in the form of Dr. Finian Tan, the then-deputy trade minister of Singapore. Finian's formidable government task? To turn Singapore into the Silicon Valley of Asia. He did it. In 2005, after a series of remarkable investments while heading the Asia-Pacific Department for Draper Fisher Jurvetson, where he oversaw a $1 billion government fund, Finian founded Vickers Venture Partners. Khalil already knew about Finian, having received five visits—with self-imposed month-long stays—from a persistent friend imploring him to get on board. Soon, Finian and Khalil met in Bordeaux.

Khalil has been the vice chairman of Vickers since. One fund, Vickers-IV, includes more than thirty start-up companies in biotechnology, telecommunications, media, and consumer and financial services. Among those companies is Samumed, the brainchild of Turkish businessman Osman Kibar (the Zen term *samu* loosely translates to "concentration while doing a routine task"). Samumed is in early- to late-stage trials on drugs designed to reverse and eradicate our most debilitating diseases and ailments (arthritis, osteoporosis, cancer, and Alzheimer's disease, among others). The focus is on the so-called Wnt gene, the communication system of our body cells. The Samumed team aims for a state of disease-free living, part of Khalil's world vision of healthy, peaceful, loving people who get along. Nothing routine about this concentrated task!

I love many things about Khalil, and this statement reflects why. He's a billionaire with endless generosity in his heart and soul. What could be more generous than reversing the paths of our most debilitating diseases and disorders—and doing so on a scale that, he says, "will change the lives of over 400 million people"?

Khalil's entry into the triathlon world began in early 2016 during a discussion with his nephew, Bashir. "Bashir was doing the Ironman 70.3 UK," Khalil recalled. "When I saw him, I asked, 'What are you doing? Why would anybody do that? You shouldn't be doing this.' I was talking to him as an orthopedic surgeon, as well as his worried uncle. He ignored me, and kept doing his sports.

"Some time later, I was having dinner with him in Hong Kong. I asked him, 'This insanity of yours . . . how long do you need to train per week?'

"'Twenty, twenty-five hours, sometimes thirty before a race.'

"'Wait a minute. Twenty-five hours a week?' Then I thought of my own sports. I was playing tennis two hours a day, training on the elliptical one hour, and lifting weights for an hour or two, six days a week. I was already putting in the time. I was also intrigued by a question: how far can a human being push their body? 'Well, I'm going to give it a try,' I told him.

"I came back to California, and saw a friend of mine, Dave Love, who's done twenty Ironmans. I said to him, 'Listen, I would like to try this, but

I would like to do it in a very professional manner. I need a coach. Can you get me a coach?' He got back to me with Terry Martin. She's been my Ironman coach since."

Khalil is the center of his family members' lives in many important ways; anything he does can affect them. Like swimming, biking, and running 140.6 miles . . . "Half of my family didn't agree with my choice, and the other half started doing it!" he chuckled. "The others are afraid something will happen to me. I address that by getting thoroughly examined every six months at UCSD, and I do nuclear medicine too, so I have a 3-D image of every cell of my body, it seems. I talk to my cardiologist, my internist. If I didn't think for a second my body could do it, I wouldn't do it. That's not what Ironman is about."

While trying to negotiate that discussion, Khalil had to run it by a more immediate family member—Gwilym. "I'm going to have to be away for four or five hours a day. Is it okay with you?" he asked.

"Not only is it okay, but I'll do it with you, so we don't have to be apart for four or five hours a day," Gwilym replied.

"Gwilym started training with me, and he lost 32 kilos [70 pounds]," Khalil said. "Eleven months after we began training, we began with a modern [Olympic] triathlon, then the Ironman 70.3 Vichy, then the Ironman Barcelona."

A few months later, we ran into each other at the Ironman 70.3 Oceanside.

I began to deeply appreciate Khalil's determination and passion in May 2017, during Ramadan. Traditionally, Ramadan lasts thirty days, but Khalil holds himself to a strict spiritual standard and always observes for forty days. As an Ironman triathlete in serious training, proper nutrition and hydration are the highest priorities, along with rest and recovery. When you can't have any food or water from midnight until the following sunset, a stretch of about nineteen hours, and you endure that body-taxing discipline for forty straight days, training can be tough. In the hot, humid May conditions of Southern California, it became a serious challenge for him to run or cycle without taking in water or calories.

For several Sunday afternoons, I arrived at Khalil's to be his running partner. We ran anywhere from ten to fifteen miles with no food or water.

I ate and drank before I arrived, but I always felt too guilty to drink or eat in front of Khalil. "How is he doing this without nourishment?" asked my coauthor after the three of us trudged up the mile-long hill to his house to end a fifteen-mile run.

Good question. Can you imagine not eating all day and still finding the energy to ride your trainer for hours or run in the late afternoon heat? Khalil may love his creature comforts, but underneath those designer labels, he is diamond tough. I learned so much about his toughness, tenacity, and devotion on those runs. I was now mentoring, befriending, *and* running, swimming, and biking with him, while leaving the overall Ironman coaching to Terry Martin, who was a fine pro in the 1990s.

We were just getting started. What moved me, and took this friendship into my heart, was his generosity of spirit despite profound calorie debt and dehydration. I imagined he'd be cranky and irritable, like most would be after running fifteen miles with no food or water, but he was the exact opposite. Khalil took the time to smile and say hello to everyone he passed. That can be a mini-event unto itself. He wears his race gear while running, so picture this man pulling up to an intersection near you in a one-piece white lycra tri-suit contrasting with his bronze skin, neon pink headband, and knee-high neon compression socks. The guy stands out. However, it's his zest for life, his joie de vivre, which shines brighter than any amount of neon. His passion is his secret weapon, along with a famously wicked sense of humor, which meshes very well with my occasionally sharp, sarcastic side. I usually find shared jokes on email very tedious, but when one arrives from Khalil, I know it will make me laugh out loud and I can hardly wait to pass it along. Khalil can tell a joke like a pro. Most of his humor suggests it could go down an adults-only road, only to take a surprising turn and finish with a positive G-rated punchline.

My support for Khalil took a comic turn when we traveled to Racine, Wisconsin, for an Ironman 70.3 in mid-summer 2017. Gwilym's darling mother, Elizabeth, was visiting them, and Gwilym was recovering from surgery to reattach a torn quadriceps, suffered when a tourist hit him during a bike ride. In his absence, I volunteered to be Khalil's sherpa.

From our first meal together, Khalil has regaled me with stories of exotic locales, first-class travel, swanky hotels, and multistarred restaurants. Let's just say our hit-and-run trip to Racine was not in the same vein as our monthlong journey six months later to Marrakesh, Gran Canaria, and Dubai—but an epic adventure nonetheless. It was more like *The Beverly Hillbillies,* one of my favorite shows as a kid, in reverse. (To summarize, the Clampett family discovers oil on their rustic property, moves to Beverly Hills, and as nouveau riche hillbillies shake up privileged society with their hayseed ways.)

Our race experiene: Envision a billionaire triathlete flying on Southwest Airlines and staying in a Comfort Inn located next to the Interstate 94 truck stop. He must plead with a local steakhouse manager to stay open past the 8:00 P.M. closing time so he can eat. He shops for the first time in a Walmart, and keeps requesting fresh squeezed orange juice, only to be told repeatedly they don't have it. Said visitor finds the restaurant bills so low, he assumes it's a mistake. Then he thinks the bill only covers food tax. Finally, he's moved to gleefully declare that, while in Racine, he will become a thirty percent tipper.

We laughed so hard that we cried in our pasteurized orange juice. With all due respect to the very nice residents of Racine, this premise would make a funny sitcom.

Then Mother Nature decided to offer her own comic relief. The temperature of Lake Michigan dropped overnight to a dangerously low 51°F. Upon arrival on race morning, we were informed the swim was canceled. The Ironman 70.3 Wisconsin triathlon became a duathlon. Rather than throwing a wrench into his plans, the decision brought a huge smile to Khalil's face and elevated his mood.

He still had to complete a 56-mile bike and 13.1-mile run in humid conditions. The race switched to a time trial start for the bike, like they do in the Tour de France prologue and Olympic road time trial. Riders started every two seconds. Khalil enjoyed an awesome ride and started the run in great form. It was so fun to run around the course, snapping pics and yelling encouragement. With about ten minutes left, I yelled, "Take the reins off and let it rip to the finish line!"

He responded like he was shot out of a cannon. I'd never seen him run that fast! However, I knew he wouldn't make it to the finish at that pace. I literally jumped in behind him, sprinting and yelling, "NOT THAT FAST!"

The next day, Khalil mentioned his leg was a bit sore from his long sprint. Turns out he sprinted so hard that he ripped a hole in his quad. Now that's someone passionate about his sport and determined to excel! The same approach has made him successful, along with his limitless mental strength.

Khalil's passion for Ironman knows no bounds, and his athletic ability is catching up to his mental strength. He is getting the hang of endurance racing and adapting beautifully to the training required to hone yourself as an Ironman. "Every day, I'm discovering things I didn't know I had. It's an incredible journey," he said. "And you find, when you are aware like this, there are many things to discover, no matter how old you are. You become really, really aware of everything. Your senses . . . I've never used drugs, and I've never drank alcohol, but now, I understand what a 'high' is. When you're training, the endorphins kick in, you have a sense of well-being, and you're really on a high. It's your own constant high. But it's a happy feeling, a very healthy feeling.

"I will give you an example. I had to fly seventeen hours back to California for six days of meetings while training for Ironman 70.3 Dubai, and woke up at 2:30 A.M. I had to wait almost four hours for daylight, so I could go on my four-hour bike ride. I did the ride, then my yoga teacher put me through a session. The next day, I woke up at 4:30, waited a couple of hours, did my 21K [half marathon] run to Fiesta Island and back, and went for a swim. The next morning, I woke up at 6:00 A.M., really tired. But I had to swim two miles. Somehow, I made myself go to that pool. The rest of the day, I was smiling, and happy, the skin looks good. You *radiate*. That's what happens with training."

Our friendship jumped to yet another level in January 2018, when I flew to Morocco, and then the Canary Islands, to train for a month with Khalil and to race the Ironman 70.3 Dubai. It was my first lead-in race to the fortieth anniversary Ironman World Championship. As with all good friendships, you share from your lives, and advise and learn from each other while also having a helluva lot of fun.

Khalil opened up this idea by visiting what I thought was an unrelated subject—my 2017 Kona race. After I returned, I headed to Khalil's to give him the blow-by-blow. In his eyes, I noticed a certain, unadulterated look of disappointment. Mats had also given me that look. I didn't feel judged by either, but confusion reflected back at me in both cases. Neither could understand my final choice to not finish. Their shared look said they would find a way to get to the finish line in Kona, no matter what. No excuses.

After dinner, Khalil surprised me. "Dahhhling, I think you need a change of scenery in the New Year." He suggested I join him and Gwilym in Marrakesh and Gran Canaria to prepare for Dubai. Talk about a change of scenery: Oui, si, ja, I was all in.

After arriving late in Gran Canaria, I learned a valuable lesson from Khalil: every second counts. In his world, that means squeezing in his planned workouts. He had a 1½-hour training run ahead. Not five minutes after we arrived, we were out the door. A couple days before, in Morocco, he ran as many intervals as possible before cutting it a bit short to meet with his banker.

I ask you, what are the odds of billionaires hammering out intervals before their first appointment of the day?

The shoe then shifted to the other foot, although I'd forgotten until Khalil raised it. "When we were on our bikes in the Canary Islands, she saw that my hips were moving ever so slightly. When you do that, you lose energy. But she didn't tell me! She moved in front of me and asked, 'Can you see if my hips are moving?'

"I said, 'No, yours aren't moving.' Then I thought, *Wait a second, she's trying to tell me something.* 'Maybe mine are moving.'

"She smiled at me. 'Yep, they're moving.' She showed me the example before she said anything.

"That's the subtlety of training with an icon. It was quite an extraordinary gesture. And it was so modest, which I appreciate seeing in all successful people. There's a saying, 'No matter how high up you go, you still sit on your butt.' The more you achieve, the more you strive for modesty and simplicity. At the end of the day, we are all the same—people trying to do the best we can with our lives that God has given us. I certainly see that in Julie.

"When you're training with an icon, your whole demeanor changes drastically," Khalil continued. "You naturally want to do well, and she's such an incredible example who's *bloody fast,* so you want to keep up with her. Everything that comes out of her mouth comes from positive energy and positive thinking. She shows you things we don't realize we're being shown, which is an incredible achievement. Not many can do that. She was naturally teaching and transmitting this incredible God-given gift without it feeling like she was coaching me.

"I look at training with Julie this way: If you're working with a regular coach, and you are a tennis player, you obviously improve. But if your coach is Roger Federer, you improve a lot more! She's done it so many times, despite so many ups and downs in her life; she always came back to training and gave triathlon even more. Again and again. You can't substitute for that life experience. You are bound to improve just by watching. I'm so privileged to be her friend and a training partner, and it's only the beginning."

I understand fully, and humbly, what Khalil is saying. I still draw from elite athletes too. The ultimate value of an elite athlete, in my view, is to inspire, to make us want to recreate that feeling. It's that simple. We take their journey with them, and they inspire us to take our own journey. It pushes you toward your best self. While on a layover in Frankfurt, Germany, I was running on the treadmill during the second set of Roger Federer's 2018 Australian Open finals victory over Marin Čilić. I've never had a faster hour on the treadmill. Then later, I watched Roger weep openly over winning his twentieth Grand Slam title. He's been at the pinnacle of his sport for so long, and letting us in to how this makes him feel inspires me. I want to *feel* that deeply.

I learned another valuable lesson from Khalil about why he's so successful—he's always available. He will answer the phone while running an interval. We were in middle of a long interval set that included a twenty-minute warm-up, and reps of a six-minute run at 10K pace with a one-minute recovery jog in between. Halfway through our third interval, the phone rang. *Surely, he's not going to answer,* I thought . . . but there he was, running swiftly at 10K speed while conversing in French.

The night before Khalil raced Dubai 70.3, he slept a total of ninety minutes. This wasn't due to prerace nerves, but because he was conducting business. He never complained. He's positively tireless on behalf of his investment partners and his family and friends.

In the short time I have known Khalil, he has become a brilliant diamond light in my life. He has unlimited potential as an Ironman triathlete, and it has been one of my greatest joys to be his friend and training partner. I'm thrilled that I can offer my experience and support to one of the most accomplished men on the planet as he continues his Ironman journey. Besides, he is my prince in shining armor!

CHAPTER 24
Be Amazing at Any Age

"Gratitude opens the door to . . . the power, the wisdom, the creativity of the universe."

—Dr. Deepak Chopra

On New Year's Day, 2018, I received an email from a yoga instructor friend, Xuyen, who spelled out her New Year's resolutions a bit differently:

The word resolution means to resolve. Consider something from within that needs to be resolved. Could be a pattern, behavior, or relationship. When we resolve from the inside first, things will start to fall in place on the outside.

- *I will resolve to be less negative and more positive so I can live my life with the glass half full.*

- *I will not be quick to judge so that I can truly appreciate the goodness of mankind that still exists.*

- *I will be kind and love myself so that I can offer and receive love from others.*

Namaste!

I thought about viewing my path forward through the prism of 2018, a year different from any other. First, I would share my story through this book, achievements, warts, and all. Also, I would race for others as well as myself; that's what my fortieth anniversary Ironman World Championship race is all about.

When I received Xuyen's message, I was two days away from jumping on a plane to spend a month in Marrakesh, Gran Canaria, and Dubai with Khalil. That began a very busy spring. In March, I joined Mats in New Zealand for *his* Ironman tune-up, the Ironman New Zealand 70.3, as well as my full Ironman qualifier. It was a great day for both of us. I won the 60–64 division by almost two hours in 11:10—the same time I ran at Kona in 1982—while Mats finished second in his division and fourth overall in the Ironman 70.3, running 4:20. He looked great! In April, Lisette and I ran the Paris Marathon together to celebrate "turning sixty," and to mark her first marathon since we ran Boston in 2004. If that wasn't enough, an idea popped into Khalil's head: "Dahhhling, you need this intercontinental event on your resume," he said, signing me up for the Bosphorus Cross Continental Swim, an open-ocean swim that starts in Europe and ends in Asia near Istanbul, Turkey.

This sequence of events is much different than my 2017 schedule; it's more like a yearlong celebration of everything triathlon has done for me. It is also indicative of my desire to share my experience with others through mentoring, conversation, group runs, and some coaching. It culminates in my primary reason for going to Kona once more, to finish the race for you and me alike. Xuyen's email was so timely and poignant.

In 2001, Santa Cruz surfer Jay Moriarity died in a diving accident in the Maldives. He was only twenty-three. Jay was already a local big-wave legend, and later the posthumous subject of *Chasing Mavericks,* starring *300* and

Olympus Has Fallen hero Gerard Butler. Even though Jay died so young, he gave so much back. When he passed, I lived a block away from Pleasure Point, where they held his paddle-out—a beautiful ritual, in which surfers paddle beyond the waves, form a circle, share stories or moments, and pay their respects. The essence of ohana. I didn't go in the water, but I did stand on the bluff, watching and wondering, "What was it about this young man that would get so many people to come out like this?"

Later, I got a chance to meet Jay's widow, Kim, while I served as an announcer for Surftech's Jay Moriarity paddle event. She was the race starter. That made such an impression on me, how Jay achieved an incredible reputation and brought out so much love because of the way he gave of himself. I wanted Mats to "Be Like Jay."

I wanted to be like Jay too. I started looking more at what I could do. In the past five years, it has taken on a new dimension, from a curiosity to part of my daily life.

It began with a question: What do I really offer and share in my work, talks, races, and appearances? I've spent a lot of time contemplating this. If my original career brand was "Never Give Up," my brand today is "Ageless Adventures: Be Amazing At Any Age."

Part of my approach crystallized during a roundtable discussion about life at fifty I shared with Kris Riley (wife of Jim Riley, my bike training partner and the man who started the first triathlon apparel line), Trisha Hegg (wife of 1984 Olympian Steve Hegg, formerly a retail employee of Scott Tinley's, now a global branding expert), and fellow branding expert Juju Hook, the author of *Hot Flashes, Carpools, and Dirty Martinis*. The title alone is catchy.

No matter how old or young we are, if we get off the couch, put one foot forward, and keep moving, we can literally change ourselves and our lives. From there, we can positively impact those around us. "Forget about age and find a role model," big-wave surfing legend Laird Hamilton told Roy Wallack, who wrote a wonderful article on me for *Triathlete* after my 2017 Ironman North American Championship.

For my part, I fell from being a world-class triathlete to struggling to walk or run more than 200 meters at age fifty-one due to depression and my clove cigarette addiction—to being where I'm at today at sixty. Age does not deter what I feel I can accomplish, and I don't listen to those who try to limit me, or themselves, with comments like, "Aren't you getting too old to keep doing that?" No, I'm not! Neither are you! I want to touch everyone with that and other messages that open the doors to empowering ourselves. Isn't that the essence of mentoring? Paying your life experience forward?

My Ageless Adventure Brand comes with a central focus, a resolution in the spirit of Xuyen's New Year's Day email: *I resolve to live every day with a can-do attitude.* When people approach me and say, "I can never do an Ironman, but maybe I can do an Olympic distance, or a sprint, or a Half Ironman," I don't downplay my abilities, but instead say, "With my inexperience in 1982, if I could get to the finish line of Ironman, anyone can."

What is this "can-do" attitude? Runners talk about being "in the zone," when the sheer joy of running merges with a copious endorphin flow to create a euphoric feeling, which we all crave. What about setting a goal that flies out of your comfort zone, way over your head, so far out there you think it's impossible? But it's something you really want? What if you chip away at it? I thought for years, "If I don't write a book . . ." I trusted I would know when the time was right, part of learning to trust that intuitive part of myself: "If I go with it, lock myself in because it's under my skin, pay attention to it, and then act, good things will come." That's being in the zone. If you think you can do it, and align your mind, heart, and body with your passion and priorities, and you're patient, you can change yourself—and the world. I'm living proof of it.

How do passion, priority, and patience work together? I had the patience to keep moving in 1982, no matter what speed. I would want to race, then have the patience to pick myself off the ground. I had passion for the young woman I was becoming in my breakthrough, the woman I wanted to be, and the kind of life I wanted to lead. In the last couple months before the race, Ironman became my priority. If you can bring passion, priority, and patience to your effort, whether it's an Ironman or another spectacular achievement for yourself, YOU CAN DO IT. That's the can-do attitude.

I also focus on our inner Wonder Woman or Superman, Übermensch, the inner super being. Prior to the 2018 Ironman 70.3 New Zealand, I told an interviewer, "My definition of a strong woman is any woman who chases her dream and is willing to risk going outside her comfort zone to make that dream come true. The bigger the dream, the riskier it can feel and the bigger the rewards. A strong woman takes all that into consideration and trusts in her choice and just begins." Later, I added, "Don't be afraid to push outside your comfort zone. It was only outside my comfort zone, on my hands and knees that I discovered what a warrior I could be. Underneath all the layer of self-doubt and settling for less, I found a well of untapped courage. At my physical limit, I discovered my self-worth was unlimited and my self-worth was worth fighting for."

Every woman deserves to know her self-worth and to access her inner champion. Often, we only discover that when we're kicked to the curb, so to speak. The hidden opportunity or nugget of possibilities lies in the falling down, then in getting back up and *never* giving in. These pieces define us. They constitute the champion side of our beings. We're not going to get it any other way. Not everyone can be a specific event champion, but anyone can find the spirit of the *life* champion within.

Let me give you a heartwarming example. In 2013, Shirin Gerami was the first Iranian woman allowed into triathlon competitions. In 2016, at age twenty-six, she made history by being the first to cross the finish line at the Ironman World Championship. Not only did Shirin train intensely like every other Ironman, but she did so in full Islamic dress. She wanted to create an opportunity for every woman to access triathlons and reap the psychological, physical, and social benefits of the sport. That's a champion. That's a Wonder Woman.

In 2013, my desire to share these positive, affirming messages found a fresh forum with the Iron Icons speaking series. It continued with various opportunities to talk with women and men about achievements, endurance sports, life lessons, and, of course, running the Ironman. In 2017, I took it a step further, attending the I Am More Than What You Sea all-women's workshop in San Diego, which helps support the Mini Mermaid Running Club. The Mini Mermaids operate throughout California. They were started in Santa Cruz by Heidi Boynton, a triathlete, mother, and cancer survivor. A Wonder Woman. What a strong message for an impressionable girl! So is this mission statement: "MMRC stands for self-worth, value, and equity. We are changing the lives of girls and young women by shifting their internal experience and the way they interact with the world around them . . ."

Empowering, isn't it? The curriculum empowers with strong engagement: girls identify with a fictional character to see ways to change their behavior, to become more empowered. They shift the typical constructs a girl confronts in society by focusing on heart, mind, *and* body strength. They work with girls to find the happy, powerful place inside themselves, and within their environment, as a foundation for lifelong fitness.

The workshop provided a safe, nurturing environment that overwhelmed me. It was so much different than a triathlon, which is a battle with yourself, your opponents, and the elements. Some day, I see myself implementing a Mini Mermaid program at Carlsbad High School, my alma mater, by working with the track and cross-country girls as student mentors.

As I rolled further into a mentor's mindset, I thought more about the women in our sport who are making that shift. Kathleen's work with Mike Levine has grown into a larger cause. Cherie Gruenfeld still competes as a seventy-something triathlete while bringing the triathlon experience to inner city kids through her foundation, Exceeding Expectations. Her mission: to encourage at-risk kids to move their lives in a positive direction. Multiple age-group Ironman World Champion Ellen Hart Peña tackles women's eating disorders, which she overcame. Her example and mentorship have touched countless lives, and turned around many troubled women to find their greater strengths.

I'm heartened by how my generation is pointing the way through their enduring passion and commitment. Take eight-time Ironman champ Paula Newby-Fraser and 1994 Ironman winner Heather Fuhr. Paula is the pro athlete liaison for Ironman and an Ironman U coach, while Heather is the pro athlete/VIP liaison. Paul Huddle and Roch Frey, their husbands, are also former triathlon stars—and involved with supporting stars of today and tomorrow. Paul is the manager of Global Operations for Ironman, and Roch is Ironman event director. Four-time Ironman World Champ Chrissie Wellington is mentoring and bringing 5K races to parks across England through Parkrun UK, a non-profit where she serves as global lead for health and wellbeing. What a great job title!

My Ageless Adventures lifestyle led to the wonderful partnership I enjoy with Hoka One One. As recently as 2012, few people in North America had heard of Hoka. Now, the brand is renowned for its highly popular, state-of-the-art running shoe line, and was the number one shoe in Kona 2017. Not to mention Hoka One One's very direct commitment to the Ironman World Championship and Postal Nationals.

My journey with Hoka One One began in late 2014, when newly appointed global triathlon consultant Eric Gilsenan called. Eric and I have known each other for twenty years and have worked together on occasion. He wanted to bring me aboard as a partner and brand ambassador, something I very much welcomed. "When I had the opportunity with Hoka One One, she was one of the first people I called," Eric said. "Many athletes send me sponsorship proposals looking for a 'mutually beneficial relationship.' It's rare that any athlete can produce anything halfway 'mutually beneficial,' but with Julie, she is the ultimate spokesperson for triathlon."

From the beginning, I liked Hoka One One's support for events, clinics, and other activities, as well as working with people like Eric and Sunny Margerum, the national team liaison. In 2016, Eric and I launched #runwithjulie, a group run in Kona, in which I take twenty to thirty women on the final two miles of the Ironman course. I also show them where I fell and crawled. "Most runners returned to the [Ironman] expo [where they started the run] with tears in their eyes," Eric said. "They were all beaming about their experience. What an opportunity to share an iconic piece of endurance sport! Who can do that? Who can deliver that?

"That's the power of trust and building a relationship like I have with Julie. I knew it was going to be a hit—and it was."

The #runwithjulie idea might be taking on even further life. A half-dozen empowered women competed as an unofficial #runwithjulie team at the 2018 Encinitas Half Marathon. As I've mentioned, when we do something powerful in our lives, we have the ability to positively impact others with our experience and passion. Sometimes the impact grows on its own.

I've since participated in a number of activities with Hoka One One, or within events they sponsor. One of my new favorites is the Hoka One One Postal Nationals, in which high school kids race two miles on the track, at night, during the heart of cross-country season. They are *fast*. I've had the privilege of attending as both an endorsed athlete and a coach. Because of the enthusiasm generated by events like this, Hoka One One is now making inroads with high school racers, as well as its strong over-thirty market.

Before my February Ironman 70.3 race in Dubai, I sat on a Women For Tri panel with Minda Dentler, the only handcyclist to complete four Ironman triathlons, including the Ironman World Championship. A wife, mother, polio survivor, and paraplegic athlete from India, Minda had a profound effect on me in Kona in 2012, when it was getting tough. As I struggled at the ninety-mile mark of the bike, cramping and struggling to push on the pedals, Minda rolled by on her handcycle, pushing and not looking back, the perfect person to yank me out of a bad stretch. Minda didn't quite make that finish line, but she returned in 2013 and became an Ironman World Champion. Her efforts were well-noticed; she was nominated for a 2014 ESPY Award for best female athlete with disability. Two years later, at Ironman Florida, Minda set the world record Ironman time by a female wheelchair athlete. In 2017, she became a gold medal–winning Ironman All World Athlete in the physically challenged division. Her public speaking appearances are just as inspirational. I was honored to join her on the panel, my first Women For Tri appearance of the year. I also participated at Ironman New Zealand.

I've spent more time with the Challenged Athletes Foundation, which has helped countless physically impaired athletes find new life through fitness and racing, raising about $65 million in the process—and counting. If you've stood on the sidelines of a triathlon or running race, you've likely seen CAF athletes run through, usually attached by a stretch cord to their guide runners. They warm up any course and inspire fans and athletes alike.

CAF started in 1997 when Jeffrey Essakow, Scott Tinley, Virginia Tinley, Bob Babbitt, Rick Kozlowski, and others organized a benefit run for future USA Triathlon Hall of Famer Jim MacLaren, who competed with one leg and a prosthetic limb—then suffered a car accident that left him paralyzed. They raised $49,000, providing MacLaren with a wheelchair van for his final competitions until he passed.

However, the phone kept ringing off the hook. More people wanted to donate. Essakow formally incorporated CAF with a goal of raising $1 million over the next ten years. Within five years, they were raising $1 million *annually*. By 2011, CAF was helping more than 1,000 challenged athletes per year, with donations from more than twenty-five countries, totaling over $6 million.

I was reminded of the profound impact of serving others when I attended the 2017 Gala for Hope in San Diego. It was held to combat Huntington's disease, a fatal genetic disorder that breaks down nerve cells in the brain. Many Los Angeles Chargers players attended, along with their longtime PR director, Bill Johnston, a beloved figure in the San Diego sports scene, whose wife of over thirty-five years suffers from the disease. Bill recently became the San Diego Padres' PR man to keep him close to home; the Padres underwrote the Gala for Hope. For years, Bill was a fixture in road races, pushing his wife in her carriage in everything from 5Ks to marathons. The event honored ESPN announcer par excellence Chris Berman, whose wife had recently died in a fatal automobile accident.

The night before the event, I received a call from Chris's friend and mine, longtime TV producer Jay Kutlow. Jay and his wife, Diana, live near me. "Hey, Julie, I have an extra seat to the Gala for Hope," Jay said.

I was tired. "Ahhh, I don't want to go."

"Diana's going down by herself. You could ride down with her."

It turned out to be a pretty big deal. Berman came to be honored, but instead, he pivoted and honored Bill Johnston—an incredibly classy move. Chris knows what it's like to lose a spouse, and he related to Bill's challenge. A few months later, on Thanksgiving Day, NBC featured Bill's story on its broadcast of the Chargers and Dallas Cowboys game. I would imagine a lot of women, and men, shed tears and gave many thanks for being healthy. Sports pieces don't get more moving. I find myself investing more time and attention into events like this.

In the past couple of years, I've also enjoyed working with some great cross-country kids at my alma mater, Carlsbad High School. One in particular, the lovely and tenacious Kendall Drisko, rose from an average prep runner to a state-level elite in one season. That's rare. "Julie helped me see that, if I wanted to get to State, I had to give everything in every workout, even two months before," said Kendall, who, in her 2016 State year, set nine personal bests in a thirteen-race season. Think about that: cross-country courses are hilly, held on differing terrain, and everyone has off-races and nagging injuries. But nine Personal Bests? How impressive is *that*? "She told me how hard it is to finish an Ironman, and I thought about it while we rode the bus to the [San Diego] CIF [Championships]," Kendall said. "That was inside me in the last mile, where I had to pass and hold off four girls who'd beaten me all year just to get into State."

"Bringing in elite athletes, if you are a lucky enough to do that, is a fantastic opportunity for the student/athletes to train under the best," Carlsbad High Athletic Director Amanda Waters said. "They get the skills necessary to get the most out of their high school sports experience, and also get insight from athletes who know what it takes. Julie is an amazing inspiration for our athletes. The kids really respond to her. There are not many people who can share those experiences."

Mentoring works best when we dial into the athlete's or person's reality, rather than our own. One of Kendall's teammates, Drew Kesslin, was a gold medalist in lacrosse in 2017 at the Maccabiah Games, sometimes called the Jewish Olympics. Drew is an amazing young lady; Google her "Insides Out" spoken-word performance at a 2016 Motivating Masses event. You'll see what I mean. Drew is not the strongest runner—she's quick to admit that—but she is a great captain. Before a junior varsity race in 2017, she threw down a prerace talk so empowering, the young freshmen and sophomores promptly improved their 5K best times by *an average of three minutes.* That's one minute per mile, per person. She was their accelerant!

The empowerment young women and men get from pushing themselves physically will translate to everything they do in life. It is the honey that draws mentors like me to work with them. I'm especially fond of working with young people in longer races, which I see as scale models of the ups, downs, fast periods, speed bumps, triumphs, and challenges of life. You want a metaphor for a long, involved work project or long-term goal? Try training for and running a marathon.

I've seen this in my own son, who qualified to experience Kona in 2018. I'm balancing mothering and mentoring, not always easy, while, for the most part, offering advice only when asked (hey, I'm only human). Mark and I both wanted to let him embrace his decision and implications on its own. "Initially, they were both a little reserved," Mats said. "They have a lot of respect about the magnitude of really doing this sport. They weren't diminishing my decision at all, but sitting back and saying, 'Let's see how it goes.'"

"From Julie, I've always gotten this feel that she's emphasized the practical aspects of the professional athlete in *triathlete*, and tried to highlight how important it is to do other things," Mats's girlfriend, Megan, continued. "She's given practical, grounded advice. She's saying to him, 'pursue this, do pursue it, but you're going to have to get really crafty, really smart.'"

The fortieth anniversary Ironman presents an interesting dynamic, one that I've been afraid might disrupt Mats's preparation. I was concerned enough about this to ask if he was okay with me racing. I originally wanted him to have his own Kona experience in 2018, but then I DNFed in 2017. His reply? "Honestly, Mom, I won't even know you're there." Ordinarily, mothers might not want to hear that, but to me, it was the perfect answer. He knew Kona would require his fullest concentration and focus, and I now knew I would not be a distraction to him.

Another thing that gives me great comfort? Mats understands and embodies the "Spirit of Ironman." He also knows something of its history. "I totally wish I could've done my first race back then, like my parents did," he said. "It was new and organic in 1982, and everyone was trying to figure it out. That's more my style. I think of my dad when he was on the JDavid [racing] team, him and a bunch of guys in their mid-twenties, riding around with their long blond hair, looking like a bunch of surf bums. And my mom was a surfer girl and college student who took a chance, jumped into the race, and changed everything. Why? She wanted to see if she could do it. That reminds me of my climbing buddies and me in the Sierras, not doing it for the money or sport, but just for the view."

Just for the view . . . *my* view is that I am racing in 2018 to celebrate our innate agelessness, the value of fitness and positivity in our lives, and to showcase the inner and outer power of finishing big. When we finish big, we open the door to something bigger. I don't feel the need to race for my own ego, though one can safely argue that my ego framed my 2017 goal of beating the 1982 time. Not in 2018.

I am using my platform to create more awareness of health and wellness, and the larger benefits of finding a fitness program and sticking to it. One day, I was running with Jim Riley and he said, "You know, people are sitting too much. They're so sedentary." I flashed back on a section of Chris McDougall's book, *Born to Run,* in which he stripped our running instincts back to their mother root: Our most distant ancestors had to slowly run down their prey over the course of many miles and hours, sometimes even a day or two; it was life or death. They had to move their bodies, constantly, in order to survive. In a sense, so do we.

Our robust endurance sports participation reflects a loss of connection with our instinctive humanity. What can be more fully human than using our skills, abilities, and physical fitness to fight for our lives, or to take on and conquer a mighty challenge like an Iditarod? An Ironman? A Western States 100-mile race? A tall mountain or the face of El Capitan? If you're a firefighter, law enforcement officer, or soldier, you know already. Outside of battling severe health issues, or a life-threatening accident or injury, though, the rest of us don't. What is it like to really have to dig down and get to the finish line? We crave that.

From Kona, I learned how quickly life can change. I also learned what people were *really* seeing, a seed that now is part of my mission. When people saw the *Wide World of Sports* footage, I thought it would repel them, but it did the opposite—it drew them in. They saw my vulnerability, limitations, and willingness to get up, no matter how many times I fell. Instead of wanting to know more about the sport, they were curious about what drove me to try so hard. I could feel them thinking, "What is out there that would make *me* want to try that hard?"

Endurance sports ask us what we can give of ourselves, in performance and potential, rather than listlessly punching a time clock and waiting for 5:00 P.M. to arrive. Endurance sports strip away how we perceive ourselves, and how others perceive us. When we're twenty-two miles into the marathon portion of an Ironman, believe me, we're not too concerned with how we look out there or the chatter running along the fans' rope line. It comes down to being in the moment: how do I feel right now? It's not an intellectual thing. To paraphrase something Lisette says about our forty-year friendship, say YES to challenges more than you say no.

In time, we circle back to the things that fully tested and connected us to our larger potential. Why do people dust off old surfboards or tennis rackets when their kids are older? Why do we start jogging again? Why does someone who never walked up a hill in their local park suddenly talk about summiting Mount Everest? What I seek is the outcome of these experiences, a "day after day after day" awareness and presence of moving forward, continually improving, expanding my potential as a woman.

It starts by signing up for a challenge, whether a 5K, hot yoga class, boot camp at your local gym, a half marathon, or Ironman. Doesn't matter. Sign up for something that requires you to stretch beyond your comfort zone. Simple intentionality begins change in your life. As soon as you commit, the universe will start to align on your behalf, from this moment to the moment you cross that finish line. Your job? To allow this to happen and to keep working out.

My friend, Diana Kutlow, bid on a race entry for the Suja Rock 'n' Roll Half Marathon in San Diego at the Gala for Hope. She hadn't run much in the past few years, yet she placed the winning bid. She used the excuse of donating to a good cause to step outside of her comfort zone and take a risk. Diana could now see her running as a way to help others, to be part of something bigger than simply getting back into shape. She can now run eight miles comfortably. I run with her a couple times a week and we chat the entire time. I have no doubt Diana will get to the finish line. Find a goal that will force you to get out of your way and feel connected to something bigger than yourself.

We never know when our next race or golden opportunity will be. Or if we'll get that opportunity. Who's to say that, after your next big challenge, you'll have another chance? What would happen if you treated your next major endeavor with that sense of urgency? My guess is that you'll have an extraordinary experience, one that either leads to something bigger or feeds your big life even further.

Elite athletes work out exhaustively and pay strict attention to detail. That's why we follow them: to watch commitment mesh with inherent greatness, and to see the athletes perform with a calm poise that seems to strengthen when it matters most. That was Mark Allen's gift. He *always* got up for big races. With Ironman, ultramarathons, or any long-term endeavor, it's not what you do in the peak or strong moments that speak to that commitment or edge, it's what you do in the valleys. Just like life!

"You see in my mom's race that spirit of never giving up, of persisting. That race really shaped the way people see Ironman. Yeah, there's fifty men and fifty women that line up for the professional race, but everyone else is out there seeing if they can do it, or how fast they can do it, seeing if they can fulfill this personal challenge. I mean, that's my mom's goal for 2018—to go back one last time and experience the race start to finish," Mats said.

Finishing gave me the keys to a world I never imagined as a girl. I've met people who populated my textbooks and the biography shelf of the library as a kid, as well as those making history today. Believe me, I felt a thrilling chill or two when I recorded a piece for Oprah Winfrey's OWN network in New York. Now, as I grow older, it has given me the opportunity to share my experience and wisdom, filled with both a larger purpose and the knowledge of what it *feels* like to stretch beyond what you think possible.

I thought I would end my career on a dramatic note in 2017, waving the athlete flag proudly, saying, "Look here, look at who I am." The young woman and little girl who nearly crossed the line a race winner in 1982 wanted, more than anything, to be a person others would notice.

I was noticed, not for winning, but for persevering. "Talk about great timing. She's the poster child," says Lisette, who's seen my life journey since I was nineteen. "The unique thing, for her, is that she was the poster child for men *and* women. It wasn't just women. Equally as many men have been in awe of her athletically. Given the times now, the time for women is ripe in many ways. She's a great role model. It's not like she's defying the odds, it's a new time, a new way of thinking, and she's so inspiring. She's doing something you never see professional athletes do;

she has become a poster child at both ends of her career, the poster child of 'you can do something!'"

I've learned to never say never when asked about competing in another Ironman. I was gently reminded of this by Scott Tinley, who read my Facebook posts after my DNF in Kona, the first saying goodbye, the second saying hello . . . again. After he read, he texted me:

ST: *How'd you feel about the day?*

JM: *Clear in my choice to stop after the bike. I didn't come to just finish by walking the marathon. I came to run and after the bike I had no run in me. I was just as clear in the light of day. No regrets, thanks for checking in.*

ST: *I believe you.*

JM: *Ha ha, there will be no do over, the chapter ends for me now, it's Mats's turn . . .*

ST: *I doubt it. People like us don't have a choice. Mats is a good person, perhaps the best amalgamation of his parents. But for you to stand in the long, dark shadow and saying nothing. . . nothing. We'll see about that. See you in the movies.*

What a sweet exchange, complete with message: It's never really over.

"That type of competitive drive really shows in these goals she sets. The fact that she can hit them, now? Amazing," Kathleen said. "In 1982, she didn't approach it so seriously. She didn't optimize her opportunity to train, although 1985, 1988, and 1989 were good years for her. Now, she's living up to her potential as an athlete. Had she applied herself then as she does now with her training, racing, business, strategy, commitment, time management, motivation, and drive to succeed? Who knows what she could have done? I'd say, without a doubt, that Paula Newby-Fraser and Erin Baker would've had a third rival at the very top."

What has it meant? I've spent more than thirty-five years trying to figure it out, seeking the outer limits of myself, possibilities, and potential, and then making the turn to work with others to help them discover the same within themselves. "Is it an accident that she fell into triathlon the way she did? Yes and no," Lisette said. "Given her background, growing up at the beach, very oriented to the ocean and outdoors . . . in the late '70s and early '80s, that's where triathletes came from. Plus, when we met, that was one of our commonalities, the ocean and the outdoors. We loved running and loved being outdoors. She already had that predisposition. I think triathlon was and is very well suited to her lifestyle. And Hawaii? Hawaii is a huge part of her life, who she is."

And now, here we are. "Julie had all the pieces then to put it together, which makes it even more beautiful now, at sixty years old, she has the time and drive, the passion, to do it," Kathleen said. "It has come together so beautifully. She obviously is discovering her greatness."

Epilogue

What will it feel like to toe the starting line at the fortieth anniversary Ironman World Championships? Will my personal history adorn me like a beautiful lei, or serve to remind me of the lava-sharpened edges of my limits? Will the wonderful conversations and people I've met through this fabulous sport and lifestyle pop into mind? Will I be digging so deeply that I'm laser-focused on putting one foot in front of the other? Or will I move smoothly, filled with thoughts of celebrating my sixtieth birthday with a strong finish?

All of these things will be with me. However, as I ponder this race, a few people and moments stand out.

I will be running for Khalil and Mats, as well as for myself. I see this race and the desire to excel in their eyes, and I want to share this experience with them—and cheer both of them on. It will be a way to connect with Mats in a very special way. He expressed very clearly that part of his legacy is to have a good Ironman experience in Kona. For me to see him racing, for the brief moment we pass each other on the course, to know his father will greet him at the finish line, and then for Mats to greet me at the finish line sometime later . . . that moment is a long time in the making. To have that moment on Ali'i Drive with my son, with his father there . . . Of all the blood, sweat, and tears, love, heartache, rejoicing, disappointments, the entirety of everything that happened with Mark and me, when all is said and done, we have Mats.

This race will be the culmination of so many dreams, time, support from family and friends, and commitment. It's also a starting point. The gifts we receive from accomplishing what we set out to do—finishing the race—remain for the rest of our lives. Use them. One of the gifts Mark and I have is Mats. To share his first Kona as a family . . . that's what a family is. Mark will be there for Mats. I will be there for Mats. Mats will be there for me. It's a great cycle. I think the moment I'll treasure most is when Mats crosses the line, followed by me.

Lisette Whitaker will once again be my roomie in Kona for Ironman Week, making it three Konas in row. I can't imagine not having Setty there or not seeing her at the finish line. My heart simply would not feel steady if she weren't there. In all our Cali-Girl adventures together over the years, from sunrises in Esalen, to sunsets in Paris, she's always been the steady one, the tortoise to my hare, the one who brings calm to my drama. However, Setty let me know that 2018 will be her last Ironman as CSS, Chief Support Sherpa. The best mahalo I can offer up, to the woman who knows me best, is to race drama-free and boringly steady in her honor.

I will also be running for my lifelong friend, Cindy Conner. In January, less than a week after I got on the plane to join Khalil and Gwilym in Morocco, I received a text. While unloading her skiing equipment curbside at LAX, Cindy was crushed between two cars. She has undergone many surgeries to repair a crushed pelvis and severe internal injuries. Here's a woman who spent thirty years in the trenches for the LA Sheriff's Department, always running straight into danger. She made it through her entire career pretty much unscathed while attending the funerals of many coworkers that were not so lucky. One year after she retired, she had this horrible accident.

Cindy has enjoyed a very active life, running half marathons, skiing, surfing, and stand-up paddling. She's a stud. Thank goodness she was in great shape when this happened. That's when training and fitness really pays off, when we're pushed up against our mortality. She was on my mind for every run and bike ride that followed her accident. Rather than feeling guilty about being on basically international traveling camp while she lay in a hospital bed, fighting for her life, I thought, "I'd better get out and work out every day, and not complain, and not whine. Cindy can't. It's going to be a very long time before she can even consider working out." I've trained with her in mind. It is a special motivation, one Shalane Flanagan used in a different way to win the 2017 New York Marathon. There's going to be a point where I can again walk with Cindy, jog with her, and run another half marathon with her. If anyone can bounce back from such horrific injuries, it is Cindy. She'll be back out there.

My brother, Marshall, tells a revealing story about her: "Years ago, we were racing sabots out of Oceanside Harbor. She'd already clinched the overall series title going into the last race, but if I won this last race, I would finish second in the overall. Cindy is one of the toughest and most athletic people I know, and I used to think even a little mean when we were in high school. During the race, I caught up to her, and she complained that her governor was jammed. She too knew how important the last race was to me. I ended up winning . . . and then, as other competitors wondered how Cindy lost that race, I thought about it. Normally, Cindy would've kept her rigging together with her teeth. From that moment, I realized that beneath her toughness is a heart that always looks out for others."

After my last bike ride on Gran Canaria, I had some extra time and was out taking pictures, and I thought, "Do I have to do that transition run?" Those are tough; they call upon you to dig right away to find a comfort level you can maintain, whether you're out thirty minutes in a workout, two hours in a Half Ironman, or four hours in an Ironman. The actual race is better, because you do it once and you're done. Whereas in training, you're doing it over and over. An image came over me: "Cindy, come run with me. Let's get you out of that hospital room." It was sort of spiritual to take her on the run. Then we "talked" for all thirty minutes.

I will also be running for you.

Will this be my final Ironman? Never say never. Scott Tinley knows me well. I've said "never" before—after 1990, 1997, 2003, and 2012. I even said it briefly, and very publicly on Facebook, after 2017. There have been too many moments of inspiration from Kona to say I'm done. When I wrote

Diana Bertsch about entering, she replied, "We're never truly done with Kona, and Kona isn't done with you."

Kona also isn't done with my family. I feel like Mark and I paved a nice road, one that Mats chose to run without prompting from either parent. He will carry the legacy forward, in whatever shape and form, while fulfilling part of his own personal legacy. And we'll be there cheering him on, remembering when we too were that young and that mighty and fast.

It's time to lace up and chase another dream. It's time to fly.

A Week in the Life of Julie Moss:
An Ironman's Training Menu

To get to the finish line in Kona, you have to complete a long swim, a long bike, and a long run.

If your goal is an eleven-hour day in Kona, then try and duplicate the time by having an eleven-hour day. These Kona-long days should take place two to three months before the race date. The volume (time) is increased by the Saturday Long Ride, the Sunday Long Run, and adding in yoga.

Ironman Training is pretty simple when you frame it simply. I have created a simple menu with which I work, and you can emulate. I plug in the workouts based on time per day and the goals I have set for weekly hours of training:

A.M. Swim Training: 3 Workout, 10,000 meters

2000 meters 2x200 Swim, 200 Paddles/Buoy, 250 Kick Fins
2000 meters 2x400 Swim, 300 Pull Buoy, 200 Paddles/Buoy, 100 Kick Fins
3000 meters 5x200 Swim, 200 Paddles/Buoy, 200 Kick Fins

3000 meters 3x400 Swim, 300 Pull Buoy, 200 Paddles/Buoy, 100 Kick Fins

4000 meters 10–12x400 on a 7-minute clock (1:40 average per 100 meters)

P.M. Swim Training (Double Swim Days)

1000 meter Swim: 1x200 Swim, 200 Paddles/Buoy, 200 Kick Fins, Swim 2000, Kick 200 Fins

1500 meter Swim: 2x500 Swim, 250 Paddles/Buoy

Bike Training: 3 Workouts, 12–15 hrs/wk

Moderate Ride on Hills with Interval 3–3.5 hrs: Group ride. Warm up on hilly start, established time-trial section of ten miles, ten-minute rest stop to regroup, second half hills for strength, warm down.

Pace will vary depending on how engaged your ego gets, but group riding provides plenty of incentive to hammer the time trial.

Moderate Ride Flat to Rolling with Intervals 3 hrs: Group ride. Warm up on flats, time trial for 7 miles. Regroup, then 5 mile second time, dead flat terrain. Rest stop. 7 mile third time trial, warm down.

Long Ride with Hills Small Group 6–9 hrs:
Go long and steady, focus on time in the saddle. Hills build strength.

Run Training

Transition Run: 30 min to 1.5 hrs

Middle Distance Run: To build speed, run second of each interval faster than first half (known as negative splitting).

Broken: 1–2 hrs
Run 15 min Walk 5 min x 3 = 1 hr
Run 20 min Walk 5 min x 3 = 1:15 hrs
Run 45 min Walk 5 min x 2 = 1:40 hrs
Run 35 min Walk 5 min x 3 = 2 hrs
Run 20 min Walk 2 min x 6 = 2:12 hrs

Long Run: To build endurance reduce rest times

Broken Long Runs: 3–4 hrs
Run 20 min Walk 5 min x 6 = Run 2:30 hrs
Run 25 min Walk 5 min x 6 = Run 3:15 hrs
Run 30 min Walk 5 min x 6 = Run 3:30 hrs
Run 30 min Walk 1 min x 6 = Run 3:06 hrs

My early season weeks are 20–28 hours. Add or subtract workouts as time demands. (Opt out of the yoga, and you subtract seven hours of training.)

Monday: 2 hrs

- Run 20 min Walk 5 min x 3 = 1:15 hrs
- 2000 meters 2x400 Swim 300, Pull Buoy, 200 Paddles/Buoy, 100 Kick = 45 min
- Yoga 1 hr

Tuesday: 5 hrs

- A.M. 2000 meters 2x200 Swim, 200 Paddles/Buoy, 250 Kick Fins = 45 min
- Moderate Ride on Hills with Interval = 3–3.5 hrs

- Tempo Run = 30 min
- Yoga = 1 hr

Wednesday: 2.5 hrs
- Run 45 min Walk 5 min x 2 = 1:40 hrs
- Yoga = 1 hr
- Massage

Thursday: 5 hrs
- 2x400 Swim, 300 Pull Buoy, 200 Paddles/Buoy, 100 Kick Fins = 45 min
- Moderate Ride Flat to Rolling with Intervals = 3 hrs
- Tempo Run = 30 min

Friday: 3 hrs
- Run 15 min Walk 5 min x 3 = 1 hr
- 3000 meters 5x 200 Swim, 200 Paddles/Buoy, 200 Kick Fins = 1 hr
- Yoga = 1 hr

Saturday: 7.5 hrs
- Long Ride with Hills Small Group = 6 hrs
- Tempo Run = 30 min
- Yoga = 1 hr

Sunday: 3 hrs
- Run 35 min Walk 5 min x 3 = 2 hrs
- Yoga = 1 hr

The bulk of my training weeks are thirty hours.

From eight to twelve weeks before Kona, I shoot for four consecutive weeks of thirty-five hours for an Ironman. These long days are based on time. The plan is to keep moving. The mantra is, "Time on the Legs."

Here is my typical training week eight weeks out from Kona. This is a high-volume week to build strength and endurance:

Monday: 2–3 Hrs
- Run 20 min Walk 5 min x 3 = 1.5 hrs
- Yoga = 1 hr

Tuesday: Brick with Hills 6 hrs
- A.M. Swim 3000 meters 5x200 Swim, 200 Paddles/Buoy, 200 Kick Fins = 1hr
- Moderate Ride Hills = 3 hrs
- Tempo Run = 30 min
- P.M. Swim 1x200 Swim, 200 Paddles/Buoy, 200 Kick Fins, Swim 2000, Kick 200 Fins = 30 min
- Yoga = 1 hr

Wednesday: Recovery 2 hrs
- Run = 1 hr EASY
- A.M. Yoga = 1 hr
- P.M. Massage

Thursday: Brick Flat with Rollers 8–8.5 min
- A.M. Swim 3000 meters 3x400 Swim, 300 Pull Buoy, 200 Paddles/Buoy, 100 Kick Fins = 1hr
- Moderate Ride Flat = 5 hrs
- Tempo Run = 45 min

- P.M. Swim 2x500 Swim, 250 Paddles/Buoy = 30 min
- Yoga = 1 hr

Friday: 3.5 hrs
- A.M. Run EASY Run 15 min walk 5 x 3 = 1 hr
- A.M. Swim 4800 meters 12x400 on 7 mins (1:40 average per 100 meters) = 1.5 hr
- Noon yoga = 1 hr

Saturday: Long Ride 9.5 hrs
- Long Ride = 8 hrs
- Tempo Run = 30 min
- Yoga = 1 hr

Sunday: 4.5 hrs
- Run Long Run 30 min Walk 5 min x 6 = 3.5 hrs
- Yoga = 1 hr

◆

Food and Nutrition:

I start most days with coffee (with half & half) and a bagel spread with almond butter and honey or mascarpone and jam.

For all my brick workouts, I pack a cooler for the day with three bars, two protein drinks (700 total calories), one Kombucha, plus water.

I have a protein drink after swimming.

My bike bottles are filled with the same drinks I pack when I race: two scoops of electrolyte (I vary the brands), two scoops of Carbo Pro, and two scoops of Base Salt. I refill on the ride with Gatorade (any flavor as long as it's blue). I carry two bars but will buy a PayDay bar or Fritos if needed. For long rides, I may buy a cheeseburger (skip the fries).

For the Tempo Run, drink half a protein drink before and carry Clif calories on the run plus more Base Salt, drink second half of protein after. I pack a bar if needed on the drive to yoga studio.

Kombucha plus water during yoga.

My traditional prerace dinner is penne pasta with roasted cherry tomatoes, good grated parm, olive oil, and red pepper flakes. (Mind you, just a few flakes to avoid a race day fire in the hole!)

Race morning is muesli (soaked overnight) served with greek yogurt and blueberries. This is also the morning meal I have on long ride days.

Race morning, I also have a protein drink an hour before the start. (I know that if I eat less before the start, my tummy will bother me on the swim.)

On Yoga:

Here's the truth: I wish I had the discipline to do yoga on my own, but I don't. I have to practice yoga in a studio with an instructor doing all my thinking and motivating. I walk into the yoga studio a mess and walk out always feeling restored. I'm a member of CorePower. (I also have my teacher certification from CorePower.) I always try and end my workout day in the yoga studio. The recovery through yoga has blown me away with how effectively it has been in helping me stay healthy. Even when I had to rehab my knee, I slapped on a brace and did one-legged yoga. Yoga makes it possible for me to handle the big buildup weeks for Kona. It is about breath, balance, strength, flexibility, building strong core, and an even stronger mind. I'm an uber-fan of yoga, not just for Ironman training, but for life. I will always practice yoga in a studio, preferably heated to over 100°F.

ACKNOWLEDGMENTS

From Julie Moss...

Robert Yehling: O Captain! My Captain! Bob, you have been my navigator and anchor during this journey. Thank you for believing in me.

Armen Keteyian: My friend, mentor, and badass correspondent and author.

Literary Agent, Dana Newman, for all your support and guiding us to Pegasus Publishing.

Jessica Case: Jessica, your insights and edits have been essential to keeping me on track. As a part of the Ironman ohana you provided the authenticity and leadership that helped give me the confidence to trust this leap of faith.

Lisette Whitaker, I love that I get to start so many mornings with you and our coffee chats. I can't fathom how much money I've saved on therapy because of our heart-to-hearts.

Khalil Binebine, my Iron Twin. Thank you for being my knight in shining armor.

My Family and "Framily," you hold me accountable and give me the heart to keep pushing my limits. Brother Marshall Moss, Sue Robison, Aunt Beverly, and Cousin Wendy, thank you for all your trips to Kona, and the great meals and laughs. Thanks also to my Carlsbad posse Jimmy Watson, Cindy Conner, and Barbie Baron.

Mahalo to all the Ironman pioneers for the times we shared while paving the way . . .

Valerie Silk, Bob Babbitt, Lois Schwartz, Mike Plant, Carol Hogan, and all the athletes that left their blood, sweat, and tears on Ali'i Drive.

A very special thanks to my sponsors, who make it possible for me to continue to live this wonderful lifestyle and race competitively: Hoka One One (Eric Gilsenan/Sunny Margerum); HERevolution Women's Triathlon and Cycling Apparel (Darcy Eaton); Base Performance (Matt Miller); Cerve'lo Cycles (Leslie Loughlin); HED Cycling (Anne Hed); XLAB Bike Gear (Candice Turner); Garmin (Talia Herman); Nytro Multisport (Skip McDowell); Action Sports (Kerry Ryan); and ROKA Sports.

Mark Allen: We shared some unforgettable moments, continuing with watching our son become his own man. I've longed to find a safe haven for the love and respect I feel for you. This book feels like I've finally found it.

Mats Allen: You amaze and inspire me, I love you unconditionally. Consider the Ironman torch passed and make it your own unique experience. I'll meet you at the finish line.

From Robert Yehling . . .

Thank you to everyone who gave so generously of your time and stories to recount an epic moment in the history of sports, one that still reverberates in all directions after 36 years. Particular thanks to Kathleen McCartney and

Scott Tinley for giving hours of background and insights, well-honed during your own legendary careers. Also to triathlon legend Wendy Ingraham, who had her own crawl to the Ironman finish line in 1997.

Additional thank yous to Julie's posse: Lisette Whitaker, Sue Robison, Cindy Conner, Jimmy Watson, and Marshall Moss, you greatly enhanced an already remarkable story. Cindy, we made it to the finish line inspired by your will to fight. Sue, I'm still laughing over your Kona stories. And Jimmy, loved walking down thirty-five years of event promotion memory lane with you.

Thank you to Carlsbad High School Athletic Director Amanda Waters, who added to the story when she enthusiastically backed my request to bring in Julie to work with my cross-country team. Two of our girls, Hannah Hartwell and Kendall Drisko, went to State thanks in part to this.

Finally, thank you to the millions who watched a young woman crawl across the finish line of a race few understood on *Wide World of Sports*, became inspired enough to focus on their own fitness, and followed Julie's career and her message. Enjoy her memories, story, and journey. You're all Wonder Women and Super Men!